False Wisdom
The Principles and Practice of Pseudo-philosophy

Gary H. Merrill

Copyright

Gary H. Merrill

False Wisdom:
The Principles and Practice of Pseudo-philosophy

First Paperback Edition

Copyright © 2021 Gary H. Merrill
All rights reserved

No part of this book may be reproduced, or stored in a retrieval system, or transmitted in any form or by any means, electronic, mechanical, photocopying, recording, or otherwise, without express written permission of the publisher.

Cover and interior design by the author

Library of Congress Control Number: 2020923787

ISBN: 978-1-7362603-2-6 (Paperback)

Attributions

Pied Piper of Hamelin images used by permission of the artist Templeton Moss:
http://fairytalesbytempleton.blogspot.com/2011/04/pied-piper-of-hamelin.html

Thinking Frog image:
www.maxpixels.net/Amphibian-Green-Thinking-Animal-Worrying-Frog-48234
(accessed November 7, 2020)

Tools icons used in Chapter 3 are by permission of Eugeny Osadchenko
www.iconfinder.com/iconsets/tools-icon-set-2
(accessed November 26, 2020)

Other images used in chapters are in the public domain.

Preface

This book is a comprehensive historical, theoretical, and practical treatment of pseudo-philosophy — a concept often encountered in both formal and popular philosophy, but rarely with any degree of seriousness and precision. It presents a theory of pseudo-philosophy through the use of models of the genuine philosopher and pseudo-philosopher, and then applies that theory to specific real-world cases.

A primary goal of this treatment is to provide readers with a set of easily applied tools for identifying pseudo-philosophy and responding appropriately to it when it is encountered. The approach I've provided is, I believe, understandable and useable by what academics would refer to as "the philosophically unsophisticated reader" while also being of interest to those same academics in terms of the "philosophical infrastructure" that was necessary to develop in pursuing this task.

I have remained focused on the "average person" as the typical reader — not assuming any background or formal training in philosophy, nor familiarity with philosophical jargon and terminology, and presenting things in a casual "non-academic" style so far as possible. In terms of references to the literature (and primarily for the purpose of pointing to additional information concerning concepts employed in the book) I have generally favored articles in the *Stanford Encyclopedia of Philosophy* and *Wikipedia* — choosing between these in each case based primarily on readability by non-philosophers so long as accuracy and completeness was sufficient. But I have not been reluctant to refer to primary sources, or more "professional" sources. when this was required for clarity or accuracy. My intention with this approach has been to make the material more accessible and transparent to those unfamiliar with it. But academics — including philosophy faculty, humanities faculty more generally, graduate students, and undergraduates perhaps majoring or minoring in philosophy — will find no lack of rigor and thoroughness.

Throughout the lengthy term of this project, several people have made my work easier and contributed in different ways. Early on, David Austin and Michael Pendlebury (both of North Carolina State University) were helpful in directing my attention towards potential subjects of investigation and in providing me with a variety of background research materials with which I otherwise would have remained unfamiliar. They also pointed me in the direction of prior work both directly and indirectly related to pseudo-philosophy, and which proved to be of substantial value in the development of my thinking on that subject and related concepts such as pseudo-science and, more generally, the concept of "the pseudo".

Later in the development of the book, Jeff Painter (who had worked with me at GlaxoSmithKline in applying methods of formal ontology to problems of drug discovery and drug safety) provided unflagging support in providing me with research materials. During the period I was working on the book, Jeff also picked up a law degree — and so provided invaluable insight into the process of patent filing and review that contributed substantially to a portion of my treatment in the case of Keith Raniere that became Chapter 10.

Special thanks are due my wife, Carla Kary Merrill for the immense effort she devoted to helping me in the process of transforming the original digital version of the book into a print version, without which this would likely not exist, and for her thorough attention to the details of editing. In addition, it was she who suggested the Raniere case as one of the practical applications of the approach developed here. Throughout, she served as a sounding board and foil for many of my ideas, listened to me rant on periodically about various topics associated with pseudo-philosophy, and continued to encourage the progress of what turned out to be a more lengthy and consuming project than I had anticipated.

Finally, Shawn Dawson was especially helpful in pointing me towards *Paint.NET* to address my needs in image editing, and this saved me untold hours of frustration and despair.

Gary Merrill
Chatham County, North Carolina
January, 2021

Contents

PART 1 HISTORY AND INTRODUCTION 1

CHAPTER 1 A PRELIMINARY VIEW 3

    1.1 Perspective 4
    1.2 Accusations of pseudo-philosophy as warnings 5
    1.3 What's the goal? 8
    1.4 The benefits of understanding pseudo-philosophy 11

CHAPTER 2 THE PHILOSOPHICAL LANDSCAPE 16

    2.1 Approaching what philosophy is 17
    2.2 Philosophy as an esoteric academic discipline 19
    2.3 Philosophy in terms of its areas 24
        Metaphysics 24
        Ethics 26
        Epistemology 28
        Logic 29
        Metaphilosophy 30
    2.4 Philosophy in terms of its schools or traditions 31
    2.5 The "anything goes" view of philosophy 36
    2.6 Some assumptions that philosophers make 37

CHAPTER 3 TOOLS OF THE PHILOSOPHER'S TRADE 40

    3.1 What is a philosopher? 41
    3.2 The philosopher's trade: products and services 45
    3.3 An illuminating philosophical problem 47
        One approach to a solution: semantics 51
        Another approach to a solution: metaphysics 53
        Lessons of the paradox 56
    3.4 The philosopher's basic tool chest 57

PART 2 PHILOSOPHER AND PSEUDO-PHILOSOPHER 75

CHAPTER 4 MODELING THE PHILOSOPHER 77

    4.1 Personas 77
    4.2 *Philo*: the philosopher persona 79
    4.3 Criteria of adequacy re-examined 81
    4.4 Markers 83
        Markers in biomedicine 83
        Markers in business and finance 84
        Markers in philosophy 85
    4.5 The logical and evidential roles of markers 86
    4.6 Markers of genuine philosophy 88

CHAPTER 5 PHILOSOPHY, ITS RELATIVES, AND IMITATORS ... 91

- 5.1 History ... 92
- 5.2 Theology ... 95
- 5.3 Religion ... 96
- 5.4 Rhetoric ... 97
- 5.5 Science ... 99
- 5.6 Psychology ... 101
- 5.7 Literature ... 103
- 5.8 Poetry ... 104
- 5.9 Philosophy or not? If not, then what? ... 105

CHAPTER 6 PERSPECTIVES ON THE PSEUDO ... 107

- 6.1 Some philosophers' views ... 107
  - *R. G. Collingwood on pseudo-art* ... 108
  - *Quine and Ullian on pseudo-science* ... 108
  - *Nicholas Rescher on pseudo-philosophy* ... 110
- 6.2 Dimensions of the pseudo ... 112
- 6.3 Mimicry and pseudo-philosophy ... 114
- 6.4 Is pseudo-philosophy a pseudo-discipline? ... 116

CHAPTER 7 A PRACTICAL MODEL OF PSEUDO-PHILOSOPHY ... 118

- 7.1 *Pseudo*: the pseudo-philosopher persona ... 118
- 7.2 Pseudo-philosophy markers ... 120
- 7.3 Pseudo-philosophy and dishonesty ... 141

PART 3 REAL-WORLD PSEUDO-PHILOSOPHY ... 145

CHAPTER 8 APPLYING THE MODELS: A USER'S GUIDE ... 147

- 8.1 What's so bad about pseudo-philosophy? ... 148
- 8.2 Reacting to pseudo-philosophy ... 148
- 8.3 The anti-sophistical stance ... 150
  - *Suspicion* ... 150
  - *Skepticism* ... 151
  - *Scrutiny* ... 151
- 8.4 Challenges in this approach ... 152
  - *Lack of familiarity with philosophy* ... 152
  - *Providing sufficiently detailed examples* ... 152
  - *Identifying markers in context* ... 153
- 8.5 Expectations and limitations ... 154
- 8.6 Abduction revisited ... 155
  - *An example of abduction* ... 156
  - *The models, abduction, and pseudo-philosophy* ... 157
  - *The simple principle of abduction* ... 158
- 8.7 Practical guidelines ... 159

Contents

CHAPTER 9 NURSING THEORY, KNOWLEDGE, AND SCIENCE 165

9.1 A brief orientation to Nursing Theory 165
9.2 The nursing theory/philosophy controversy 167
    Suspicions and skepticism 169
9.3 Silva's philosophy of nursing knowledge 171
    Setting a context for pseudo-philosophy 171
    A pseudo-philosophy of nursing knowledge 179
    Fatal philosophical flaws 181
    Results and motives 187
9.4 Consequences of pseudo-philosophy for Nursing Theory 192

CHAPTER 10 THE CURIOUS CASE OF KEITH RANIERE 195

10.1 Background 196
10.2 Raniere as a philosopher 199
10.3 Where is Raniere's philosophy? 201
10.4 The *Conocimiento* corpus 203
    Raniere's articles and books 204
    Why publish in Conocimiento? 206
    An initial impression: philosophy or pseudo-philosophy? 207
    Digging in: "When the Justice of Man Meets the Justice of God" 208
    Raniere's views on science vs. religion 210
    Two more samples from Conocimiento 221
    The Conocimiento corpus: a summary 224
10.5 The YouTube performances 224
    What to conclude from the YouTube videos 230
10.6 It's all about Rational Inquiry™ 231
    The Rational Inquiry videos 232
    The Rational Inquiry patent 234
10.7 Making a judgment 237
10.8 A final appraisal 239

CHAPTER 11 AYN RAND: MOSTLY BORROWED, NOTHING NEW? 242

11.1 Background 242
11.2 The hurling of epithets 245
    An alternative 247
11.3 Simplifying our investigation 248
    Limiting the scope 249
    Filtering out commentaries 250
    Rand quoting Rand 253
    Guidelines for appraising Rand's philosophy 255
11.4 *For the New Intellectual* 257
    The Randian view of intellectualism 257
    A perspective on Rand's style 265
    Attila, the Witch Doctor, and the conjuring of demons 269

Conjuring the logical positivist demon 272
What should we have expected? 276
11.5 THE VIRTUE OF SELFISHNESS 280
An introductory look at Rand's ethical principles and concepts 281
Ambiguities and equivocations 287
Prelude to the Shuffle 295
The Shuffle 299
11.6 DETERMINATIONS AND EXPLANATIONS 305
Rand's pseudo-philosophy: origins, impetus, and irony 307

A CONCLUDING METAPHILOSOPHICAL POSTSCRIPT 317
The Pragmatic Model of pseudo-philosophy 318
Lessons learned 320

NOTES 325
REFERENCES 335
INDEX 347
ABOUT THE AUTHOR 351

Part 1

History and Introduction

Chapter 1

A Preliminary View

> *In this chapter:*
> - What does "pseudo" mean?
> - Why is recognizing pseudo-philosophy so important?
> - Where are we going in this book, and what should we expect?

This book is about pseudo-philosophy: whether there is such a thing and — if there is — exactly what characterizes it and distinguishes it from "real" philosophy. Saying that something is "pseudo" is suggesting that it's false, pretentious, misleading, deceptive, or dishonest:

Pseudo-history is "fake history": a kind of "revising" of history that departs from the conventional standards of historical investigation and reporting . Examples include claims that it was Chinese sailors who discovered America, that the Holocaust didn't occur, and that extraterrestrials constructed the Egyptian pyramids.

To say that something is pseudo-artistic is to say that it's falsely portrayed as artistic: it pretends to be artistic, but it's not (Collingwood, 1958). And in art and literature the *pseudo-classical* involves an "imitative use" of the classical style (found, for example, in the 18th century). In the same artistic domains, pseudo-realism (Wikipedia 2020m) refers to works that purport to provide a realistic portrayal of their subjects and content, but may leave out certain critical elements, distort the result, or use "artificial means" (such as animation or altered images) to accomplish the *appearance* of reality.

Numerology, alchemy, and astrology are often cited as examples of pseudo-science. And there's a rich collection of mathematical humor that makes use of pseudo-mathematical reasoning (Dudley 1992) to "prove" pseudo-theorems (such as that all positive odd numbers are prime, that the circle may be squared, that an angle may be trisected by geometrical means alone, or that $1 = 2$). A pseudo-science is pseudo because while it pretends to provide the reliable and intelligible sorts of explanation, prediction, and understanding that a genuine science does (along with methods that support those features), it does not.

In this vein, pseudo-philosophy is fake philosophy: something that pretends to be philosophy but is not.

1.1 Perspective

This project is an exploratory journey of discovery, speculation, hypothesizing, theory-making, analysis, application, testing, and confirmation — concerning whether there's a viable distinction between genuine philosophy and pseudo-philosophy, what that difference is, and how we can tell when we see it. It involves a lot of poking and prodding of ideas, arguments, and theories — as well as some degree of uncertainty, backtracking, and (at times) revision. But to remove some of the mystery and uncertainty, here are some hints regarding how that journey will end.

- There is indeed a viable distinction between genuine philosophy and pseudo-philosophy.

- There are methods that can be applied to see where that line is in general, and to determine when we're dealing with something that's genuinely philosophical and when, instead, we're being confronted with pseudo-philosophy. That is, there's a practical application and value to what we're doing here.

- Rather than ending up with a set of ad hoc guidelines or principles, or a definition of either "philosophy" or "pseudo-philosophy", we'll converge on coherent models of philosophy, pseudo-philosophy, and the relations between them and among them and other disciplines. And these models will then be used as the basis for making judgments about philosophers and pseudo-philosopher in specific cases.

- The models will meet certain criteria of adequacy that we lay out as requirements for succeeding in our journey.

- Even though our models may not yield an absolute and unquestionably clear distinction between the philosophical and pseudo-philosophical in all cases, in those cases where they do not, this will provide a clear sliding scale that can be used in a practical way to decide on whether you want to view a particular work or author as genuinely philosophical or, instead, as pseudo-philosophical.

More important: it will provide a solid foundation on which that debate can be carried out rationally, with substantial clarity and precision, and on the basis of which your genuine/pseudo-philosophy judgment can be argued and justified in each case. In short, it doesn't leave you with just the ability to "express your opinion".

The chapters here are oriented toward readers who have little or no direct experience with philosophy: people who have read few (if any) original sources in the history of philosophy and who haven't taken a course in philosophy, but who still may have an interest in philosophy and what it is, or what they think it is. This is particularly true of Chapter 2 (*The Philosophical Landscape*) although that chapter contains some insight and perspective that may be interesting or unfamiliar even to those with rather broad knowledge of philosophy.

In this and the next chapter we'll provide a basic background to philosophy and a fairly quick and rough comparison of pseudo-philosophy and genuine philosophy that will give us an initial feeling for what some of the fundamental similarities and differences are. We'll ask, and in part answer, such questions as: What is a philosopher? Why is an understanding of pseudo-philosophy important? What's the best way to view the nature of genuine philosophy? What are the major features that distinguish pseudo-philosophy from it? We'll also discuss what we'll be trying to do and to understand in the remainder of the book, what we should expect from that, and how we'll go about it.

With this preliminary view and strategy in hand, then in Part 2 we'll delve into much more detail as we develop a more careful and detailed account (a *theory* or *model*) of pseudo-philosophy: what makes it *pseudo*, how you can identify it when you see it, and how you can avoid falling prey to the trickery of pseudo-philosophers. Along the way we'll illustrate our points with examples taken from the history of philosophy and other fields. Finally, in Part 3, we'll apply this model in identifying the presence of pseudo-philosophy (and pseudo-philosophical writers and techniques) in three detailed real-world cases.

1.2 Accusations of pseudo-philosophy as warnings

The word "philosophy" comes from two Ancient Greek roots — "φιλία" ("philia": *love*, or *love of*) and σοφία ("sophia": *wisdom*) — and means *the love of wisdom*. "Pseudo" comes to us from the Ancient Greek root "ψευδής", and the meaning most commonly given for it is *false*. But the connotation of "pseudo" goes well beyond that of mere falsity, and includes such meanings as *lying, deceptive, sham, fake, bogus, pretending, unauthentic, fraudulent*, and other terms indicating intentional dishonesty for a purpose. Pseudo-philosophy is counterfeit philosophy, and the illusion of knowledge and understanding that comes from it is not genuine wisdom, but *false wisdom*.

There's a lengthy history of philosophers complaining that certain other teachers and writers are not *really* philosophers — that what they offer as philosophy is not *really* philosophy, and often worse: that these pseudo-philosophers seek to dupe their students and readers through a cynical and imitative approach with the purpose of ensnaring followers in an attitude, a world view, or an ideology that's neither well-founded nor even coherently expressed. The pseudo-philosopher seeks to use the hard-earned respect of genuine philosophy to achieve his or her own goals, and to manipulate the minds of the unsuspecting with trickery, dishonesty, and deceit. From this perspective, the pseudo-philosopher is like the construction worker who shows up in a community after a hurricane, promises to repair major damage to your house, does some minor cosmetic fixes, and then takes your money and disappears.

A number of complaints have been made by philosophers about pseudo-philosophy in different periods of history. In 393 BC, Isocrates wrote *Against the Sophists* — a speech in which he exposes the deceptive and self-serving practices of the Greek Sophists who were a group of what we might now think of as "intellectual trainers" or "professional educators". They charged fees to teach "virtue and wisdom" to those (typically the young nobility) who could afford such an education. And originally the term "sophist" itself was intended to refer to a person of wisdom who was in the business of communicating that wisdom to students. But a number of their contemporaries (whom we regard as founding fathers of Western philosophy) accused the Sophists at some length of being pseudo-philosophical, of being dishonest and deceitful in their methods, and of teaching clever methods of rhetoric and persuasion rather than true wisdom. As a result of these sustained attacks by Isocrates (an orator and rhetorician who was technically a Sophist himself), Plato, Xenophon, Aristotle, and (according to Plato in at least some places) Socrates, the word "sophist" came to have the very negative connotation it does today in referring to someone who uses trickery and deceitful (though often entertaining) methods to convince the unwary and leave them with the faulty impression that they'd gained wisdom. Even ancient Greece was rife with accusations of pseudo-philosophy, and emotions could run high.

In the nineteenth century, Arthur Schopenhauer attacked the well-known philosophers Hegel, Schelling, and Fichte as being pseudo-philosophers for using obscure jargon and twisted argumentation to mislead their students and readers. In the twentieth century and continuing into the twenty-first, Jacques Derrida (and so-called "postmodernists" more generally) have been attacked for their unintelligible "philosophical" writings by a number of what we might call "establishment philosophers" (and by scientists as well, for practicing pseudo-science). And popular writers such as Eric Fromm and Ayn Rand have been held — on the one hand — to be innovative thinkers successfully addressing fundamental problems in metaphysics, ethics, and political philosophy, and — on the other — to be hopelessly pretentious pseudo-philosophers in the tradition of the Sophists.

In Part 2 we'll look much more closely at the nature of pseudo-philosophy and its distinctive characteristics. But at this early stage we can sense the following core of complaints against it:

- Pseudo-philosophy results in incoherent and incomprehensible (or "mystical") accounts and explanations that don't yield genuine knowledge and wisdom.
- Embracing it will reduce your "mental powers" (leading you into believing things that aren't true and that don't make sense).
- It has "no merit" in truly understanding the world and the issues it purports to address.
- It's pretentious and deceptive in giving the illusion (but not the reality) of clarifying important problems and issues, and in proposing solutions to them.
- It violates the accepted norms and principles of genuine and honest scholarship while cloaking itself in the respectable trappings of these in order to gain a respect it hasn't earned and doesn't deserve.

These complaints in fact represent warnings about the consequences of pseudo-philosophy that are similar to ones you might see about counterfeit currency, counterfeit brand clothing, counterfeit software, or counterfeit medicines: these are not the real thing, you can't depend on their purity, features, or effect, their properties haven't been "validated" (e.g., by organizations such as the U.S. Food and Drug Administration or various standards organizations), and they're dangerous to the degree that they may result in your making poor decisions, may make you sick, or may kill you. In this way, the complaints against pseudo-philosophy are similar to a mental health warning that genuine philosophy issues against it: *if you drink this Kool-Aid, it will adversely affect your mind and your powers of thinking and reasoning.*

We can see, then, why an understanding of pseudo-philosophy — and the ability to recognize it — is so important:

Chapter 1: A Preliminary View

The Importance of Recognizing Pseudo-philosophy

- It helps you avoid being fooled by intellectual tricksters, duped into holding faulty beliefs, and falling for unsupported or incoherent views, theories, and explanations.

- It puts guards in place to prevent you from acting on the basis of fundamentally faulty thinking and drawing erroneous conclusions.

- It protects you from devoting your time and money to causes or subjects that are based on nonsensical or fake intellectual sleight of hand, intimidation, and groundless appeals to authority.

- It contributes to your acquiring an accurate and useful understanding of genuine philosophy and philosophers, and to adopting a healthy critical and skeptical attitude towards the false wisdom offered by their pseudo-philosophical counterparts.

1.3 What's the goal?

What are we to make of this? Is "pseudo-philosophy" just a nasty term hurled at an opponent whose philosophy you find incorrect or objectionable? Or is there a genuine distinction between philosophy and pseudo-philosophy?

These are a couple of the fundamental questions we'll face, and for which we expect to have answers by the time we arrive at our destination. But even in just thinking about them, we can see that they give rise to a host of other questions we'll need to deal with along the way. One of these is the obvious question "What is philosophy?" And don't we need to answer this question before we can do anything else? How can we possibly provide an account (and criticism) of pseudo-philosophy if we don't first know what philosophy is so that we can contrast pseudo-philosophy to it?

The question as to the nature and definition of philosophy may seem to present us immediately with a very serious, if not insurmountable, obstacle since philosophy has defied a comprehensive and universally accepted definition for over two thousand years. And taking virtually any position on this would leave us open to the accusation that we're prejudiced in one way or another. So if we're to proceed in that direction, we must tread carefully. But first there's the question of exactly what we think our destination is, and there's the related question of what we can reasonably expect to achieve by getting there.

♦ THERE IS NO UNCONTROVERSIAL ACCOUNT

Ideally, we might hope to arrive at definitions of *philosophy* and *pseudo-philosophy* that are universally acceptable and are clear enough for us to apply them to specific cases in an uncontroversial way. But just a moment's reflection will show that such a goal seems entirely unreasonable and unrealistic. To begin, *no one* will want to be judged to be a pseudo-philosopher, and so no matter what our characterization of pseudo-philosophy is, the people who turn out to be pseudo-philosophers according to it are likely to find it unacceptable (or to argue that we haven't applied it correctly). So we can't expect to achieve an uncontroversial and universally acceptable account of pseudo-philosophy. And, as we shall see, there's even a question concerning whether there *is* a clear distinction that can be drawn between philosophy and pseudo-philosophy.

Instead, we can hope at best to arrive at characterizations (which will not be *definitions*) of philosophy and pseudo-philosophy that are *acceptable* to most interested parties and that can be *applied* (in what is acknowledged as a reasonably objective manner) to make *defensible judgments* about whether a work or a writer is genuinely philosophical or pseudo-philosophical. Who are the "interested parties"? Well, these must include a significant plurality of recognized academic philosophers who, after all, have the strongest claim to the title of "philosopher" because of their formal studies, professional activities, and intellectual pedigrees stretching back through the ages. These interested parties should also include academics from other disciplines — including the arts, the humanities, and the sciences — who are sensitive to philosophical issues and questions, and who may often use philosophy themselves. To be sure, we can't expect *everyone* to be satisfied with our account of the nature of pseudo-philosophy, but this is in part a consequence of the nature of any intellectual discipline. However, we should expect that our account will find broad acceptance among professional philosophers, their students, and those in other disciplines who have philosophical interests.

♦ AN HISTORICAL CONSTRAINT

There's another important constraint to be imposed in determining where we're going and how we'll know we've succeeded: whatever our characterization of pseudo-philosophy turns out to be, the preponderance of what professional philosophers regard as genuine philosophy over the past two millennia must turn out — according to our characterization — to be genuine philosophy and not pseudo-philosophy. If we don't accomplish this, then what we mean by *philosophy* won't be what it means either historically, academically, or in its core meaning in current parlance. However, this does *not* mean that the applications of our characterization may not have some surprising results when applied to various parts of the history of philosophy. But overwhelmingly — *for the most part* — our approach should not end up judging as pseudo-philosophical a significant portion of what previously has been regarded as genuine philosophy.

Thus while we don't want our account of pseudo-philosophy to be merely a defense of "establishment" or "institutional" philosophy, it's precisely establishment and institutional philosophy, stretched across two thousand years, that has given the term "philosophy" whatever objective meaning it has. And we do assume that this term *is* meaningful in a non-subjective way, and that this meaning is shared by practicing philosophers, their students, and others in the arts, humanities, and sciences. Moreover, even the alleged pseudo-philosophers acknowledge and share this meaning (as we shall see repeatedly) since it's the very thing they want to "borrow" for themselves!

♦ THE GOAL

Our ultimate goal, then, is to arrive at a comprehensive account of pseudo-philosophy that satisfies several criteria:

Criteria for an Account of the Nature of Pseudo-philosophy

Distinctness Criterion: The account must provide a clear distinction between pseudo-philosophy and genuine philosophy. This *doesn't* mean that there won't be some fuzzy or borderline cases. We can also expect there to be cases in which some good arguments — based on our principles — can be given for classifying something as pseudo-philosophy and some good arguments given for classifying it as genuine philosophy, so that a final judgment may need to be made on the "preponderance of the evidence". But it *does* mean that there will be a number of clear (and among them, well-known) cases in which the classification — based on our principles — is uncontroversial.

Applicability Criterion: The account must provide guidelines that can be applied in specific cases to justify classifying a writer or a work as pseudo-philosophical. That is, the account must be sufficiently clear and precise that we can use it to make judgments in specific cases, and that people can agree on these judgments and the reasons supporting them.

Compatibility Criterion: It must be compatible with how philosophy has been viewed throughout its history. This is a kind of "conservation principle" that ensures that we don't achieve our intended goal through cheating by changing the meaning of the word "philosophy" to be something other than its recognized historical sense.

Acceptability Criterion: The account must be acceptable to the vast majority of professional philosophers and academics in other disciplines to the degree that they're concerned with philosophical matters and philosophical questions pertaining to their disciplines.

Neutrality Criterion: The account must be as ideologically neutral as possible in terms of taking a perspective on the nature of philosophy.

1.4 The benefits of understanding pseudo-philosophy

Achieving this goal, and satisfying these criteria, will yield three fundamental benefits. First, it will provide us with a clear, comprehensive, and applicable characterization of pseudo-philosophy that has so far been lacking in the philosophical literature (where accounts of pseudo-philosophy are brief, episodic, incomplete, often vague, and generally oriented towards attacks on one writer or a particular "school" of writers). Second, it will provide us with a coherent and principled basis upon which we can render a judgment of pseudo-philosophy. And third, it (and the process we go through in achieving this goal) will yield a fuller understanding not just of pseudo-philosophy, but of the nature of philosophy itself and its distinctive character. Moreover, this list is an example of a set of *criteria of adequacy* for a philosophical inquiry that we'll discuss more fully in Chapter 4 and that will serve as an important component in our treatment of the distinction between genuine philosophy and pseudo-philosophy.

♦ QUESTIONS TO BE ANSWERED

We expect our account will enable us to answer — *in a principled and justifiable manner* — such questions as:

- *Why* is a particular work reasonably thought of as an example of pseudo-philosophy?
- Are there *objective reasons* for classifying the work as pseudo-philosophy? What principles are used in making this judgment? Are these principles reasonable?
- What *part* of a particular author's writings are pseudo-philosophical?

- Although they're talking about the same subject matter and saying many of the same things, why is the work of *one* author pseudo-philosophical and the work of *another* author genuinely philosophical?
- What, in general, is the *difference* between genuine philosophy and pseudo-philosophy?
- What's the difference between pseudo-philosophy and philosophy that's just *poorly done*?
- *What would it take* to turn a particular author's pseudo-philosophy into genuine philosophy? Can it be "repaired", or is it hopelessly pseudo-philosophical?

We'll begin by assuming that there *is* a difference between philosophy and pseudo-philosophy — and we have some evidence for this in explicit comments and criticisms by philosophers across two millennia. Then we'll attempt to provide additional support for that assumption. But we can also begin by offering a brief argument that such an assumption is both necessary and of value, and that it offers some insight into why we should care about understanding the difference between philosophy and pseudo-philosophy. This argument will also expose some dangers in what we're attempting to do, and these must be kept in mind as we progress through the rest of the book. Here is the preliminary argument:

Philosophy is an intellectual and academic discipline (we'll talk more about this — at some length — in the Chapter 2 and provide additional illustrations in Chapters 5 and 6). It's a domain that you may study — like physics or biology or chemistry or music or sculpture or mathematics or pig farming. Some things are chemistry and some things are not. When I play my tuba I'm involved in music, and not in chemistry (although various chemical processes may be going on in both my body and my tuba). When I run an experiment in a chemical laboratory to identify an unknown substance, I'm involved in chemistry and not in music or tuba playing — although I could be involved in both if I'm humming or whistling at the time. When I take a course in chemistry, I'll be very puzzled if one day the instructor brings her flute into the classroom and gives a recital as a chemistry class. I should be similarly surprised if my philosophy instructor brings her flute into my metaphysics class and delivers a recital rather than a lecture or discussion in metaphysics. Flute playing is not metaphysics, and metaphysics is not flute playing. I might be sufficiently shocked that I would go to the department chairman or to the dean and say "I signed up for a course in chemistry and got flute playing. Something is wrong here. I need a course in chemistry." Or "I need a course in metaphysics to complete my requirements. The flute recitals aren't helping with this, however nice they otherwise are." Of course, the flute playing would be perfectly appropriate in a course in flute performance, and a chemistry experiment would be perfectly appropriate in a chemistry course (though not in a music performance course).

These admittedly silly examples illustrate the point that there are genuine differences among disciplines in terms of their scopes and their subject matters. Certainly I'd like my biology professor to have studied biology and to have an advanced degree and some experience in biology — and not in, say, romantic poetry (unless he *also* has a degree in biology!). And just as we acknowledge a fundamental difference between music and chemistry, between chemistry and mathematics, and between sculpture and physics, so we should acknowledge a difference between philosophy and each of these disciplines. And this means that *some things are philosophy and some things are not*, and that should seem quite obvious — though we'll return to the details of such differences in Chapter 5.

Now if *some things are philosophy and some things are not*, then it's possible for something that is *not* philosophy to *appear* to be philosophy — or to *try* to appear to be philosophy. Pseudo-philosophy is such a thing, and it bears the same relation to philosophy that pseudo-science bears to science (a similarity that we'll explore more fully a bit further on in the book). And all of this goes to provide some support for our initial assumption that there *is* a difference between philosophy and pseudo-philosophy. But why go to all this trouble to support the reasonableness of our assumption? Isn't it, after all, pretty obvious?

The answer is that it may not be so obvious if you start to think about it a bit too much — which philosophers, particularly, are prone to do. The problem lies in the nature and scope of philosophy itself. We could easily take the view that because philosophy is so broad in its scope, because it permits of so many alternative (and at times conflicting) approaches, and because there are philosophical problems and issues in every discipline, then there really is nothing that is *not* philosophy in some way or other, or to some degree or other. This may not be an incoherent view (although it's a little vague), but it does render the term "philosophy" rather meaningless; and it's incompatible with how the term has been used historically and continues to be used today. Just *because* there may be "gray" areas concerning what is philosophy and what is not (so that in some cases it's difficult to decide), it doesn't follow from this that there's *no* fruitful distinction that may be drawn between the philosophical (genuine philosophy), the non-philosophical (music, chemistry, etc.), and the pseudo-philosophical. So we shall begin by assuming that there *is* such a distinction — even though we may not (yet) have a very clear idea of *just what this is*, or *where or how we can draw the line*. And part of the work in this book is to clarify that distinction in a useful way.

So if there *is* a difference between philosophy and pseudo-philosophy, then how can we get at it? How may we discover (if it's a matter of discovering) or decide (if it's a matter of deciding) what this difference is or ought to be? For this, we'll need to make use of several different methods.

♦ THE PATH AHEAD

First (in Chapter 2 and again more deeply in Chapters 4 and 6), we'll look at what philosophers *say* when they accuse someone of creating pseudo-philosophy or of being a pseudo-philosopher. We'll see that this is, in general, quite different from what they say when they're criticizing another philosopher for making a (philosophical) *mistake*, for misunderstanding, for employing a faulty methodology, or for misapplying a methodology. What is it, we'll ask, that really irritated the likes of Isocrates, Plato, Xenophon, Aristotle, and others about the Sophists? What were they really complaining about? What is it that so upset Schopenhauer about the work of Fichte, Schelling, and Hegel? Why were a group of philosophy professors so upset with the work of Jacques Derrida that in 1992 they wrote a letter to the *The Times* of London, protesting in very strong language the proposed award of an honorary degree to Derrida by the University of Cambridge? Answers to these questions will provide us with an initial understanding of what philosophers traditionally have regarded as central features of pseudo-philosophy, but to some degree this will serve only to focus our attention on the accused.

Our second method (introduced in Chapter 2 and used more extensively in Chapters 4 and 6) will then be to look directly at the philosophers and writings that have been accused of being pseudo-philosophical. We'll compare these with one another and scrutinize them in the light of the accusations against them, attempting to extract similarities and to abstract general themes, techniques, and principles. We'll augment this approach by also looking more closely at the common characteristics of other pseudo-disciplines such as pseudo-science and pseudo-history, in an attempt to identify a broader pattern shared by writers in pseudo-disciplines.

This process will lead naturally to our third method where (in Chapter 6) we'll begin to make some hypotheses about the pseudo-philosophical and its relation to the genuinely philosophical, and on that basis in Chapter 7 we'll create a list of *themes* and *symptoms* that seem to be displayed in these writings. In turn, these themes, techniques, principles, and hypotheses will then begin to yield a *model* of the nature of pseudo-philosophy. And this model will be refined and tested as the book progresses and as we consider specific cases of philosophy and pseudo-philosophy. With this method we may in turn take our model to be the diagnosis of a disease or medical condition (the condition of pseudo-philosophy) and our goal will be to arrive at a characteristic set of symptoms or "markers" of the condition that we'll be able to use in identifying the condition in new cases. This is a good approach for a couple of reasons. Pseudo-philosophy may be regarded as a kind pathological condition afflicting true philosophy, and — just as in the case of disease diagnosis and classification — a diagnosis may be (and may need to be) made on the grounds of several symptoms being present, even when the patient isn't exhibiting all of the symptoms that may be manifested by the disease. We'll return to this analogy from time to time as our journey progresses.

All this means that we'll be taking what philosophers have said about pseudo-philosophy, as well as what the alleged pseudo-philosophers themselves have said (both in what they purport to be philosophy and in their defenses against their accusers), and we'll be using this as "data" in arriving at (and testing) our model of pseudo-philosophy. This model (or theory, or characterization) of pseudo-philosophy ultimately will be expressed in the form of a set of inter-related criteria and guidelines to be used in identifying pseudo-philosophy and making judgments with regard to specific works and authors.

Chapter 2

The Philosophical Landscape

> *In this chapter:*
> - How should we look at philosophy as an area of study or knowledge?
> - Characterizing philosophy without "defining" it
> - Views of what philosophy is and what philosophers do
> - The philosopher persona: a useful representation and tool

Richard Taylor opens his great little book *Metaphysics* (Taylor 1992) with the observation that while it's sometimes said that everyone has a philosophy, in fact "nothing could be sillier": that people have *opinions*, and that some of these (in the areas of religion, morals, the meaning of life, etc.) border on philosophy, but in general people have no idea of what philosophy really is or what philosophers do. And indeed it seems true that people have one of two views about philosophy.

The first is that everyone is entitled to his or her own philosophical opinions, which are at least as good as those anyone else may express; and the second is that philosophy is a deep, dark, excessively complicated subject that's impossible for the average reasonably intelligent person to understand and may, in fact, be incoherent. While I won't say that nothing could be sillier, each of these views presents a challenge we'll have to confront here. Such an attitude and perception of philosophy can make philosophy difficult for you to approach and understand, can stand in the way of your understanding philosophy and what it is, and can make you more susceptible to the lure of pseudo-philosophy. Ignorance of what you're being sold always puts you at a disadvantage to a clever salesman. But understanding philosophy — and understanding *how* to understand it — isn't any more difficult than understanding basic science, mathematics, literature, music, art, poetry, or history. The initial stumbling block is that while people are introduced to those other subjects from a very early age in school (beginning in elementary school), they typically encounter philosophy only at a much later age, and in a way (perhaps in university courses) where the initial level of it is more complex. We're going to try to bypass that kind of "intellectual shock" here, cover the basics in a way that — while admittedly incomplete — is accurate and adequate for our purposes, and use that to move on in our approach to pseudo-philosophy.

2.1 Approaching what philosophy is

Defining what philosophy is, or answering the question "What is philosophy?", are notoriously difficult tasks — historically open to intense, seemingly unbounded, and unresolved debate. But we still need some reasonably clear and practical characterization of philosophy that can be applied in specific cases and will make what we say about philosophy (and pseudo-philosophy) intelligible. For our purposes, we can achieve a pretty good initial approximation of such a characterization by looking at what people regarded as philosophers *do* and have done, what they *say* they do, and what they say are their *goals and methods*.

Even this is tricky because the first step in this process appears to lie in deciding which writers count as philosophers. So it appears that what we need first is a characterization of philosophy in order to tell *who* the philosophers are, in order to get a characterization of philosophy. This seems circular since it makes it look like we need a characterization of philosophy in order to get a characterization of philosophy. And this is the kind of problem that makes philosophy (whatever it is) difficult. It's exactly the sort of twisted handwringing situation that philosophers and philosophy students can get into if they think they're looking for a *definition* of philosophy. If we think that we need an adequate, precise, and acceptable *definition* of philosophy in order to begin to draw an intelligible distinction between philosophy and pseudo-philosophy, then we're sunk.

But it's not hopeless — because *we're not looking for a definition of philosophy*! And it's true that to some degree we do need to *start* with *some* characterization of philosophy in order to get *the* characterization of philosophy we need. But that's all right! It's all right because we can regard the *first* characterization we start with as a (possibly somewhat imprecise and incomplete) *working hypothesis* of what philosophy is, and as we use and test that provisional characterization, we'll probably change it and sharpen it up. We'll throw some things out of it and include other things. Ultimately, we'll arrive at a *final* characterization that does the job we need it to. In doing this (which is *not* a circular process, but a convergent one), we may need to make some decisions at the beginning that might appear to be arbitrary in some ways, and they certainly may be provisional and subject to revision — but in the end we should either be able to provide good grounds for these and keep them, or else discover that they really were arbitrary and throw them out. So, much like a scientist, we can investigate the nature of philosophy and arrive at a good characterization of it by proceeding with hypotheses about it, confirming or refuting those hypotheses, fitting those hypotheses to history and the facts, and successively refining the characterization in order to make it better and more accurate.

In addition — as we'll discover again and again — the pseudo-philosophers themselves generally agree with the genuine philosophers concerning the characteristics (or many of them) of genuine philosophy. And in fact they want to leverage this agreement in order to bring respect to their own works. So we won't be "begging the question" (which means "assuming what we're trying to prove") against the pseudo-philosophers. We want to avoid both arbitrariness (simply defining by fiat, either explicitly or implicitly, "what philosophy really is") and meaninglessness (ending in the view that "anything counts as philosophy") as a consequence of a too–liberal and broad characterization. And remember: whatever we do come up with must satisfy the *Applicability Criterion* and be generally acceptable to the "philosophical community" (in which for this purpose we can include the pseudo-philosophers as well). With these considerations, let's proceed with building our initial characterization of philosophy.

Our approach to characterizing philosophy

- We won't try to provide a *definition* of philosophy.

- Instead, we'll work towards providing a *characterization* of philosophy that will become increasingly more precise through an iterative process of successive refinement, and will be

- *acceptable* to the preponderance of historical and contemporary professional philosophers

- *consistent* with how philosophy and pseudo-philosophy have been viewed throughout history

- *applicable* in assessing whether a particular work (or particular writer) is genuinely philosophical or pseudo-philosophical

- *applied* to a number of specific test cases drawn from several academic/intellectual domains

- *evaluated* in terms of its success in analyzing these cases as being either genuine philosophy or pseudo-philosophy.

To do this, we'll look at philosophy, philosophers, and the history of these from several different perspectives, we'll look at other proposed definitions or characterizations of philosophy, and we'll develop some additional and new methods for distinguishing between genuine philosophy and pseudo-philosophy.

Certainly the common view of philosophy is of a body of knowledge, or an approach to understanding the world, that's esoteric, difficult to understand, and difficult to see as applying to the everyday world. Philosophers, it is often felt, think "deep thoughts" about such things as truth, meaning, what "good" means, what it means to have a "right", the nature of God (and gods), whether we have free will (and what that means), what really exists and what only seems to exist, how we think and how to think correctly, and a number of other abstract topics.

If you want to become a philosopher — or to gain some knowledge and appreciation of philosophy, its history, and practice — then you might take one or more courses in philosophy, or perhaps even pursue philosophy as your minor or major subject in school. In that case you'll study philosophy from several different perspectives, including the history of philosophy, what philosophers have regarded as the major problems to be addressed (and hopefully solved), and methods that philosophers use to pursue those problems and solutions. This would at least give you a good view of a representative cross-section of "mainstream philosophy" as it appears at this point in history and from the perspective of professional university philosophers.

Aristotle begins his book *Metaphysics* by observing that "All men, by nature, desire to know," and he goes on immediately to clarify that the sort of knowledge he's talking about is a deep sense of knowledge that becomes wisdom because of the depth of understanding that it represents: we have wisdom when we know the 'why' of things. To Aristotle, the philosopher's deepest duty is to pursue knowledge (and the truth on which it's based) in order to attain — so far as possible — wisdom. "Clearly then Wisdom is knowledge about certain principles and causes," he says. Genuine philosophy (and a genuine philosopher) is then compelled to pursue knowledge and wisdom, distinguishing what is true from what is not true, and developing methods that will take us in a reliable way to genuine knowledge and wisdom. As we progress through later chapters, we'll see that this one sentence contains the elements (truth, knowledge, method) that lie at the foundation of distinguishing philosophy from pseudo-philosophy.

Other than this, at the moment, we don't need to settle such questions as "What is philosophy? " or "What distinguishes philosophy from other pursuits or disciplines?" or "What precisely are the distinctive characteristics of philosophy?" This will be just the skeleton of a starting point that will enable us to begin moving forward and adding flesh to these bones as we proceed.

2.2 Philosophy as an esoteric academic discipline

Suppose that we wanted to find some philosophers — perhaps to ask questions about their jobs, what they do every day, and the nature of philosophy. Where would we look?

If we wanted to find a plumber, we'd perhaps look in a telephone directory or we'd search online for plumbers in our area. A number of plumbers would come to our attention in this way, and we could then choose one for the work needed. Similarly for electricians, or auto mechanics, or doctors, or police officers, or dentists. But where are the philosophers, and how do we find them?

Everyone knows the answer to this, of course (and it would become apparent if we did that online search for philosophers): they're all in the universities and colleges. If you want a philosopher, that's where you have to go (aside from trying to find an unemployed philosopher, which shouldn't be difficult because there are so many, but is in fact very difficult because they don't advertise). Nowadays, in virtually the entire world, a professional philosopher can be found only in a department of philosophy in a university (or perhaps in a department of religion, or a combined department of philosophy and religious studies, or perhaps in a seminary, or maybe in a department of cognitive science). Professional mathematicians and engineers and scientists and golf course designers and artists and musicians, etc. may be found in myriad places across the globe. But philosophers are holed up behind the walls of academia. If you're making a living as a philosopher, you're doing it by being a philosophy professor (or instructor) in a university. This was not always so.[1]

Socrates (c. 470-399 BC) — often thought of as the father of Greek and Western philosophy — was the son of a stone mason and worked as a mason for some time. He also served in the Athenian military as a hoplite infantryman for a number of years, during which he participated in three major campaigns and earned a reputation for his courage in battle. There's significant dispute in the historical record (from the perspectives of his two major students) concerning whether Socrates was ever paid as a professional philosopher. Plato indicates that Socrates didn't accept payment for his role as a philosophy teacher, but Xenophon (another of Socrates' students) reports that he was paid for teaching (Aristophanes agrees with this). On the other hand, Xenophon also reports that Socrates' wife Xanthippe complained that he wasn't making enough as a philosopher to support the family.

Xenophon (c. 430-354 BC), a student of Socrates who's primarily thought of as an historian, but something of a philosopher as well, made his living mostly as a soldier and mercenary, and is regarded as the greatest military strategist prior to Alexander. Plato (c. 423– 327 BC) was from a very wealthy and politically influential family, and so doesn't seem to have had any money worries. There is some evidence that he made money early in his life as a professional wrestler (and in fact that the name "Plato" is really a nickname, meaning *broad* or *broad-shouldered*, given to him by a wrestling coach). But the origins of his name, and exactly what his real name was, are obscure. At about age 40, Plato returned from lengthy travels to establish a school (*The Academy*), becoming the functional equivalent of a philosophy professor. Later, Plato ran afoul of some political intrigue, was sold into slavery, bought out of slavery, then became a prisoner of the King in Syracuse for several years before making it back to Athens. For someone with such an education, well-placed friends, and an excellent résumé in philosophy, he seems to have had a really rocky career path.

Rene Descartes (1596–1650) — "I think, therefore I am." — was a professional military officer from 1618 until 1620, and then invested his savings in bonds which provided him with a reasonable income for the remainder of his life.

Baruch Spinoza (1632-1677) was a lens grinder, producing lenses for microscopes and telescopes; but he didn't make a lot of money at it although his lenses were regarded as very high quality. He was also supported, in part, by charitable donations from his friends.

Although his father had been a professor of moral philosophy, and he had himself received prestigious graduate degrees in philosophy, Gottfried Wilhelm Leibniz (1646–1716) worked as a secretary at a society for alchemists, then worked as an administrator in a Court of Appeal, as a diplomat, and finally as a Counselor for Justice.

David Hume (1711–1776) worked as an office assistant and did some tutoring. He later got a job as a librarian in the University of Edinburgh, which paid practically nothing but gave him access to a great library. In later years he became Secretary to the British Embassy in Paris, then served as a *Charges d'affaires* (which was largely a letter-writing job), and as Under Secretary of State for a region in northern England. He was, basically, an academic and government bureaucrat. But it gave him time to make major and lasting contributions to philosophy.

The American philosopher C. S. Peirce (1839–1914) — who made truly significant contributions to mathematics, statistics, scientific methodology, semantics (then called "semiotics"), and logic — worked for about 30 years in a scientific capacity for the United States Coast Survey and (what it later became) the United States Coast and Geodetic Survey. He also worked during this period in Harvard's astronomical observatory and devoted significant amounts of time (detracting substantially from his job performance) to generating what turned out to be voluminous writings on philosophical topics that interested him. Because he spent so much time on what was non–job–related work, in 1891 he was asked to resign from the U.S. Coast Survey and never had reliable employment again. In 1879 he had landed a part-time untenured position as a lecturer in logic at Johns Hopkins University. Unfortunately, he was fired from this position in 1884 for living with the woman (who was to become his second wife) while still technically married to his first wife. He continued to do and publish excellent philosophical work, but without benefit of an academic position from which to do it, and he died in abject poverty.

These examples, and a number of others we could list, show us three things about people who are regarded as philosophers. First, we see that, historically, a significant number of philosophers didn't actually work as philosophers in the sense of deriving their income and livelihood from either teaching or publishing philosophy. They may have devoted a substantial amount of time to their philosophical activities (perhaps even more than to their regular jobs), but they didn't make a living from these activities. In this sense they weren't *professional* philosophers as we think of this term today. And this group of *non-professional* (or perhaps even *amateur*) philosophers included some of the truly *major* figures in the history of Western philosophy.

Second, we see that things have changed over the past 2,000 years in terms of the roles and positions of philosophers in our society. Philosophy has become an almost purely academic discipline, exhibiting the common features of academic disciplines.

Third, this results in a kind of control of the dissemination of research and information in the field by determining who gets appointed to editorial boards and to positions as referees for professional journals, research grant applications, and respected book publishers. And this in turn imposes various constraints on what gets published as "real philosophy" — which means that it's very difficult for a non-professional philosopher (i.e., one without a university affiliation of some kind, if not an appointment as a professor at some rank) to get an entirely fair hearing and consideration; and the publication of philosophical work is pretty heavily slanted in the direction of whatever the fashionable trends are in terms of the hottest topics and problems that are currently being recognized by "professional philosophers" and their students (who are hoping to become professional philosophers themselves).

This has always been true (at least for several hundred years), but it progressed substantially in the 20th century and has become much more pronounced today. To some degree it has to be this way since it's the only way to establish and make sense of the notion of professional standards and standards of scholarship in a given discipline. But this means that there are strong forces oriented against according respect (as representing "genuine philosophy") to the work of someone who isn't part of this closed community of "certified" professional philosophers and who isn't participating in the "academic game" (involving university affiliation, conferences of professional philosophical societies such as the American Philosophical Association, research grants, awards by professional associations, publications, pursuit of promotion and tenure, and so on).

For us, this means that in analyzing and characterizing the differences between genuine philosophy and pseudo-philosophy, while we must use the practice and works of "recognized" philosophers as a basis and touchstone for our conception of philosophy and its distinctive characteristics, we must also beware of going too far in this direction and falling victim to an attitude of authoritarianism which takes accepted academic philosophy as the only measure of genuine philosophy. In part we must do this because one of the very first responses of the pseudo-philosopher, pseudo-historian, or pseudo-scientist is to claim that the reason his or her work doesn't have the respect it deserves is simply because the author isn't a member of the current academically privileged "in group". Of course this is always an easy charge to make. But there may be something to it in particular cases, and philosophy faces a more difficult response to such a charge simply because of the general (or seeming) lack of objective standards that's broadly acknowledged by the "establishment philosophers" themselves. If you can't provide clear lines delineating what you do from things that other people do, then you can't make a very convincing case that someone has crossed those vague or non-existent lines. And this is perhaps one reason that so little attention has been devoted by philosophers to the notion of pseudo-philosophy. Sometimes it's wiser to ignore the pig than to wrestle with it in the mud. We'll deal with some of these challenging problems in Chapter 5.

With such caveats in mind, let's take a cursory look at academic philosophy and how it's organized. The sketch drawn here won't be exhaustive, but more complete accounts can easily be found elsewhere, and we just need to hit the highlights in order to provide some background for later chapters.

There are several different ways in which philosophers, philosophical problems, works in philosophy, and philosophy courses can be organized or categorized. These include: the different *areas* of philosophy (such as ethics, metaphysics, logic, etc.), different *historical periods* (pre-Socratic, ancient, medieval, modern, etc.), different *methodological types* or "schools" (analytic, existentialist, logical positivist, phenomenologist, idealist, etc.), philosophy that's characteristic of a *geographical/political/national region*, perhaps during a given historical period (British, American, Continental, French, 19th Century German, etc.), and others. For our purposes, we don't need to dwell on these distinctions or many of the details that they involve. But to get a better idea of the philosophical landscape and how it may relate to pseudo-philosophy, we'll look briefly at two approaches to how philosophy may be organized or categorized.

2.3 Philosophy in terms of its areas

In order to get a degree in philosophy, your education must cover at least what are regarded as the basic areas of the subject (sometimes referred to as *areas of specialization* or *areas of expertise*). If you look at the PhilPapers.org site (a Web site and organization intended primarily for professional academic philosophers and their students), you'll see that works in philosophy are split up into six primary areas, over forty secondary areas, and a huge number of more specific areas. As an example, the primary area of *Value Theory* has a secondary area of *Social and Political Philosophy* which in turn has a sub-area of *Culture and Cultures* which in turn has a sub-area of *Cultural Relativism*. Philosophers, as we'll see, are good at splitting hairs. In addition, the organization of philosophical areas on PhilPapers reflects the perspective of its editors and would appear at least somewhat differently if done by a different set of philosophers. The view we'll take here is very similar to that of PhilPapers, but much simpler in that we'll look only at the highest level of how the various areas of philosophy can be characterized.

Traditionally, the broadest areas are:

Metaphysics

Immediately we run into a problem because this area and the meaning of the term "metaphysics" are notoriously difficult to characterize and delimit. Very informally we can say that metaphysics has to do with the "ultimate reality" that "underlies" what we experience in the world. I've put these terms inside quotation marks (scare quotes) to indicate that the meanings of these critical terms are unclear and open to much debate. In fact, it's the metaphysician's job to clarify what ultimate reality is and what it means for it to underlie the normal experience we have in the world. This, of course, requires a great deal of "deep thought" and corresponding jargon and complex expressions of that thought — things that most people take to be hallmarks of philosophy.

Without looking into the details of metaphysical theories or analyses themselves, we can get at least a glimpse and rough understanding of this area by looking at the sorts of questions and problems metaphysicians traditionally have dealt with:

- What are causes? What is the relation between cause and effect? Are there *really* causes, or are we just fooled into believing this by what we see in the world?

- Does God exist? What arguments are there for and against the existence of God? What is God's relation to people? What are God's attributes? If God exists and is good, then how can so many bad things happen in the world?

- Do we have free will? What does it mean to have free will? How can we tell if we have free will?

- What is the nature of our minds? Do we really have minds, or is this just an illusion? What's the relation of my mind with my body? Could androids or robots have minds?

- What's the nature of space? How does this affect us?

- What's the nature of time? How does this affect us? Is time travel possible?

- Is there only one correct way to look at space and time, or are there alternate incompatible ways of doing this, each of which "works"?

- How is change possible? Even before the time of Socrates, some philosophers had offered arguments that change (movement, flowing of a river, change in size or color, etc.) wasn't possible, and *the problem of change* (explaining what it is and how it's possible) became an important topic of philosophical thought.

- The problem of universals. Universals are "what is common" to a number of individuals that have the "same property". A typical example is *color*. Other examples drawn from the history of philosophy are *being a man* and *being a triangle*. What is it that makes all red things red? What makes all men be men? And what makes each triangle a triangle? One answer to this is that in addition to individuals (such as *this* red ball, *this* man, and *this* triangle), there are abstract and "general" *features* or *properties* that individuals share: redness, being a man, and triangularity. These are "universal" across many particulars or individuals and account for the similarities that we see in individual things. This is a very crude description of universals, and the details of any theory of universals become complicated very quickly. Some philosophers (often called "nominalists") deny the existence, and even the coherence, of universals, and seek to provide a basis and account of similarity in different ways.

- Does life have meaning? What meaning does it have? If it doesn't have meaning, what am I doing here?

- What's the difference between fact, possibility, and necessity? Are there some things (facts about the world, about our nature, about the nature of numbers, about science, about how we see and understand the world) that are necessary? Why are these things necessary while other things are not?

From a philosophical point of view, metaphysics grapples with fundamental questions about the nature and structure of the world that may not — or that some philosophers say cannot — be understood in other ways (such as through science or religion), or at least cannot be completely understood in those other ways. Other philosophers question whether metaphysics, in this sense, is even possible or makes sense; or whether it really amounts to attempting to provide indeterminable and obscure or unintelligible answers to *pseudo-questions* (questions that look like genuine questions that should have answers but turn out to be unintelligible or nonsensical when you start to dig into them).

Ethics

Ethics deals with the good and the bad, morality, rights and obligations, actions and their consequences. It's often referred to as *moral philosophy*. In more contemporary times, the conception of it has been generalized to *Value Theory* and it bears strong relations to *social and political philosophy* and the *philosophy of law* which can be thought of either as specialized areas of ethics (to some degree) or areas in which ethics, ethical theory, and value theory are applied to certain more specific philosophical domains. Other narrower, more specialized, or "application" areas of ethics now present in academic philosophy include business ethics, environmental ethics, computer/information ethics, engineering ethics, medical ethics, bioethics, internet ethics, and others. At this point, if there is an area in which people may be faced with some sort of moral decision at one point or another (which includes just about any area you can think of), academic ethicists have created a sub-area of ethics in which to ply their craft.

Ethics, in its various forms and orientations, has become extremely popular in academic philosophy over the past 30 years, and now a significant number of philosophy departments are heavily weighted (in terms of the proportion of their faculty devoted to the different areas of philosophy) to offering courses and programs in ethics and its related areas and sub-areas. In the geographical area in which I live there are three major universities — two large state universities and a large and highly respected private university. An examination of the philosophy departments of these schools shows that in the private university about 38% of its faculty work and teach in ethics and its associated areas, while in each of the two public universities, at least 50% of the philosophy faculty work in these areas! This significantly disproportionate representation of ethics in faculty and

Section 2.3: Philosophy in terms of its areas

in course offerings is partly a sign of the effect that philosophers in these areas have had on real world issues and problems (in the domains of medical ethics, environmental ethics, business ethics, and fashionable issues and problems) while the other areas of philosophy still tend to be regarded as "esoteric", "difficult" and "other worldly" (not *relevant* to normal people and their lives). We'll say more about this in later chapters where we consider examples of pseudo-philosophy.

We can't begin to approach a characterization of all of these different domains in which a philosophical approach to ethics is being practiced today. Instead, we'll provide a brief (and hopefully useful) account of good old *Ethics*, and leave further investigation of its details and descendants as an exercise for the ambitious reader. The sorts of questions and problems with which an ethicist traditionally has been concerned include:

- Can virtue (i.e., goodness) be taught? That is, can you learn to be good? Or is it something you're either born with or without?
- Can we draw a coherent distinction between good and bad (or good and evil) without an appeal to God (or some supreme being or authority)? How can we do that?
- What principles and guidelines can be used to make ethical decisions in our daily lives?
- If we encounter a conflict in our duties or responsibilities, how can we resolve this?
- What's the relationship between morality and happiness?
- Is there a *natural law* concerning right and wrong? How can we come to know it?
- Is it possible to base ethics on self-interest?
- In making ethical choices, is it reasonable to equate what's *right* (or good) with the greatest individual good for the greatest number of people ("The good of the many outweighs the good of the few.")? Or does such an approach end up violating the rights of individuals in unjustified ways and with deplorable consequences (such as sacrificing the rights of minorities because they are "the few")?
- Is there such a thing as moral sense?
- Which ethical theories (bases for morality) are compatible with various political philosophies and forms of government (socialism,

capitalism, Marxism, theocracy, libertarianism, monarchy, democracy, ...)?

Epistemology

Epistemology is also known as the *theory of knowledge* and it focuses on what "knowledge" means, what "belief" means, whether and how it's possible to have knowledge, and what the grounds are for *rational belief*. Epistemological problems, analyses, and theories are often closely related to problems and theories in metaphysics, logic, and the philosophy of science. Example questions addressed by epistemologists include:

- Is it possible to have knowledge that's more certain than merely justified belief?
- How can we attain true knowledge and how can we know when we have it?
- Do certain beliefs, by their nature, guarantee that they represent knowledge (e.g., beliefs about God or about mathematics)?
- Does science provide us with a kind of belief that is knowledge, or that at least is more reliable than other beliefs we may have? How does it do this? How reliable is it?
- What's the role of perception (information from our senses: seeing, hearing, feeling) in belief and knowledge?
- Is it even possible to define what knowledge really is? Do we need to? Why should we want to?
- What role does logic play in belief and knowledge?
- How important is the concept of truth in understanding knowledge and belief?

In contemporary philosophy, a great deal of research and publication in epistemology falls under the philosophy of science and related sub-fields. In addition, a number of issues and questions in epistemology that arose for philosophers in the past have more recently been taken over by cognitive scientists and brain researchers. In fact, the philosophy department in which I received my bachelor's degree in philosophy no longer exists, and degrees in philosophy are now awarded within the Cognitive Science department.

Logic

Logic is sometimes referred to as the "laws of thought" or "laws of reasoning". The primary goal of logic is to provide us with a set of rules or principles or guidelines on the basis of which we can, in a *reliable way*, draw conclusions from other things that we already know (or have good reason to believe). As part of this, the logician also has the task of characterizing and clarifying the notion of *argument* as a process from things that are known or assumed (called *premises*) to reliable *conclusions* that *follow from (*or are *inferred from*) these.

Formal logic is a rigid and precise system of definitions and rules that can be applied to premises in order to draw correct inferences from them. Part of the role of the formal logician is to characterize the notion of *proof* (of a conclusion from a set of premises) — which is similar to the notion of proof used in mathematics, but frequently more precise and rigorous (many mathematicians might say "picky"). Formal logic was invented by Aristotle, and is called "*formal* logic" because it characterizes the goodness of an argument based on the *forms* of the argument, its premises, and its conclusion. Basically this means that if an argument fits a particular template (a form), then it's good (reliable). And if it doesn't, then it's bad (unreliable).

Formal logic was improved a bit (though not much) throughout the middle ages, and was advanced substantially in the late 19th century by Gottlob Frege, followed by additional advances by Alfred North Whitehead, Bertrand Russell, and (in the early 20th century) various members of the Vienna Circle and "Polish Schools" of logic. It has continued to expand since then and forms part of the critical methodological foundations of philosophy, computer science, information retrieval, database theory and systems, electrical engineering, and the empirical sciences.

In philosophy, (formal) logicians occupy a peculiar niche and frequently are viewed with some apprehension by other philosophers. In part, this is because a number of philosophers don't regard a logician as a genuine philosopher, but instead as some kind of aberrant mathematician (all those puzzling symbols, you know, and proofs, and all that!). Unfortunately, mathematicians tend to have a very similar attitude and don't regard logic as genuine mathematics, but something along the lines of disguised philosophy dressed up in mathematical clothing. Also, logicians tend to be disturbingly picky about proofs. So logicians often end up not being seen as philosophers and also not being seen as mathematicians — but as being bastard children of both philosophy and mathematics.

Over the past few decades, as there's been an increase in the relative number of ethics professors in philosophy departments, there's also been a noticeable decrease of logicians in philosophy departments (and in fact in mathematics departments as well). Philosophy departments still offer courses on a regular basis in elementary formal logic, and perhaps in "advanced logic" (though it's not often what many logicians would think of as advanced); but beyond that, more advanced courses in logic, set theory, formal semantics, and related areas have been disappearing from philosophy departments. If you want to find logicians today, a good place to look for them is in mathematics departments (where, however, they unsurprisingly tend to work in the area of foundations of mathematics), or in departments of cognitive science — where they team up with computer scientists, linguists, neuroscientists, and some escaped epistemologists and philosophers of science — to make advances in such areas as artificial intelligence, data mining, robotics, and machine learning. They're still heavily involved in genuine philosophy, but just doing it somewhere else.

In contrast to formal logic, *informal logic* takes a ... well ... informal approach to what counts as reliable reasoning and how to do it. And this approach has a very comfortable home in university departments of philosophy, often under such titles as "critical thinking", "representation and reasoning", "thinking logically", and "reason and argument". Informal logic is closely related to rhetoric in terms of how it analyzes and evaluates arguments and inferences. Courses in it often do include descriptions of some purely formal fallacies, but its primary focus is on what historically has been called "informal fallacies of relevance" that focus on the *content* of an argument rather than its form, and in showing how the content of a particular premise is irrelevant to establishing its conclusion.

I'll note in passing that PhilPapers lumps *Metaphysics and Epistemology* into one topic (which seems odd, though I understand some of the motivation), takes *Ethics* to be a secondary area to the broader one of *Value Theory* (which seems reasonable in light of contemporary thought on the scope of these), and throws *Logic* in with *Science, Logic and Mathematics* (which gives the false impression that logic is somehow related to these in ways it's not related to areas of philosophy). But there are many ways of seeing how philosophical works fall into different categories, and virtually any philosophical work will fall into more than one category, no matter how you split things up. The view I present here is just a particularly simple (but historically accurate) one that's designed mostly to get us going with sufficient understanding while avoiding unnecessary complexity and confusion.

Metaphilosophy

An obvious question in this context is "Under what category of philosophy does this book fall?" The quick answer to this is that it falls into the area of *metaphilosophy*: philosophizing about philosophy, or examining and analyzing the methodology of philosophy. But metaphilosophy isn't one of the categories we just discussed and claimed to comprise the fundamental areas of philosophy. So where does metaphilosophy fit into those?

Unsurprisingly, there's some disagreement about this. Some philosophers feel that metaphilosophy isn't really philosophy, but is something else. But what else could it be? It uses the methods of philosophy to reflect on and analyze itself. What we're doing in this book is reflecting on, analyzing, and characterizing the natures (to some extent) of philosophy and pseudo-philosophy in order to draw an informative and useful distinction between these — if we can. And that's a philosophical task and a philosophical goal.

Some philosophers seem very confused about what the term *metaphilosophy* could or should mean. As an illustration of this, consider that PhilPapers sticks *Metaphilosophy* directly under *Metaphysics and Epistemology*. There must have been quite a bit of debate about this (and probably a lot of dissatisfaction when it came time to vote on where it should end up) because they seem to have got it wrong. Metaphilosophy isn't just about metaphysics and epistemology, nor does it make use of only techniques drawn from metaphysics and epistemology. Rather, it can be about any area of philosophy (including metaphilosophy itself!), and it may use techniques or appeal to concepts, theories, and arguments from virtually any philosophical area. So we can see there's the potential for much debate and disagreement, and perhaps some danger, in specifying what are the categories or areas of philosophy.

Let's not go down that rabbit hole just now, or we won't make any progress at all. Instead, we'll take the simple way out with our streamlined view of philosophy being split amongst *Metaphysics*, *Ethics*, *Epistemology*, and *Logic*. That's not as precise and fine-boned as many philosophers might like, but it will serve our limited purpose here, it's understandable to non-professionals and non-experts, and it's not inaccurate or wrong. For now, let's also acknowledge that what's going on here is metaphilosophy (if we need a label for it), that it's some kind of philosophy (certainly it's conceptual analysis), and that (as we'll see) it's related to at least logic and epistemology. And we'll argue that in our case it's also related to ethics, and perhaps to metaphysics. The details of just how it's related remain to be seen and won't matter to us for some time, and won't matter much for our program here overall.

2.4 Philosophy in terms of its schools or traditions

Another way of looking at the broad area of philosophy is in terms of its "schools", traditions, or perspectives. A school, in any particular academic discipline (philosophy, history, political theory, economics, literary analysis, psychology, etc.), can be thought of as a collection of people (professors, writers, researchers) who share a certain perspective involving goals, principles, methods, and criteria of success. So in this sense "school" doesn't refer to any particular college or university, but rather to a "school of thought" — a particular ideology or view of what to do and how to accomplish that, usually combined with related views of what *not* to do, what's *not* important, and what methods are lacking in value. Often such schools are also associated with a particular region or geographical location or a university or set of universities. But it's the goals, views, principles, and methods that bind together the members of the school — who may not even think of themselves as forming a school, but rather have this categorization imposed on them by others studying their works.

Just to get a quick grip on this way of slicing up the philosophical spectrum, let's take a brief look at some examples.

One of the oldest schools (which yet has its adherents today, to varying degrees) is the Aristotelian School. Adherents of this school follow Aristotle (in metaphysics, for example) in seeing reality as composed of both individuals and universals, and in seeing the concepts of *substance* and *essence* as being necessary to explaining such things as *universals*, shared properties among individuals, and how a thing can persist (be the *same* thing) over time. Aristotle's philosophy, and the school that formed around this, developed largely in response to severe problems that Aristotle found in his teacher Plato's view of the nature of reality (particularly the notion of a Platonic *form* — an idea that Plato had introduced to address these problems of "the one and the many" (Rickless 2015) in pre-Platonic philosophy. Aristotle's metaphysics is complex and arcane, and very few contemporary philosophers would count themselves as full adherents of the school, but a prominent one is Barry Smith, who has sought to apply the Aristotelian view (concepts, principles, and jargon) to problems in contemporary biomedical science.

There is also an Aristotelian school of ethics, with its view that ethics is more of a practical field than a theoretical one; and this evolved into what might be called the "virtue school of ethics" which faded from the scene in the early 20th century. There was, at least through most of the middle ages, an Aristotelian school of logic (which is reasonable since Aristotle invented formal logic). This emphasized the syllogism (Bobzien 2010) as capturing the valid forms of reasoning. But it was highly criticized for various obvious weaknesses in the later middle ages and ultimately superseded by modern formal logic as developed by Frege (Zalta 2019) in the late 19th century.

Two major schools/traditions that developed in the middle ages were Thomism (based on the philosophy of Thomas Aquinas (McInerny and O'Callaghan 2014)), an extension and improvement to Aristotelianism, and Nominalism

(Rodriguez-Pereyra 2015) which arose as an attack on, and alternative to, the Realism of Thomas and others (Miller 2019).

Other schools often encountered in the study of philosophy and in philosophy courses include:

- *The Vienna Circle*: Centered in Vienna, Austria but with members or sympathizers extending into Germany, Czechoslovakia, England, and the United States), characterized by a heavily empiricist (i.e., scientific and formal) approach to philosophy and the rejection of much or all of metaphysics as meaningless. The orientation of the Vienna Circle is often referred to as "logical empiricism" or "logical positivism". A similar approach is represented by the *Lvov-Warsaw school* — primarily an approach (empiricist/nominalist) to metaphysics, logic, semantics, and science. It contained strong currents of nominalism and shared various principles and views with the Vienna Circle, though not its hyper-intense rejection of metaphysics as entirely senseless. We'll revisit some aspects of the Vienna Circle in Chapter 11.

- *Marxism*: Primarily a socio-political school of thought and philosophy based on the anti-capitalist writings of Karl Marx and his views on such things as the notions of private property, class struggle, and the means of creating and sustaining products, services, and wealth in society. Marx's thought, in turn, owed a lot to the Hegelian school.

- *Analytic philosophy*: Often referred to with a regional flavor as *anglo-american analytic philosophy*, analytic philosophy takes as a fundamental tenet that the goal of philosophy is analysis in some precise meaning of that term. This refers to analysis in the sense of conceptual analysis: the analysis of concepts, their content, their relations to one another, their clarification, and their use in dealing with problems of a philosophical nature. Such an approach may, and often will, result in complex (but precise) theories that expose the nature and properties of these concepts and relations among them. The concept of meaning (and indeed other semantic concepts such as reference and truth) are central to the analytic philosopher's approach, and contemporary formal logic (and alternative formal logics) are frequently used or developed as analytical tools to aid the philosopher's exploration, expression, and explanation. The use of such methods and the focus on analysis in this sense is often criticized by competing approaches (particularly existentialism and phenomenology) as being sterile, puerile, or devoid of much interest.

- *Phenomenology*: Phenomenologists have an annoying tendency to deny that phenomenology is a unified movement or a school, while still insisting on referring to themselves as phenomenologists and touting the phenomenological approach. There is sufficient variation in focus and methods that it's difficult to pin down what the core of phenomenology amounts to, but generally it's felt that a phenomenologist is concerned with analyzing, interpreting, and understanding "experience" (or experiences) that people have, constructing models or theories of "consciousness" and its "structures", and of the phenomena that appear in events or experiences of consciousness. As such, it often appears to be inwardly agent-focused rather than outwardly focused on objective reality.

  A short list of phenomenologists would typically include Edmund Husserl (credited with founding the approach), Roman Ingarden, Martin Heidegger, Maurice Merleau-Ponty, Paul Ricoeur, and Jacques Derrida. Phenomenology is a continental (European) school of philosophy that has spread widely beyond its original borders. Like existentialists, phenomenologists typically view logical empiricism and analytic philosophy as sterile or at least severely limited and misguided.

- *Existentialism*: This is an intensely humanistically oriented approach to philosophy which takes its focus to be on the individual, individual acts, and the feelings that individuals have. It's about an attitude (the existential attitude) or state of mind, and about considering and coming to understand human existence, how humans feel, and how they interact with other feeling humans. This will yield, so existentialists believe, an understanding of what it means to be human, and yield it on both a cognitive and emotional level. In pursuit of that goal, the existential philosopher seeks to develop a set of categories (distinct from those typically found elsewhere in the history of philosophy) in terms of which this problem may be explored and a solution found. As a consequence, existentialists historically find analytic philosophers to be anathema, but find a compatibility with phenomenology, and a use for it in their own pursuits.

- *Ordinary language philosophy*: Arising in the early to mid-20th century, this approach is generally regarded as originating with Ludwig Wittgenstein and being expanded by his students at

Cambridge. The students who carried on Wittgenstein's approach into a tradition are sometimes referred to as "disciples" because of their devotion to him and to analyzing and explaining his often-confusing writings. Ironically, Wittgenstein felt that his disciples generally misunderstood and distorted much of what he had to say. His lectures were not quite lectures and his books were not quite books — often being, instead, lists of observations, aphorisms, argument sketches, questions, and reflections.

A concise rendering of the foundation of this approach would be to say that it holds that throughout history, philosophers have been "bewitched" (Wittgenstein's term) by their words, and in fact have unnecessarily manufactured many of the problems that they then have had a difficult time solving. The job of the philosopher — in so far as he or she has a job — is to untangle this misuse of words and thus "dissolve" (rather than solve) philosophical problems (which are, after all, fake problems of the philosopher's own making). If this is an approach to philosophy, it's an approach to philosophy as linguistic therapy, and one which seeks to eliminate the classic philosopher from the picture through change of language.

A later thread of ordinary language philosophy was developed by philosophers like J. L. Austin who retained some features of the approach taken by Wittgenstein, but did not feel an overt intellectual debt to him, did not adopt his view of the nature of philosophy, and did not participate in the Cambridge personality cult ("disciples") comprising Wittgenstein's students.

- A number of other "isms" such as Fatalism, Rationalism, Skepticism, Empiricism, Idealism, Hegelianism, Formalism, Conceptualism, Altruism, Consequentialism, Conventionalism, Naturalism, Materialism, and on and on. For details of these (and more!) see the variety of articles available in the *Stanford Encyclopedia of Philosophy* (Zalta 2020).

Notice that the view of philosophy as an academic discipline and the view of philosophy as a set of schools, perspectives, or traditions are not incompatible with one another. These are just two ways of looking at what's regarded as the domain of philosophy throughout history.

2.5 The "anything goes" view of philosophy

A third view of philosophy that you're likely to encounter from time to time is that philosophy is a discipline, a subject, or an area in which "anything goes" — and that this is precisely why philosophical problems never have solutions and can't be decided: you can't tell (or even characterize in any way) what's good philosophy as opposed to bad philosophy. In this view, philosophy is just the expressing of opinions that can never be evaluated in any objective way, and so it's all equally good, or equally bad, or equally meaningless. Or put more bluntly, philosophy is just bullshit. Bertrand Russell, for example, mentions such a view and says that many people, being "under the influence of science or of practical affairs," often think that philosophy is just an intellectual game of abstract distinctions and disputes about things that can't really be resolved (areas in which "knowledge is impossible").

This attitude is often exhibited by people who've never actually devoted any time to a study of any part of philosophy, and who may as easily feel that Einstein's Special Theory of Relativity is nonsense (because they've seen some informal accounts of some unintuitive consequences to it), that Darwinian Evolutionary Theory is "just opinion" since they've never studied its details and how it fits into the rest of biological science, or that quantum mechanics is bullshit even though it's used in making their cell phones work. Or these people might fit in well with the crackpots who believe that *pi* is an integer (or at least a rational number) because they just never learned enough mathematics to understand how it can't be. They all have a "right" to *holding* these goofy beliefs, but having that right doesn't make the *beliefs* right. You have every right (in a legal and moral sense) to believe false and stupid things.

I'm not going to press an argument against the "anything goes" view of philosophy at the moment, in part because it's a digression that would slow us down, and in part because we'll actually be seeing how this view is false as we move further through the book (including the very next chapter). If the "anything goes" view is correct, then it's simply not possible to distinguish between genuine philosophy and pseudo-philosophy on an objective basis, nor to convince anyone that there's a meaningful distinction between the two. So in fact if we succeed here in drawing and defending such a distinction, that will serve as an argument refuting the "anything goes" view itself — because we'll have identified something that "doesn't go" in philosophy, and that's pseudo-philosophy.

As a consequence of this attitude, we're going to assume — at least provisionally, and as what you might think of as a working hypothesis — that the "anything goes" view of philosophy is incorrect, and see where that takes us and how we may be able to support this hypothesis in the end.

2.6 Some assumptions that philosophers make

It's sometimes said that philosophers make no assumptions and instead "question everything". But this involves a fundamental confusion. Philosophers may question everything (though no particular philosopher can really question *everything* and still get through a normal day!). This just means that they hold (or at least *try* to hold, since no one's perfect) all of their beliefs, assumptions, and conclusions open to examination, criticism, testing, and reconsideration. But they do make assumptions — and they have to make assumptions in order to get anywhere, even though those assumptions may be adopted temporarily, provisionally, and subject to later rejection or revision. And philosophers do their best to expose what those assumptions are, to make them explicit, to see what their consequences are, and to determine whether they can be justified or should be rejected or modified.

Given all that, and in the context of these first two chapters and the broad history of philosophy, we can see at this point that there are some basic assumptions that philosophers make and that are necessary in order to pursue philosophical investigation itself, or at least to facilitate that investigation.

Assumptions philosophers make

Assumption 1: The goals of knowledge and wisdom

The primary goals of philosophy are finding truth, knowledge, and wisdom about us and the world around us. And these concepts are taken in an objective sense where truth, knowledge, and wisdom can be expressed, communicated to others and shared with them.

Assumption 2: The true/false distinction

The assumption of truth, knowledge, and wisdom as goals is closely related to a distinction between truth and falsity, between what's true and what's false, and to an assumption that we're able to determine these differences in an objective manner that can be communicated, learned, and shared among individuals.

Assumption 3: Consistency

Consistency then emerges (as we've argued and illustrated in earlier sections) as an important factor in drawing and maintaining the true/false distinction and supporting our goals of knowledge and wisdom, for without it we appear to lose all of that.

Assumption 4: Rationality

Philosophers assume that rationality (as characterized by communicable principles of logic and rational belief) matters in — indeed, is fundamental to — achieving knowledge and wisdom. This comes along with a view and belief that we can't achieve coherence outside of a rational approach, and that without coherence we certainly can't have knowledge or wisdom. So the philosophical enterprise is assumed to require rationality.

Assumption 5: The role of logic and argument

Philosophers also assume that logic is fundamental to the exercise of rational thought, to the establishing and support of conclusions, and to convincing others (in a *reliable manner*) of the truth of those conclusions. Logic and its use in arguments are then taken to be essential characteristics and tools of philosophical thought in its pursuit of knowledge and wisdom. They are also fundamental in exposing assumptions and flaws in philosophical positions and theories, and so in analyzing and evaluating both a philosopher's own work and the work of others. Logic, however, need not mean any particular form or system of logic, but only a system of rules that support rational reasoning in drawing conclusions and avoid inconsistency and paradox.

Assumption 6: The possibility of achieving the goals

Philosophers assume (at least provisionally) that they can succeed at achieving their goals: that knowledge and wisdom can be achieved, at least in some significant sense and to some degree. They assume further that philosophical positions and theories can be objectively evaluated, and that objective decisions about the goodness of a position or theory can be made on grounds that can be agreed to by other philosophers.

These assumptions are obviously very basic and quite general. And it's true that at times certain philosophers have questioned them. But remember, that's what philosophers do: they question basic assumptions. So they'll question their own basic assumptions. And you can find some philosophers who question the value of rationality, or philosophers who question the value of logic (or certainly of this or that particular approach to logic), or philosophers who question what role rationality should play in philosophy. But for the most part, these assumptions are shared by philosophers, and we'll see that violating them can be symptomatic of pseudo-philosophy.

It might be argued that not all of these are assumptions, and instead that some of them follow (logically, of course) from others. This may be the case, or might be made to be the case with a little extra work. But that's not important for us here, and if you'd rather not think of them as "assumptions", then think of them instead as interlocking principles and concepts on which philosophy, philosophical investigation, and philosophical analysis rest. We'll just be using them in later chapters as touchstones and landmarks to help navigate the twisty channels between philosophy and pseudo-philosophy.

You might also stop and think that "Wait a minute! Don't people in disciplines other than philosophy make these assumptions?". And the answer to this is that yes, they do — at least in some other disciplines (notably scientific ones) — although there may generally be a difference in focus and scope when it comes to Assumption 1. So Assumptions 1-6 by themselves don't carve out philosophy as a distinct and distinctive discipline, but we'll see in Chapter 5 that they do manage to carve at least a partial border between philosophy and other areas.

Chapter 3

Tools of the Philosopher's Trade

> *In this chapter:*
> - What is a philosopher?
> - Philosophy as a trade: the philosopher's craft
> - A sample philosophical problem
> - The philosopher's basic tool chest — what's in it, and why

The previous chapter has given us a view of philosophy as an academic discipline in which professional philosophers function as teachers and researchers, involved in "scholarly activities". But there's another view of philosophy, philosophers, and philosophical work that will provide us with an additional valuable perspective in understanding some of the essential characteristics of philosophy and how pseudo-philosophy relates to it. From this perspective we'll view philosophy as a *trade* or *craft* which seeks to provide *products* or *services* within the philosophical domain.

A tradesman (or tradeswoman, or craftsman, or craftswoman, or artisan) is a worker who has special training and skills needed in order to do a particular kind of work, often referred to as a *skilled trade*. A number of skilled trades were organized in the middle ages in the form of craft guilds (which evolved into the trade unions common in more recent times), and the trades included such areas of specialization as wheelwrights (who made wheels), masons, carpenters, shoemakers, coopers (barrel makers), barbers, farriers (horse shoers), truck drivers (teamsters), various kinds of smiths (blacksmiths, goldsmiths, silversmiths, etc.), musicians, and so on. Later the trades expanded to include electricians, plumbers, pipe fitters, boilermakers, millwrights, autoworkers, and a host of other specialties. And then "professions" developed — marked by advanced training, certification, often government requirements, and various specialized academic degrees. But a profession is just a trade with pretensions and more paperwork.

It doesn't take much effort to see aspects of trades and guilds in how philosophers are organized within departments of philosophy in colleges and universities — requiring specialized training (college and graduate courses), certification (usually represented by advanced academic degrees), proof of "mastering the craft" (research grants, dissertations for the Ph.D. degree, and publications), final full acceptance into the guild (tenure, after an apprenticeship as an assistant professor), and promotion to its higher ranks (associate professor = journeyman, full professor = master craftsman, research professor, distinguished professor, etc.). Considering the trade or craft aspect of philosophy also allows us to detach the philosopher from a number of political considerations pertaining to his or her work in the university, and to focus instead on the nature of this work. Without doing something like this, we could easily be accused of classifying someone as a pseudo-philosopher just because she isn't a member of the "guild". In fact, not surprisingly, *most* authors who are accused of being pseudo-philosophers are not members of the guild of professional university philosophers. But we shouldn't make the mistake of thinking that someone is a pseudo-philosopher just *because* she isn't a member of the guild — or is a genuine philosopher just because he *is* a member of the guild. The relation of genuine philosophy to pseudo-philosophy is much more complex than that!

Let's get back to thinking about philosophy as a trade and about how the philosopher is similar to a plumber, an electrician, a carpenter, or another type of artisan. What we'll discover is that this has to do with *problems*, *solutions* to those problems, and *how to get from a problem to one of its solutions*. Then later we'll use that insight to help us distinguish philosophy from pseudo-philosophy, and to provide more careful characterizations of both. But to start down this path, there's a preliminary and challenging question we have to answer.

3.1 What is a philosopher?

We've already conceded in earlier chapters that the question "What is philosophy?" is notoriously difficult to answer. But we may move towards an approximate answer to it from several directions by asking related questions. One of these is "What is a philosoph*er*?" Certainly the quick answer to this is "Someone who philosophizes," but that's not helpful since it just spins us in a circle! We'll need to dig a little deeper, and our answer to this question may still be somewhat approximate or fuzzy around the edges. That will turn out to be okay for our purposes here, and we'll see why shortly.

A problem faced by anyone who's trying to define a word is that we can make a word mean whatever we want it to. But it's not helpful to do this (to make use of a *stipulative definition*) in a situation like the one we're facing where we're trying to achieve a generally acceptable and informative understanding of the term "philosopher". If we simply, by fiat, say what this word will mean for us, then people will just focus on what they may find objectionable about that definition, and we'll be bogged down arguing about the definition and not get anywhere with an attempt to achieve our broader goal of understanding the distinction between philosophy and pseudo-philosophy.

Instead, we need to find some characterization of the term on which everyone can at least mostly agree, even if there may be some minor disputes around the edges of our agreement. We can do this — at least for our current purpose — with our term "philosopher".

One common and casual sense of the word "philosopher" can be found in such remarks as "My old grand-dad was quite a philosopher. He always had something to say about the best way to lead your life." Or "Aunt Mary's a real philosopher. She's got a lot of insight and a saying or aphorism to help you out in any difficult situation."

Here, "philosopher" has a meaning close to *someone who offers valuable insight and advice in problems or decisions you may encounter in life*. We can think of this as the *colloquial sense* of "philosopher", and there's nothing wrong with it. But it won't help us toward an understanding of what pseudo-philosophy is, and it's pretty far afield from the senses of "philosopher" and "philosophy" we need. Notice, for example, that if you substitute "psychologist", or "advisor", or "counselor", or even "coach" for "philosopher" in the statements about grand-dad and Aunt Mary, these statements make as much sense and mean pretty much the same thing. We need something better, something clearer, and something that matches up at least broadly with our initial characterization of philosophy in Chapters 1 and 2.

We've already seen in previous sections that you don't need a degree in philosophy in order to be a philosopher, and you don't need to have a job as a philosopher in order to be a philosopher. And now we've seen that we don't want to count you as a philosopher just because you try to offer insight and advice on life's problems. So what's left? What *should* it take to be thought of as a philosopher?

In Chapters 4 and 7 we'll offer some specific indicators (or *markers*) that help to classify someone correctly as a philosopher or as a pseudo-philosopher, but now let's change perspective and see if we can find some help by looking at an area other than philosophy — one that isn't so abstract and that may not be felt to be so "fuzzy" in its outlines. What, for example, does it mean to be an *astronomer*? This question is in fact a bit easier to answer, although it exhibits surprising similarities in some respects to the philosopher question. And answering it will provide us with some useful insight in approaching the question of what a philosopher is.

Section 3.1: What is a philosopher?

Let's say that I want to be an astronomer. Step 1 seems obvious: Get a telescope. So I get a telescope, say one that's advertised as being good for at least looking at the moon, planets, comets that visit the earth, moons of planets such as those around Jupiter, etc. This scope gets great reviews, even by experienced amateur and professional astronomers. I'm confident that it's good equipment, and I start looking at the night sky with it.

Am I an astronomer? No — not any more than I'm a world-class tennis player because I bought a tennis racket or that I'm a successful NFL quarterback because I bought a football. I'm just a guy with a telescope. Having the telescope, and my interest in astronomy, might be a good start, but it seems I'm a long way from being an astronomer. I might be an astronomy *fan*, but I'm not an astronomy *player*. What do I need to do in order for me to become an astronomer and for others to see me as a *genuine* astronomer? Well, in part that depends on how far I want to go. But in general, going from the status of a fan to the status of a player (whether in tennis, football, astronomy, or philosophy) requires two things: training and the acquisition of skills.

If I want to become a professional-level astronomer, publish papers in peer-reviewed astronomy journals, and have the acknowledged respect of astronomers who teach in universities or work in research organizations such as NASA, JPL, and the U.S. Naval Observatory, then I'd better put a lot of long-term effort and formal study into getting an advanced degree in astronomy from a recognized university astronomy department. That would certainly make me an astronomer, even if I make my living by herding sheep in Montana. (Remember that Spinoza was a lens grinder, Descartes and Socrates were soldiers, and that for a time Plato was a wrestler.) But that's a *lot* of effort and commitment (and perhaps expense), and I may not want to go that far.

Maybe I'm interested in astronomy but don't want to do it as a career. I want to be an *amateur* astronomer, but still be well respected among other amateur and professional astronomers. I might want to publish an article in some astronomy magazine or journal from time to time, perhaps teach an astronomy course at a community college or in an adult learning program now and then, and maybe even get lucky and make some genuine contribution to astronomy by discovering something new (like an asteroid, comet, or some orbital or stellar phenomenon that hasn't been noticed previously).

In this case, I won't need an advanced degree (though I still might want to pursue one in my spare time), and I won't even need an undergraduate degree in astronomy (though I might want to get one just to be sure I feel confident that I've learned "enough" about the field), but I do still need to put serious effort into learning some of the core of astronomy as that field has been studied and conducted historically and as it is today. I need to learn at least the basics of what astronomers now know, and I need to learn enough about astronomy so that I can go on and learn more. Otherwise, I'm just a guy with a telescope.

There's a certain *body of knowledge* that any astronomer possesses and without which I can't be considered to be an astronomer. There's also a set of *methods and techniques* with which any astronomer must be familiar — and this includes a certain foundation in mathematics comprising at least the basics of analytic geometry and calculus, and a similar foundation in physics comprising basic Newtonian mechanics, orbital mechanics, and gravitation. Finally, there's a set of *astronomical facts, problems, and theories* that any astronomer must be familiar with in order to be seen as having genuine fundamental knowledge of astronomy. For example, ancient astronomers believed that the earth was the center of the solar system (and in fact the center of the universe) and the planets and stars revolved around it; but now we know that the sun is the center of the solar system and the planets (including the earth) revolve around *it*. Without such basic knowledge of the subject of astronomy, I may call myself an astronomer; but I'm not an astronomer. And — worse — I'm in serious danger of being a crank or crackpot who holds bizarre or disreputable views. Without this basic knowledge, my understanding of astronomy and my beliefs about it almost certainly will be incorrect and, to at least some degree, "nutty". No genuine astronomer (professional or amateur) will take me seriously when I offer opinions in the area of astronomy, and I might be regarded as a *pseudo-astronomer* — someone who's pretending to be an astronomer but isn't one.

Even if I decide that what I want to do is to become a "hobbyist" in astronomy, I still need a certain degree of familiarity with the body of knowledge, methods and techniques, and the facts, problems and theories. Without that, I'm just a guy with a telescope, and I'm no kind of astronomer.

Requirements for competence

To be competent in a given field, and to be taken seriously when you speak or write about things in that field, you at least need to:

- Understand and be able to use the basic methods and techniques of experts in the field,

- Have command of the fundamental facts regarded as established in the field,

- Know and understand the basic problems that historically have been dealt with in the field,

- Be aware of what problems and unsettled questions are recognized in the field today, and what attempts have been made to address these,

- Be aware of, be able to express, and understand major theories that have been developed in the field, how and to what degree they succeeded, and how and to what degree they failed.

Now let's switch back to our consideration of philosophy in light of this look at astronomy and what it means to be an astronomer. What we've seen in the case of becoming an astronomer is also true for anyone who wants to be — and to be considered as — a philosopher. To be a philosopher — even at the hobbyist or amateur level — I *must* be familiar with (and correctly understand to some significant degree) a certain body of knowledge, certain methods and techniques, and certain facts, problems, and theories. In the case of philosophy, we've briefly sketched some of the body of knowledge and the problems and theories in Chapter 1. We'll return to these in more detail in later chapters, but now we'll pause to look, first, at what are the products and services of the philosopher-as-tradesman, and, second, at the methods and techniques of philosophers in providing these products and services. These are the basic tools of the philosopher's trade, and an understanding and use of these (together with the body of knowledge and "philosophical facts") is what it "means" to be a philosopher. What it will mean to be a pseudo-philosopher is to misunderstand or misuse this body of knowledge, methods and techniques, and philosophical facts — and we'll explore the details of such misunderstanding and misuse in later chapters.

3.2 The philosopher's trade: products and services

If we view the philosopher as a tradesman or artisan, then what are the *products* that the philosopher produces and what are the *services* that the philosopher provides? If we look at contemporary academic philosophers in universities, it appears that the primary product of the philosopher is publications (books or papers published in peer-reviewed philosophy journals) and the primary service is instruction (in philosophy). Certainly the academic philosopher is paid specifically to teach courses in the school where he or she is employed, and the philosopher's advancement in the academic world is linked directly to the number of publications, the journals in which these have appeared, citations of those papers, and research grants the philosopher has received. In fact, several online sources provide "rankings" of the "best" journals. And the tenure and promotion policies of any philosophy department discuss explicitly how both tenure and promotion depend on such publication. There is no doubt that publication and teaching are the most visible products and services of the academic philosopher.

But this is a very shallow view, and really is useful only to university administrations in evaluating their faculty members. Also, it takes no account of those philosophers (contemporary and throughout history) who did not hold university positions. So what were (and are) the products and services of *those* philosophers — and moreover, what are the real products and services of philosophers which are only shallowly represented by publication, teaching, and research "metrics"? Publication and teaching are still involved, but there is something more, since publication and teaching provide only modes of communication for the true underlying products and services.

Of course, we've already seen the answer to these questions: the products of the philosopher's trade include insight, knowledge, and understanding (even useful understanding) of important and usually complex and abstract things and ideas that affect our lives and account for how we see the world around us and what we see (and can do) in it. The services include analyses (and methods of analysis) that yield ways of making dependable decisions and ways of choosing among alternative beliefs, explanations, and conceptual schemes or theories.

These philosophical analyses are similar to the sort of analyses that geologists provide for stone or ceramic objects, rock formations, and underground structures — which may then be used for such purposes as oil exploration, gemstone and precious metal discovery, and the drilling of different kinds of wells. Chemists provide a similar service with their chemical analyses that expose the make-up and properties of substances, and financial analysts deliver careful analyses of companies, stocks, bonds, and markets for the purpose of making informed and guided economic and investment decisions.

Likewise, researchers in the fundamental areas of science also provide analyses and explanations of a wide variety of phenomena encountered in the world (such as electricity, different forms of energy, weather, chemical reactions, biological organisms and systems, disease and treatment, and so on) in the form of *scientific theories* and *explanations and predictions* based on those theories. Although what philosophers do isn't quite the same as what scientists, engineers, and financial analysts do in certain important respects, it's very similar in others; and it provides us with insight, understanding, and knowledge in very similar ways. This is why the philosopher can be seen as a tradesman or artisan whose products include the clarification and analysis of concepts, accounts of how critical concepts are related to one another, the consequences of adopting certain principles, views, ideologies, or belief systems, and rich and complex theories or "philosophical systems" on which these analyses are based.

While scientists and engineers focus on natural phenomena we observe in the world (and on predicting and explaining these phenomena), the philosopher focuses on "concepts" and "fundamental principles", on clarifying these, on how these are (or might be) related, and on how different theories and explanations concerning these may be compared, evaluated, and applied by us in a broad variety of different domains ranging from law, politics, business, and religion through the biomedical and physical sciences and their applications — all in the service of enhancing our *understanding* and *wisdom* in these domains. It is often said that "philosophy is conceptual analysis," and historically this is as good a one-phrase description as can be had, if it's understood in this way. And someone who is purporting to do this type of work (to provide these products and services) either is a philosopher or at least is purporting to be a philosopher.

Although this provides us with a general characterization of philosophy as a trade, with some broad descriptions of the philosopher's products and services, and with some helpful analogies to the products and services of contributors in other disciplines, it's still pretty vague. When we talk about a philosophical analysis, a philosophical problem, or a philosophical theory, what do we really mean by this? We need some examples to make this at least a bit specific and to understand a bit better what philosophers do and what they strive for. While this book isn't a philosophy textbook or an introduction to philosophy, and while we can't divert attention to very detailed examples from the history of philosophy, we can at least look briefly at some details of a few typical philosophical problems and what philosophers have delivered in the form of analyses, theories, and solutions to them. Our examination will, of necessity in the current context, be simplistic and incomplete. But it will at least provide some basic illustrations of what we're talking about, some examples we can later refer back to in considerations of pseudo-philosophy, and references to more detailed treatments of the examples we'll consider here.

3.3 An illuminating philosophical problem

Let's begin with a classic example in logic and metaphysics. In various contexts it's referred to as "the problem of personal identity", "the problem of identity over time", and "the problem of change". It dates back at least to Parmenides of Elea (5th century BC) who, in a poem, argues that change isn't possible! What Parmenides means by this, and what he means to establish, is the shocking conclusion that whenever you change something *in any way*, that makes it *a different thing*! So nothing can ever change and yet be *the same thing*. His student Zeno later argued (by presenting a series of paradoxes now called — of course — "Zeno's paradoxes") that motion is impossible! — that nothing can ever move even though it appears that things move all the time. These paradoxes presented sufficiently troublesome problems to physicists and mathematicians over the ages that numerous attempts were made to dismiss them as mere "tricks", but in his work *The Principles of Mathematics* (Russell 1996), Bertrand Russell remarks that after two thousand years of such troublesome arguments, mathematicians and philosophers finally buckled down and solved the paradoxes.

♦ WHY CONSTRUCT A PARADOX?

Why are Parmenides and Zeno offering us arguments and trying to convince us of conclusions that are so utterly goofy? Do they really believe that it's impossible to say coherently that the car parked outside my house is the *same one* that was there yesterday (or an hour ago, or a millisecond ago)? Do they really believe, despite the evidence of our senses and our interaction with things in the world, that *movement is impossible*? *Then how can we watch football games?* No, of course they don't. Then why are they trying to confuse us with these arguments? And why have we spent thousands of years at this point analyzing and re-analyzing the arguments?

The answer to these questions is that these apparently goofy logical/philosophical arguments expose *fundamental problems* with our understanding of certain concepts that are essential to our understanding of the world. They expose flaws or "holes" in our knowledge and wisdom, and those flaws need to be repaired in order for us to attain the genuine knowledge and wisdom that we seek — not just in philosophy, but also in science, other disciplines, and our everyday knowledge of the world. If there's something incoherent, for example, about our concept of the *same thing* (same car, same person, same real estate, etc.), this can have serious consequences for us in everyday life in terms of disputes about ownership of property (What is owned? How much of it is owned?), insurance coverage (Is this the same disease or a different one? Was damage done to the same property that was originally insured, or to a different one?), and criminal law (If I'm not the *same person* I was when the crime was committed, then how can I be found guilty of that crime?). So this is an important point at which the rubber of philosophy meets the road of reality and everyday life. Also, of course, from the philosopher's point of view, these are just nifty and challenging puzzles.

The problem of change is a serious problem that dates back to the beginning of Western philosophy, has been approached by a huge number of philosophers over the years, and is still problematic and of interest today in several contexts. The problem appears in many guises and it broadens out into a more general *problem of individuation* of which we've just seen examples in the previous paragraph. For other examples of this, dealt with in an interesting and informal way from both scientific and philosophical perspectives, take a look at some of the *Star Trek* episodes and movies dealt with in Lawrence Krauss's book *The Physics of Star Trek* (Krauss 2007) and by a number of other authors (try a Web search for "Star Trek transporter identity").

Section 3.3: An illuminating philosophical problem

◆ THE SHIP(S) OF THESEUS

The example we'll look at now is what's often referred to as *The Ship of Theseus Paradox*, and it's first described by the 2nd century (AD) historian and philosopher Plutarch in his account of the mythic Greek hero Theseus. In accord with being a mythic Greek hero, Theseus had many heroic adventures that we won't try to enumerate here. Leaving out a great deal of detail, we can say that one of Theseus's adventures involved a lengthy and trying (and of course heroic) journey from Athens to Crete where Theseus killed the Minotaur (a half-man and half-bull monster to whom the Athenians had been forced to make human sacrifices on a yearly basis). Then Theseus and his men sailed back to Athens in a ship. Plutarch, who seems inclined to regard Theseus as a real person in Greek history, remarks that

> "The ship on which Theseus sailed with the youths and returned in safety, the thirty-oared galley, was preserved by the Athenians down to the time of Demetrius Phalereus. They took away the old timbers from time to time, and put new and sound ones in their places, so that the vessel became a standing illustration for the philosophers in the mooted question of growth, some declaring that it remained the same, others that it was not the same vessel." (Plutarch 2013)

What Plutarch describes here is a process by which, over time, each individual component of the original ship (which was kept in Athens as a memorial) was replaced by a new version of that component: a part–by–part replacement of the entire ship. At a certain point years later, then, *every piece of the original ship had been replaced*, and this gives rise to the questions "Was this ship the *same ship* that Theseus had sailed to Athens on his voyage?".

Plutarch reports that there was disagreement among the philosophers about this. Some felt that this was "the ship of Theseus": that there was only one ship that the crew had sailed on the voyage. It left Crete, sailed to Athens, and thereafter it was kept in the harbor as a memorial. Sure, each of its parts needed to be replaced as they degraded over time, but each act of replacing a single part didn't result in a different ship (so they say). Note that — while Plutarch and the philosophers apparently didn't consider this — exactly the same question could have been raised about members of the crew: they were older, maybe had suffered injuries, had grown longer hair and perhaps cut it, had lost or gained weight, etc. Were they the *same people* who had left on that voyage so long ago?

Other philosophers felt that since all the ship's parts were different after a number of years, the repaired memorial ship *couldn't* be the same ship as the one Theseus came back in. Later, in the 17th century, Thomas Hobbes created a "stronger" version of the paradox in which he imagined that as the old parts were being individually replaced over time, they were each taken and stored. Then, when every part had been replaced, all the old parts were retrieved from storage and used to reassemble the "original ship". So which was the "real" Ship of Theseus: the one that was complete all along (having its parts replaced one at a time over a span of years), or the one that was made of all the original parts? Neither of these appears to be the obviously correct and unproblematic answer.

Voyages of the Ship of Theseus

Keith Wiley, a software engineer and computer scientist, has a wonderful video on the Ship of Theseus Paradox and a number of its variations that's well worth watching (Wiley 2020). Wiley's video cleverly illustrates the complexity of the problem in a degree of detail that would be a diversion for us here. And it shows a number of questions that have to be answered no matter which way you decide to go. He concludes, quite rightly, that "conventional theories of identity" are shown to be inadequate by this paradox. It shows us that our prior understanding of the concepts of identity and sameness are flawed in some fundamental way — that the concepts of identity and sameness aren't as simple as we thought — and that we need new and better concepts in order to avoid the paradox and to understand in a coherent way what "same" means.

This is an example of a *philosophical* problem. It's not a problem that we can understand or solve simply by examining facts about the world. The facts aren't in dispute. There's nothing wrong with the facts. Something must be wrong with our *thinking* — and it's the job of the philosopher to find out what this is and figure out how to fix it.

It's also important to see that while we're looking at this as a clever little logical puzzle, that puzzle represents a significant problem and confusion that can (and at times does) affect us in the real world: under what conditions do we want or need to say that things are *the same* and under what conditions do we want to say they're *different*? Solving that puzzle in a variety of contexts (legal, medical, scientific, engineering, educational, advertising, business, etc.) is necessary to solving some very practical problems that confront us in daily life: Is this *generic form* of the drug *atorvastatin* the same as its branded form *Lipitor*? In my hospital bill for recent surgery, did I have just *one procedure* (as the doctor's bill indicates), or did I have *two* procedures (as the insurance company claims while paying for only one of them)? Can I register my old car as the *same car* with the Department of Motor Vehicles even though I put a new motor in it? Can I register my old car as *the same car* if the motor and chassis are the same, but I changed the old body for a new one? And by the way, what does it mean to say that the motor and chassis are *the same* if I've changed spark plugs, water pump, tires, broken windshield, and shock absorbers? It's in answering (or at least analyzing) questions such as these that esoteric and abstract philosophy can make substantial contributions to everyday life.

One approach to a solution: semantics

Philosophers might look at this paradoxical result and say "Well, what this demonstrates is that while we *thought* the word 'same' meant something obvious and simple, we now realize that it can have two very different senses. Using one sense of 'same', the old ship and the new ship are the same; but using the other sense of the word, they're not the same."

According to this diagnosis of the paradox, the problem arises because of a previously unnoticed *equivocation*[2] on the word "same" in which the two senses conflict with one another in terms of their consequences. Realizing that "same" is used with two different meanings allows us to escape the paradox. How?

One meaning of "same" in the paradox is "has the same parts arranged in the same way". Let's call this the *composition sense*, and the people who favor it *compositionists*. We're very familiar with this sense. If you take your car in for an inspection in order to renew its registration, the mechanic will look it over and perform several tests. He may take the wheels off and check that your brakes aren't worn out, for example. He may check your oil level by removing the dipstick. Then he replaces the dipstick and the wheels, and the wheel nuts, and of course your car is the same car. It has the same parts arranged in the same way as when you came in. Its *composition* hasn't changed. This would be true even if the mechanic took the car apart into every single part that makes it up, and then reassembled it. It would be the same car because it would be comprised of the same parts in the same arrangement.

The other meaning of "same" in the paradox is "has a continuity involving changes of parts over time". And we're familiar with this sense of sameness as well. Let's call it the *continuity sense* of sameness, and the people who favor it *continuists*. The Department of Motor Vehicles doesn't regard your car as a different car after you've replaced a headlight bulb or a muffler on it. And if you have your car for a number of years, you'll replace quite a number of things. War criminals have been prosecuted decades after they committed their crimes on the grounds that they were the *same people* as the ones who committed the crimes. And no defense would be successful if based on the grounds that the authorities had captured a different person — even though that person was different in various respects and a number of his parts had changed (cells in his body, removal of appendix, artificial joint replacement, etc.). The bodies of people change constantly over time, and yet they remain "the same person". If they didn't, society would be impossible. Likewise, your house remains your house

Chapter 3: Tools of the Philosopher's Trade

— and the *same* house — from the point of the bank that holds your mortgage and the point of view of the county tax authorities, even though you've made various improvements to it over time (such as remodeling your kitchen and bathroom, adding an extra room, and so on).

But there's a deeper philosophical lesson to be drawn from this apparently simple semantic solution — and this is really the major contribution of the philosopher here: *there is no single sense of* "the same"; *there is no single relation of sameness*. Things are a *lot* more complicated than we thought they were. And this is an important — and deep — realization. It's not something we started out with — it's something that the paradox forces us to realize as a result of our philosophical analysis. And apparently it's not something that the philosophers in Plutarch's time understood. However, there's still something unsatisfying about this as a final answer. Why? Because we sense that there's some important relation between the two meanings of "the same" — or, in the case of the compositionists' argument, between the two ships. After all, it still seems (intuitively, at least) that we're still — in some sense — talking about the *same ship*. Or at least if we're talking about two different ships, then these ships are related in a close and interesting way that different ships aren't normally related.

This is a *semantic* solution to the paradox since it shows how an apparent contradiction (two things are the same and yet not the same) arises simply from being careless in how we use a word ("same") when it turns out to be ambiguous. And the solution rests on finding *principles* by which it can be phrased and explained. In this case, the principles are

> (**Continuity Principle**) If an object at a later time results from an object at an earlier time by the *sequential replacement of one part by another*, then the objects are the same.

> (**Composition Principle**) If an object at one time *has exactly the same parts as* an object at a later time, then the objects are the same.

As we'll see in later chapters, the discovery of principles used in solving philosophical problems is a fundamental technique that philosophers use, and it often distinguishes their work from the work of others.

Everyone agrees it was the same ship in the beginning, but it now appears that *that* ship has somehow disappeared even though there's one "just like it" except for being made of different parts. So at some point did the original Ship of Theseus stop existing, and then each time some part of it was replaced, *another* Ship of Theseus came into existence? This attitude seems to take us back to Parmenides' view that change just isn't possible: we may *call* different things "The Ship of Theseus", but they're really *not* the same thing at all. And this makes us wonder if there ever was *one* Ship of Theseus, and at what point this could have been and what made it uniquely *that* ship (since apparently it wasn't the parts it was made of, or their arrangement). Among that lengthy sequence of slightly different ships, which ones get to be The (real) Ship of Theseus, and by what rules?[3] Then it starts to look as though the compositionists are really just Parmenideans, holding the view that *change isn't possible* — and that leads us into other problems and paradoxes because we also seem to know that change *is* possible (and happens all the time). Pesky paradox!

At this point, many people will want to just stop thinking about it. And many people do. But it's not just a silly philosophical puzzle, and a number of different types of people have to solve it and problems like it for real-world reasons in everyday life: lawyers, psychologists, judges and juries, insurance companies, geneticists, and so on.

While our initial solution — and our quite accurate realization that there's no single meaning of sameness that makes sense — might have been a solution to the limited problem found in The Ship of Theseus Paradox, our analysis of the paradox shows us that some more general sort of solution is needed. And this should be a solution that clearly relates the two senses of sameness represented by the Continuity Answer and the Composition Answer. Without any more handwringing, let's sketch the basics of such a solution as a continuing illustration of the kind of thing philosophers do and why they do it.

Another approach to a solution: metaphysics

Another way of looking at the Ship of Theseus Paradox is to see it as calling into question what a *thing* (i.e., a physical object) is, or how we think of things, and how we think of things existing and changing over time. Maybe the problem which the paradox presents isn't just about what "same" may mean, but about what "ship" (or more generally, "thing") means. Or maybe it's more fundamentally about what a thing *is*. And maybe the paradox illustrates that our concept of *sameness* (or "being the same thing as") is tightly tied to our concept of *thing* and what "really" makes one thing different from another. This moves us away from our initial semantic solution and towards a solution in metaphysics — out of the area of what *words mean* and into the area of *what there really is* and how things in reality are related to one another. Following that line of thought, let's offer an alternative solution to the paradox by sketching a "theory of things and sameness" that answers these puzzles.

When we look at the arguments in the paradox, it's apparent that a thing (the ship in this case) is thought of as a three-dimensional (3-D) object that has a number of different properties and exists over a period of time. In fact, this is the common sense concept of a material thing, and it's seemed to have worked well for us in everyday life. Properties of things include size, color, number of parts, relations among the parts, various other properties of the parts such a hardness, reflectivity, etc. Some of these may be thought of as "essential properties" of the thing (i.e., properties without which it wouldn't be *that* thing, or at least that *kind* of thing), while other properties may be thought of as "incidental properties" (properties that could be different without that affecting the identity of the thing or what kind of thing it is). If Theseus paints his ship pink or paints it in a camouflage pattern, people wouldn't say "Look! Theseus has a different ship." They'd say "Look! Theseus painted his ship. The ship is now a different color." While the ship has changed (in color), it's the same ship. Color is taken to be an incidental (or in philosophy-speak, *accidental*) property — at least most of the time. It might be argued, for example, that the color (red) is an essential property of a stop sign or stop light, as we understand these things. But you can see how this distinction between essential and incidental properties can quickly take us down a very confusing rat hole (and, in the history of philosophy, it has).

If we think of a thing as a 3-D object that occupies a certain amount of space in a certain location, then it's pretty easy to construct the paradox of the ship: if we change any of the properties or parts of that object from one time to another we end up with a *different* (in terms of properties or parts) 3-D object. It's that simple. So maybe a lesson to be taken from the paradox is that we shouldn't think of a thing as a 3-D object. Maybe thinking of the ship as a 3-D object is like thinking of a cube as a square — it misses essential features of the object. Then what's the alternative? Well, how about a 4-D object? Let's see what happens when we think of things as four-dimensional objects; and in particular, let's see what happens to the paradox when we think of the ship as a 4-D object. What does this mean?

In this theory, we think of a thing (material object) existing across, or throughout, a span of time. An object has the usual three dimensions *plus* the dimension of time. Think of a building that was constructed in 1975 and then demolished in 2015 so it could be replaced by a different and more modern building. We don't think of the building as just a volume of space occupied by concrete blocks, steel girders, windows, elevator shafts, and so on (that would be a 3-D object), but rather as a 4-D object stretching across time. We think of the building as a kind of concrete/steel/glass "temporal salami" in four dimensions (the usual three plus time), and when we slice that salami-building at any particular time, we get a 3-D slice that's the-building-at-that-time. And the *real building* isn't any of these individual time slices (although they're all *real slices*): the real building is the whole (4-D) salami and each of the slices is a *temporal part* of the building.

In the case of the Ship of Theseus, if we think of ships as 4-D objects in space–time, and we think of the 3-D ship we'd get on at one point and sail away as a *slice* of such a 4-D object (at a single time), then what we started out thinking of as the *original Ship of Theseus* and as the *final Ship of Theseus* are really two (different!) slices of the *one* (same!) 4-D ship. And using this theory, the paradox disappears because while the two (3-D) slices are different, they're slices of the same (single) 4-D object, and ... well ... that 4-D ship is always the same as itself. Of course, in order to really make this theory work, we have to make it detailed and precise enough to explain carefully the relations between the slices and the temporal "salami" 4-D objects that they're part of, and to account for how all those relations and sameness work in the case of the possible branching of a 4-D object over time. And this will require developing *principles* relating 3-D to 4-D objects.

While that works for the Continuists, things are a little tougher for the Compositionists on this view. The Continuists have a nice coherent and understandable theory of change over time and what "the same ship" means. But how do things look for the Compositionists if we think of objects as 4-D things extending over time? The Compositionists still have two different *slices* of a ship that they want to (somehow) turn out to be the *same ship*, but what happens to the ship in between? Where's their 4-D object — of which these two slices (the original ship at the beginning and the reassembled ship at the end) are parts?

One approach for the Compositionist is to reject the theory that physical objects are 4-D in nature, but another approach is to recognize scattered objects that exist over time. So once the replacement of parts begins, the ship is regarded as a collection of parts that reside in different locations and don't (together) resemble what we would normally think of as a ship: the set of parts isn't in the *form* of a ship, and in fact the parts end up as just a pile of parts until much later when they're *reassembled*. Then at the end, that collection of (original) parts is reassembled into the proper shape of a ship — but for the Compositionist, the 4-D object that's the ship is at times ship-shaped and at other times just a heap of ship parts and at other times a partly ship-shaped bunch of parts together with a (separately located) heap of stored parts. So the 4-D ship of the Compositionist is a *different 4-D object* than the 4-D ship of the Continuist. This need not be an insurmountable problem for the Compositionist, but it may mean that he needs to introduce more things into his ontology,[4] and more distinctions and relations between them and the other things, and more principles of individuation for all those things.

Again, this is a *metaphysical* solution to the paradox in that it's based on how we view *what exists in the world* and how it's organized — rather than a semantic solution based on what "same ship" *means*. But notice that the metaphysical and semantic solutions parallel one another: the metaphysical solution provides a basis for explaining the need for different senses of sameness. And we can see that in terms of this model/theory, what the Continuists regard as the ship and what the Compositionists regard as the ship are the same (slices) at the beginning of the 4-D salami, but are different after the salami branches (at the point that parts begin to be replaced). As a result of this theory and solution to the paradox, *we're looking at the world in a very different way* — and it's the philosopher who's provided this new and needed insight.

We won't pursue any more details of such a theory of 4-D objects here, but we can see that one is possible, and that — while being complex in its details and initially somewhat counterintuitive — it may offer certain advantages over our earlier simpler semantic solution to the paradox. In fact, such a precise theory was created as long ago as 1954 by the philosopher Rudolph Carnap, and the *principles* that make up the theory appear in chapters describing theories of space-time topology in his book *Introduction to Symbolic Logic and Its Applications* (Carnap 1958), where he mentions its connection to the physics of space-time, and the special theory of relativity.

Lessons of the paradox

There are several lessons about what philosophers do and how they do it that we should take away from this paradox, our analysis, and our proposed solutions. The first of these is that, in addition to being a kind of esoteric academic discipline often divorced from real-world considerations and practiced in an "ivory tower" environment, philosophy is also a *craft* or a *trade*. And we should be able to see how the puzzle presented by the Ship of Theseus Paradox, and the philosopher's solutions to it, will also appear in such contexts as determining whether one car is the same as another, whether one contract is the same as another, whether one building is the same as another, and whether one algorithm is the same as another. We've also seen how the philosopher is a craftsman, with goals, and tools for achieving those goals, and with products and services to be delivered. And being a philosopher means knowing what these goals are, what the tools are, how to use the tools, and then using the tools to deliver those products and services.

Our treatment of the paradox has also illustrated that the questions with which philosophers are confronted often can't be provided with a single answer or a single theory, but instead may have multiple answers depending on what may be of particular value to you and what your theoretical or practical goals are. A computer scientist looking at this situation might say that "Correct or useful answers to philosophical questions are *context-dependent*." So there may be no single "right" answer in these cases since success is relative to a goal and there can be multiple goals — although this doesn't mean that there aren't a lot of *wrong* answers that may be proposed! Again, it's the philosopher's job to present the right (or potentially right) ones, and to provide clear grounds for rejecting the wrong ones.

As an initial and partial answer to our question at the beginning of this chapter ("What is a philosopher?"), we can see that a philosopher is someone who knows and understands certain things (about reasoning, ideas, and relations among ideas), recognizes certain problems and types of problems, and has a certain set of tools (for example, paradox, consistency, logic, concept analysis, and theory construction) and skills to deliver solutions to those problems. Now — using this paradox as an example — we'll take steps to make this answer more complete by filling in the details of what the philosopher's tool set is. And this will take us one step closer to an ability to distinguish between genuine philosophy and pseudo-philosophy.

3.4 The philosopher's basic tool chest

Philosophers have a number of tools to use in their tasks of problem analysis, analysis of philosophical positions and proposed solutions, criticism, and construction of their own solutions. An impressive array of almost 100 such tools is covered in *The Philosopher's Toolkit* (Baggini and Fosl 2010). But the highly detailed and granular treatment Baggini and Fosl provide is way beyond our requirements here, and we'll need to understand the nature and use of only about 10 tools altogether — and at a much less challenging level of detail. In addition, most of the tools covered in *The Philosophers Toolkit* (which I encourage you to look at for more depth and detail), can be seen to fall under the broader characterizations of tools in this section.

A quick introductory description of construction and maintenance tools wouldn't need to delve into the details and differences concerning claw hammers, framing hammers, masonry hammers, brick hammers, sledge hammers, ball peen hammers, cross peen hammers, upholstery hammers, gunsmithing hammers, dead blow hammers, tack hammers, etc. (not to mention mallets!). So likewise I won't go into the details of the myriad kinds of logic (some reasonable, some esoteric, and some just plain weird) that a philosopher might use, or all of the subtle concepts that might appear in those logics, or different kinds of paradoxes and dilemmas, or a surprisingly broad variety of informal fallacies, or a bunch of different concepts of the notion of concept, or different theories of knowledge and perception, or different styles of dialectic and "critique".

Instead, we'll take the view that a hammer is just (pretty much) a hammer, it's used for hitting or pounding, and any other details necessary can be handled in context as work proceeds. And we'll take the similar view that there are certain fundamental tools of use to the philosopher, that we need a very basic understanding of these to get where we're going, and that any other details will be introduced and dealt with as necessary.

In the next chapter we'll also look at a couple of specialized tools that will be used throughout the rest of the book (and that aren't covered by Baggini's and Fosl's treatment). But for now, let's proceed to a survey of the fundamental philosopher's tools we'll need in examining the differences between genuine philosophy and pseudo-philosophy.

Consistency and truth

Consistency depends on some type of logic and on some approach to, and understanding of, the concept of truth. But fundamentally, it means that you don't get to be taken seriously if you say something and then deny the truth of what you just said — or if you say something and then say things that contradict (are inconsistent with) what you just said. Put another way: If you want to act rationally — if you want to *be* rational, if you want to be *seen* as being rational and intelligible, and if you want to be *understood* by others, then you must be consistent in what you say and what you think.

This particular idea of consistency we may think of as *logical consistency* (not tolerating the assertion of a contradiction or of statements that mutually imply a contradiction) or as *epistemic consistency* (not *believing* a contradiction or a set of statements that are collectively contradictory). In our Ship of Theseus example, consistency is at the heart of the problem, and inconsistency is a tool used in constructing the paradox — forcing us to the original intolerable conclusion that there are two distinct ships and yet only one ship. This conclusion is inconsistent — a contradiction.

This sort of *logico-epistemic consistency* can be contrasted with another common meaning of consistency where the term refers to *uniformity* or *constancy* in thought or action, and where we might refer to consistency in training a dog or a horse (not changing methods, rewards, or punishments), or consistency in a business management situation or in applying the law (not changing how principles or processes apply from case to case). This is a kind of *pragmatic consistency* which may ultimately rest on an underlying logical consistency (of laws, rules, guidelines, etc.), but it's concerned with uniformity of action rather than the avoidance of contradiction and the loss of coherence. We'll be concerned here with the logico-epistemic sense of consistency since this is the one that applies most directly to statements, discussions, analyses, arguments, and beliefs.

Now some people will tell you that consistency in thought and belief is "over-rated" or is a "false ideal" — that it confines our thought in narrow channels and that the truly intelligent thinker shouldn't be bound by it. This is absolute nonsense (in the most literal meaning of that term), and these people are just trying to trick you into believing or acting as they want you to in order to achieve some goals of their own. But this trickery can be alluring and difficult to resist (or even to detect), and so we need to spend some time thinking about consistency, inconsistency, truth, and reasonable belief in order to be thoroughly grounded on the value (and indeed the necessity) of consistency in expression, debate, analysis, and argument.

The ghost of the poet Ralph Waldo Emerson is often invoked as a shield against the demand for consistency in thought and reasoning. What Emerson had to say about this is

> "A foolish consistency is the hobgoblin of little minds, adored by little statesmen and philosophers and divines. With consistency a great soul has simply nothing to do. He may as well concern himself with his shadow on the wall. Out upon your guarded lips! Sew them up with packthread, do. Else, if you would be a man, speak what you think to-day in words as hard as cannon balls, and to-morrow speak what to-morrow thinks in hard words again, though it contradict every thing you said to-day. Ah, then, exclaim the aged ladies, you shall be sure to be misunderstood. Misunderstood! It is a right fool's word. Is it so bad then to be misunderstood? Pythagoras was misunderstood, and Socrates, and Jesus, and Luther, and Copernicus, and Galileo, and Newton, and every pure and wise spirit that ever took flesh. To be great is to be misunderstood." (Emerson 2016)

A number of similarly expressed denigrations of consistency (by the likes of Aldous Huxley, Oscar Wilde, and others) occur scattered throughout the history of literature, and we'll use Emerson's frequently quoted passage as representative of the sentiment shared by these. In this passage Emerson is just being clever, playing a game, and being a trickster. If Copernicus, Galileo, and Newton were "misunderstood", precisely what did this have to do with inconsistency? Isn't what Emerson is doing here just saying — in poetic language — that we should always be open to changing our beliefs in the light of new knowledge, new evidence, and alternative beliefs that may work as well or better than the old? Why does he shift in his first sentence from "*foolish* consistency" to "consistency"? *Of course* "foolish" consistency would be foolish, but when *is* consistency "foolish"? Could we see an example, please? Apparently not.[5]

And then he suggests that if you "speak what you think ... in hard words," and then change your mind later, you will then be "misunderstood." But this flies in the face of experience and reason. What's the nature of this misunderstanding that he holds up as a requirement for being "pure and wise" and "a great soul?"

Emerson's tone and style in this passage are also worthy of some attention. They're demeaning to those who may have very good reasons for valuing consistency, and they're clearly intimidating in their attempt to get the reader to side with Emerson's view — on the pain that otherwise you'd be guilty of having a "little mind," of failing "to be a man," or being among "the aged ladies." And certainly you wouldn't be great in insisting on consistency because you might not be misunderstood. Just think, for a moment, of how nutty that claim is! Well, Emerson is regarded as a great poet. His status as a philosopher is much more in question; and as we proceed in later chapters, we'll see how intimidation of this sort is a hallmark of pseudo-philosophy. But let's try to ignore the tone of this passage and attempt to treat it seriously and give Emerson the benefit of the doubt.

It seems that what Emerson may really mean here (or perhaps *should* mean) is not that consistency is a mark of stupidity and the mundane — or that inconsistency is a mark of superior intelligence and courage — but that a "foolish consistency" *with what others believe* (that is, going along with the crowd) is a mark of those. What Copernicus, Galileo, Newton and the rest mentioned by Emerson did was to use the inconsistency in the current beliefs of others to demonstrate that something was *wrong* with those belief systems and that they needed to be changed in some way. And then those thinkers went on to produce such results as the Copernican revolution in astronomy (yielding a heliocentric view of our solar system and abandoning the earth-centered view of our existence), the replacement of flat earth theories of our world, the almost incalculable changes wrought by abandoning Aristotelian physics in favor of Newton's theories, etc. This didn't happen because Copernicus, Galileo, Newton, Pythagoras, and others held inconsistent beliefs, but because the *consistent beliefs* they held were superior to the beliefs of others which *were* inconsistent and otherwise inadequate in ways that needed fixing — in part for the purpose of *removing* those inconsistencies. This is perhaps a good illustration that when a poet is taken to be making accurate and factual claims about the world of objective experience, then *he* is likely to be misunderstood, or perhaps even to misunderstand himself, or perhaps not to care. We'll return briefly to such considerations in Chapter 5.

An even less charitable response to Emerson has been made by U.S. Supreme Court Justice Antonin Scalia. After some rather uncomplimentary remarks concerning Emerson's view on consistency and concerning law professors who frequently quote these, he continues with his argument that Emerson's view "is, in the legal culture, an unacceptable proposition," and that further, "it is a pretty silly proposition in any context." Scalia, then goes on to amplify these observations with

Antonin Scalia on Emerson's view of consistency

"... [I]t is quite impossible to forgive the line 'To be great is to be misunderstood,' which can only be matched for banality by 'Love means never having to say you're sorry.' As for substance: It should be noted that Emerson is condemning not just that portion of consistency he considers 'foolish.' His point is that all desire for consistency is foolish. 'With consistency a great soul has nothing to do.' At the risk of being considered a little statesman, a philosopher, a divine or even an aged lady (at least many of the last category, by the way, seem quite wise to me), this strikes me as unmitigated nonsense. One should assuredly not shrink from changing his views when persuaded that they are wrong. But the person who finds himself repeatedly in that situation — who quite readily speaks today what he thinks today, and tomorrow what he thinks tomorrow, with no concern for, with simply nothing to do with, the inconsistency between the two — is rightly regarded, it seems to me, not as a 'great soul,' but as one who habitually speaks without reflection, that is to say, a right fool. It is an even bet, of course, that Emerson would agree with this. Since he undoubtedly considered himself a great soul rather than a little statesman, etc., there is no reason to believe that what he thought yesterday has anything to do with what he might think today.

Now all of this would not have been worth commenting upon if Emerson had not been inflicted upon the law. I think it generally sound policy to leave poets alone if they leave you alone. But the fact is that Emerson's aphorism — which, as I have observed, is even inaccurate in its more general application — has been regularly and repeatedly applied to the law, where its message is destructive beyond measure. Consistency is the very foundation of the rule of law." (Scalia 1989)

Scalia argues that Emerson ends up rejecting not only *foolish* consistency, but *all* consistency; and that he makes no attempt to link changing your views with any requirements for changing evidence, with logic, or with any rational process. In urging us that inconsistency is not only a mark of greatness, but a prerequisite for it, Emerson leads us to embrace a form of *irrationalism* that's inconsistent with the rule of law (which should be fine with Emerson since he sees inconsistency as admirable). In this, Scalia also links logico-epistemic consistency with pragmatic consistency since the law requires the former in order to achieve the latter and thereby guarantee uniformity and fairness in how the law has been applied and will be applied in all cases that come before a court.

Losing this fundamental feature of the law he sees as being "destructive beyond measure". He goes on in his essay to illustrate exactly how this is the case, how consistency in reasoning and application is required by the U.S. Constitution and legal system, and what are the consequences of losing it.

Scalia even injects a bit of a joke in the middle of this assault on Emerson's thoughts when he remarks that since Emerson "undoubtedly considered himself a great soul," then "there is no reason to believe that what he thought yesterday has anything to do with what he might think today." It follows from this, of course, that Emerson — either from striving to be inconsistent in his own views (in order to be "great"), or just from being inconsistent as part of his greatness — would likely at some point deny the views he expresses in this very essay about the value of inconsistency, and instead demand consistency of us. This is one of the immediate dangers of inconsistency, as we'll see shortly: that it tends to devour itself and leave us with nothing to believe because we can't tell what's true, what's false, or even what the difference is. Regarding Scalia's remark that he finds it generally good policy to leave poets alone if they leave you alone, we shall return to this in Chapter 5 when we examine the differences between philosophy and poetry.

Given these two different perspectives on what are argued to be fundamental flaws in Emerson's famous (or perhaps infamous) remarks concerning the benefits of inconsistency, let's dismiss these rhetorical "small minds" arguments about the attractiveness and value of inconsistency, and about how consistency confines your capabilities and thought. But then let's ask "So, what is it about consistency that's good; and what is it about inconsistency that's bad?" The answer to these questions has all to do with truth, and logic, rational belief, and the pursuit of wisdom.

To begin, let's agree that some things are true and some things are false, and that something can't be both true and false. It's a feature of logic since its invention by Aristotle that from a contradiction, anything (and everything) follows — that is, if a contradiction is one of your premises in an argument, or can be inferred from the premises in your argument, then *anything* can be inferred from those premises. And what this means is that if a contradiction comes to be viewed as true, then *every* statement must be viewed as true since any statement can be inferred from it. This feature even has a nice Latin name: *ex contradictione sequitur quodlibet* ("from a contradiction anything follows"). It is also called "the principle of non-contradiction" or the "principle of explosion". So inconsistency in a set of statements or in our beliefs (which leads either directly or indirectly to an explicit contradiction) removes any distinction we can hope to make between truth and falsity. The result is that we have to go back and give up our original (and seemingly obvious and necessary) starting point that "some things are true and some things are false".

Being unable to distinguish truth and falsity (and what's true from what's false) is an intolerable situation in our system of belief and our attempt to describe the world around us. It prohibits us from attaining wisdom — or at the very least it prohibits us from knowing (or reasonably believing) that we've attained wisdom. This is the fundamental reason that inconsistency can't be tolerated by philosophers — who are seeking truth, knowledge, and wisdom, and who are unwilling to tolerate in their place incoherence and deceit. Error is pardonable, but embracing inconsistency is not. Mistakes that we may make can be corrected (in part by using consistency as a guide), but embracing inconsistency sacrifices the ability to determine what is error and what is not, and what is a mistake when we have made one.

Now when I say that this feature (of anything following from a contradiction) "is a feature of logic since its invention by Aristotle," I have to admit that I've taken a bit of liberty with total accuracy. In more modern times, and particularly since the mid-20th century, a spectrum of "alternative logics" has been explored by philosophers, and some of these attempt to accommodate (in one way or another) the presence of contradictions without losing the true/false distinction as I've described.

Several different logical and semantic techniques have been used by logicians to construct "non-classical" logics in which the principle of non-contradiction doesn't hold. Basically, a logician will start to tinker with some of the fundamental principles of logic or features of semantics. For example, the non-standard logic may be one in which the Law of the Excluded Middle (that a statement is either true or false) isn't enforced. Or it may modify exactly what "not" means and how it can be used. Such changes result in a logic that's "weaker" than classical logic (you can't prove as many things in it), but one in which (because you can't prove as many things in it) a contradiction can be regarded as true, or at least as "not false", at least in certain contexts and uses. Such systems of logic involve different trade-offs over classical logic, frequently end up endowing such logical words as "and", "or", and "not" with peculiar and unintuitive senses, or introduce additional truth values (such as allowing statements to be either true, false, or "meaningless"). This is an interesting formal and intellectual pursuit, and a fun-filled way for logicians to spend their time and publish papers (I know, since I've done that myself), but I'll just make a sweeping statement about this now, and then move on without spending a lot of additional time on it. Here's why:

A study of alternatives to classical logic (and especially of logics that attempt to dodge the consequences of the principle of non-contradiction) will quickly show that every one of these has some weird feature, some odd trade-off that many philosophers are unwilling to make, highly unintuitive features and results, and no obvious benefit compared to classical logic with its principle of non-contradiction (which also possesses strong intuitive support). Decades of experience by highly qualified and committed logicians, mathematicians, and philosophers have yielded no alternative found to be acceptable other than in restricted contexts with certain specific goals. This includes such attempts as multi-valued logics, intuitionistic logics, relevance logics, fuzzy logic, paraconsistent logics, and others. Sometimes these logics are referred to (especially by logicians themselves) as *deviant* logics (Haack 1974) — which will give you an idea of how they're often viewed

There are some areas (e.g., in computer science, electrical engineering, or quantum physics) where non-standard logics have found some useful applications or uses for modeling reasoning or inference in constrained domains, but no system of non-standard logic has found anywhere near universal, or even broad, acceptance; and this is certainly true of systems that attempt primarily to dodge the principle of non-contradiction. It turns out that it's *very* (*very*!) difficult to make something "locally inconsistent" in a logic or set of beliefs so that the inconsistency is somehow isolated, doesn't infect the entire system, and yet results in a useful and intelligible mechanism for reasoning, argument, and inference. For a more extended analysis of the benefits of classical logic, including the principle of non-contradiction, see W. V. Quine's easily understood book *Philosophy of Logic* (Quine 1986).

The bottom line for us here is that someone who holds that an inconsistency in his or her views isn't harmful must demonstrate how this view itself does in fact not lead to harm — since there is a strong *prima facie* and historical case, based on many examples and substantial research, that it will. Inconsistency is incompatible (inconsistent) with the true/false distinction, and so with knowledge and wisdom as we typically understand these — all fundamental goals of the philosopher. Any genuine philosopher who wishes to abandon the principle of non-contradiction owes us a highly convincing argument that the proposed alternative is a genuine and acceptable alternative (accompanied by a rigorous development with clear and broad applications of it) that eliminates the principle in an intelligible way and offers clear benefits to the traditional approach.

Regarding arguments such as that offered by Emerson that consistency is somehow limiting, we can happily concede that this is true — though not in the sense that seems to have attracted Emerson. Consistency limits us to the truth, to intelligibility, and to rationality. It will not by itself yield truth and wisdom, but without it there can be none. It tethers us to these when we might otherwise be subject to poetic, mystical, or drug-induced illusions, delusions, or flights of fancy. It provides the very basis for, and a critical guideline to, wisdom. This is why it's treasured by philosophers and is perhaps the most basic tool in their collection — used time and again to demonstrate that a proposed analysis, principle, concept, theory, or philosophical system is fundamentally flawed.

 Logic

Logic provides us with the rules of reasoning, and its job is to ensure that we don't draw faulty (i.e., false) conclusions from true premises. Deductive logic is a highly formal presentation of these rules that originated with Aristotle and his syllogisms. Aristotle sought to provide a set of patterns of reasoning which, if applied to true premises would guarantee the truth of the conclusion. Later, this syllogistic approach was expanded by medieval philosophers, and still later (in the 19th century) what we now call modern formal logic was developed by the German mathematician/philosopher Gottlob Frege (Zalta 2019). The limitations of the Aristotelian approach had been known for millennia, and Frege's logic was a significant advance over Aristotelian/medieval logic in that it enabled the characterization of more complex forms of inference that could be applied to the worlds of mathematics, science, and philosophy. The logic that Frege spawned is also frequently referred to as "symbolic logic" (although Aristotle's logic was symbolic in a very minor manner) or "mathematical logic" (although a lot of mathematicians don't regard logic as mathematics, and mathematics is only one domain where logic finds fruitful application).

Aristotle's logic captured such simple inferences as:

- All men are mortal.
- All Greeks are men.
- Therefore, all Greeks are mortal.

and

- All birds have feathers.
- Some pets are birds.
- Hence some pets have feathers.

But it couldn't come close to handling arguments involving more complex relationships such as:

Heads of horses are heads of animals because horses are animals

- All horses are animals.
- Therefore, every head of a horse is a head of an animal.

or this formulation of the *Omnipotence Paradox* (Hoffman and Rosenkrantz 2017), or the *Paradox of the Stone* (Savage 1967) — which purports to show that God can't be omnipotent:

The Paradox of the Stone

- Either God *can* create a stone which He can't lift, or He *can't* create a stone which He can't lift.
- If God *can* create a stone which He can't lift, then He *isn't omnipotent.*
- If God *can't* create a stone which He *can't* lift, then He *isn't* omnipotent
- So God is not omnipotent.

Both of these examples are easily seen to be valid arguments in contemporary formal logic even though they can't even be formulated reasonably in the logic of Aristotle and the Medievals. Contemporary logic is also "expressive enough" and "strong enough" to serve as a foundation for the formalization of mathematics (which was really Frege's goal in the first place), and it leads into such areas as axiomatic set theory, category theory, the theory of types, algorithms, and computability. Bertrand Russell has characterized it as providing "the skeleton or framework within which the test of coherence applies," and Donald Kalish and Richard Montague have said

> "Logic is concerned with arguments, good and bad. With the docile and the reasonable, arguments are sometimes useful in settling disputes. With the reasonable, this utility attaches only to good arguments. It is the logician's business to serve the reasonable. Therefore, in the realm of arguments, it is the logician who distinguishes good from bad." (Kalish and Montague 1980)

The other side of the traditional logic coin is *informal* logic, which often also appears in treatments of rhetoric (there will be more about this in a later chapter) and focuses on certain traditional fallacies of reasoning. These include what are called *fallacies of relevance*: personal attacks on your opponent, appeals to emotion or prejudice, appeal to authority, using ignorance as justification ("You can't prove otherwise; so what I'm saying is true."), circular argument, complex questions, "straw man" arguments, etc. The informal fallacies also include the *fallacies of insufficient evidence* such as the *post hoc* fallacy ("after this, therefore because of this"), special pleading (ignoring facts or reasoning that undermine your case and support your opponents), the fallacy of hasty generalization (leaping to a general conclusion based on too few examples), and a number of others.

Rather than attempting to introduce even the basic foundations of either contemporary formal logic or traditional informal logic at this point (each of which has itself been the subject of many books), we'll be content with this minimal sketch of the area and a promise to look into further details as these are required in later chapters. But we can clearly see at this point how philosophers feel logic (as a set of rules for reliable reasoning) is a fundamental part of their methodology.

Arguments

To the philosopher, an argument is a set of statements (or sentences, or propositions) that typically contains one set of statements taken to be true at the outset, called the *premises* of the argument, and a (possibly complex) statement that's claimed to *follow from* these by the rules of logic (called the *conclusion* of the argument). It's also not uncommon, as part of constructing an argument, to either provide *evidence* establishing (or supporting) the truth of the premises, or to provide other arguments to support the premises themselves.

An argument may have one of two goals or results (or it may more likely have both): (1) to support or demonstrate the truth of its conclusion; or (2) to persuade others that the conclusion is true (or that it's more likely true than not). As we'll see in the case of some disciplines and areas other than philosophy, and particularly in the case of pseudo-philosophy, these goals are often related but can be quite distinct.

A good argument changes "I think that ..." and "I believe that ..." into "I have good reason for believing that ..." and "Here's why you should believe this too ...". Without an argument, you just have feeling and opinion — and everyone is perfectly free to have his or her own feelings and opinions. But an argument can bring us together in sharing our beliefs and opinions, and in finding truth and wisdom.

Semantics

Semantics is the study of meaning in language. But, you may ask, what does "mean" mean? Yes! Now you have it! That's semantics — the study of, and construction of theories concerning the concept of meaning in several senses. It deals with a number of related concepts which together comprise what we see as representing the broader concept of meaning as this applies to our utterances and written expressions. The primary set of concepts treated by the discipline of semantics are:

- **Reference**: a word *stands for* or *designates* something in the world. As examples, we say that " 'Red' *refers to* a color, and 'color' *refers* to a property that things may have."

- **Sense**: a word or phrase has a *sense* or *meaning* that in different circumstances or contexts determines what it refers to. The phrase "the President of the United States" refers to different people at different times although its meaning is constant in that it always picks out the chief executive of the United States government. Likewise, the word "red" always picks out the set of all red things whenever it is used, although the members of that change constantly over time. And the phrase "square circle" picks out nothing because the properties it attempts to attribute to its referents are contradictory. We might be tempted to say that such a term is *senseless*, but a reasonable alternative to this is to concede that although the term can never have a *referent*, part of its sense is *square* and part of its sense is *circle* — and it's in virtue of the incompatibility of these two components of its sense that the term cannot *refer* to anything.

- **Truth**: a property that a sentence (or statement, or proposition, or utterance) has when what it says (its sense) corresponds to reality. The statements "Two plus two equals four." and "The earth has a single moon." are both true while the statement "The moon is composed of green cheese." is false.

Other issues that are dealt with in semantics are synonymy (sameness of meaning), ambiguity (multiple meanings of the same expression), vagueness, self-reference ("This sentence contains exactly six words."), an imposing variety of semantic paradoxes that seem to arise from what initially appear to be simple and unproblematic uses of language ("This sentence is false." — which is false if it's true, and true if it's false; and "the smallest number that can't be referred to in fewer than fourteen words" — which refers to that number in only

13 words), soundness of logical arguments, completeness of logical theories, translation, concepts (what they are and how they work), propositions (as abstract meanings of sentences or statements), truth values (True, False, and others), and a number of lesser notions that are related to these.

Semantics is an important tool of the philosopher because philosophical arguments depend for their intelligibility and strength on the meanings of the words and statements in them. Consequently, it is rare to encounter a philosophical analysis, argument, or theory that doesn't appeal to semantic concepts and issues at some point. We've already seen an example of this in one of our solutions to the Ship of Theseus Paradox.

Definitions

In normal everyday life, the role of a definition is to establish (or declare) the meaning of a word (or phrase), at least within a particular context, so that everyone concerned with using it has the same understanding of it.

In the context of your medical, automobile, or home insurance, it's important to know what "coverage", or "covered event" means. In insurance contexts, it can be important even to have a clear and specific definition of "day" since hospital charges are often paid on the basis of how many days are spent in a hospital room, an ICU, etc.

In the community of international diplomacy, it's important to define such terms as "terrorism" and "anti-Semitism" in order to arrive at effective legislation and procedures concerning these. In criminal law, it's critical to provide a definition of "felony" because conviction for a felony has some clear consequences for a defendant that don't pertain to conviction for a misdemeanor. In education, a definition of having "special needs" or being "advanced and gifted" is required in order to classify and place children in appropriate classes and programs in school.

In philosophy, the concept of a definition becomes much more complex and diffuse, and it's safe to say that there's no general definition of "definition" in that context. Nor is there a single use of definitions in philosophy. In ages past, there was a tendency for philosophers to see the finding of a definition as a major (if not the primary) goal of a philosophical analysis, or else to see the seeking of a definition as a sound philosophical technique, although even Plato in his dialogues had pointed out some severe problems with this.

While definitions can settle meaning and achieve agreement, they are very limited in what they contribute to an informative analysis, a true understanding of concepts, or to wisdom. Attempting to view definition as a fundamental tool of the philosopher presents a significant danger because of the ever-present threat of infinite regress: you can always ask for a definition of the more basic words or things in terms of which you're providing the definition; and either this will go on in a never-ending way (threatening an "infinite regress") or it must be terminated arbitrarily — at which point you have to concede that at least some terms can't be defined and must be understood or analyzed in some other way.

We'll return to considerations of this sort in later chapters. Definition may be valuable in establishing the basis of exposition and argument. And an attempt to find satisfactory definitions can help to highlight or to discover fundamental concepts or principles, or to expose inconsistencies and paradoxes. But a dependency on definition as a philosophical methodology— together with a misunderstanding of what it contributes to philosophical analysis — is often a sign of pseudo-philosophy.

 ## *Dialectic*

Dialectic is truly one of the ancient arts, beginning at least in Plato (and according to him, in Socrates), and then evolving in several distinctive ways over a couple of millennia. Fundamentally, dialectic involves a discussion or dialogue between two people (or among more than that) and in fact is a kind of debate. Each side (or participant) presents his or her view or position, and then argues for that against the other positions that are presented.

Aristotle seems to suggest that while dialectic is similar to (and related to) rhetoric, it differs from rhetoric in being more honorable and more objective in that its focus is on truth, knowledge, and wisdom rather than on persuading, compelling, or simply winning an argument. In Plato's dialogues, the Socratic method is employed in a dialectical manner to expose and then address confusions, conflations, inadequate definitions, and poor reasoning. Clarity of terms and concepts results from this dialectical process, leading to the philosopher's overall goal of improving knowledge and wisdom.

Dialectic is of course also related to logic since logic is used in the discursive process and argumentation that is an essential part of dialectic. And dialectic is also viewed as a primary method for bringing together incompatible or conflicting views into a "synthesis" or compromise view that is consistent while benefiting from the strong points of each position. Consequently, dialectic is often viewed as being comprised of two steps: an analytic step (*analysis*) in which clarity, goals, and inconsistency are addressed; and a synthetic/constructive step (*synthesis*) in which a consistent and merged position results. We'll come across dialectic again, though briefly, in Chapter 11.

Theories, models, and explanations

In science, the concepts of *theory* and *explanation* (based on, or supported by, a theory) are quite well known. Some examples of theories that people are often familiar with include Galileo's theory of falling bodies (which can explain how far a thrown ball will travel or how long it will take a dropped weight to hit the ground), Semmelweiss's theory of cadaverous poisoning (a precursor to Pasteur's germ theory of disease that explained why some women died of *puerperal fever* shortly after giving birth), Ptolemy's geocentric theory of the solar system and Copernicus's heliocentric theory that replaced it (both of which sought to explain astronomical observations), Torricelli's sea of air theory that lead to the discovery of air pressure and barometers, and Einstein's theory of the equivalence between mass and energy (often finding expression in the equation $E = mc^2$). A scientific theory is usually considered to be a framework consisting of a set of statements (called the *laws* of the theory) and guidelines or procedures for applying those laws to specific phenomena or events. It explains and predicts events and phenomena in the world, and gives us knowledge by relating a set of concepts to one another (such as *mass, force, velocity, germ, disease, symptom; gene, phenotype, evolution; radio wave, frequency, refraction, magnetism*, etc.).

Philosophical theories strive for the same sort of organization and structure as scientific theories, although they aren't (except in some isolated and usually indirect cases) tied to empirical or experimental evidence. Plato's Theory of Forms (Wikipedia 2020p), Aristotle's Theory of Universals (Wikipedia 2020a), D. M Armstrong's Theory of Universals (Wikipedia 2020b), and David Lewis's theory of properties in his *New Work for a Theory of Universals* (Hall 2020) are all theories of this sort intended to analyze and solve The Problem of the One and The Many that we've mentioned briefly in Chapter 2. Similarly, in ethics and political philosophy we find John Locke's Theory of Property (Tuckness 2016) and John Rawl's Theory of Justice (Wikipedia 2020n); in the philosophy of language we find a number of theories of truth (Glanzberg 2018); epistemology is full of theories of knowledge and belief (Wikipedia 2020d); and so on. The role of a philosophical theory (like that of a scientific theory) is to collect a set of basic and critical concepts into a set of *principles* (philosophical theories rarely describe these as *laws*), and then make use of this set of principles and concepts to *explain* and to *provide* a solution to a particular philosophical problem or set of problems.

The advantage to using the theory as a fundamental tool for analysis, explication, clarification, explanation, and problem solution in philosophy is that it's a much more powerful and effective approach to these goals than simply seeking a "definition" (whatever that may mean), and it turns out that definitions — in so far as they're enlightening and helpful — can be given clarity and precision in the context of a theory that explicates the terms used in the definitions. Employing a theory in this way also avoids the problem of an infinite regress that the approach of analysis by means of definitions otherwise faces. It's the theory that bestows meaning on the terms and expressions that appear in its laws or principles (by relating these together in potentially complex ways), and then a definition within the theory may summarize or abbreviate some of those complex relationships.

With a theory, we speak of *acceptance* rather than *truth*. This makes a theory about knowledge or, better, rational or reasonable belief — and only indirectly about reality in some fundamental metaphysical sense (whatever that might mean). Theories are always subject to criticism, additional support, or overthrow and replacement if they turn out to be inadequate in one way or another.

There is a second sense of theory that's also commonly encountered, and this is one in which the principles of the theory are presented more in the manor of recommendations or guidelines for accomplishing something. It's in this sense that people refer to *music theory, poetry theory, literary theory, theory of art*, etc. So poetry theory attempts to provide a set of rules, suggestions, or guidelines for creating good poetry. Music theory presents an array of principles and practices (regarding such notions as pitch, chord, melody, chord progression, harmony, etc.) for creating "good music" or a "good musical composition", literary theory proposes a body of ideas and methods to be used in the practical reading and understanding of literature, and a theory of art provides concepts and relations among these used to draw a distinction between art and non-art, and to characterize what counts as *good* art.

In such cases, the theory is offered as a kind of *perspective* or *method* for accomplishing a particular task (e.g., creating good poetry, composing or performing music, writing a play or novel, etc.), and not as a set of principles or laws having descriptive content about the objective world in which we live. However, the line between these two types of theories (the scientific/philosophical variety and the artistic/practical variety) can become blurred; and even Aristotle dealt extensively with both senses of theories in treating not only of Analytics, Physics, Categories, and Metaphysics, but also of Rhetoric and Poetics. And normative ethics (that part of ethics that seeks to say what particular acts or choices are good and right, or bad and wrong) feels a very strong tension between both types of theory, in contrast to metaethics (which instead seeks to explore the *meanings* of moral terms without attempting to provide practical rules and guidelines about how to act or what you *ought* to do).

In our discussions and analysis of philosophy versus pseudo-philosophy, we'll generally have in mind the philosopher's use of theories in the first (scientific/philosophical) sense I've just described. But in the end, the theory of pseudo-philosophy developed here will fall at least as much under the second (practical) sense of theory; and so it will be a merging of the abstract and practical features of these two types of theories. In this, we'll be guided by Goethe's dictum that "It is not enough to know; one must also apply. It is not enough to will; one must also do."

Paradoxes and counterexamples

We've already seen one paradox, in the case of the Ship of Theseus, and seen how the paradox appears as a contradiction that follows from what seem to be true premises by what appear to be valid rules of logic — forcing us to realize that our views of sameness aren't altogether consistent. There are a number of well known paradoxes and types of paradoxes whose subject matter spans virtually all intellectual disciplines from mathematics through various sciences, philosophy, religion, economics, politics, and others.

Some paradoxes require a high degree of detail and complexity just in order to show that they follow from a certain set of beliefs, and others — like the Liar Paradox: "This sentence is false." — are easily and quickly expressed (though not at all easily solved!). But in each case, revealing the paradox is tantamount to shouting "Something here is very wrong!" And this is the value of paradox, as a tool, to philosophers: it demonstrates and draws attention to something fundamental that needs to be understood better, and fixed. It can also be employed as a defensive maneuver against a philosophical concept, theory, or position that you're trying to attack. So paradox — when it can be applied — is one of the most powerful tools in the philosopher's tool chest.

The same is true of counterexamples, which in certain ways are similar to paradoxes, although not quite as devastating. In a counterexample, you demonstrate not that a position, theory, or set of beliefs results in a contradiction, but that it results in a conclusion that is *unacceptable*. And here, "unacceptable" means either that the result clashes sharply with intuition and is therefore, at least initially, regarded as *wrong*, or that the conclusion conflicts with (is incompatible with) a criterion of adequacy or some principle that was adopted earlier.

Consider a simple theory of utilitarian ethics which attempts to use as a fundamental component the principle, immortalized outside of academic philosophy in the *Star Trek* series (Wikiquote 2020), that "The needs of the many outweigh the needs of the few." In philosophy, this principle often finds expression as "The good of the many outweighs the good of the few," or in Jeremy Bentham's ethical dictum that "It is the greatest good to the greatest number of people which is the measure of right and wrong." And this principle, or something like it, forms the foundation of what are called *utilitarian* (Driver 2014) or *consequentialist* (Sinnott-Armstrong 2019) theories of ethics and morality.

Many people are attracted to such a view, and it does seem to have a certain common sense to it. But in the end, it's fraught with danger and invites confusion and paradox through some rather obvious counterexamples. Let's take a quick look at one.

Imagine a post-apocalyptic world in which large tribes of flesh-eating zombies roam the earth. One of these tribes comes upon a barricaded small town (whose inhabitants they outnumber) and say to the townspeople "Hey! Give us just one of your babies that we can torture and eat, and we'll go away and leave you alone. Otherwise, we'll overrun your measly defenses and kill you all, and then eat everyone anyway." Let's also assume (stay with me here), that this particular tribe of zombies, regardless of their other repugnant habits, is well known to be honest and to keep their promises (they just have some really bad personal and social inclinations, but at least they're honest). Imagine you're one of the townspeople, maybe even with a baby of your own who's now up for grabs. What do you do? It's obvious that in this case the good/needs of the many will determine that you hand over a (your?) baby to this horde. How does *that* sound to you?

It doesn't matter too much how it sounds to you (and this is a key to how counterexamples work) because it's made you *stop and think* about how to solve this problem. You've either got to somehow dismiss the counterexample as faulty or incoherent (pretty difficult, if not impossible, in this case) or you've got to acknowledge that your dearly held principle about the *good of the many* has gotten you into some really hot water — and now you either need to reject that principle ("Seemed like a good idea in the beginning, but didn't work out.") or try to modify it in some way ("Maybe there's really something to this idea of individual rights transcending social welfare, or maybe you can't have the one without the other?"). The counterexample brings you up short with the realization that things weren't as simple as they seemed, and that you didn't do as good a job with your philosophy as you thought you did. Again, as in the case of a paradox, the counterexample forces you to reexamine your entire approach or solution in order to figure out *what went wrong*. Similar to paradoxes, counterexamples point to some sort of inconsistency in your concepts, your principles, your logic, your evidence, or your (perhaps as yet not explicitly expressed) beliefs or facts. Ultimately, a counterexample will expose a paradox lurking in the details of your approach. And so it demands careful and immediate attention.

We'll see more about counterexamples, and how philosophers respond to them, in later chapters.

Part 2

Philosopher and Pseudo-philosopher

Chapter 4
Modeling the Philosopher

> *In this chapter:*
> - Personas
> - The philosopher persona
> - Criteria of adequacy re-examined
> - Markers
> - The roles of markers
> - Markers of the genuine philosopher

With our look at the philosophical landscape and philosophers' assumptions in Chapter 2, and our survey of philosophers' tools in Chapter 3, we have some understanding of what sorts of things interest philosophers, what they strive for, and what they value. We begin to see a broad set of characteristics of philosophy and philosophers emerge. Let's add some more of those characteristics and tighten our focus a bit as we paint a better picture of the philosopher. We'll do this by introducing a couple of metaphilosophical tools that will be especially helpful in comparing and contrasting genuine philosophy with pseudo-philosophy, and in contrasting the discipline of philosophy with other intellectual/academic disciplines in the next chapter. Together, these tools will constitute a model of the genuine philosopher.

4.1 Personas

We'll begin by thinking in terms of a *philosopher persona*, and borrow the persona concept from the areas of marketing (where a persona represents a "demographic" or group of customers) and user experience design (where a persona represents a "typical user" or target for the design of a product). This concept is also similar in some fundamental respects to that of a personal "profile" that's employed in crime analysis by such organizations as the FBI. In the more traditional sense, a persona may be taken to be a collection of attributes or aspects of someone's character that, at least in some loose sense, "defines" that person (or type of person) or tries to capture in a succinct way important aspects of the person. In our sense, however, the persona can more accurately be thought of as an abstract *model* of a person, or a *representation* of a person.

Sometimes personas in this sense are used (explicitly or implicitly) in job descriptions and hiring. You'll encounter such phrases as "The ideal candidate will have an advanced degree and three or more years of experience in biochemistry," or "Successful applicants will have experience in preparing French cuisine, in designing and maintaining high-speed digital networks, and will be reliable translators of Egyptian hieroglyphs." Hiring managers and Human Resources departments then go through job applications and filter them by comparing them to the persona, looking for the *type* of person (and the set of characteristics or attributes) needed for the job to be filled. Similarly, we'll be investigating what type of person a philosopher is, and what type of person a pseudo-philosopher is.

The concept and use of a persona in user interaction (UI) design and user experience design (UX), which is the design of products based on goals and principles intended to provide the best experience for a user of products or services) was pioneered by Alan Cooper in 1995, presented in some detail in *The Inmates are Running the Asylum* (Cooper 2004), and expanded in three editions of his *About Face* books, including *About Face: The Essentials of Interaction Design* (Cooper 2014). It developed into a sophisticated, though largely informal, approach to modelling the goals, needs, and characteristics of an individual or a type of individual, in which a kind of *virtual person* is constructed to represent these personal features in order to support predictions, explanations, and reasoning about that person, and to facilitate comparison of that *representative person* with other persons or types of persons.

Although we won't employ all aspects of a persona as described by Cooper, we'll use a significant portion of his approach to model and understand both the philosopher and the pseudo-philosopher (and hence philosophy and pseudo-philosophy). We'll follow Cooper, for example, in agreeing that "Personas must, like any model, be based on real-world observation" (in our case, of philosophers and pseudo-philosophers and some others), that "Personas are represented as individuals" (*the philosopher* and *the pseudo-philosopher*), that personas are construed as *personifications*, meaning that while a persona is *represented as* an individual, he or she *represents* a class or type (e.g., the persona of the individual philosopher represents the class of philosophers: what is common to them or typical of them), and that personas (like the persons they represent) have goals and motivations.

Cooper urges us to revisit the persona as we apply and use it, treating it as a hypothesis that may require revision. More properly, we should view the persona (at least in many cases) as *him* or *her* (or at least as *him–or–her*) since the persona represents a *person*.

4.2 *Philo*: the philosopher persona

Let's begin by naming our philosopher persona "*Philo*" and deciding that his or her gender is indeterminate. Later, we'll construct a pseudo-philosopher persona and name him or her "*Pseudo*".

We know that Philo is interested in attaining wisdom (which includes a certain kind of knowledge), and that he values logic, rationality, and consistency in pursuing that goal. He also wants to share this wisdom with others, and even to convince them that what he's found is the real thing: wisdom. In doing this, then, he wants to avoid emotion both as a goal and as a tool in getting others to follow him in his views.

Likewise, Philo wants to avoid any other tricks or deceptions in advancing her arguments and convincing others of the knowledge and wisdom that she's discovered. Truth is valued over agreement or acceptance; and when attained, agreement and acceptance should follow from the truth Philo presents, and from logic, arguments, and evidence she offers to support it. False belief — and false, fake, or bogus wisdom — is not the philosopher's goal. False belief should be avoided wherever possible, though as a practical matter we know that some of our beliefs will be false. But *false wisdom* is *incoherent* and not to be tolerated. Philo wants her own beliefs (and the knowledge and wisdom they lead to) to result from, and be supported by, rationality and rational methods. So she'll strive to avoid dogmatism and irrationality in any form. This includes avoiding the use of emotion, fear, or intimidation as techniques of argument or persuasion. The only compulsion should be the compulsion of reason, where logic and critical reasoning win the day. As Bertrand Russell remarks:

> "The pursuit of philosophy is founded on the belief that knowledge is good, even if what is known is painful. A man imbued with the philosophic spirit, whether a professional philosopher or not, will wish his beliefs to be as true as he can make them, and will, in equal measure, love to know and hate to be in error." "Philosophy for the Layman" (Russell 1946)

And so Philo will not only be open to criticism from others, but also will be actively self-critical in order to avoid error, or at least to reduce the chance of error, in his thoughts, positions, theories, and arguments. And he'll be committed to respond to that criticism in a reasonable and reasoned manner — avoiding the use of *ad hoc* attacks on his opponent, and avoiding deception or dishonesty of any sort. It's only in this way that Philo can hope to achieve genuine knowledge and wisdom. To do otherwise would be the philosophical analog of a scientist's faking data in an experiment in order to get his paper published or to get an additional grant — again, a kind of cheating that can lead only to false wisdom.

Along with this approach to her own work, Philo must take a similar approach to the work of others. This means being fair and objective in interpreting that work, even to the point of investigating ways in which it could be made better or its mistakes or weaknesses could be corrected. But most important, it means not imposing an interpretation on a statement, argument, position, or theory of another philosopher (or anyone else) which doesn't put it in the best light possible (and hence make it as difficult for Philo to defeat as possible). What's at work here is often referred to as the *Principle of Charity* (or the *Principle of Rational Accommodation*), and the idea is that when criticizing someone else's work you should do that on the basis of the best (strongest and most sensible) interpretation of the work — even if you have to tidy it up a bit yourself in order to make it reasonable.

More succinctly, we might summarize the Principle of Charity as

---

Principle of Charity

In interpreting your opponent's work, give it a break — so far as this is reasonable and possible without distorting the original expression of it.

We'll return to this in later chapters when we encounter specific examples where the Principle of Charity applies.

Philosophers are problem-oriented, and this is obvious even in the oldest fragments of text we have from the pre-Socratics such as Zeno, Empedocles, Anaxagoras, Pythagoras, and Heraclitus. Philo isn't out just to tell you a story that you can choose to believe or not. He doesn't think of himself as an entertainer. He may in fact be telling you a story, but it's the same kind of story that a scientist tells you: one that's intended to be *true*, to *communicate knowledge* about the real world, to provide some *explanation and understanding,* to provide you with *wisdom,* and perhaps even to be useful in various ways. This philosophical story begins with a *problem* (or often a question that lacks a reasonable or acceptable answer).

The story the philosopher tells isn't just an expression of opinion, and it isn't intended to divert or entertain you, and its goal isn't to make you *feel* some particular way (though it may have that effect as well). Explanation and understanding are the goals (along with the broader and deeper goal of wisdom as well). As part of this, Philo will reject mythological explanations (which may be offered appropriately by dramatists and entertainers), and if he offers you an account involving a deity, then he'll support that with rational arguments (e.g., in the tradition of Anselm, Aquinas, Spinoza, and Berkeley). In Part 3, we'll look in detail at comparisons of this type of story with very different types of stories incompatible with Philo and genuine philosophy.

4.3 Criteria of adequacy re-examined

Philo's problem orientation will also force her to think in terms of criteria of adequacy, which are — informally put — conditions that her story has to meet in order to be a *good* story (accurate, and yielding knowledge and wisdom). We've already seen that for Philo, consistency is a fundamental criterion of adequacy for any philosophical "product" she may produce. But for a particular problem she's approaching, she'll need to state (or at least recognize or acknowledge) specific criteria of adequacy for that problem.

In the *Ship of Theseus* example of Chapter 3, we looked at a specific philosophical problem that involves the concept of the identity of material objects over time, and at that point we saw how to introduce criteria of adequacy into a problem statement and how to use them. But here's another quick and illustrative example, without going into it in detail: Any moral theory should be able to be applied to concrete situations and tell us what actions or decisions are good in those situations, what actions are bad in those situations, and what actions are morally neutral (neither good nor bad, or equally good and bad). This in itself is a fairly general criterion for any moral theory a philosopher may develop. But more specifically, if we're to make a judgment about whether this general criterion is satisfied, we may want to list a number of critical sample cases that we know the theory should decide, and then see whether we can in fact apply the theory with adequate results.

We might then consider the question of abortion and what the theory says about a specific case: Is abortion morally permissible? Under what conditions, or are there no constraints? What about abortion in the case of rape? What about abortion in the case of a deformed fetus which everyone agrees won't survive outside the womb? What about abortion in order to avoid having a female rather than a male child? We could quite reasonably adopt as a criterion of adequacy for our moral theory that it must provide clear and definite answers to each of these questions. We could go even further and adopt for each of these questions a criterion about exactly *what* answer our theory should give: for example, "yes" in the general ("not otherwise specified") case, "yes" in the case of rape, "yes" in the case of the deformed fetus, and "no" in the case of sex selection of the baby. If our moral theory answers all of these questions, and answers the specific ones as we've indicated, then it satisfies our criteria of adequacy and is judged to be *adequate* and *acceptable*. Otherwise it fails to one degree or another.

Now note that these criteria of adequacy are debatable. If Philo adopts these criteria, other philosophers might argue against them. One philosopher might argue that one of the criteria is too strong (requires too much of the theory), and another philosopher might argue that it's too weak (doesn't require enough). Or it might be argued that a particular criterion doesn't make sense or shouldn't be included on one ground or another. Or it might be argued that the entire set of criteria of adequacy taken together violate the basic criterion of consistency. All of this is up for discussion, criticism, argument, and debate. All of it is an important part of philosophical methodology. But once Philo adopts a set of criteria of adequacy for his solution to the problem he's attempting to solve, these both constrain and direct him.

Philosophers like challenges and like to respond to them. Philo does. This isn't a matter of personality (or isn't simply that), but one of goals and methods, and being able to tell whether you've succeeded in your philosophical task — whether you've really solved the problem you set out to solve; whether you're good at what you do. Only criteria of adequacy allow you to do that — because they are part of defining your goals (to yourself and others) and defining what counts as achieving those goals, and so they're the measure of success. If you specify good criteria of adequacy for your challenging problem, and then your solution (analysis, theory, or explanation) is shown to satisfy those criteria, you win! There's no other way to tell that you've succeeded in the arena of truth, logic, knowledge and wisdom. There has to be a way to create that arena and draw its borders. Criteria of adequacy do that, or at least are an essential part of doing it.

So Philo knows that for any of her philosophical problems, she needs to develop criteria of adequacy that can be shown to be worthy, that will serve to specify the goals of her proposed problem solution, and that can be demonstrated to be met by that solution. She also knows — philosophical investigation being what it is in terms of exploring, clarifying, and analyzing — that she may need to revise her criteria over time (as she learns new things about the problem, her solution, and the criteria), and she may discover that some are unreachable and that others should be added. That's all part of the game, and part of achieving knowledge and wisdom. She also knows that a bait–and–switch approach to her criteria of adequacy can't be allowed: she can't get to the end, discover that her work fails to satisfy some of her criteria of adequacy, and then say "Well, those weren't important after all". If she does this, then she at least has to *show* how they turned out not to be important, *how* she learned this, and what *justifies* withdrawing them as criteria. And all of that, of course, takes place in the arena where the unalterable goals for Philo are truth, knowledge, and wisdom.

4.4 Markers

The second critical concept we'll use in analyzing both the genuine philosopher and the pseudo-philosopher — and comparing the two — is that of a *marker*. We'll borrow this from its use in chemistry, biomedical science, and other fields. A marker, in this sense, can also be thought of as an *indicator*, or an *indirect measure*, or a *sign* of something. For us, a marker is a rather simple concept, but one which provides some significant power and clarity in our task of identifying and characterizing pseudo-philosophy and pseudo-philosophers.

Our approach will be that there are certain markers that are characteristic of genuine philosophers, and certain other markers that are characteristic of pseudo-philosophers, and that whether someone should be considered a genuine philosopher or a pseudo-philosopher can in general be determined by identifying which markers apply and which predominate. We can also go further than this — as our exploration of markers progresses and as we apply them to specific cases in philosophy and pseudo-philosophy — and see markers in many cases as being *constitutive* of pseudo-philosophy. That is, the presence of certain markers (and how, and how frequently they appear) will not only *indicate* that a work is pseudo-philosophy, but they will be what *renders* that work to be pseudo-philosophical.

Markers in biomedicine

In biomedicine a *biomarker* (Strimbu and Tavel 2010) is a property found in an individual or specimen that indicates the presence of some disease, biological state, or medical condition. It isn't a direct observation of the disease, state, or condition itself, but it's an indirect *sign* or *clue* that the condition is present. For example, if you go to a doctor and as part of your physical examination have blood tests performed, a high level of cholesterol in your blood may indicate that you have or are developing a coronary condition that could threaten your circulation and heart. A high level of glucose (sugar) may point to the development of diabetes. And if you're a man, a high level of PSA (Prostate-specific Antigen) may indicate prostate cancer.

There are a few important features and distinctions that apply to biomarkers. One important feature is that biomarkers are *objectively observable or measurable*. In medical parlance, they're *signs* rather than *symptoms* since a sign is objectively observable or measurable while a symptom is a condition that's "self-reported" by a patient or subject. For example, "I feel hot." or "I'm feeling light-headed." are reports of symptoms, but your body temperature and your blood pressure are objectively measurable signs of your current condition (and are regarded as biomarkers). A second important feature is that a biomarker is a *fallible* indicator of the disease or condition that it "points to". You may have a relatively high PSA level, but this may be associated with some condition other than prostate cancer (for example, prostatitis or benign prostatic hyperplasia). An elevated white cell count may point to leukemia, but it may also point to a raging infection, to a reaction to some drug you're taking, to myelofibrosis, or to rheumatoid arthritis. Or it may simply be a result of your smoking habit or of stress. So a single biomarker points a finger, but more work typically needs to be done to identify any specific condition that's related to it or to identify an underlying cause.

However, biomarkers tend to acquire more reliability as they aggregate. That is, when a patient exhibits multiple biomarkers, each of which points (at least to some degree) at the same underlying disease or condition, then the likelihood of that disease or condition being present is increased. So, for example, *clusters* of biomarkers are now being used by cardiologists to produce more accurate risk scores in diagnosing and predicting the seriousness of cardiovascular disease in patients. And when the biomarkers of a high white cell count and high eosinophil count are coupled with night sweats and the symptom of severe itching, this *combination* of biomarkers and symptoms points with high accuracy to an underlying cause of Hodgkin's Lymphoma. There just aren't many cases in which *all* these things appear that aren't Hodgkin's Lymphoma.

Markers in business and finance

Similarly, in business and finance, markers are again *observable indicators* of underlying (or more complex and abstract) conditions such as fraud, theft, corruption, or embezzlement. These conditions aren't the kinds of things that can be directly observed ("Look! There's some corruption!"), but they can be inferred (and the prosecution of them justified) on the basis of *indicators* that are directly observable. As an example, in its *Fraud and Corruption Policy* (University of Western Australia 2015c), The University of Western Australia identifies a number of conditions that constitute fraud or corruption. These include *fraud* ("dishonest activity causing actual or potential financial loss"), *misconduct* (which involves a lengthy and complex definition), and *corruption* ("dishonest activity in which a University Officer acts contrary to the interests of the University and abuses their [*sic*] position of trust"), in highly legalistic language, pertaining to actions and failures to act).[6] But how is a member of the university community able to determine that fraud, misconduct, or corruption has been committed in a specific case? What *counts* as fraud, misconduct, or corruption?

The answer to this question for the case of fraud is to be found in an addendum to the Policy — Appendix D: Possible indicators of fraud (The University of Western Australia 2015b) — which provides *applicable guidelines* for inferring that fraud has occurred. A number of indicators (or in our terms, markers) are described which suggest (and should act as warning signs) that the conditions are present in some act or event or process. Further, the guidelines go on to say, "the more indicators present, the higher is the risk of fraud taking place." But they then warn that the presence of the indicators does not strictly imply the presence of the condition of fraud. Rather, the indicators should "raise awareness of risk" and trigger a heightened scrutiny and monitoring of the systems or processes in which they've been observed. Examples of these markers include: missing vouchers and official records, excessive variations to budgets or contracts, excessive movements of cash funds, unauthorized changes to systems or work practices, lost assets, evasive behavior by an employee, managers bypassing subordinates or subordinates bypassing managers, and excessive control of records by one officer. When markers like these are observed, fraud should be suspected and steps should be taken to pursue its exposure.

Markers in philosophy

We'll follow this same approach in developing a set of markers (*philosophy markers*) for philosophy and a similar set of markers (*pseudo-philosophy markers*) for pseudo-philosophy. Then in Chapter 8 we'll introduce guidelines for using these markers, and in Chapters 9-11 we'll apply those guidelines and sets of markers in analyzing and evaluating the works of several writers in the area of philosophy, and in supporting judgments concerning whether a given work (or writer) falls into the camp of genuine philosophy or the camp of the pseudo-philosophers. Given the nature of markers as we've just explained it, we may expect there to be difficult calls in some of these cases if the aggregate of markers doesn't point strongly in one direction or the other. But in general this approach should yield some clear, understandable, and defensible judgments, and otherwise focus attention on remaining areas of dispute.

We'll also adopt the view (consistent with the historical record) that the practice of pseudo-philosophy by a given writer may not be uniform: that some of his or her works (or portions of those works) may be genuinely philosophical while some may be pseudo-philosophical in nature. And this will yield a kind of "sliding scale" according to which a writer may be judged to be pseudo-philosophical in some works, but not others, and may be judged to be either fundamentally pseudo-philosophical or only occasionally pseudo-philosophical. Thus we're allowing for lapses of judgment on the part of a writer without committing her to the wholesale condemnation of being "a pseudo-philosopher", and this seems reasonable. In accord with this approach, we'll adopt the following broad attitudes and principles in our approach to pseudo-philosophy and to the use of markers in identifying and characterizing it:

Markers of philosophy and pseudo-philosophy: their features and use

- Philosophy markers and pseudo-philosophy markers are objectively observable features of an author's writings and presentations.

- A judgment of pseudo-philosophy against a particular work requires the clear presence of pseudo-philosophy markers in that work; and support for that judgment is strengthened both by multiple occurrences of the same marker, and by occurrences of multiple markers.

- A broad judgment characterizing an author as pseudo-philosophical requires demonstrating the presence of pseudo-philosophy markers throughout his or her works (a pattern of behavior); and support for that judgment is strengthened in proportion to the pervasiveness and variety of those markers.

We may then view pseudo-philosophy as a pathological condition of works that are purportedly genuinely philosophical, and one that can be identified through objective means.

4.5 The logical and evidential roles of markers

Whenever we think of something as a marker, we must also think of it as a marker *of something*; and we'll adopt the neutral term "condition" or "characteristic" to refer to what a marker is taken to *indicate*. A marker is a visible, or easily seen, indicator of a more subtle, indirect, or less directly determinable condition or characteristic. Markers are clues to the presence of that condition or characteristic. In the case of markers in biology and medicine, the conditions are often medical conditions such as a disease, and so your elevated level of A1C is a marker of your Type 2 diabetes condition, and PSA level is a marker that you may have prostate cancer. In business, evasive behavior and missing records are markers of fraud and corruption.

Still, an observation of a marker only raises the suspicion of the presence of a condition; and we have to concede that the marker may be present without the particular condition it flags actually occurring. Records can go missing through carelessness or accidents, evasive behavior may result from some emotional disturbance an employee is temporarily suffering, and a PSA level may be higher than normal either through a faulty test or from an underlying condition (such as prostatitis or a urinary tract infection) that doesn't involve cancer. A high PSA level isn't like a prostate biopsy in determining the presence of cancer. With a biopsy, you can see the cancer cells; but with a PSA test you *infer* that there's a good possibility that cancer is present. The marker doesn't show us the cancer cells that constitute the cancer itself, and it doesn't provide us with direct or deductive evidence that cancer is present. This is because a high PSA is *associated* (in fact, fairly strongly associated) with prostate cancer, but it isn't necessarily tied in a causal way to prostate cancer.

Similarly for other markers. In each case the marker is *associated* with the condition or characteristic it indicates, but is not deductively or necessarily related to that condition or characteristic. The presence of the condition doesn't *follow from* the observation of the marker.

But this raises the question "What makes something a marker rather than merely an association?". And following on this are two important epistemic questions about the value of markers: If a marker is a clue, how can it go on from being just a clue to being something that provides us with *evidence* of the presence of a condition? Or even further: How can it go on to become *constitutive* of the condition as we'll see in the case of pseudo-philosophy. And how can the use of markers *justify* our inference of a conclusion based on their presence? How can markers incline or compel us to believe (and believe rationally) that a certain condition is present?

The answer to these questions lies, in part, in an area of logic and epistemology called *abductive reasoning*. Abductive reasoning is a kind of non-deductive (and also non-inductive) reasoning that is often referred to — especially within the philosophy of science — as *inference to the best explanation*. Very informally, here's the way it works in the form of an example:

- You know that a certain *condition* (say, Hodgkin's Lymphoma) is associated with a number of *indicators*.

- You know that these indicators include the presentation of a lump (generally at the site of a lymph node, and frequently in the neck, armpit, or groin), drenching night sweats reported by the patient, an elevated temperature that may come and go, unexplained itching of the skin on some parts of the body, loss of appetite, a constant feeling of fatigue, and an elevated eosinophil count.

- You also know that each of these markers *may* be caused by some other condition, but that a *combination of the markers* is rarely seen except in cases of Hodgkin's Lymphoma.

- A patient comes to you complaining of a lump in the neck, pronounced itching of his forearms, severe night sweats, and constant tiredness.

- You conclude that it's very likely that the patient is suffering from Hodgkin's Lymphoma. This is the *best explanation* under the circumstance that you've observed, and it's the *most reasonable thing to believe* given those circumstances.

Our markers of genuine philosophy and markers of pseudo-philosophy will serve this same role in the case of determining whether a work or author is genuinely philosophical or pseudo-philosophical, and I'll cover this in much more detail in Chapter 8.

4.6 Markers of genuine philosophy

Given our characterization of philosophy and philosophers in Chapters 1–3, and our construction of the philosopher persona Philo in this chapter, we can now take the following to be a summary — in terms of markers — of the distinctive goals, characteristics, and methods of the genuine philosopher. The true philosopher will (in the aggregate) exhibit these markers, and *not* exhibit the markers of the pseudo-philosopher (Pseudo) whose markers we'll discuss in Chapter 6. And in the case of genuine philosophy, what these markers indicate are commitment to the *pursuit of wisdom*, *integrity*, and *competence*.

 *Markers of the pursuit of wisdom*

Φ **Inquiry**

Philo remains open to new and further inquiry into problems and solutions, and to where that inquiry takes her — even if (or especially if) it's incompatible with previously accepted analyses, theories, and solutions.

Φ Explanation

Philo seeks the ability to provide intelligible, rational, and enlightening explanations as basic components of the wisdom that she pursues.

Φ Rationality

Philo insists on arguments conforming to the canons of rational reasoning and the principles of rational epistemology.

Markers of integrity

Φ Objectivity

Objectivity requires the fair and reasonable interpretation of positions, arguments, theories, and the views of others (as expressed in the *Principle of Charity*). Communication and the presentation of Philo's own problem statements, theories, and proposed solutions demand that these admit of a shared interpretation and understanding that all participants can agree to and employ fruitfully with one another.

Φ Critical Appraisal

Philo constantly exposes her own work to self-criticism, and is open to (and actively invites) the criticism of others. Sincere efforts are then made to address these criticisms, and may result in either a defense of the work, or in alterations of either minor or major proportions. The same is true in applying a high degree of critical appraisal to the terms, concepts, positions, and arguments advanced in the work of others. The genuine philosopher does not accept, or attempt to make use of, such work until it is carefully understood (along with its consequences) to the best of his ability. Critical appraisal is in fact a hallmark of philosophy.

Φ Adequacy

Philo develops criteria of adequacy in order to formulate goals with clarity and precision, and as measures of the success or failure of his proposed solutions.

Markers of competence

Φ Problem Orientation

Philo has an orientation towards identifying problems, characterizing them carefully and clearly, and posing solutions to them as part of the pursuit of explanations and wisdom.

Φ Clarity

Philo prizes (and requires) clarity in expression of his views, the analysis of his concepts, the statements of problems, criticism of himself and others, and in the presentation of proposed solutions.

Φ Consistency

The pursuit of wisdom demands consistency among Philo's principles, arguments, and beliefs.

Φ Methods

Philo is committed to understanding basic methods and techniques in philosophy (as, for example, these are briefly summarized in Section 3.4) and to having familiarity and skill in employing these methods.

Φ Domain Awareness

Philo is familiar with the basic problems that historically have concerned philosophers, the major approaches to dealing with these, and the strengths and weaknesses of those approaches. In addition, she's aware of major unsettled problems and disputes about proposed solutions.

In the next chapter we'll make use of the Philo persona and these philosophy markers to compare and contrast philosophy with other disciplines that are seen as being related to it.

Chapter 5
Philosophy, Its Relatives, and Imitators

> *In this chapter:*
> - More on markers and their role in distinguishing boundaries
> - How philosophy is related to history, theology, religion, rhetoric, science, psychology, literature, and poetry
> - The good, the bad, and the just plain different

In preparation for applying our methods to possible cases of pseudo-philosophy in Part 3 of this book, it will be helpful to look at a number of disciplines that are *not* philosophy but are related to philosophy in one way or another. This will help us refine our understanding of the boundaries between philosophy and other disciplines, and see how our using the Philo persona and markers applies in practice.

When we look at a particular work or a particular thinker or author, and wonder whether genuine philosophy or pseudo-philosophy is being exhibited, there are several possibilities. We may see that genuine philosophy is being practiced by the author in that work. Or we may see that pseudo-philosophy is present instead. Or we may see that some parts of the work exhibit genuine philosophy and other parts exhibit pseudo-philosophy. But of at least equal importance, we may see that *something else* is being done by the author in that work: something perfectly legitimate that's not philosophy but yet isn't pseudo-philosophy either — even though it may have philosophical (or perhaps pseudo-philosophical) elements in it. The world of thought, after all, is much broader than just philosophy and pseudo-philosophy.

That's the focus of this chapter: to get a bit better grip on the boundaries between philosophy and "not-philosophy" in such a way that we avoid the danger of classifying anything that's not "good philosophy" as pseudo-philosophy. And this is an important step in satisfying the criteria of adequacy we set out for ourselves in Chapter 1. Let's proceed to a consideration of several disciplines and comparisons of them to philosophy. We'll begin with history, and treat that as a paradigm case that we can then apply (at least by analogy in places) to other disciplines.

5.1 History

History is the study of the past: past events, past civilizations, past societies. It's the story of what has been, and historians are the writers of this story. We all know that. It's a very dry and fact-oriented subject involving a lot of memorization that requires excellent skills of recall.

Except historians don't seem to know this; and that perspective has changed substantially in the 20th century. Historians think that in addition to keeping track of historical facts, it's their job to provide interpretation, explanation, and (to some degree) prediction. They also feel that they're serving up at least some kind (or some degree) of wisdom in terms of what history can teach us in understanding the world around us — at least when it comes to certain types of events and social or political changes. Such a view is championed, for example, by E. H. Carr in his 1961 book *What is History?* (Carr 1961). Not all historians agree fully (or perhaps even largely) with Carr's view of history and its practice, but it's undeniable that history, as a discipline, is (and seemingly always has been) something more than simply recording "the facts" in very long and boring books.

Another view of the nature of history — and how to pursue it — is found in Jarrod Diamond's book *Guns, Germs, and Steel: The Fates of Human Societies* (Diamond 2017). Here, Diamond (who has had professional careers as a professor of physiology, an ornithologist and ecologist, and a professor of geography) draws a fascinating picture of how modern science (particularly plant biology, genetics, linguistics, meteorology, and geography) can contribute insights and explanations for historical, societal, and political events and processes that have previously defied our understanding in terms of more classical approaches. Again, not all historians are entirely enthusiastic about Diamond's techniques or vision.

The point of these examples of the work of Carr and Diamond is that history (and its methodology and practice) isn't nearly as simple as most people think. And as part of their trade, historians use philosophy (often predominantly social and political philosophy, but also aspects of metaphysics and epistemology as well), both in reflecting on and evaluating their own methods, and in constructing their interpretations of the historical record. This is an example of how philosophy tends to intrude to some degree in any other discipline: it appears to be applicable *everywhere*.

Moreover, there is probably no discipline more concerned with its own history — and with constantly reviewing it, teaching it, reusing it, applying it, and in general dwelling on it — than philosophy is. So we have to concede a very close relationship between philosophy and history. They are at least very close cousins, if not siblings. Yet there are some fundamental differences which make history not-philosophy and make philosophy not-history. And the differences are of such a nature that history (properly practiced, as historians are inclined) is also not pseudo-philosophy. History isn't fake philosophy or bad philosophy. It's something else.

The discipline of history isn't just, or even mostly, philosophy applied to the historical record (although historians do a certain amount of this as part of their work). And the history of philosophy — or history of ideas— isn't just a set of facts in the historical record devoid of any interpretation or analysis. Some writers may be regarded as, and referred to as, philosopher-historians — indicating that they involve themselves frequently both in philosophical analyses and in historical ones. And likewise, a philosopher whose specialty is the history of philosophy will have a foot solidly in both camps and traditions. Nonetheless, it's important to distinguish between the two disciplines in terms, at least, of their concerns, their scopes, their techniques, and their goals.

Whatever else we may believe about history as a discipline, it does have a focus on historical facts. These are the fodder of history. This is not true of philosophy. Even when philosophy is being done in (or as) the history of philosophy, it's not historical facts that are either the focus or the important components. Instead, it's the development of philosophical concepts, arguments, theories, counterexamples, and so on, *through an historical lens*, that is the focus. And the primary focus in all of these isn't a mere description of events (or some sort of historical explanation of the sequence of events), but the philosophy that's involved. A book on Kant's ethics, for example, will devote most of it's time to understanding Kant's thinking about ethical concepts, principles, and their applications. It will employ the history of Kant's development of these, and the historical context of Kant's time and what preceded it — in order to understand Kant's thinking — but the focus will be on the philosophy.

To the degree that the history of philosophy deals with such a sequence (or evolution, or change over time) of philosophical ideas and theories, it is an exercise in history, and not in philosophy. But to the degree that it focuses on the details of the problems, how these problems are approached at each point, what concepts and theories are introduced and explicated, what arguments were made for and against philosophical positions, what problems and consequences there are for such positions, etc., then it's an exercise in philosophy and not in history. In part this is because what the historian of philosophy wants to analyze and explain is the ideas, problems, theories, and concepts — and their *philosophical* relationships to one another. He makes use of history in doing this, but history is the sauce and not the main dish. He does both history and philosophy, but these remain very different things to do.

Chapter 5: Philosophy, Its Relatives, and Imitators

A result of this is that if you take historical considerations (and references) out of philosophy, what you have left is still the body and content of philosophy (in the form of the problems, concepts, arguments, positions, counter-arguments, counter-examples, paradoxes, and theories). You lose some historical insight into how those things came to be over time, but you still have the philosophy. Similarly with history (or an historical treatment or analysis): if you take away any philosophy you find in it (as we've characterized that in earlier chapters), you still have all the history, and the insight and explanations that come from that. History and philosophy can contribute to one another — use one to elucidate the other — but they are not at all the same disciplines in terms of content, focus, and methodology.

This same relationship (primarily the use of philosophy to elucidate the content and methods of other areas), is found repeatedly across other disciplines and domains. This is one reason that philosophy is often said to be "more fundamental" than other disciplines and sometimes referred to as "the queen of the disciplines". In *Science, Perception, and Reality* (Sellars 1991), for example, Wilfrid Sellars makes the point that philosophy doesn't have a "special subject-matter", but that philosophers must *know their way around* the subject-matters of the various special disciplines; and this is certainly true with regard to the disciplines in which they intend to apply their own philosophical work. So a philosopher specializing in medical ethics had better know more than a little about the theory and practice of medicine, surgery, and pharmaceutical development and drug use; a philosopher of science must be conversant at a reasonably high level (and be able to read the peer-reviewed literature) in whatever area of science his work may apply to (physics, chemistry, biology, genetics, cosmology, gravitational theory); and so on. And in general (we see this even — or especially — in Aristotle) the philosopher must "know his way around" in areas of the real world and the domains of other disciplines if his work isn't to remain irrelevant and sterile. In this sense, we can think of philosophy as a kind of matrix into which other disciplines can be inserted in order to see them in certain critical, expository, and evaluative ways — and it alone provides a structured context for comparing those special disciplines to one another in an objective way.

In the case of the relation of history and philosophy, Sellars draws the distinction on the basis of what questions the historian is concerned to address versus what questions are of concern to the philosopher, and *how* the historian and philosopher each approach answering those questions. The historian, Sellars observes, not only reflects on historical events, but also on "what it is to think historically ... its aims, its criteria, its pitfalls". And the philosopher has the same orientation with respect to philosophical issues and what it means to think philosophically. These are distinct disciplines, but in some sense they are co-dependent in how they make fruitful (and in fact critical) use of one another.

Having, with this example of history, established the peculiar role that philosophy plays in regard to other disciplines, we won't need to do this repeatedly as we consider additional areas that are acknowledged to have especially close relationships with philosophy. And we can more quickly characterize the relations of these disciplines to philosophy as well.

5.2 Theology

Theology is typically said to be the study of "the divine", the nature of the divine, the nature of God, or the nature of religious belief. It would not be inaccurate to say that in the general sense, theology is the study of God, or gods, or god-like (supernatural) creatures — except that (in the general sense) the concept of god in such contexts is itself vague and can range from the classic Judeo/Christian/Islamic conception of an all-powerful all-knowing creature (concerned in some personal way with the existence of humans) to much lesser gods who lack full omnipotence and omniscience but may "specialize" in intervening in certain areas of life and existence for a variety of motives that they may have.

Even beyond that, theology as a discipline must be broad enough and liberal enough to include divinities (or spirits or forces) which are impersonal and highly abstract (as Aristotle's prime mover may well be). But regardless of the broad range of possibilities here, theology does have the underlying assumption that its focus is on some sort of "being" or "force" that is beyond what we understand as nature and that has direct effects within nature (and the universe) as we know it.

This assumption is the primary critical and fundamental difference between philosophy and theology — since philosophy makes no such assumption, and doing so would be incompatible with several of the philosophy-markers listed in Section 4.4. In fact, it could legitimately be argued that for each of those philosophy-markers, we could find a perfectly acceptable example of theology that violates it, though we won't delve into the details of that argument here. Theology *always* involves a certain kind of ideology (often referred to as "faith" or "true belief"), and is — with respect to this ideology — a *justificatory* tool rather than a set of methods and tools employed in open-minded and objective exploration of the sort that the philosopher requires in his pursuit of wisdom and his sincere willingness to question all assumptions. Theology is, by its nature, a closed or limited investigation in a way that philosophy is not.

Certainly theologians often concern themselves with understanding and even with some sense of explanation, but this is always in the context of the fundamental assumption of the divine and the exploration of its nature. Even the great philosophical theologians such as Thomas Aquinas (often a paragon of reason and rationality, insisting that faith must be consistent with reason) retained this focus. Philosophers of religion may cross the line into theology in their investigations and comparisons of theological systems from a philosophical perspective. But the goals of theology (primarily justification of belief, and elucidation of the nature of faith), assumptions (that there is divinity in one sense or another), and methods (e.g., the use of scripture, revelation, myth, and the interpretation of these) are fully outside the scope of philosophical investigation and of our philosophy-markers. Certainly some great theologians have been great philosophers, and some great philosophers have been great theologians, but that was because they were great within each of these distinct disciplines and able to use one to inform their work in the other.

5.3 Religion

Religion is even further divorced from philosophy than is theology. As theology is the theory of the divine, so religion is the operational implementation of the theory. Religion is thus twice-divorced from philosophy, and is at best a second cousin.

Religion (or a religion) is typically characterized as a social or cultural system in which beliefs about the divine (and related notions of faith, spirituality, morality, and behavior towards the divine) are codified in a set of rules, doctrines, and rituals. This is true even (or sometimes especially) in the case of natural religion, non-denominational religion, and primitive religion — some of which may lack a scriptural or doctrinal basis.

Clark Glymour has remarked that religion is a practice and not a discipline, and certainly there is a lot to be said for this view. While philosophy and philosophical techniques may be employed by religious practitioners (priests, prophets, ministers, rabbis, shamans, et al.) in the execution of their duties, they are used under even more severe constraints than the fundamental and broad assumptions found in theology. In such cases these are again employed in a justificatory manner, but also in an explanatory role for the sake of communicating and clarifying any theological foundation underlying the particular religion being practiced. Questioning of fundamental beliefs or assumptions — and philosophical practice in accord with our philosophy-markers — are not within the scope of religion or its practice. While religion is not inherently pseudo-philosophical, there is a danger of it slipping into that darkness whenever belief and conformance is regarded as more important than truth and wisdom.

5.4 Rhetoric

Rhetoric has a very long relationship with philosophy, and a number of attempts have been made by scholars to absorb rhetoric into philosophy (fundamentally, as a philosophical tool, as logic is). Even Aristotle himself wrote the original definitive analysis of rhetoric and it's included in his philosophical corpus. So isn't rhetoric really philosophy, or a kind of philosophy, or part of philosophy? The answer to this question is that no, it's not: it's philosophy's evil twin. And this answer rests on how rhetoric is characterized (even by rhetoricians themselves), on what its goals are, what its methods are, and what its consequences are.

Philosophy, as we've seen in earlier chapters (and explicitly in Chapter 4), is focused on achieving, sharing, and teaching *wisdom*. Look at the markers of genuine philosophy listed in Chapter 4 and you'll see that philosophy is an exercise in understanding what is true and what is the nature of that truth. It prizes and requires rationality and objectivity, consistency, honesty, and the fair and open consideration of alternative views, accounts, and explanations. Rhetoric does not. Rhetoric isn't about that. Rhetoric is about thought control: making (or at least encouraging) you to think a certain way, independent of whether that thinking is sound and consistent with truth and wisdom (and often specifically when it is not).

In his dialog *Gorgias*, Plato characterizes rhetoric as the art of persuading an "ignorant multitude" of people about the rightness or wrongness of a matter, even though the rhetorician himself is ignorant of such matters and may have no care about the rightness, wrongness, truth, falsity, honor or dishonor of what he's working to get people to believe. The rhetorician, according to Plato, has no concern to impart any "real instruction" (anything that is true), but sees his job (the role of rhetoric) as *persuasion*: getting people to think a certain thing, to think in a certain way, or to take a certain action *independent* of whether this persuasion is based on *truth* and *wisdom*. To Plato, the rhetorician is an intellectual soldier of fortune.

Xenophon (another student of Socrates, mentioned briefly in Chapter 1) devoted a portion of his work *On Hunting* to excoriating the Sophists (who were viewed as rhetoricians rather than true philosophers). He says of the Sophist:

> "[W]ords with him are for the sake of deception, writing for personal gain; to benefit any other living soul at all is quite beside his mark. There never was nor is there now a sage among them to whom the title "wise" could be applied. No! the appellation "sophist" suffices for each and all, which among men of common sense sounds like a stigma. My advice then is to mistrust the sonorous catch-words of the

sophist, and not to despise the reasoned conclusions of the philosopher; for the sophist is a hunter after the rich and young, the philosopher is the common friend of all; he neither honours nor despises the fortunes of men." (*On Hunting*, (Xenophon 2013 Chapter VII))

Here again we see the complaint that rhetoricians are deceitful, write and work for personal gain, and lack wisdom. They should be mistrusted and despised. But, says Xenophon, you shouldn't let this affect your attitude towards philosophers — because philosophers pursue wisdom and truth, and they're completely neutral when it comes to any consideration of wealth or monetary reward ("the fortunes of men"). To Xenophon, sophists/rhetoricians are hired mind-benders, out to make a quick buck.

In the 17th century, British empiricist John Locke remarks that the words of rhetoricians are for no other purpose than to "insinuate wrong ideas", "move the passions", and "mislead judgment". And so the words of rhetoricians are "perfect cheats". In the 18th century, Immanuel Kant chimes in with the observation that rhetoric (which in one place he calls "the art of deluding") is a "fine art of playing for one's own purpose upon the weaknesses of men" and "merits no *respect* whatever". In the early 20th century, Charles Caleb Colton (an English cleric, later apparently a wine-merchant, art investor, gambler, and highly popular essayist) offers in his book *Lacon, or Many Things in Few Words, addressed to those who think* (Colton 2017) that "rhetoric is the creature of art, which he who feels least will most excel in; it is the quackery of eloquence, and deals in nostrums, not in cures". And Wayne Booth, a mid-20th century literary critic, professor of English and literature, and something of an icon for his 1961 book *The Rhetoric of Fiction* (Booth 1983), remarks that "Rhetoric is the art of finding and employing the most effective means of persuasion on any subject, considered independently of intellectual mastery of that subject," a clear indication that truth and wisdom are not concerns of the rhetorician (and as clear a statement as you can find of precisely the attitude which has so distressed philosophers throughout history).

There appears to be a convergence of thinking, over the ages, concerning what rhetoric amounts to and what's wrong with it. Even rhetoricians themselves acknowledge this in describing their own subject, often as they attempt to recast it in modern times as a "communication art". And they frequently seem not to realize that they're confessing to the sins of which the philosophers accuse them (see "What is Rhetoric?" (San Diego State University, 2020)) — perhaps because they don't recognize them as sins.

In fact, of course, philosophers and rhetoricians share the use of certain techniques such as logic, argumentation, analysis, explanation, counterexample, and theory construction. But it's what they do with these techniques and *how* and *why* they do it that makes the difference.

Rhetoricians recommend (and teach) precisely the techniques of persuasion that philosophers condemn. And philosophers condemn them because those techniques not only fail to lead to wisdom and understanding, but in fact lead to (and often seek) the replacement of wisdom and understanding by false beliefs based on faulty and irrational reasoning. These techniques include the appeal to emotion (including such emotions as empathy and fear), equivocation (basing conclusions on shifting the meaning of a word in your argument), persuasive definitions (which have built-in assumptions and prejudices), ambiguity and vagueness (depending on the lack of precision to obscure obvious flaws and counterexamples), the time-honored technique of "lying with statistics", employing classical fallacies of relevance such as the *ad hominem* (personal attack on your opponent rather than addressing his or her claims and arguments), appeal to authority, intimidation (e.g., "If you don't agree with what I'm saying, then you're not smart enough to understand it."), and others.

Rhetoric isn't applied only to, or within philosophy, but broadly within other fields as well, whenever persuasion is required. However, when it does appear in a philosophical context it may result directly in false wisdom (pseudo-philosophy) as it's used to imitate genuine philosophy. We'll see the details of this in later chapters.

5.5 Science

Science is closely related to philosophy — or at least it's related to a lot of philosophy such as metaphysics, logic, epistemology, and (of course) the philosophy of science. But there was a time when not only was science related to philosophy: it actually *was* philosophy. Our word "science" comes from a Latin root meaning *knowledge*. But the meaning that we attach to "science" today — as a set of related domains (biology, chemistry, physics, psychology, etc.) with careful methodologies focused on understanding natural phenomena in the world, explaining and predicting those phenomena, and having direct practical effects in such areas as the production of energy, agriculture, medicine, transportation, communication, and entertainment — was introduced only in the early 1700s. Prior to that, what we call science was referred to as "natural philosophy". And beyond this history of nomenclature, science (i.e., natural philosophy) was practiced by philosophers at least since the time of Aristotle, who seems to have been as much of a naturalist and biologist as he was a philosopher. When Isaac Newton (certainly a paradigmatic scientist, and one of the greatest in our history) published his master work *Principia Mathematica* in 1687, the full title of this work was *Philosophiæ Naturalis Principia Mathematica* or, in English, *Mathematical Principles of Natural Philosophy*.

Newton's avowed goal was to "discover the forces of nature" and to "demonstrate the other phenomena from these forces." This is a succinct description of the goals (and implicitly the methods) of empirical science as we know it, and it lies at the root of the division of science and philosophy. Science swerved onto a path of being "about the world" in a direction that philosophy did not (and did not want to) follow. It became focused on empirical observation, exact measurement of phenomena and their properties, precise theories for predicting and explaining observable events, related methodologies for confirming, refuting, accepting, and rejecting those theories. And together with engineering, science extended its domain to include applications of those theories both to enhance understanding the observable world around us and to create practical devices and processes to enhance our lives. If we were to construct a scientist persona, as we have a philosopher persona, that persona would reflect these fundamental differences. The markers for a scientist will overlap those for a philosopher, but they would be phrased in terms of the scientist's measurement-oriented methods and direct focus on observable reality, rather than on the more abstract and conceptual goals and methods of the philosopher.

Still, the intellectual bond between science and philosophy is strong. Any competent theoretical scientist (no matter her sub-discipline) must also be philosophically competent to some degree in order to develop the scientific concepts, models, and theories necessary in contemporary science. And likewise, any competent philosopher of science must be competent in at least some area of science.

In his 1912 *The Problems of Philosophy*, Bertrand Russell remarks that

> "... as soon as definite knowledge concerning any subject becomes possible, this subject ceases to be called philosophy, and becomes a separate science. The whole study of the heavens, which now belongs to astronomy was once included in philosophy; Newton's great work was called the mathematical principles of natural philosophy. Similarly the study of the human mind, which was a part of philosophy has now been separated from philosophy and has become the science of psychology." (Russell 2001)

What Russell means here by "definite knowledge" is the sort of objective knowledge that results from measurable empirical data and yields reliable (and repeatable) explanation and prediction of observable phenomena in the world; and the history of philosophy and science is a sequence of such "separations". Even as early as 1912 Russell had a vision of philosophy getting smaller in the sense of having specific areas of it detach into their own (scientific) disciplines; and this appears to be happening at an accelerated rate in the late 20th and early 21st centuries.

One such separation taking place today is the emergence of the discipline of cognitive science from the disciplines of computer science, psychology, philosophy, mathematics, and brain research. Another lies in the area of ontology — one of the original and fundamental pillars of metaphysics that deals with what exists, what kinds (categories) of things there are, and how the things and the categories are related to one another. But now, while philosophers continue to pursue ontology at an abstract level, it's being widely developed and used in other disciplines (both scientific and humanistic) to formalize, represent, and analyze the knowledge and methods in those areas (see (Merrill 2011)). Philosophy still retains a grip on ontology, but that grip is weakening even to the point that a contemporary philosopher such as Thomas Hofweber worries very seriously about "defending ontology as a philosopher's project," whether ontology is just "esoteric metaphysics," and what "follows for our beloved discipline of ontology" (Hofweber 2009). And there are interesting questions about what philosophy's role is in contemporary ontology, and how that relates to the role that ontology is now playing in science.

Science and philosophy remain closely related — at times with philosophy spawning new scientific disciplines, and at other times with science brightening the usefulness of philosophy — but these are different paths to different kinds of knowledge, employing different methods, and having different goals. Today, it is likely that they're capable of contributing to one another more than at any other time in history.

5.6 Psychology

Not only is psychology closely related to philosophy, but it actually was a part of philosophy for about 2,500 years. Throughout much of that period it was referred to also as "philosophical psychology" or the "philosophy of mind". Much thought, research, and publication effort is still devoted to the philosophy of mind within philosophy itself, and *MIND* — one of the most respected philosophy journals since the late 19th century — continues to be published by the Mind Association, which describes itself as a "generalist philosophy journal," but continues (as many philosophy journals do) to publish articles in the philosophy of mind and related fields. In its early days, a focus of the journal was on the question of whether psychology could truly be established as a natural science, and the editors took as their primary goal a convincing determination of the answer to this question. Much has changed over the intervening years (in psychology, philosophy, and related fields), but recently *MIND* has published a

Chapter 5: Philosophy, Its Relatives, and Imitators

special virtual edition on *Emotions* which illustrates the continuing closeness of philosophers' interests to psychological topics.

So what happened after 2,500 years to break up this relationship and cause psychology to strike out on its own? There's a one-word answer to this (again alluded to by Russell): science. In the 18th century — with the rise of modern science following the history of such luminaries as Isaac Newton (16th century), Evangilista Torricelli (17th century), various members of the Bernoulli family (17th-18th centuries), Antoine Lavoisier (18th century), Carl Linnaeus (18th century), Joseph Priestley (18th century), Charles Darwin (19th century), Nikola Tesla (19th-20th century), Albert Einstein (19th-20th century), Marie Curie (19th century), Louis Pasteur (19th century), and a host of others, the time was ripe for genuine empirical science to turn its attention to the human mind. Philosophy, for millennia, had grappled with conceptual problems and analyses of what the mind was or might be; but the experimental and measurement-based tools of modern science could both formulate and answer questions that the philosophers never could (and often didn't want to).

Both experimental and clinical laboratories for psychology (and the related field of psychiatry) began to be established in the 1890s, and psychology broke off as an independent discipline, developing its own methodologies, concepts, theories, and research programs. The child discipline was strongly influenced in its formation and infancy by the parent (in the writings of such philosophers as John Locke, George Berkeley, David Hume, Gottfried Wilhelm Leibniz, and some of the early existentialists), but it was off on its own, with its own goals and approaches. And this is how psychology came to be distinct from philosophy. In addition, as things progressed with the laboratory approach, much was learned about how the brain and central nervous system really function, and increasingly (with the collaborative work being done in psychology, computer science, philosophy, biology/physiology, and cognitive science) how the brain is related to what we think of as "the mind".

Psychology left philosophy and became an empirical science, though there may remain some debate concerning the degree to which certain areas of psychology genuinely have attained that goal. And so the quick answer to the question of how psychology differs from philosophy is to invoke what we've seen in the previous section concerning the difference between science (broadly construed) and psychology (as either a natural or social science). As in the more general scientific case, the markers for a psychologist and the practice of psychology would be quite similar to the philosophy markers of the previous chapter, but the psychologist persona would be quite different in fundamental ways, and the psychology markers would need to include a heavy emphasis on empirical, laboratory, measurement-oriented methods and their use in the criteria of adequacy for psychological answers to psychological questions.

5.7 Literature

Literature can be viewed as an expressive and narrative art that yet has (or can have) substantive cognitive content, even if indirectly through the narrative or the dialog of its characters. Some philosophers (or writers sometimes felt to be philosophers) have dabbled, or in some cases "doubled", in literature. Notable examples are Plato (*The Republic*, the *Death of Socrates* dialogs), Jean-Paul Sartre, Ayn Rand, and Voltaire. On the other hand, such iconic philosophers as Aristotle, Descartes, Hume, Locke, Hegel, and Marx aren't known for authoring riveting stories or other works of literature. It's not uncommon for philosophers to approach their philosophical writings as dialogs (Plato, Berkeley, Hume, Malebranche, and David and Stephanie Lewis are examples) but this doesn't always transform the work into a literary effort — as anyone who has read many philosophical dialogs would tell you. Reading a philosophical dialog is more often like watching a chess match than reading a narrative account of characters who have motives, desires, and feelings (all hallmarks of a literary work).

It could even be claimed that our introduction of the Philo character is a literary device which makes this book a work of literature. No harm comes from such a view, except perhaps in disturbing genuine writers of literature, but it misses the point here of what our main goals and methodologies are — and how that makes this a work of philosophy rather than one of literature. As with poetry, the primary difference between philosophy and literature is not merely one of style. Instead — as is always the case in drawing a distinction between intellectual disciplines — it's a matter of goals, methods, and criteria of success or what makes the work "good" or "bad" as an example of its type. Kant's *Critique of Pure Reason* is rightly revered as a monumental work of philosophy; but viewed as a literary effort, it's so dreadful that no one would seriously consider it from that perspective.

It's also true (as in the case of poetry, which is a variety of literature) that writers of literature often "deal with" or "offer insight into" problems and areas of specifically philosophical interest. But the literary persona (were we to construct one), and the markers of literature (were we to list them) would be quite different from their philosophical counterparts. Literature strives not to achieve explicit analyses and explanations as science and philosophy do, but rather to entertain, suggest, and inform in a certain way. It may also seek to teach, in its narrative and discursive manner, in such areas as morals, politics, religion, and psychology; and to teach us about "the human experience". Literature may also aid in teaching more technical subjects such as science, mathematics, and engineering. But it is none of these subjects itself, and does not share their goals or methodologies. While literature is not inherently pseudo-philosophical, it can drift in that direction if an author attempts to go too far in attempting to provide a philosophical analysis and solution to a problem while violating those requirements of the philosopher that we've described in the Philo persona and enumerated in our philosophy markers. Emerson's comments on consistency that we examined in Chapter 3 serve as an example of this, and we will see another example in Chapter 11.

5.8 Poetry

Poetry is also often felt to overlap philosophy, sometimes in very close ways. Poets often express philosophical ideas, views, or theories. And in many cases the poet's goal (somewhat like the rhetorician's) is to encourage, convince, or persuade the reader to adopt these views. For the most part, the views expressed in poetry are of a personal nature, having to do with trials we face in life, hope, expectations, personal pain and tragedy, love, relationships of various sorts, and (directly or indirectly) "the meaning of life". Or sometimes poetry is meant to entertain or provide different sorts of insight into daily life.

Plato certainly had an axe to grind against poetry, and he spent a lot of time grinding it in *The Republic* (Plato 2016). Indeed, it seems that one thing raising Plato's hackles was a kind of jealousy of the poet who gets to express his ideas without the precision and constraints imposed on the philosopher, and yet who seems to reach out more (and more effectively) to "the people." Imagine that you spend a lot of effort to write a long book with a complex theory of metaphysics, ethics. politics and society, and you just know some guy is going to write some one-page poem, and people won't read your book but will *memorize* the poem! It just doesn't seem fair! But we have to concede that reading just about any poem and getting at least something out of it is easier than reading just about any philosophical analysis (whether you get anything out of it or not). Such is the nature of philosophy versus poetry. Perhaps Plato got the last laugh in the end since *The Republic* was a big hit over time, and a lot of students have to read it (or at least pieces of it). Ironically, Plato is generally thought to be a fairly "poetic" writer of philosophy (as compared, for example, to his student Aristotle).

Aristotle treats poetry in a more even-handed way, and allows that the poet is more "philosophical" than the historian, and that poetry is "more momentous" (!) than history, by which he may have meant that it's not as dull and it's easier to read. Other philosophers have offered thoughtful analyses of poetry, and its relation to philosophy as well, but we won't go any further down that road here.

While it would be unfair to prosecute poetry for the sort of anti-philosophical sins attributed to rhetoric, there are some interesting parallels between poetry and what philosophers find objectionable about rhetoric. As in the case of rhetoric, poetry makes strong appeals to the emotions. In fact, it can be argued (and frequently is) that it is emotional expression and the evoking of feelings that's fundamental to poetry: that the poet paints ideas and perspectives with emotions through the use of words. And so it's neither unfair nor inaccurate to say that poetry depends in an essential way on subjective (at least highly non-objective) evocation of emotions and feelings — which may lead to genuine insight of a sort (and which might even be accurately characterized as a kind of "personal wisdom"), but may equally well lead to a faulty understanding.

This is, again, the nature of poetic art: it's not objective (and doesn't pretend to be), it's emotional (and intends to be), and it doesn't involve the use of argumentation, nor does it care (except incidentally in passing) about rationality, evidence, or logic. The poet wants to *move* people as her primary goal rather than to persuade or convince them, or to provide them with a careful analysis of concepts and their relations.

If poetry provides to us a kind of wisdom, it's not the kind of wisdom that's the focus of the philosopher — and similarly for any sort of insight or "explanation" it may provide. Being subjective and emotional, it's at best unreliable in providing us with an objective view of worldly reality. It isn't philosophy, but neither is it pseudo-philosophy, though it might be used by a pseudo-philosopher in an attempt to escape the demands of a truly philosophical analysis. If we look at the Philo persona and ask which of her attributes fit the poet, it's clear that few of them do — with the exceptions of a commitment to the pursuit of wisdom (of a sort, but not the sort that we'd find in the Poet persona), and possibly Problem Orientation (if focus is on problems of the human condition in an emotive sense).

5.9 Philosophy or not? If not, then what?

In earlier chapters we've seen a number of criticisms and complaints by philosophers about pseudo-philosophy and also about certain disciplines other than philosophy. But pseudo-philosophy, whatever it is, isn't just something that's not philosophy; and this chapter gives examples illustrating the accuracy of that view. We now know that mere incompatibility with the goals and methods of philosophers isn't sufficient to condemn something as pseudo-philosophy. We know that the absence of philosophy markers from an author's works doesn't imply that those works are pseudo-philosophical. We can see clearly that there are perfectly coherent personas for practitioners of disciplines other than philosophy. We know that something isn't pseudo-philosophy just because it's different from philosophy. These realizations are all important in pursuing the goals and criteria of adequacy we enumerated in Section 1.4. But now what?

Chapter 5: Philosophy, Its Relatives, and Imitators

In moving forward we need a characterization of pseudo-philosophy that's not just a litany of complaints. We also can't come to an understanding of what pseudo-philosophy is by focusing entirely on what it's not. What we need is a characterization of pseudo-philosophy that closely resembles (or mirrors) our account of philosophy in Chapter 4, and that provides us with a persona for the pseudo-philosopher and a set of pseudo-philosophy markers. We'll do this in Chapter 7, but first we need to reflect in a bit more detail on "the nature of the pseudo".

Chapter 6

Perspectives on the Pseudo

> *In this chapter:*
> - Additional perspectives on pseudo-philosophy
> - The dimensions of pseudo-philosophy
> - Pseudo-philosophy as mimicry
> - Is pseudo-philosophy a pseudo-discipline?

Earlier chapters have provided a detailed view of what philosophy is, what philosophers are, and what they do. There have also been glimpses of what the nature of pseudo-philosophy may be, and a litany of complaints that philosophers have made against it and its alleged practitioners. But these have so far been fragmentary and dredged from several periods in the history of philosophy and intellectual thought, some as many as 2,000 years ago. The time has come to turn our attention to more specific and more modern perspectives on the nature and practice of pseudo-philosophy, and to get a better view of it: more along the lines of what it is, rather than what it's not. We've been affirmative about what philosophy is, and if pseudo-philosophy isn't just bad philosophy or inept philosophy or the absence of philosophy, then we need a more affirmative account of what it is.

6.1 Some philosophers' views

Several 20th-century philosophers have views on the nature of pseudo-disciplines that apply to, or extend quite directly to, the pseudo-philosopher. One is in the area of pseudo-art, one is in the area of pseudo-science, and one is in the area of pseudo-philosophy itself. These will provide us with some additional insight into the nature of pseudo-philosophy and, more generally, "the pseudo".

R. G. Collingwood on pseudo-art

In 1938, British philosopher R. G. Collingwood published his book *The Principles of Art* (Collingwood 1958), a famous but somewhat murky and confused work in which he spends some time distinguishing genuine art from pseudo-art. Collingwood offers the view that pseudo-art refers to something that is *not art*, but is *mistaken for art*; and further, that *something* can be mistaken for art only if there's some *reason* to make that mistake. You have to somehow get (or be given) the idea that there's art going on — for example, by being told or having it suggested to you that what you're seeing is art — and then mistakenly think (or be led to think) that what you're looking at is really art even though it's not. He gives an example of the use of art in religion (representing religious figures, events, or ideas), and warns us that using art in such a way results in a combination of art with religion where we can fall into a confusion in which we treat religious aspects of the work as if they're artistic aspects; but they're not. We *mistake* religious aspects for artistic ones. Today in colloquial circles we would refer to this as a "bait and switch".

We've already seen something similar to this in the account given in Chapter 5 where careful lines have been drawn between other disciplines (including religion) and how philosophy may be *used* (or misused) in them. There's a danger in such cases of the other discipline (or its practitioners) "borrowing" philosophy to the degree that it ceases to be philosophical and deviates from the characterization we've provided of it in Chapters 3 and 4.

Collingwood goes on to say that in order for the *pseudo* version of art to arise, two things must happen. First, there must exist the pure form of art, with its own goals and criteria of goodness. And second, there must be some *non-artistic goal* (he says "some utilitarian end") that the practitioner has in mind, and for which he or she can make use of art, in a *misleading* way, to accomplish. So Collingwood sees pseudo-art as arising from certain *uses* of art for goals that are *not artistic,* and he sees pseudo-art as a perversion or misuse of genuine art.

Quine and Ullian on pseudo-science

Willard Quine and Joseph Ullian make a similar point in *The Web of Belief* (Quine and Ullian 1978) regarding pseudo-science, and this extends to pseudo-philosophy as well. They view pseudo-science as involving the development of "anti-rational doctrines" that are "masquerading as science" while attracting their own cults of "devout followers". They then ask themselves how this could happen if the doctrines are so wrong. How can people be led to believe such bogus accounts of reality?

Section 6.1: Some philosophers' views

A part of the answer is that contemporary science is (to many people) so incomprehensible, so difficult to understand and evaluate, that the pseudo-scientist sees a void into which she can throw a distorted, outrageously wrong, or even unintelligible theory which may nonetheless seem plausible if presented to the average person in just the right way. And even the unintelligibility of the fake science may, Quine and Ullian observe, be "mistaken as a sign of authenticity": it's complicated like real science is, and may make about the same amount of sense to those lacking much experience with real science.

When asked if a heavier (e.g., lead) ball will fall faster than a lighter ball of the same size (e.g., a baseball), most people without any knowledge of simple physics will quickly say that the heavier ball will of course fall faster. It doesn't. Galileo knew this and demonstrated it in the 17th century. But that was an *interesting* discovery because it's counter-intuitive, and most people are inclined (by their intuitions) to believe that heavier things fall faster than lighter things. Even this very simple example of a scientific phenomenon illustrates how complicated (or at least unintuitive) science can be to many people, and how they might fall prey to a pseudo-scientific trickster, who (for example) might propose a complicated theory concerning the generation of excess energy by using something like a perpetual motion machine (Wikipedia 2020h) to solve the world's energy crisis. The media-fueled Cold Fusion Fiasco of 1989 (Rational Wiki 2020) is another example of how something "scientific" can make sense to a lot of people who know little about science, or even to scientists who are working outside their own domain of expertise. It also illustrates how easy it is for people to believe what they want so very much to be true (in this case, "free energy"), and so can fall prey to a "likely story" pitched by someone who may initially appear to be credible.

Descriptions of scientific processes and events (such as "global warming", or "climate change", or how cell phones work and why you can't get good signal strength where you live) are difficult to follow, even when they're presented by scientific experts who are trying their best to communicate with those lacking intimate knowledge of atmospheric physics, meteorology, and electromagnetic radiation. Scientists speak a different language, and judgments are difficult for a layman to make — both for lack of understanding and because science still faces a number of questions that it's unable to answer (or at least unable to answer in a decisive way). And in cases of pseudo-science there's always a "hook" offered by the pseudo-scientist to get believers and followers: something like free or low-cost energy, the ability to reliably predict the future, why so many airplanes disappear in the Bermuda Triangle, the ability to find gold or water with a simple handheld device, better eyesight through relaxing eye "strain", better gas mileage by using a magnet to "align" fuel molecules, and on and on. Something is offered that "normal" science can't provide.

Certainly the same thing is true in philosophy — where arriving at an objective determination of truth, or deciding which theory is better than another, is even more difficult for the untutored and inexperienced. Indeed, substituting "philosophy" for "art" in the case of Collingwood, or for "science" in the case of Quine and Ullian results in perfectly accurate statements concerning philosophy and pseudo-philosophy. And so (as in art and pseudo-art, and science and pseudo-science) it becomes easy for the pseudo-discipline to "borrow" from the genuine one and weave a seemingly plausible story that may captivate the unwary, the uninitiated, and the inexpert (i.e., "normal" people: your "average" man or woman).

It's fairly obvious what, in the case of pseudo-science, can be dangled as bait in front of the unwary in order to attract them as believers. But what about pseudo-philosophy? What can the pseudo-philosopher offer that normal philosophy doesn't provide? What's the bait? Well, how about certain knowledge — that is, some knowledge or kind of knowledge that's absolutely certain and can't be doubted? It's even better if this is knowledge about something like moral choice or political systems! How about an offer that if you believe this very simple system of metaphysics — which you're told you can easily understand — then all of the mysteries of modern science will be revealed to you in astonishing clarity? Or what about a simple doctrine that could get you out from under having to think hard and apply logic and careful reasoning in making decisions? Consistency? Who needs it? It's just a crutch used by the mentally lame! Simply embrace a few basic principles, your intellectual life becomes a breeze, and you can win arguments with anyone. Yes, pseudo-philosophy has as much to offer us as pseudo-art and pseudo-science do.

Nicholas Rescher on pseudo-philosophy

Perhaps the best-known concise characterization of pseudo-philosophy in print is the entry on it written, originally in 1995, by Nicholas Rescher in *The Oxford Companion to Philosophy* (Rescher 2005). Rescher is a philosopher of great repute, and it appears that his brief characterization is so highly regarded that it's had some effect in discouraging further serious inquiry by professional (academic) philosophers into the topic of pseudo-philosophy.

Rescher begins by saying that pseudo-philosophy *masquerades* as philosophy, and he identifies three primary components of pseudo-philosophy: ineptness, incompetence, and the lack of "intellectual seriousness." Certainly his critique of pseudo-philosophy isn't unfamiliar, and seems to be a recasting in different language of at least some of the historical complaints of the ancients and other philosophers through the 19th century: the complaints about inappropriate or deceptive practices and techniques used by the Sophists and rhetoricians, for example.

One peculiar feature of Rescher's treatment is that he focuses on ineptitude, incompetence, and a lack of seriousness — all which we might regard as "passive sins" or certain kinds of *error*, and this doesn't seem consistent with characterizing pseudo-philosophy as involving a *masquerade*. He does attempt, in a brief three sentences, to accuse and convict Derrida (Wikipedia 2020f) and his followers of incoherence and self-contradiction; and he does come down hard on irrationalist threads throughout the history of pseudo-philosophy. But he refrains from explicitly attributing anything like *intentional deception* or *malfeasance* to pseudo-philosophers. In this he seems to deviate sharply from other genuine philosophers throughout history who have felt that often it's precisely malfeasance that's motivated and driven the misapplication of philosophical methods which Rescher recognizes.

You have to wonder if Rescher just didn't quite get what Plato, Isocrates, Xenophon, Schopenhauer, and others were saying when they complained about the evil and self-serving motives of the pseudo-philosophers. But perhaps his accusation of deceit and malfeasance towards pseudo-philosophy is just less direct and more subtle than what those earlier philosophers have said, and he observes (similar to Collingwood) that it's "the fostering of power interests or ideological influence or literary *éclat* or some such" that lies at the root of the pseudo-philosophical errors — which means that, for Rescher as well, pseudo-philosophy involves some extra-philosophical goals, deceit, and malfeasance rather than just accident and error indicative of mere ineptness or incompetence.

This is a bit confusing because "incompetence" in this context suggests the *unintentional* misuse or misapplication of philosophical techniques and methods. But "masquerade" implies an intentional deception. Which is it: a bumbling ineptness or a clever masquerade? And Rescher then says that this incompetence and ineptness is *reflective* of an "insufficient commitment to the pursuit of truth.j" But this seems to get the cause/effect relationship the wrong way in the case of pseudo-philosophy. It's as though the ineptness and incompetence result in the masquerade. But that can't be right, and in fact it's the masquerading that's employed as a deceptive way to misuse philosophical techniques that normally (for the genuine philosopher) are always used in the pursuit of truth and wisdom.

The masquerading and misuse aren't merely *reflective* of a failure to pursue wisdom and to do things in a philosophically correct manner. They don't just happen as a result of incompetence and ineptness. Plato, Isocrates, Xenophon, and others were very clear about this. Rescher seems to have it backwards. *Masquerading* is an *intentional* action. It's not an accident or an inability. Instead, it's the pseudo-philosopher's *means of achieving his unphilosophical goals* related to power and attention — or as Rescher puts it, to "the fostering of power interests or ideological influence or literary *éclat* or some such." And it's the lack of commitment to the pursuit of truth coupled with the *fostering* of power interests, etc. that leads the pseudo-philosopher to masquerade as a genuine philosopher as an effective and intentional way of achieving his unphilosophical (or even anti-philosophical) goals. This tension or confusion that's apparent in Rescher's account of pseudo-philosophy — between accusing the pseudo-philosopher of incompetence, on the one hand, or malfeasance on the other — is one that permeates the discussion of pseudo-philosophy through the ages. Let's try to sort it out and clarify things a bit.

6.2 Dimensions of the pseudo

After seeing the attacks made on pseudo-philosophy by the ancients, other philosophers through the 20th century, Collingwood, and Quine and Ullian — and then trying to unravel Rescher's seemingly discordant perspective on pseudo-philosophy — we're left facing a blunt question about pseudo-philosophy and pseudo-philosophers: *Is the pseudo-philosopher an inept and bumbling fool; or is he an evil genius, skillfully twisting philosophy to achieve his own ignoble goals?* The answer to this question is, very simply, "Yes". Given how the term "pseudo-philosophy" has been used across the millennia, and where and how different philosophers want to draw the line between genuine and pseudo-philosophy, it's only reasonable to concede that some pseudo-philosophers may create their "art" through incompetence, some may create it through clever thought, distortion, and manipulation, and some may create it through a combination of these: part ineptness and part mischievous or malevolent design.

This gives rise to a kind of 2-dimensional model of pseudo-philosophical practice in terms of which we can think of the *axes of incompetence and exploitation* as these appear in the pseudo-philosopher's use of philosophical methods:

Dimensions of the Pseudo

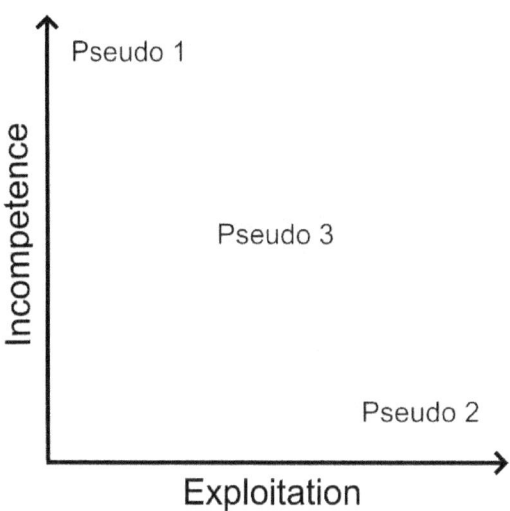

Here, position along the *axis of incompetence* can be seen as a measure of the lack of understanding or expertise that the pseudo-philosopher has and exhibits, while position along the *axis of exploitation* can be viewed as representing the degree to which *anti-philosophical goals are being pursued* or to which *philosophical methods are being distorted* to support such goals. Placement of a particular writer or work at a position along the incompetence axis is a (rough) measure of her lack of understanding or skill in philosophy, and placement along the exploitation axis is a (rough) measure of the degree to which the pseudo-philosopher is exploiting the methods, goals, and reputation of the genuine philosopher.

So in this little graph, *Pseudo 1* represents an author (the Bumbling Fool) who has no ulterior (anti-philosophical) motives or goals, but has an extremely low degree of competence and understanding; and *Pseudo 2* represents an author (the Evil Genius) with a high degree of competence but an extreme commitment to some unphilosophical goal or to the misuse of philosophical methods in achieving her goals. And *Pseudo 3* represents someone who has a mixture of impure goals and lack of competence.

This is intended only as an aid to our intuitions, and as an informal guide for applying criteria to be set out in the next chapter. It obviously involves no genuine metric of one writer being more or less competent or exploitative than another, or of being either philosophical or pseudo-philosophical to a specific degree. But it can effectively and suggestively represent how both incompetence and exploitation (including dishonesty and malfeasance) contribute to the practice of pseudo-philosophy. And in doing this it can remove some of the confusion evident in Rescher's otherwise perceptive remarks. Part of what we get out of this is the ability to see the ways in which pseudo-philosophy isn't just bad philosophy or philosophy poorly done — which is one of the questions we set ourselves to pursue in Chapter 1. The moral here is that the misuse or misapplication of philosophy and philosophical techniques can be either a result (of incompetence), or a means (for exploitation or malevolence), and there will almost certainly be a mixture of these in anyone we'll identify as a pseudo-philosopher. Here, *Pseudo 1* and *Pseudo 2* are the extreme cases, and we wouldn't expect to encounter them frequently in practice. Pseudo-philosophers will fall somewhere within the plane defined by the dimensions of incompetence and exploitation.

As an example, a student taking an introductory philosophy course (or series of such courses) wouldn't be accused of pseudo-philosophy for writing papers or answers to essay questions that misused philosophical principles or techniques, or mistook what the philosopher's goals should be. Why? Because there's no intention to mislead or deceive in such cases. It wouldn't be any more reasonable to accuse the philosophy student (or a student ignorant of philosophy) of pseudo-philosophy than it would be to accuse an elementary chemistry student of pseudo-science because she made repeated errors in balancing equations. But a more advanced student or a graduate student might well be reasonably accused of pseudo-philosophy if his competence was sufficiently high and there were clues in his work concerning suspicious unphilosophical goals or motives. This reflects the difference between trying to do good philosophy (and possibly failing) and trying to do something else (while pretending to maintain a genuinely philosophical stance).

6.3 Mimicry and pseudo-philosophy

One thread throughout all these accounts is that pseudo-philosophy pretends to be, or presents itself as, genuine philosophy. In large part it does this by purporting to share the goals of the genuine philosopher (though, at least in part, it does not), to share the standards of the genuine philosopher, to share the attitude and stance of the genuine philosopher, and to share an interest in the problems addressed by the genuine philosopher (which is at least sometimes true). This is particularly clear in the complaints of the ancient philosophers who felt that those they accused of pseudo-philosophy were, with the use of guile and pretense, trespassing on their own turf.

Why do pseudo-philosophers do what they do? And why do they choose to use (or misuse) *philosophy* in order to do it?

Section 6.3: Mimicry and pseudo-philosophy

We've seen a number of cases in which what the pseudo-philosopher does is described as a *masquerade* or a *pretense*. Another term for masquerade would be "mimicry" which comes from a Greek work meaning "imitate", and again indicates acting as something that one is not. Quite a bit is known about the phenomenon of mimicry in evolutionary biology, and this can be informative in gaining some insight into the attitudes and actions of pseudo-philosophers, and in answering these questions about why pseudo-philosophers do what they do.

Among biological organisms, mimics evolve (of course typically over long periods of time through genetic change) because there's "something in it for them" (evolutionary advantage). Appearing as something they're not gains them some advantage. This includes advantages such as making them less susceptible to predators (defensive mimicry), being able to be more effective predators themselves (aggressive mimicry), or becoming attractive to potential targets for mating (sexual mimicry). Evolving to mimic a toxic organism, for example, may discourage predator attacks, while evolving to appear to be one of your own prey can facilitate luring the prey to your attack. Numerous examples of such mimicry exist in species of insects, spiders, fish, snakes, and birds. And the opossum is a well known example of a defensive mimic that benefits from convincing predators that it's already dead.

In the biological case, there are three components to the relation of mimicry. The first is the *model*, which is the organism to be imitated. The second is the *mimic*, which of course is the one doing the imitating by pretending to be the model. And the third is the *dupe* (or less disrespectfully, the *receiver* or the *operator*), which is the one that gets fooled and taken advantage of. In the case of pseudo-philosophy, the genuine philosopher is the model, the pseudo-philosopher is the mimic, and you are the dupe — assuming you're not playing either the philosopher or pseudo-philosopher roll in this drama. And even then, if you're a philosopher who isn't paying close enough attention, you could still end up as the dupe.

The biological model of mimicry fits the pseudo-philosopher well. He gets the *cachet* of being admired as a genuine philosopher, and the respect that comes with that. The pseudo-philosopher's imitation of a philosopher immediately puts the dupe in a frame of mind to be disposed towards giving the pseudo-philosopher at least a fair hearing without being alert to any trickery or deceit. And it provides the pseudo-philosopher with a ready-made and well-tested tool chest (Chapter 3) from which he may borrow tools to use in deceptive and inappropriate, but effective, ways. As a bonus, in responding to criticism he can appeal to the historical difficulty philosophers have had in describing their own discipline and justifying it; and he can challenge others (particularly the dupe) to show how what he's doing *isn't* philosophy and isn't as dependable and respectable as the work of genuine philosophers — which is an appeal to the "anything goes" view of philosophy mentioned in Section 2.5.

Ideally, if he's a good enough mimic (high on the competence scale and skilled at exploitation), the pseudo-philosopher can hope to get away with his imitation and achieve his goals — possibly (or frequently) being ignored by genuine philosophers as someone not worthy of their attention. As a kind of predator, the pseudo-philosopher typically maintains an aggressive approach to winning over the dupes while the genuine philosopher in her ivory tower adopts the attitude that students should come to her in order to be instructed in the customary way. Thus, perhaps aside from some passing treatment in critical thinking courses, combating pseudo-philosophers is outside the job description of the genuine (academic) philosopher. After all, pseudo-philosophy isn't philosophy, is it?

6.4 Is pseudo-philosophy a pseudo-discipline?

If pseudo-philosophy isn't philosophy, and it's not a lot of other things as well (it's not religion, it's not theology, it's not rhetoric, etc.), then what is it? Or at least what sort of thing is it? Is it, for example, its own discipline with its own practitioners, and its own goals and principles and rules of conduct? If we ask the question "Is pseudo-philosophy a pseudo-discipline?" what might we even mean by this? What sort of answer might we expect?

Well, we might mean "Is pseudo-philosophy a discipline like philosophy, except different in some fundamental ways?" We are, after all, going through a lengthy exercise to pin down what pseudo-philosophy is — in the same way that we might try to pin down what mathematics is. If we succeed in characterizing pseudo-philosophy and pseudo-philosophers, haven't we, by doing that, characterized a pseudo-discipline — a domain of study with its own subject matter? Shouldn't there then be departments of pseudo-philosophy in universities, and professors of pseudo-philosophy, and courses in pseudo-philosophy, and journals in which the pseudo-philosophy professors can publish their pseudo-philosophical contributions, and grants for pseudo-philosophical research, and, of course, pseudo-philosophy conferences and conventions? Those are a lot of questions, and the answer to each of them is "No!". In part this answer is the only reasonable one because, were pseudo-philosophers to adopt such an approach, it would their own goals and exploitative use of philosophical methodology. But there, as well, are other reasons why this is the correct answer.

Pseudo-philosophy isn't philosophy, and it's not even (or merely) bad philosophy. Even if it were, we couldn't very well expect there to be a *Department of Bad Philosophy* in the university. That would be taking the idea of diversity too far. A *Department of Pseudo-philosophy* wouldn't make any more sense. Pseudo-philosophy also isn't an *alternative* to philosophy. In Section 3.1 we observed that for any discipline or domain of study — such as astronomy or music or philosophy — there's a certain *body of knowledge* and a certain set of *methods and techniques* with which experts in that discipline need to be familiar and in command of in order to count themselves as genuine experts in that domain. Without such an acknowledged body of knowledge, and without such a set of methods and techniques, the domain of expertise simply can't exist.

Ironically, and somewhat humorously, we can argue that pseudo-philosophy *does* possess a set of techniques — and these are just the techniques that the pseudo-philosopher employs to mimic the genuine philosopher. And they are generally the employment of various rhetorical and sophistical techniques to divert our attention and provide faulty arguments and bogus reasoning in support of pseudo-philosophical positions and goals. In fact, we'll enumerate these and discuss them in some detail in the next chapter. But this isn't enough to make pseudo-philosophy a discipline in its own right.

Pseudo-philosophy lacks the necessary body of knowledge, and the only general goal of pseudo-philosophy is to subvert the genuine body of knowledge found in genuine philosophy and mimic the genuine philosopher. There's nothing to serve as its foundation — nothing to "hold it together". There is no body of pseudo-philosophical knowledge, no set of guiding pseudo-philosophical principles, and no set of unifying goals among pseudo-philosophers. Anything that may appear to be in common is borrowed from genuine philosophy (in order to mimic it), and will promptly be misapplied by the pseudo-philosopher to achieve his own immediate goals (which may not be shared by any other pseudo-philosopher, as we'll see in Chapters 9-11.

So pseudo-philosophy isn't any kind of discipline or domain of study or compendium of knowledge (even pseudo-knowledge). But that doesn't mean that we can't characterize the motives, goals, and techniques of the pseudo-philosopher in a manner that will allow us to identify his craft when we see it. And that's what we'll do in the next chapter.

Chapter 7
A Practical Model of Pseudo-philosophy

> ***In this chapter:***
> - *Pseudo*: the pseudo-philosopher persona
> - Pseudo-philosophy markers
> - Pseudo-philosophy and dishonesty

We're now going to tie together work that's been done in previous chapters and proceed towards a model of pseudo-philosophy and the pseudo-philosopher that we'll then apply in Part 3. Again, our model will consist of a persona together with a set of markers that allow us to determine when we're seeing that persona in action. We begin with the construction of Pseudo — the pseudo-philosopher persona, proceed to listing the markers of pseudo-philosophy, and then discuss the use of these markers and the consequences of applying the model to real-world cases.

7.1 *Pseudo*: the pseudo-philosopher persona

Think of the terms that have been used to describe what's been referred to as *pseudo* over the past two millennia: mimicry, masquerade, deceit, trickery, inauthentic, incompetent, inept, incoherent. *Pseudo* — our pseudo-philosophy persona; is someone who wants to *appear* to be a genuine philosopher and who wants to *appear* to use genuine philosophical methods correctly, but who isn't *authentic* in either of these respects. Philo's goal of pursuing wisdom with consistency, objectivity, clarity, and openness to criticism is not Pseudo's goal — which is to convince you of a particular view, unrelated to wisdom or understanding, through the use of philosophical methods (or apparent philosophical methods) that involve trickery and deceit. This much, at least, is the convergent view of pseudo-philosophers that we have from genuine philosophers and other critics who have attempted to expose pseudo-philosophers for more than 2,000 years.

Section 7.1: Pseudo: the pseudo-philosopher persona

But there are problems in attempting to provide a coherent and useful characterization of Pseudo. We can't simply say, however tempting it might be, something like "Pseudo is the antithesis of Philo" because being a pseudo-philosopher doesn't require you to violate *every* feature of the Philo persona, or *every* principal or characteristic of genuine philosophy; and it doesn't require you to violate the canons of genuine philosophy *all the time*.

Pseudo isn't, in general, the anti-Philo, but instead is more like a faulty variant of Philo who is defective in certain ways — but not in all ways, and not even necessarily in all significant ways. Pseudo may be pseudo-philosophical in certain ways, but not in others; and she may be pseudo-philosophical to some degree or other, or at some times but not others. Moreover, in order to identify Pseudo by her writings and presentations, we'll need some positive characteristics rather than just a litany of complaints concerning how various characteristics of Philo are absent. Pseudo-philosophy isn't the absence of philosophy, and it's not even the presence of poorly done philosophy. It's *pseudo*: fake, deceptive, misleading, and inauthentic.

Pseudo will pursue a goal that deviates from the pursuit of wisdom. This will often involve an attempt at establishing himself as a genuine expert who is making some new or innovative contribution to philosophy or the use of philosophy — a project in which (he'll say) "establishment philosophers" have so far failed.[7] He'll employ techniques that are either genuine philosophical methods improperly applied, or are mimics of genuine philosophical methods intended to mislead you by their similarity to the real ones. He'll attempt to manipulate your feelings and emotions, and confuse you with misstatements of the views and arguments of others (particular genuine philosophers). He'll likely do this with the aid of jargon (crafted to appear similar to the jargon of genuine philosophy) which remains obscure and impossible to apply in any specific cases, or which allows him to subtly switch the meanings of terms and reach an unjustified conclusion.

Pseudo will often resort to tactics of intimidation to get you to go along with her view and accept the beliefs or theories that she's presenting. She may imply — or suggest explicitly — that if you don't "understand" her approach and agree with it, then you just aren't very smart, or you're ignorant of some basic issues. This is an attempt to replace trust based on rationality and evidence with an unsupported trust based on emotion and faulty reasoning.

Where Philo will be open to criticisms of his work, Pseudo will be resistant, will deflect these without responding to them, and will discourage further inquiry and requests for more clarity. In the case where she does respond to a critique of her work, this may be superficial and dismissive rather than serious and thoughtful; and in general she may prefer to avoid delving into consequences of her views that may appear incompatible with principles she's claimed to hold or with other views or consequences that she's embraced. She may have a fundamental problem with being consistent in what she says, and she may retreat to a position of attacking the value of consistency itself.

Finally, Pseudo may fail to meet certain standards of competence or scholarship of the genuine philosopher. These may include, for example, inaccurate or totally bogus citations to the work of others (used to support Pseudo's own views and arguments), failure to give credit to earlier work and claim the ideas in it as his own (either through ignorance or deceit), and failure to be familiar with prior work that anyone wanting to be regarded as philosophically competent must have well in hand.

7.2 Pseudo-philosophy markers

We're now in a position to extract the markers that alert us to the Pseudo persona and characterize pseudo-philosophy and its practitioners. Each marker is viewed as an *indicator* of the presence (in a given work) of pseudo-philosophy, which we might also think of as a kind of pathological condition that's afflicting the use of philosophy in that work. We also know (Chapter 4) that a marker by itself is just an indication, and that a single marker, or a single instance of a marker, can't be used to distinguish philosophy from several other disciplines, or to justify applying the judgment of pseudo-philosophy to a work or a writer. Instead a single marker is just a clue, and it's the presence of multiple different markers and multiple instances of individual markers (repeated throughout a work or set of works) that serves as increasingly strong reason to classify a work as philosophy or as pseudo-philosophy.

This is similar to the situation (in science and the law, and in certain theories of epistemology in philosophy) where it's ultimately the *preponderance of the evidence* that supports a judgment in a specific case and determines what is most reasonable to believe. In our case, the ultimate question is "Is it reasonable — or is it more reasonable than not — to conclude that this work or this writer is involved in the practice of pseudo-philosophy?"

Adopting a set of pseudo-philosophy markers is one step in creating a *theory* of pseudo-philosophy in the same sense that constructing the Philo persona and the list of philosophy of markers of Chapter 4 represents part of a theory of philosophy. While this theory of pseudo-philosophy will bear some similarities to a scientific theory, it's more like what's seen in the case of music theory, a theory of art, a theory of literature, a theory of poetry, or "chess theory": a set of principles and guidelines to be applied in order to achieve a certain understanding and beneficial results, where our personas and markers express those

Section 7.2: Pseudo-philosophy markers

principles and guidelines. Within the theory of pseudo-philosophy that emerges, the difference between philosophy and pseudo-philosophy may be seen as similar to the difference between music and noise or (in the case of the genuine philosopher versus the pseudo-philosopher) as the difference between an authentic performer and one who is "faking it". Lack of authenticity is a fundamental component of the pseudo.

But how should you use these markers — how should you apply this theory — in evaluating writers and their works? That question will be answered in detail in Part 3 when we turn our attention to some specific case studies of alleged pseudo-philosophy. For now, think of using these markers (together with the philosophy markers of Chapter 4) as you would similar sorts of markers, guidelines, features, and techniques in other contexts you might be familiar with. See which philosophy markers are present in a work and which pseudo-philosophy markers are present. If you suspect a work of being pseudo-philosophical, then look more closely to see which philosophy markers are absent, and to what degree.

This process is comparable to other critical activities that confront us in our everyday lives or work: looking at a company balance sheet in order to detect any bookkeeping abnormalities; examining a musical composition to identify any problems with rhythm, harmony, chords, chord progressions, improper scoring for instruments, etc.; reading an epidemiological study to identify any faulty assumptions or misapplications of statistical models and methods; checking a tax return for irregularities in conforming to the IRS code; performing a design or code review prior to testing and releasing a piece of software; reviewing a user interface for inconsistency, abnormalities, or difficulties in use and navigation; scrutinizing a company's financial statement in order to determine whether its prospectus is accurate and consistent; or checking your grocery bill to be sure it's accurate. It's a kind of "philosophical accounting".

Here, then, are the markers of pseudo-philosophy that we'll use as a basis for judging a work or writer to be pseudo-philosophical. I'll separate these into a few broad categories that represent the major types of methods or major kinds of flaws found in pseudo-philosophy. These categories fit the account of pseudo-philosophy developed in previous chapters, but there's nothing deep or magical about them. They're just a handy way of thinking of types of markers that appear in pseudo-philosophical works, and they may make it a bit easier to see what the pseudo-philosopher is attempting to accomplish. Clashes of these markers with the philosophy markers of Section 4.4 are also listed in order to aid in comparing philosophy markers with pseudo-philosophy markers, and in seeing how a suspected pseudo-philosopher is failing to exhibit the Philo persona.

 *Markers of trickery*

One of the primary and continuing criticisms of pseudo-philosophers is that they're dishonest and deceitful concerning the presentation of their own work, their true goals, and their characterizations and criticisms of the works of others. Here are some markers that indicate the presence of such deceit and are indicative of an attempt to get you to believe something or act in a way that isn't supported by reasonable argument or evidence.

⊘ Obscurantism
(Clashes with: Φ *Explanation*, Φ *Clarity*)

To make something obscure is to make it unclear, make it difficult to understand, or to conceal its true or complete meaning. Obscurantism is the practice of being obscure in order to achieve that lack of clarity and understanding. It's a policy of deliberately withholding clarity, precision, and knowledge in order to leave you confused about exactly what's being said, what claims are being made, what basis is being offered for those claims, and whether that basis is relevant and sufficient for you to understand and make decisions.

Obscurantism may also include denying the *value* of clarity in expressing philosophical views — saying, for example, that being unclear in your use of terminology or in your explanation of a concept or in the details of an argument leads to a kind of freedom and insight (a "liberating" effect on our thought) that can't be achieved through clarity and precision. We've seen something similar to this from Ralph Waldo Emerson in Section 3.4 where he asks "Is it so bad then to be misunderstood?". The answer is that yes, in the context of attempting to pursue wisdom and propose a philosophical theory or analysis or solution to a problem, it *is* bad! And the use or tolerance of obscurity and misunderstanding in a systematic way is a sign of pseudo-philosophy.

Obscurity in philosophy and philosophical writing is bad because it leaves us unable to make rational judgments about what's being said. Obscurantism is the intentional and systematic "weaponizing" of obscurity, and its only motivation is to achieve agreement through trickery. It's a technique used by the pseudo-philosopher to hide behind a linguistic smoke screen in order to dodge criticisms of his views, arguments, and theories.

⊘ Misrepresentation
(Clashes with: Φ *Integrity*, Φ *Objectivity*)

A pseudo-philosopher may misrepresent a number of different things in order to put her own views in a better light and persuade you that they're preferable or more reasonable than the views of others. Pseudo may misrepresent Philo's *concept* of person in an argument concerning abortion to make Philo's position appear confused or inconsistent. She may intentionally misinterpret Philo's *theory* of causation in an argument regarding doctor-assisted suicide. And she may provide an inaccurate summary of Philo's *method* of inductive inference in order to undercut his account of scientific knowledge.

Misrepresentation often occurs (and is used as a rhetorical technique) when a pseudo-philosopher has some non-philosophical goal in mind and wants to borrow the influence and respectability of known philosophers in an attempt to support that view. For example, a writer concerned to support a "liberal" political position may misrepresent a utilitarian or consequentialist theory of morality ("The good of the many outweighs the good of the few.") by skimming over the effect of some of its unattractive consequences or by ignoring well-known problems or counterexamples. And similarly, a "conservative" political theorist may ignore or distort the beneficial aspects of a utilitarian morality and distort the advantages of moral theories emphasizing personal responsibility, independence, and individual rights that can't be violated on the grounds of group benefit.

Misrepresentation to one degree or another is a frequent criticism by philosophers — both of non-philosophers and professional philosophers as well. Sometimes a misrepresentation is simply an error or an oversight, and at other times it's a knowing deception. For assessing its significance in the case of determining whether a work is pseudo-philosophical, it's important to look at how often the author misrepresents things, how obvious those misrepresentations should be to a genuine philosopher, the motivation for the misrepresentations, and the overall significance of the misrepresentations in the author's work.

⊘ Exaggerated Claims
(Conflicts with: Φ *Objectivity*, Φ *Domain Awareness*)

Exaggerated claims are common to pseudo-philosophy. This is because, in general, the pseudo-philosopher wants to "make his mark" in the world of respectable philosophy by being seen as finding some new philosophical problem, solving some long-standing problem that's resisted resolution, finding a fatal flaw in the work of some well-known philosopher, or coming up with a significant contribution to some existing discussion or debate. An exaggerated claim may also be seen — depending on how it's presented, or the nature of the support offered for it — as a violation of professional standards (see the section on *Standards markers* below).

Exaggerated claims often appear to be both grandiose and self-aggrandizing, and so are easy to spot even if you may have no (or little) understanding of the particular domain to which they apply. The mere presence of any exaggerated claims in the writings of someone purporting to be a philosopher should immediately alert the reader to look for other signs of pseudo-philosophy. The more highly exaggerated the claims are, and less well articulated and supported they are, the more your suspicions should be raised. Our examples in Chapters 10 and 11 illustrate this.

⊘ Special Pleading
(Clashes with: Φ *Critical Appraisal*, Φ *Objectivity*, Φ *Inquiry*)

Special Pleading is regarded as one of the classical informal fallacies of *insufficient evidence*, and so could be included as a ⊘ *Known Fallacy* below. I include it here because of its highly common weaponization by rhetoricians and pseudo-philosophers. In general, the special pleading fallacy always involves an author's *leaving out* of a description, analysis, or argument something that is relevant to it — in order to enhance the reader's perception of the author's own particular view.

Several slightly different characterizations of special pleading can be found, but two we'll focus on here are where a case is made for something (a view, an opinion, a theory, a philosophical principle, the definition of a term or concept, etc.), and then *either*

1. [*Ignoring unfavorable facts or consequences*] Features, arguments, or consequences that are *favorable* to the author's own position are treated explicitly and in detail, but

unfavorable features or consequences, or known counter-arguments or counter-examples are not considered.... *or...*

2. [*Weak representation*] A description or analysis of something is offered that includes (or emphasizes) certain features of it while excluding (or de-emphasizing) other features that are at least potentially relevant to its characterization. The classical fallacy of *False Analogy* may be seen to fall under this variant of special pleading.

People not versed in logical and philosophical jargon typically refer to special pleading as "slanted argument" or "cherry picking".

Example: An argument that police departments should be "defunded" or eliminated in order to prohibit the abuse of police power, but without considering any of the consequences of that for the protection of citizens and their property against criminals, spousal abuse, and mob actions. Alternatively, an argument that police organizations must have broad autonomy and special powers, but without considering the possibility and history of the abuse of such powers.

⊘ Superficial Response
(Clashes with: Φ *Critical Appraisal*, Φ *Clarity*, Φ *Objectivity*, Φ *Inquiry*)

A superficial response to a criticism occurs when insufficient attention is paid to that criticism or to the consequences of it for an argument that's been offered or a position that's being defended. Not displaying concern for legitimate criticisms that expose problems or weaknesses in your approach is often a sign of pseudo-philosophy, where the pseudo-philosopher wants to weave a one-sided story on her own behalf. Responses to critics may also be construed as superficial if they amount to some sort of misdirection away from the points being made, rather than a direct approach dealing explicitly and in detail with the criticism.

A common example of this is when a respondent employs something akin to an *ad hominem* ("to the man") or *tu quoque* ("you too") response. The first of these is a response in which the critic himself is attacked directly (generally for something unrelated to the criticism he's offering) rather than responding to the actual criticism and either conceding it or refuting it. And the second is a response in which it's claimed that the critic himself is (or has been) guilty of the same thing that he's now criticizing. These are well known fallacies of relevance and are not indulged in by competent philosophers.

Markers of manipulation

As we've seen repeatedly in earlier chapters and particularly in Section 5.4, a common complaint against pseudo-philosophers is that they constantly and programmatically attempt to manipulate their targets, victims, readers, students, and followers into accepting their views — not based on rational argument, clear explanation, or the presentation of relevant evidence — but through means of psychological manipulation typically involving fear, intimidation, or emotions. These markers act as signs of this sort of manipulation and indicate an absence of good faith in the actions of an author who exhibits them:

⊘ Intimidation
(Clashes with: Φ *Critical Appraisal*, Φ *Objectivity*, Φ *Methods*, Φ *Inquiry*)

In pseudo-philosophical works, intimidation most often takes the form of implications or outright statements that if you don't understand or agree with the author, then you're not very smart, or at least you're ignorant in some way, or you're not very well educated — because any intelligent thoughtful person would see the correctness of what the pseudo-philosopher is offering. This goes well together with similar implications or direct statements that if you're inclined to seriously consider criticisms of the author, then you've been duped into this — probably by some sort of "establishment" that benefits from suppressing the views of the author.

⊘ Discouraging Inquiry
(Clashes with: Φ *Critical Appraisal*, Φ *Objectivity*, Φ *Inquiry*)

Here, the pseudo-philosopher will attempt to prevent critics from asking questions about what she's saying. This often takes place in the context of in-person meetings or presentations, or perhaps in the context of a publication in which the author is purporting to "respond" to critics. An appeal to authority may be invoked, and this may take the form of references to the writer's position, previous publications, number of "followers", testimonials, grants that she's been awarded, etc. In these cases, some sort of intimidation will usually be employed as part of the discouragement. Otherwise, an artful dodge may be used to misdirect or to put off to a "later time" any responses to issues that a critic (or curious questioner) attempts to raise. Or the pseudo-philosopher may try a simple brush-off, or a more intimidating dismissal intended to cow the inquisitor into silence.

Another method of discouraging inquiry is for the pseudo-philosopher to make the statements and use of his own ideas (concepts, methods, principles, positions, theories, and arguments) *inaccessible* to others who might want to examine them for the purposes of understanding, analysis, or criticism. While some pseudo-philosophers do their very best to publish their (often crackpot) views as publicly and as frequently as possible, others do their best to hold exposition of their views tightly within an "inner circle" of devoted followers (we'll see a blatant case of this in Chapter 10, and in a different way in Chapter 11). As a result, a kind of cult-like bubble of inaccessibility protects the pseudo-philosopher from criticism and from exposure of his goals and methods.

Finally, inquiry may be discouraged in a more subtle way through the use of ⊘ *Obscurantism* as a rhetorical technique to suppress your natural critical reaction and instead encourage agreement and acceptance. Lack of clarity in the use of terminology or concepts can be employed to encourage the reader into provisional acceptance of what's being said, whereby she — although perhaps uncertain to some degree about exactly what is being said — is led to suspend any initial suspicion or skepticism pending more complete development. When (if) that clarity is later provided, it may well not be compatible with the reader's own assumptions on which she was willing to base her provisional acceptance.

⊘ Known Fallacy
(Clashes with: Φ *Explanation*, Φ *Rationality*, Φ *Methods*)

Part of the required domain knowledge for a *competent* philosopher involves awareness and understanding of a number of classic fallacies and modes of reasoning. And one of the requirements imposed on a *genuine* philosopher is not using such fallacies in arguments — such use being, after all, inconsistent with the pursuit of truth and wisdom. Our short list of these includes:

- *False dichotomy* (or *false dilemma*): presenting a situation or problem in which you claim that there are only two possible ways of understanding it, or only two possible choices for pursuing a solution. This is a favorite rhetorical move of pseudo-philosophers since it's an effective tool not only for avoiding criticism of their own positions, but for immediately narrowing the discussion to only those areas and points they want you to consider. While, strictly speaking, the "di" in "dichotomy" and "dilemma" refers to a choice between only two possibilities, this fallacy may occur in cases where a different number of possibilities are (falsely) presented as *limiting the range of choices*.

Example: "There are only two possibilities: choose Marxism and suppress individual rights, or choose unconstrained capitalism and oppress the poor."

- *Weak analogy*: This is an argument that because two things are alike in one (or more) respects, then they are alike in another. While analogies can be useful and powerful means of reasoning, and provide strong support to their conclusions, the strength of the analogy depends on how many (and sometimes which) similarities are shared between the things being considered. Some similarities will also be regarded as more relevant than others with regard to the conclusion, and so there is danger in inferring something about relevant similarities or dissimilarities from irrelevant ones.

Example: "Wolves are mammals and cows are mammals. Wolves are carnivores. Therefore cows are carnivores." In this case, highly significant dissimilarities are ignored in comparing wolves with cows.

- *Straw man*: arguing against something that no one has actually said, this often involves misinterpreting (or distorting) your opponent's position and then arguing against the misinterpretation. It's a favorite tactic in attacking a position that competes with the one being pitched by the pseudo-philosopher, or in responding to a criticism of the pseudo-philosopher.

Example: "[T]he writings of Charles Darwin, the father of evolution, promoted the justification of racism, and his books *On the Origin of Species* and *The Descent of Man* postulate a hierarchy of superior and inferior races."

This is a direct quote from an early draft of a bill considered by the Louisiana Legislature in 2001. Darwin's writings contain no such assertions, promotions, or postulations; and neither do they imply such a position. To the credit of the Louisiana Legislature, this straw man attack was recognized and removed from the bill.

- *Ad hominem* (*to the man*): attacking the person instead of her views, evidence, or arguments. This both dodges having to provide a direct response to criticism and also (mis)directs attention elsewhere

  Example: "We should ignore the entirety of Heidegger's philosophy because he was anti-democracy, anti-Semitic, and a member of the Nazi party."

  It's true that Heidegger was anti-Semitic in some of his writings, that he was anti-democracy as a form of government, and that he was a member of the Nazi Party. And it may be true that there are good reasons for ignoring or rejecting most or all of Heidegger's philosophical works. But his own relations to democracy, anti-Semitism, and Naziism simply aren't relevant to ignoring the substance of his philosophical work, which should be judged on its own merits — although knowing those relations might reasonably make us more cautious in reading his works and analyzing their consequences.

- *Tu quoque* (*"you too"*): accusing your opponent of the same thing he's accusing you of doing — another misdirection of attention.

- *Appeal to fear* (*"Ad metum"*): Often in the case of pseudo-philosophers using this fallacy, they argue that if you don't adopt the position or belief they're encouraging you to, then you're exhibiting a lack of understanding or intelligence.

  Example: "If you don't accept the idea that everyone should have a guaranteed minimum wage, then you're no smarter than the crazies who believe the government shouldn't be able to tax anything."

- *Petitio principii* (*circular argument*, also called "*begging the question*"): assuming, possibly indirectly, what you're claiming to demonstrate.

  Classic Example: "He says he loves me, and I know he does because he wouldn't lie to someone he loves."

- *Ignoratio elenchi* (*feigned ignorance* or *playing dumb*): providing a distraction by intentionally misinterpreting a criticism or pretending that you don't understand the point.

There are a number of others you're likely to encounter as well. Any good course in informal logic or critical thinking should deal with the entire set. Anyone can slip up from time to time and fall into a subtle version of one of the classic fallacies. But the frequent occurrence of such fallacies, or the obviously intentional use of them, in a writer's work says either that she lacks competence or that she's intentionally attempting to sway your beliefs in a dishonest way.

⊘ Accusations and Excuses
(Clashes with: Φ *Integrity*, Φ *Rationality*, Φ *Methods*)

Pseudo-philosophers (and pseudo-scientists, pseudo-artists, pseudo-historians, and others) will often attempt to provide some explanation of why their views aren't widely endorsed or respected in the broader intellectual community (which generally means the community of university teachers and researchers). Or a pseudo-philosopher may claim that a particularly bothersome (and likely accurate) critic bears some personal animosity towards him. Sometimes the problem is claimed to be embodied in "the establishment" which controls the publication of philosophical works and won't give the pseudo-philosopher a fair hearing. You'll recognize this marker when you see it. It's hard to miss and generally is delivered with excessive passion and resentment.

 *Markers of language abuse*

Much of the pseudo-philosopher's trickery is accomplished by using language in vague, peculiar, or incorrect ways. Her goal here is to give the impression of clarity where in fact there's ambiguity and confusion. This can involve a move from something that seems reasonable to something that isn't quite supported by that and ends up being unreasonable — even though you don't realize this because of the clever linguistic slight of hand. This often turns out as well to be a kind of intimidation since it seeks to put you in a position of feeling that you don't quite understand what's being said, but that this is probably your fault, and so it encourages you to retain some faith in what the pseudo-philosopher is saying rather than to take a critical stance towards it.

It's important to identify these abuses of language as early as possible, or you'll be swept along by them to an illusion of understanding, veering off course from truth and wisdom to error and false belief. Both the misuse of terminology and (our next marker) puzzling terminology are used by the pseudo-philosopher to accomplish ⊘ Obscurantism.

⊘ Misuse of Terminology
(Clashes with: Φ *Clarity*, Φ *Methods*)

Philosophy is full of specialized jargon. In a significant sense, to be a philosopher is to understand the jargon of philosophy — just as to be a physicist is to understand and correctly use the jargon of physics, or to be a chef is to understand the jargon of food and its preparation. Pseudo-philosophers frequently give themselves away by the improper or incoherent use of philosophical jargon.

Common examples of terms misused by pseudo-philosophers include "logic", "inference", "evidence", "knowledge", "argument", "proof", "counterexample", "perception", "definition", "cause", "right" and "explanation". And this doesn't begin to even touch the possibilities for misuse of special terminology introduced (very carefully and precisely) by individual philosophers such as Plato, Aristotle, Descartes, Kant, Leibniz, and all of the others. Often a genuine philosopher (or even a student with experience in a couple of philosophy courses) can quickly spot a pseudo-philosopher by his hilarious misuse of well-established philosophical terminology. We'll see examples of this in Part 3.

⊘ Puzzling Terminology
(Clashes with: Φ *Explanation*, Φ *Clarity*, Φ *Methods*)

Philosophers use a lot of technical terminology — meaning that they either make up new terms ("deontic logic", "consequentialism", "anti-realism", "epistemic necessity", etc.) or they use common everyday terms in either unusual senses or in much more precise senses than these are used in normal conversation ("meaning", "reference", "perceive", "infer", "real", "concept", etc.). There are genuinely good reasons for this (at least for a lot of it) rooted in the facts that philosophers are frequently attempting to express ideas and make distinctions that aren't found in everyday language, discussions, or disputes. And in addition, philosophers are (for the most part) trying to be much more precise with their terms, how they're used, and what they mean, in order to meet their requirements for clarity in the pursuit of knowledge, truth, and wisdom. Our example of the Ship of Theseus paradox in Section 3.3, and the solutions to it, illustrate this. New terminology was introduced (and old terminology treated more carefully and precisely) in order to craft the correct analyses and solutions to that puzzle.

This is one of the features of philosophy that makes philosophy so difficult (and irritating) for "normal people" to understand and evaluate. But it needs to be tolerated, at least up to a point, in order for the philosopher to accomplish his goals. A mark of the pseudo-philosopher, however, is the introduction of unfamiliar (and sometimes outright goofy) terminology in an attempt to mislead the reader and to get away with claims and reasoning that without the strange jargon would obviously be fallacious. The best clue that this is what's happening is that the new terminology (or the new meaning or use of familiar terminology) isn't well-explained — since genuine philosophers normally take great (some would say *excessive*) care to explain their new terms and concepts.

⊘ Vagueness and Equivocation
(Clashes with: Φ *Explanation*, Φ *Clarity*, Φ *Methods*)

Everyone knows what it means for a word to be *vague* or *ambiguous*: it has several possible meanings and you're just not sure which one is intended in the use of it that you're looking at. Pseudo-philosophers and rhetoricians are happy to make use of vagueness, and it's easy to do. Its success in achieving their goals depends on the reader's *assuming* that a particular meaning of the word is intended even though this isn't the case. But equivocation is something a bit different, and more powerful and deceptive.

Equivocation is the weaponization of ambiguity and vagueness — sometimes referred to as "doubletalk". It's often the *intentional* use of an expression (word or phrase) with multiple meanings, but without making clear which meaning is being attached to that word in each of its uses in a given context — and then *knowingly* using that ambiguity to *appear* to justify inferences or conclusions that simply have no basis. In other cases, equivocation is a *careless* use of terminology that a genuine philosopher would avoid in order to ensure clarity and avoid ⊘ *Obscurantism*.

Suppose, for example, someone says that "Everyone knows the value of the liberal arts and a liberal education. So no one should ever vote for conservative political candidates because their conservative views are anti-liberal." However you feel about liberal arts, a liberal education, and liberal and conservative politicians, it's important to recognize these two sentences as a logical and semantic disaster involving equivocation.

The first sentence uses "liberal" in the sense of "wide" or "broad" or "not specialized", and a classic liberal education is one in which both the arts and sciences are studied and mastered. In the ancient world, this meant such subjects as grammar, logic, rhetoric, poetry, and philosophy. In more modern times it came to include the natural and social sciences, and mathematics. A liberal education was supposed to be a *broad education* in all of these subjects that would serve as the foundation for further learning and for being a "good citizen" and "well-rounded person".

But the use of "liberal" in the second sentence has *nothing* to do with this classic sense of its use in "liberal arts". Instead, that second use of "liberal" refers to a type of *political ideology* or system based on certain principles, goals, and beliefs which is often said to center on the nature of "liberty" (in the sense of "freedom") and equality (in one or more possibly vague senses). Many *strongly* "conservative" politicians and individuals *strongly endorse* the value of the liberal arts and a liberal education; and to characterize them as "anti-liberal" in the sense of being against a liberal education based on this sort of equivocation is outrightly dishonest.

In a like vein in Shakespeare's play, *Macbeth* runs afoul of a nasty use of equivocation that results in his death when he's told by the witches that "none of woman born shall harm Macbeth". He quite reasonably believes that this prophecy means that no man can kill him. But the witches are *equivocating* since "of woman born" had two meanings at that time. The broader meaning was "child of a woman", but the narrower one was "child born in the normal (natural) way". Macduff, who ultimately kills Macbeth, was certainly a child of a woman, but not *born in the normal way*. Instead, he was "from his mother's womb untimely ripp'd" (delivered by Caesarian section). This didn't count as being born in the narrower sense, and the witches had their equivocation joke on Macbeth.

 *Markers of incompetence*

In Section 3.1 we considered the question "What is a philosopher?", and came up with a short list of characteristics that are required in order for someone to be viewed as a competent philosopher. These were incorporated in the philosophy-markers of Section 4.4, and any indication of their absence should incline us to suspect that what we're dealing with may be pseudo-philosophy. But now we need, in addition to these, some specific pseudo-philosophy markers of incompetence. Here they are:

⊘ **Failure to Give Fair Hearing**
(Clashes with: Φ *Critical Appraisal*, Φ *Objectivity*, Φ *Inquiry*)

This marker highlights a violation of the Principle of Charity as discussed in Section 4.2.

⊘ **Inadequate Understanding**
(Clashes with: Φ *Domain Awareness*)

Certainly this is the primary marker of incompetence. It appears not merely as an occasional mistake in representing an opponent's claims, positions, or arguments — or in the misuse of philosophical methods — but as repeated or very severe errors of this sort. Often it takes the form of the pseudo-philosopher's misapplying well-known methods and rules of logic, or demonstrating ignorance of the details and consequences of a particular ethical theory, or not understanding significant differences between types of metaphysical theories, or being unfamiliar with fundamental counterexamples involving knowledge and justified belief. However, in order to make your own judgments about incompetence of this sort, you need to possess some degree of competence yourself — or at least be able to understand the criticisms that others have made of the suspect pseudo-philosopher. We'll see specific examples of this in Chapters 9 and 11.

⊘ Ignorance of Prior Work
(Clashes with: Φ *Domain Awareness*)

While this may count as a variety of the inadequate understanding of philosophy, it's worth listing by itself since it's so often encountered in any context where pseudo-philosophy may be presented. In philosophical matters, ignorance of prior work leads to a false sense of innovation, and perhaps to self-importance — and then perhaps to resentment when "the establishment" doesn't recognize your genius. Ignorance of prior work doesn't mean that the work of an amateur or relatively inexperienced philosopher lacks quality, but it's like being the second (or third, or fourth, or ...) person to break an Olympic record. And in the case of prior work of recognized historical importance to philosophy — such as problems and proposed solutions typically covered in introductory philosophy courses — this marker can be highly suggestive of pseudo-philosophy.

People tend to become very agitated when they're told that what they thought was their brilliant work in solving a previously unsolved problem not only wasn't the first solution to that problem, but that the first solution was accomplished a century earlier. Worse, ignorance of prior work on a problem can — even if that problem remains to be solved — allow you to spend time going down a path to a solution that's been demonstrated to be inadequate or to face very serious problems that you're ignoring or failing to address adequately. And these can be signs of pseudo-philosophy as they lead to ⊘ *Inadequate Understanding*, ⊘ *Exaggerated Claims* and other pseudo-philosophy markers as well.

 *Standards markers*

While philosophers often refer to standards, it's quite difficult to find where they provide any very clear account of the professional standards that they want to impose on their own discipline. Most talk of standards applies to standards that students must meet, rather than standards that professors and other professionals are expected to meet. Even in cases where you can find standards policies or guides for philosophy faculties, these pertain only to what we might think of as "social behavior" (how faculty should act towards one another), or to legal and political issues such as those surrounding the freedom of speech and academic freedom, sexual (and other) harassment, rights of faculty and students, etc. These include the American Philosophical Association's *Good Practices Guide* (Railton et al. 2020), *Code of Conduct* (Holland et al. 2016), and *Statement on valuing public philosophy* (American Philosophical Association 2017). Such efforts have nothing to do with the quality of professional work as exhibited in presentations, publications, and research, or with any principles on which such standards might be based.

A number of specific "standards" are included in the policies for promotion and tenure at individual universities, but these are only indirect standards (more like "markers of professional success"). They involve what degree(s) the candidate should have, how the quality of research should be judged by publications in certain types of journals or books, teaching excellence and how that's to be evaluated, recommendations from colleagues in the philosopher's own institution or outside of it, etc., and how meeting these requirements or guidelines should be accomplished through "validation by peers." So the members of the club get to judge the other members (or proposed members) of the club. Presentations and arguments are made, and criticisms offered, at faculty meetings for the purpose of making tenure and promotion decisions. Records and letters of recommendation are reviewed. A vote is taken and consensus rules the day.

This situation is workable if you're dealing with professional philosophers as they're embedded in university and professional communities. But it doesn't do us any good here because (most) pseudo-philosophers aren't members of those communities. If we were to use these criteria for identifying pseudo-philosophers, it would be easy: "Do you have a job in a university philosophy department (or at least a Ph.D. in philosophy)? Then you're a genuine philosopher. Otherwise — if you think you're doing philosophy — then you're a pseudo-philosopher." Of course (as I've pointed out in Chapters 2 and 3) that's not how it works, and it's not how it's worked in the history of philosophy either.

Interestingly, professional societies in other disciplines don't seem to be so shy about laying out more explicit professional standards and expectations. The American Chemical Society, for example, has a set of Academic Professional Guidelines dating back to 1991 (American Chemical Society 2016) in which responsibilities of all chemical scientists are discussed in terms of "high standards of honesty, integrity, ethics, and diligence in the conduct of teaching, research, and all other professional activities," "communicating with scientists and non-scientists accurately, using good oral and written skills," "participating in life-long learning," contributing to "building a collegial atmosphere," being "a role model for students," and being involved in "broad self-education" both within and outside of their own discipline as well as within and outside of academia. A number of these standards are not specific to chemistry or to science, and seem to apply equally well to philosophy.

There are professional standards in philosophy — even if professional philosophers don't want to talk about them. These are also standards for anyone (professional or not) who claims to be involved in participating in philosophy and philosophical writing and presentation, and who wants to be seen as a genuine philosopher, even if just an amateur one. You can't ignore these standards and claim to be producing genuine philosophy any more than you could (Chapter 3) ignore similar standards for astronomy and claim to be even a competent amateur astronomer.

Here is a set of markers that indicate the violation of commonly accepted standards for the genuine philosopher:

⊘ **Misleading Citation**
(Clashes with: Φ *Methods*, Φ *Domain Awareness*)

It's common for genuine philosophers to refer to prior work (usually in the form of publications) — both to support their own views and arguments, and to provide examples of these that they're contesting. In fact, journal referees and editors will require a certain degree (sometimes an excessive degree) of citation in almost any article accepted for publication in a reputable journal.[8] In part this is required in order to place your own work within the history and context of the work of others in order to establish its "significance"; and in part it's required in order for the reader to determine whether what you're saying about others is accurate, and to facilitate the evaluation of your proposals and arguments (not just by readers in general, but also for tenure and promotion committees that may be judging the work). More broadly, this is a mark of conforming to the expected standards of scholarship and competence.

Pseudo, in seeking to mimic Philo, often will provide a number of references to prior work supposedly related to his own, but these may be found either to be bogus in certain regards (e.g., the references can't be found or they don't at all say what the pseudo-philosopher claims they do), or they'll be misleadingly and inaccurately interpreted. That is, they'll be references intended to impress and misguide you, or they'll demonstrate fundamental misunderstandings by Pseudo of the works being cited. This may apply even to Pseudo's own prior work, cited in such contexts as "As I've already shown in ...," or "In ... I established that ...,". While anyone can make a mistake in citing a reference from time to time, and a faulty one may not be caught by referees or editors, recurrent faulty citations should alert you to the likelihood of either incompetence or deceit. We will see several examples of these different types of misleading citations in Chapters 9-11.

⊘ Discreditation
(Clashes with: Φ *Domain Awareness*)

While you may be reading the works of Pseudo in the area of philosophy, and they may be making sense to you (at least initially or at some elementary level), you also may be unaware that Pseudo has written in other (possibly related) areas and been discredited in those. This should at least raise a red flag for you, and make you look much more closely and critically at Pseudo's approach to philosophical problems and views; and it's of particular significance when the discredited work is, or involves citations in, an area that Pseudo uses in an attempt to support his work in philosophy.

For example, you might be looking at some of Pseudo's writings in the area of ethics and political philosophy in which she's arguing for a particular moral theory and how our legal and political system should be structured in order to support and express that theory. Her views may, for all you can see, make sense — given what she says — and so you're inclined to go along with them, at least provisionally. But it turns out that in other contexts (publications or online forums, for example) Pseudo's views concerning the law and legal systems have been discredited by reputable attorneys, judges, and legal scholars — on the basis of factual observations and arguments that you can see and evaluate for yourself. This, of course, is related in a highly relevant way to Pseudo's positions and arguments in ethical and political philosophy. What should you do — immediately conclude that Pseudo's moral views and arguments amount to pseudo-philosophy? No. That would be unjustified. But the discovery that Pseudo has been discredited in another (and closely related) domain is a marker that her work in ethics and political philosophy is suspect and deserves added scrutiny. We'll see examples like this in Chapters 10 and 11.

An example of this type of discrediting can be found in the work of Dr. Deepak Chopra (Wikipedia 2020c), often regarded as a New Age philosopher, whose views and teaching overlap the areas of medicine, alternative medicine, wellness, spirituality, metaphysics, philosophy of mind, and quantum mechanics, among others.

He expresses and champions a number of views in the areas of science and philosophy that have strong consequences for how we should live, how we should understand the empirical world, the relations of our minds to it, and how medicine should be practiced. His approach and writings are elaborate, complicated, and difficult to evaluate without significant effort. But Chopra's views in some areas (such as science and medicine) that are fundamental to his philosophical views have been thoroughly discredited by multiple experts, and this should cause us to be very cautious in accepting any of those views without closer examination; and we might reasonably suspect him of pseudo-philosophy.

An *indirect discreditation* may take place when Pseudo cites the works of other authors as supporting her own views, but those works have been discredited (in, for example, reviews or critiques) in other publicly available sources while these criticisms have either been ignored or inadequately addressed by Pseudo. Some very clear and simple examples of this will be found in Chapter 9.

⊘ Lack of Rigor
(Clashes with: Φ *Clarity*, Φ *Objectivity*, Φ *Rationality*, Φ *Methods*)

Lack of rigor is often cited as a flaw in cases of both pseudo-philosophy and inept philosophy. Rigor is absolutely critical in achieving clarity and coherence in philosophical works because without it, the special terminology introduced by the philosopher, the arguments employed, and the evidence, theories and counter-examples offered become unintelligible and worthless. But what is rigor?

Fundamentally, lack of rigor is just another description for sloppiness in writing, thinking, presenting ideas and concepts, distinguishing them from one another, and presenting their consequences in a clear and understandable way. Rigor, on the other hand, is marked by carefulness, thoroughness, and clarity in analysis, exposition, and presentation. And as a pseudo-philosophy marker, lack of rigor sits on a foundation of several markers of genuine philosophy — or rather it sits on the collective absence or violation of these markers.

A judgment of lack of rigor is therefore more properly made against an entire work (or even an entire corpus of works); and the characterization can be thought of as shorthand for the presence of a number (and a number of different types) of errors, oversights, misunderstandings, and misguided criticisms that are pervasive in that work. In the case of pseudo-philosophy, lack of rigor may result from the pseudo-philosopher's failure to understand what rigor is (and so how to achieve it). But it also may be that the pseudo-philosopher understands fully what rigor is, and consciously chooses to avoid it in order to achieve a more immediately persuasive presentation.

A detailed example of this is to be found in the use of philosophy in the areas of holistic medicine and Nursing Theory as these are examined in Chapter 9. It is particularly interesting to see the arguments advanced in that context that rigor should somehow *not* be viewed as important in certain approaches to "knowing", and that in fact it can be detrimental to the acquisition of knowledge.

⊘ Misappropriation
(Clashes with: Φ *Methods*)

The *misappropriation of ideas* can take several forms, but always refers to the borrowing or use of someone else's work in a way that's central to your own (particularly to a part of your work that you claim is insightful or innovative), but *without acknowledgment*. The phrase "misappropriation of ideas" seems to be the new and preferred way to refer to *plagiarism* (at least in its general sense), and doesn't require the actual copying of words, sentences, and paragraphs for its commission. For example, if I had introduced the idea of a persona in Chapter 4 and claimed (or given the impression) that I had come up with this concept myself, then that would be misappropriation of the concept of persona that we're making use of here.

This *illicit borrowing* feature of misappropriation is made abundantly clear in the U.S. government Office of Research Integrity's primary document on plagiarism and ethical writing (Roig 2015) where in the Plagiarism section there's a separate topic on "Acknowledging the Source of Our Ideas." There, the concept of misappropriation is introduced and explored. It's made clear that (from the point of view of the government and current academic thinking, at least) you can be guilty of *unconscious* plagiarism of ideas, even though you're unaware of this and had no intention to misappropriate those ideas. However, the example given in that section to support the idea of unconscious plagiarism (or unintentional misappropriation) seems entirely unconvincing, and this seems wholly inconsistent with a lengthy history of the recognition of simultaneous or independent discovery that appears in such areas as mathematics.

We're going to side-step any controversy concerning whether the notion of unconscious misappropriation makes sense, and instead make use of a concept of law in which responsibility is imposed on an agent if she *knew or should have known* that she was acting improperly. This doctrine applies to people who, because of their authority or position, are assumed (or required) to have a degree of knowledge or competence in a given domain, and who therefore either *know or should know* about certain parts of that domain. And this is especially appropriate in the case of potential instances of pseudo-philosophy because (Section 3.1) the requirement that any genuine philosopher be competent in the domain of philosophy means that misappropriation (especially repeated misappropriation) of ideas is an overt sign of a pseudo-philosopher at work: if he *knowingly* misappropriates ideas of other thinkers, then he's being dishonest and deceptive; and if he *unknowingly* misappropriates ideas, then he's being incompetent. For this reason, ⊘ *Misappropriation* is closely related to ⊘ *Ignorance of prior work* and ⊘ *Misunderstanding*. This conundrum is illustrated in parts of Chapter 11.

7.3 Pseudo-philosophy and dishonesty

Is dishonesty an essential feature of pseudo-philosophy?

This is a question I skirted in Chapter 6, but we must consider it more fully now and come to some decision regarding its answer. In Section 6.2 I laid out a representation of pseudo-philosophy (or, more generally, *the pseudo*) according to which it includes the two components of *incompetence* and *exploitation*. And at that point I said that pseudo-philosophers will fall somewhere on the plane delimited by these two axes. But should we be willing to regard someone who is merely approaching philosophy in an entirely incompetent manner as pseudo-philosophical? Or should we take the view that pseudo-philosophy (and the pseudo-philosopher who practices it) must exhibit at least some degree of exploitation (and hence dishonesty)?

The answer to this question isn't a matter of discovery, but one of decision. There's no single and absolutely "correct" answer here, but there are reasons to prefer one answer over another. And I'm going to adopt the view that a judgment of pseudo-philosophy against an author or work both requires and implies a judgment of intentional, or at least culpable, deceit and dishonesty. That view better suits the goals of this book, and it's arguably more consistent with the view held by genuine philosophers throughout history. Along these lines, for example, when asked what the proper role of philosophy is in relation to other disciplines (e.g., those reviewed in Chapter 5), Adolf Grünbaum replied that "In a nutshell, philosophy should serve as their intellectual conscience," (Grünbaum 2005 75). This is precisely what pseudo-philosophy does not, and cannot, do.

The ancients — such as Plato, Xenophon, Aristotle, Isocrates and others — clearly felt that the Sophists and their like were being intentionally deceptive about what they could provide as, or in the place of, philosophy; and they were explicit in their writings about this view. Later philosophers such as Schopenhauer were likewise direct and vocal about how pseudo-philosophers "mislead" their students and readers. In the early 20th century, R. G. Collingwood takes deceit to be an essential element of the pseudo; and in the late 20th century, even Nicholas Rescher ultimately suggests that what drives the pseudo-philosopher is a desire for power, influence, or attention; and he explicitly accuses pseudo-philosophy of employing a technique of *masquerade*.

Additionally, one of the goals we set for ourselves in Section 1.4 was to be able to express the difference between pseudo-philosophy, on the one hand, and philosophy that's just poorly done, on the other. This is an intuitive and reasonable distinction to make, and it's required in order not to be compelled to count virtually all beginning undergraduate philosophy students (and many other students as well) as pseudo-philosophers. But this distinction can't be maintained — and hence this goal can't be met — if we allow ourselves to see merely incompetent philosophy as a kind of pseudo-philosophy. Incompetence may play a significant role in the pseudo, but it doesn't make something pseudo. That requires a particular stance involving the use of deception and masquerade.[9]

There's one exception we may make to this decision — if it really is an exception rather than just a variation of it — and that's the case of the crackpot, sometimes also called cranks or kooks (Dudley 1992). Crackpots seem to be distinguished by an unshakeable faith in their own insight and understanding of a domain, however incompatible this is with the well established and broadly accepted views of experts and professionals. This faith is coupled with a stubbornness in refusing to look at the details of fundamental problems and consequences of their own ideas, often an apparent inability to grasp technical details of what they're criticizing, a fundamental misunderstanding of critical principles or arguments, and an overwhelming desire to show some well-known figure to be "wrong". But other than the desire for recognition and acknowledgment of their own brilliance, crackpots have no desire or intent to deceive. They really think they're exposing the truth. Crackpots are perhaps most commonly found attempting to make a mark in scientific areas (a wonderful brief summary of this has been done by Stephanie Chasteen (Chasteen 2008)), but they appear from time to time in philosophy as well.

Part 3

Real-world Pseudo-philosophy

Chapter 8
Applying the Models: A User's Guide

> **In this chapter:**
> - Reacting to pseudo-philosophy
> - The *anti-sophistical stance*
> - Challenges in this approach to pseudo-philosophy
> - Expectations and limitations
> - Abduction revisited: its role and use
> - Practical guidelines

Prior chapters have been setting the stage and developing some special "philosophical technology" to help achieve the goals laid out in Chapter 1. That technology includes the *personas* of the genuine philosopher and pseudo-philosopher as well as the sets of *markers* (for both pseudo-philosophy and genuine philosophy) that distinguish the pseudo-philosopher from the real thing. Together, the personas and the markers serve as components of the different *models* of the philosopher and the pseudo-philosopher that we'll use in making *judgments* as to whether something is an example of genuine philosophy or of pseudo-philosophy.

In this chapter we talk about what our expectations should be when analyzing works and writers, mention some limitations that we'll encounter and the consequences of these, look at one more piece of technology that will play a critical role in our methodology, and offer practical guidelines for applying our models and methods to real-world cases. In Chapter 9 we'll look at how our models and techniques can be applied to a relatively simple example of a contemporary writer, discuss some criticisms that this example may raise for our approach, leave you with some open questions you may want to revisit after completing the book, and then move on to some more substantial examples in Chapters 10 and 11.

Chapter 8: Applying the Models: A User's Guide

8.1 What's so bad about pseudo-philosophy?

The goal of the pseudo-philosopher is, first, to get you to believe something and then, typically, to get you to act on that belief in one way or another. Of course, phrased in that general and neutral way, that's the goal of the genuine philosopher as well. But the pseudo-philosopher seeks to accomplish this goal through means unconnected to wisdom and truth, and this is exactly what makes his enterprise pseudo. If you're taken in by the pseudo-philosopher, there will be consequences to this, and these may range from emotional, psychological, and intellectual ones to social, financial, legal, and physical ones that can alter your life in either minor or major ways. Often, your discovery of being taken in and tricked into believing a "false philosophy" is simply embarrassment and the compensating realization that you've learned something and are better for the experience. But sometimes there is genuine harm, and we'll see examples of this in the following chapters.

On the receiving side of pseudo-philosophy, effects will include your embracing of unreliable and unfounded conclusions — presented to you as coherent and meaningful, but in fact misleading and potentially dangerous. You'll suffer a *false confidence in your beliefs and understanding* — meaning that your confidence in understanding (or thinking that you understand) what the pseudo-philosopher is teaching you is misplaced, unjustified, and dangerous to use in making decisions. You may become convinced to *believe things incompatible with your more fundamental goals and beliefs*, and so, on the basis of that belief, endanger your safety, support causes, contribute money, or join organizations that you otherwise would not. Such decisions and actions may have either trivial and temporary effects on you, or they may have much deeper and lasting effects. And embracing a pseudo-philosophical approach will also tend to *blind you to principles, views, and ways of reasoning that would lead you towards genuine wisdom* and its benefits in your life.

All considered, it's best to learn to recognize pseudo-philosophy when you encounter it, and to reject it quickly and decisively.

8.2 Reacting to pseudo-philosophy

When we look back across the history of accusations of pseudo-philosophy from the ancient Greeks through contemporary philosophers, we can identify several different reactions that philosophers (and other critical writers) have had towards pseudo-philosophy and pseudo-philosophers. These include criticism, complaint, outrage, and demands for action.

Section 8.2: Reacting to pseudo-philosophy

♦ CRITICISM

Of course, a frequent reaction to pseudo-philosophy has been *criticism*, with one or more genuine philosophers providing careful analyses and critiques of the pseudo-philosopher's work in an attempt to show how it's faulty, misleading, and incompatible with the goals and principles of genuine philosophy. We see this in Plato's criticisms concerning poets and sophists in the *Republic*, the *Gorgias*, the *Ion*, and the *Phaedrus*. Plato criticizes poets for inconsistency and presenting themselves as knowledgeable experts in areas where they lack knowledge. In this they not only fail to be wise (and to pursue wisdom), but they're also guilty of deception in what they purport to know, what they teach, and what their motives are. We'll see similar example of this sort of reaction (this one from the 19th century) in Guideline #4 of Section 8.7 below.

♦ OUTRAGE

Another response to pseudo-philosophy can be found in the final book of the *Republic* where there's a sense of *outrage* as Plato says of poets that they "maim the thought of those who hear them and do not as a remedy have the knowledge of how they [the poets] really are." This is a direct accusation that the pseudo-philosophy of the poets (and rhetoricians as well) is *knowingly harmful* in leading people, through deceit, to think poorly, incorrectly, and dangerously. And it's also a direct accusation of taking advantage of people who aren't equipped through education or training ("do not as a remedy have the knowledge") to resist the deceptive assault of the poets and rhetoricians.

♦ COMPLAINTS

We find a similar emotion and sense of outrage — along with criticisms, complaints, and a demand for action — in the 1992 letter from Barry Smith and other academic philosophers to the *Times* of London (Smith 1992), decrying The University of Cambridge's proposal to award an honorary degree to Jacques Derrida. The letter characterizes Derrida's published work as consisting of "tricks and gimmicks", sarcastically concedes that "Certainly he has shown considerable originality in this respect", and opines that "Many French philosophers see in M. Derrida only cause for silent embarrassment, his antics having contributed significantly to the widespread impression that contemporary French philosophy is little more than an object of ridicule." It ends with what is essentially a demand to deny the honorary degree to Derrida — though this is phrased in academic jargon as a *reason* for the Cambridge faculty not to proceed. Note that all this (outrage, complaint, and demand) is not in fact submitted directly to

Cambridge University for its consideration, but is published *publicly* in the *Times* for all to see — making it more of a political and rhetorical approach than an academic, intellectual, or philosophical approach or argument. It was, in any event, unsuccessful; and Cambridge awarded the honorary degree to Derrida.

The reactions of complaint, outrage, and demand for action are emotional, political, and professional responses. They're quite understandable and well-established reactions to pseudo-philosophy. But they're the reactions of professional philosophers rather than the reactions to pseudo-philosophy of an "inexpert" or "average" reader — or one who has only minor experience with philosophy. They're also primarily emotional reactions — in part driven by the expert's knowledge and understanding of what the pseudo-philosopher is doing and why it's bad. Underlying them are more important responses that we all should have when confronted with pseudo-philosophy — and these are epistemic, psychological, rational, and practical responses.

The question here isn't what the reaction of a professional philosopher or knowledgeable philosophy student should be. Rather, it's what should *your* reaction be when you *begin to suspect* that you're reading the work of a pseudo-philosopher? When you see the presence of pseudo-philosophy markers in something you're reading, or when you see what you think is the Pseudo persona emerging, what should you think and what should you do?

8.3 The anti-sophistical stance

There are three fundamental reactions you should have in the presence of something you think might be pseudo-philosophical. Each of these is a step that — while applying other guidelines for our models — will move you either towards or away from a final judgment that you are confronted with pseudo-philosophy and its dangers. Together they comprise what you may think of as *the anti-sophistical stance*:

Suspicion

This is the first leg of the anti-sophistical stance, and in fact it should always be with you in reading or listening to *anything* that's presented as philosophical — whether that's in written form, in a class, in a public lecture or business presentation, or in an informal discussion. Suspicion manifests itself as the feeling of "Wait. Is there something wrong here? Is there something that doesn't quite make sense? What am I being told, and why am I being told that?"

You may get this feeling simply from listening to, or reading, something and thinking it's not quite right and doesn't make sense. But (or in addition to that) our pseudo-philosophy markers and the guidelines presented below will help to trigger or support suspicion in cases where it's deserved. So it's important to learn what these markers are and to keep them in mind.

Skepticism

Once you become suspicious, the next part of the anti-sophistical stance is skepticism, and this is nothing more than an attitude of doubt together with the desire to have that doubt resolved in one way or another. Most people aren't, by nature, initially suspicious or skeptical. But once you become suspicious, then it's natural to become skeptical as well; and this means adopting more of an attitude of critical thought than of uncritical acceptance. Becoming skeptical, you begin to pay closer attention and ask yourself clearer and more careful questions about what you're hearing or reading — and why you should believe it or why you should not. You no longer entirely trust the author or presenter — because you've discovered reason not to. Trust may be rebuilt, but it will take some effort. In order to resolve your doubt and make a determination of whether what you're seeing is genuine philosophy or pseudo-philosophy, you need either to find clear and significant flaws in what you're being presented, or you need to somehow enhance it, repair it, or at least come to a different understanding of it that eliminates your suspicion and skepticism. This leads you to ...

Scrutiny

Now armed with an attitude of suspicion and skepticism, you apply scrutiny (enhanced attention to detail, and a more careful interpretation and analysis) to what the author or presenter is saying. This is where our models come into play by guiding your skepticism and scrutiny, and focusing on questions that need to be asked and answered. You'll use the *pseudo-philosophy markers* to sensitize you to symptoms of pseudo-philosophy and identify specific examples as you come across them. And you'll use the *genuine philosophy markers* to likewise identify the examples of genuine philosophy. At the same time, and using the markers and other characteristics of the Philo and Pseudo *personas*, you'll build a persona (let's call it the *subject persona*) of the author or presenter. That *subject persona* and the markers it exhibits can then be compared to Philo and to Pseudo in order to see how well it fits each of those, and so how close it is to being a persona of a genuine philosopher or of a pseudo-philosopher.

The next chapter contains a relatively simple — and not particularly "deep" — example in which we'll apply this method of adopting the anti–sophistical stance and then scrutinize one author's work by applying our models to it, ending with a judgment that's justified by this method. Later chapters contain more complex and "high profile" examples.

8.4 Challenges in this approach

As soon as we start to employ our methods in a practical context, it will become clear that there are a number of challenges in doing this. It's best to highlight these briefly here so that we're prepared for them and know how to respond when they appear.

Lack of familiarity with philosophy

Keeping in mind that this book isn't intended primarily for professional philosophers, advanced students of philosophy, or even those who may have taken several philosophy courses, we have to recognize that you may encounter difficulty in understanding some of the arguments, analyses, and jargon both in the examples in the following chapters and more generally when you try to apply these methods on your own.

You won't need a Ph.D. in philosophy or any significant experience in philosophy or in philosophy courses. I do have some presumption that since you're reading this book, then you already have an *interest* in philosophy and in pseudo-philosophy and may have *some* degree of familiarity with philosophy. Other than that, however, no assumptions will be made in the examples; and effort has been devoted to introducing any philosophy jargon that may be unfamiliar to you. This includes different kinds of philosophical theories (in, say, metaphysics, ethics, epistemology, and logic), any philosophical terminology that's employed in the examples, methodological rules or principles that philosophers may use and that may be relevant to an example, and so on. In addition, I'll provide pointers (in the form of links to other sources such as books, articles, Web sites, and videos) where you can get more detailed — and *understandable* — information and explanations without this being overly burdensome.

Providing sufficiently detailed examples

A significant challenge in presenting the kinds of examples we'll be looking at in the following chapters is to make them short enough and simple enough to illustrate the methods and points we'll be making, and yet detailed and clear enough both to be fair to the author who is under scrutiny and to clearly apply the methods and show how the results justify the conclusions we reach. Because of the nature of what we're doing here, and because the examples are intended as illustrations of how to employ our methods, certain trade-offs will need to be made in achieving the goals of being sufficiently detailed while remaining intelligible and not requiring undue effort on your part.

The consequence of this is that the examples given in the remaining chapters may lack a degree of completeness in the analysis itself — so that not *all* of a particular author's work or works will be considered in the example, nor even all of that work that *might* be relevant. But pointers will always be included so that you may dig more deeply if you want to.

The examples will also lack an exhaustive treatment of all *possible* arguments or counter-arguments both in favor of and against the authors' views. Selections of what we focus on will need to be made based on what the example seeks to illustrate, and every effort will be made to ensure that these examples are accurate and illustrative.

Overall, our goals with the examples (our own criteria of adequacy) are to achieve a high degree of intelligible illustration while presenting a fair representation of the authors' views without attempting to provide an exhaustive treatment of those and the alternatives. But some simplification in presentation for the purposes of clarity, readability, and succinctness must be tolerated.

Identifying markers in context

In earlier chapters we've seen clear descriptions of the markers of genuine philosophy and pseudo-philosophy as well as some brief examples. But in practice — in the context of looking at the details and complexity of a real-world case where new or unfamiliar terminology may be used, or where odd forms of expression may be employed — it can be difficult to recognize a marker based on the brief examples I've provided so far. This is an initial challenge that will succumb to a careful approach in which we indicate *why and how* a marker is attributable at a particular point in a specific case, what arguments there might be that the marker should *not* be attributed, and how best to resolve that conflict.

Remember: the point of the next three chapters isn't to *test* your existing knowledge — as though at the end of Part 2 of the book you understand how the models work in practice and need only apply them in the wild. Instead, the examples serve as additional *illustrations* for the purpose of *learning* how to apply the models. So a substantive role of the examples is to serve as tools in that learning process.

8.5 Expectations and limitations

Looking back at the goals and criteria of adequacy that were stated in Section 4 of Chapter 1, as you proceed through the examples in the final chapters you should see those criteria being satisfied and those goals being met. I'll point out details of this as we make our way through the examples.

On the other hand, you shouldn't expect the distinction between genuine philosophy and pseudo-philosophy to be any better, clearer, or more decidable than the distinction between philosophy and not-philosophy — in part because pseudo-philosophy is not-philosophy, but rather is masquerading as philosophy. But to the degree that the theory of pseudo-philosophy presented here is successful and useful, it should also illuminate the philosophy/not-philosophy distinction. And so you should expect to learn some important distinctions among philosophy, pseudo-philosophy, and other domains that are not philosophy — contributing to, and enhancing, the kinds of distinctions that have been advanced historically and summarized in Chapter 5. In this way, our project of providing a coherent and practical account of pseudo-philosophy should be seen as contributing to a deeper understanding of what philosophy is and how it differs from other academic and intellectual disciplines. So by using this methodology you'll gain a better understanding of real philosophy by gaining a better understanding of pseudo-philosophy.

Regarding using our methodology to reach a conclusion and make a judgment in cases of suspected pseudo-philosophy, you should expect mixed results and varying degrees of uncertainty in individual cases. There are several reasons for this.

Our theoretical framework (markers, models, and personas) allows not only for cases in which there's a firm and strongly defensible judgment of pseudo-philosophy, but also for cases in which there must be a judgment of genuine philosophy. Even some cases that may initially seem to be pseudo-philosophical may under careful scrutiny be shown to be examples of genuine philosophy. And some cases may exhibit both significant evidence in favor of the pseudo-philosophy judgment while also exhibiting some significant evidence against it — so that no confident and general judgment about the case can be made overall. In each case, the judgment is rendered on the basis of how each of the models applies to that case. What this means is that for any case under scrutiny, the result may turn out to be either "This is a case of pseudo-philosophy," "This is a case of genuine philosophy," or "It's not clear what our judgment should be." There's also, of course (and in the context of Chapter 5) the possibility that the example is neither genuine philosophy nor pseudo-philosophy, and is something different — such as poetry, literature, religion, or science.

The power of our approach is not that it provides an infallible method for determining whether what we're presented with is genuine philosophy or pseudo-philosophy. Nothing can do that, owing to the nature of philosophy and the variety of perspectives that can be taken in characterizing it.

Rather the methodology proposed here provides applicable and practical methods of evaluation and justification for making that judgment -- instead of attempting to provide brief and all-encompassing definitions of what philosophy and pseudo-philosophy are, and attempting to draw a narrow line between them. So our approach won't always succeed in removing all doubt. Nor will it always succeed in removing even significant or reasonable doubt. But it does succeed in providing a coherent and historically compatible theoretical foundation and methodology within which any judgment and any remaining doubt can be debated in a principled way — and within which those principles may themselves be debated, refined, or modified. It may not end debate in all cases, but it provides a rational and objective context for enabling and continuing a debate rather than simply having a disagreement that rests on what may be wildly differing goals and underlying principles — or, perhaps more frequently, on no recognized goals or principles at all. And in a preponderance of cases, it allows us to identify examples of pseudo-philosophy and justify those judgments on the basis of sound principles.

8.6 Abduction revisited

In our discussion of markers in Section 4.5 we briefly mentioned the method of *abductive reasoning*, provided a sketch of how it works in relation to markers, and promised a more detailed treatment of it in Chapter 8. Now is the time.

Abduction is a method (or a logic) that can be used either for arriving at a hypothesis or for justifying the acceptance of a hypothesis that's under consideration. In this book, we'll ignore the (more historical) use of abduction as a hypothesis-generating tool and focus on the (more contemporary) use of abduction as a method of justifying a hypothesis in science and epistemology. In this use of abduction, abductive reasoning is often referred to as "inference to the best explanation" because it's used to choose the *best explanation* (of an event, an observation, a relation, the truth or falsity of a statement, etc.) from several alternatives under consideration. Abduction will be our primary tool in judging a work or author to be either philosophical or pseudo-philosophical, and so it's important to understand how it works and why it's a good and reliable tool in this context.

Chapter 8: Applying the Models: A User's Guide

An example of abduction

Here's a simple example of using abduction to justify a hypothesis (or a choice among hypotheses or possible causes): Suppose you're out hiking along a path on a large horse ranch. Up ahead, and crossing your path is a dirt road. You can't yet see the road that you're approaching, but suddenly you hear what sounds like hoof beats coming along the road at high speed, passing the intersection with your path (which you can't see yet), and then moving off in the distance along the road. By the time you get to the intersection, nothing is in sight. You look at the road surface and there are a number of what appear to be tracks of different kinds in the road. Some deer tracks cross it; some cow tracks appear to follow it; there are a few bear tracks and moose tracks; and of course some horse tracks (it is a horse ranch, after all).

What is it *most reasonable* for you to conclude about what you just heard and what, if anything, just happened along that road? There are a number of possibilities:

1. Nothing happened. I had an unexplained auditory hallucination, or perhaps I had a cerebral mini-stroke that made me think I heard something.

2. Something ran along the road, but I have no way of knowing what that might be.

3. I heard a horse running along the road.

4. I heard a deer, a moose, a bear, a cow, ... (i.e., some other animal) running along the road.

It's not reasonable to believe 1 since you have no independent evidence for it. You haven't previously had any hallucinations or perceptual problems, and you didn't feel odd in any way. So, given your experience and what you know, it would be silly to think that 1 is true. You're really only considering 1 as a "logical possibility" for the sake of completeness.

Now 2 is a more reasonable possibility — or it would be in the absence of other things you already know. For example, you know what a galloping horse sounds like, you know you're on a horse ranch, you know that people ride horses along trails and roads on the ranch, and that this wouldn't at all be unusual. So you have substantial indirect evidence and background knowledge suggesting that what you heard was in fact a horse.

Number 3 certainly appears to be the most reasonable conclusion unless (number 4) what you heard *sounded* like a horse, but was really something else. So 4 is the best competitor to 3. But it's not that good a competitor because (as you know) none of those other animals sound like a horse galloping. Possibly you heard a mule, and so you might consider expanding 3 to include that, but you also know that the ranch doesn't have mules that are commonly ridden along the trails. And of course, there's always the possibility that a zebra has escaped from a nearby zoo, managed to make its way to the ranch, and then gallop along the road just as you were approaching it. But again that's grasping at straws (unless the ranch is in certain parts of Africa).

As a result, you conclude that there *was* a horse galloping along that road because *that's the best explanation among the available alternatives*. And that's abduction in action.

Have you *proven* that you heard a horse galloping along a road while you were out hiking? No. But outside of a few very restricted contexts (such as logic and mathematics), you won't find any proofs. Epistemology (the theory of knowledge) is about *reasonable belief* more often than it's about knowledge in some more "certain" sense, and what it's most reasonable to believe (and to act on) given available prior knowledge and the evidence you have at hand. Abduction can provide that to you, and it's commonly used in such areas as medicine (What's the best explanation for these symptoms and test results?), forensics (Which suspect provides the best explanation for the evidence and testimony we have?), broadly throughout the empirical sciences, and constantly throughout our everyday lives.

The models, abduction, and pseudo-philosophy

In our case, abduction is even more powerful, dependable, and confidence-inspiring because of the *constrained manner* in which we'll use it. Abductive reasoning becomes more dependable as the number of alternative hypotheses decreases, and as those hypotheses become more distinct from one another (so that there won't be any possible overlaps among the cases that may be overlooked)

In applying abductive reasoning in the context of our models and task of judging works or authors in being either genuinely philosophical or pseudo-philosophical, there are always just four distinct possibilities: (1) the models show that the case is one of genuine philosophy, (2) the models show that the case is one of pseudo-philosophy, (3) the models show a mixed result, or (4) the case simply isn't either philosophy or pseudo-philosophy at all. And application of the models will show which of these is, in any specific case, the *best explanation* of what we observe in that case. In short, we'll judge an author (or his work) genuinely philosophical if the model of genuine philosophy best fits (by the preponderance of the evidence) that author; and we'll judge it to be pseudo-philosophical if it is a best fit to the model of pseudo-philosophy. And then there will perhaps be some cases where neither model fits better than the other, and so there is no best explanation in that case — which we may also view as the judgment that the author is in some ways (or at some times, or in some works) genuinely philosophical and, in others, pseudo-philosophical.

Remember that one coherent and suggestive way of viewing pseudo-philosophy is as a kind of fundamental failing on the part of the pseudo-philosopher to satisfy the attitudes, goals, and standards of the genuine philosopher. In light of Chapters 4–7 and the repeated criticisms of philosophers throughout history, pseudo-philosophy may also be seen as the result or goal of a character flaw (or moral weakness, or perhaps a pathological psychology) of the pseudo-philosopher as much as it may be seen as a fundamental error of philosophical methodology or as ineptness in applying correct philosophical methodology. An analog to this view in science and pseudo-science can be found in the distinction between the demented evil genius and the bumbling amateur. At some point, and in some way, the practice of pseudo-philosophy requires the intention to ignore or to subvert the fundamental principles of philosophy that are oriented towards truth and wisdom, and to turn instead — for one reason or another — down a path of trickery and deceit in order to render the pseudo-philosopher's analyses and teachings attractive and plausible.

We can then think of the pseudo-philosophy markers enumerated in Chapter 7 as the *symptoms* of this aberrant condition. We can likewise think of the genuine philosophy markers of Chapter 4 as symptoms (or better, *indicators* or *qualities*) of genuine philosophy. And so — for methodological purposes — we can look at any case of purported pseudo-philosophy as a subject (a writer or the writer's work) who presents us with symptoms and conditions to which we can apply principles of abduction in order to make and justify one of the judgments of philosophy or pseudo-philosophy.[10]

The simple principle of abduction

In practice, our evaluation of potential pseudo-philosophy cases will involve just one simple principle of abduction to be applied on the basis of our models (markers and personas) in deciding whether pseudo-philosophy is exhibited and whether the preponderance of the evidence justifies an overall judgment that the example is pseudo-philosophical.

The Simple Principle of Abduction (SPA)

1. Given the possible judgments of *genuine philosophy* and *pseudo-philosophy*, and results of matching pseudo-philosophy markers, genuine philosophy markers, and the Philo and Pseudo personas to an example, then
2. Conclude that the judgment of pseudo-philosophy is justified if the best match of the example is to pseudo-philosophy markers and the Pseudo persona,
3. Conclude that the judgment of genuine philosophy is justified if the best match of the example is to the genuine philosophy markers and the Philo persona,
4. Otherwise (in the absence of a clear preponderance of conformance to one model or the other) conclude that there are elements of both genuine philosophy and pseudo-philosophy in the example.

A somewhat oversimplified, but accurate summary of how we'll use this principle is

Using the Simple Principle of Abduction to make a judgment of genuine philosophy or pseudo-philosophy

Given a source that's being considered as a possible example of pseudo-philosophy, make the judgment as to whether it's pseudo-philosophy, genuine philosophy, or neither based on whether it's a better match to our model of Philo and genuine philosophy markers or to our model of Pseudo and the pseudo-philosophy markers.

In the case that neither is a more compelling match than the other, conclude that an objective overall judgment can't be made.

And now we can look at some guidelines to help us use our models and methods in detecting and determining when we're being presented with material of a pseudo-philosophical nature.

8.7 Practical guidelines

Let's begin by assuming that you're reading some material that's supposedly "philosophical in nature". The same approach will apply to listening to a talk or watching a video; so we can simplify things by just talking about reading something. Let's call that "*the article*" or "*the source*", and it could as easily be a book, a set of articles, a video or audio recording, a set of those, a Web page, a blog, and so on. Here are some broad hints of how to proceed in understanding and evaluating that article or source, with an eye towards deciding whether it contains pseudo-philosophy or is fundamentally pseudo-philosophical.

Guideline #1
Adopt the right stance

Adopt a philosophical and anti-sophistical stance, and become sensitive to any rhetorical or sophistical stance being used to sway your thought.

Using Guideline #1: In the case of reading philosophical material (or sources that employ some use of a philosophical approach), it's reasonable to assume that you're reading that material in order to learn or understand something that it seeks to teach, or that it claims to offer an insight into some problem or issue that concerns you. You should not, however come to it with a naive attitude and an unconstrained willingness to accept what you're being told. Adopt the anti-sophistical stance described in Section 3 above, beware of a lack of clarity, and identify questions that should be answered by the article or presentation (see Guideline #4 below).

Guideline #2
Pay attention to common signs of pseudo-philosophy

As we've seen in a number of examples drawn from the history of philosophy and complaints about pseudo-philosophy, pseudo-philosophers share several different tendencies or behaviors in common. Be alert to these behaviors as you assess any work with regard to its philosophical or pseudo-philosophical content. It's often easier to spot these broad behaviors than immediately to identify a specific marker in a particular example, and they can act as guides for further scrutiny.

Using Guideline #2: Our pseudo-philosophy markers enumerate behaviors and techniques that are sufficiently specific to be used in making definite judgments about the presence of pseudo-philosophy. But there are also tendencies and behaviors — more broadly and vaguely characterized — which may be more intuitive and more easily noticed by most people, and which can be used to guide your attention to our more specific markers and features of the Philo and Pseudo personas.

Frequently encountered ways in which a writer's pseudo-philosophical tendencies are exposed include attention-getting behavior, unreasonable criticisms or personal attacks on opponents, substantial time spent on garnering credit or admiration rather than on pursuing wisdom or problems and solutions. Underlying the pseudo-philosopher's pitch is often the message that "You should believe me because I have special skills, insights, abilities, and talents. Trust me."

Recall (from Chapter 6) that a strong component of pseudo-philosophy is one of *masquerade* — in the sense that the pseudo-philosopher is *pretending* to be a genuine philosopher, or to "pass herself off" as one. This will frequently appear as the pseudo-philosopher attempts to inflate his own degree of education, professional credentials and expertise, skills, experience, or list of publications. Most readers are inclined to believe what they're being told by an author. After all, who would lie about such things when surely it would be easy to see through them? But pseudo-philosophers do lie about (or heavily distort) their own accomplishments and credentials, and they often do so in such a way that it's difficult for the average reader to check up on them. We see an excellent example of this in Chapter 10.

If the pseudo-philosopher lists a number of publications that he claims to have authored — perhaps in rather important-sounding academic journals, and perhaps even in a foreign language — who but an academic researcher would go to the trouble of finding those references, verifying that they exist, verifying that the content of the publications is what it's claimed to be, that they've appeared in reputable journals, and that in fact the articles were written by the author claiming them? No: no normal reader would do this — which is to say that the typical targets of the pseudo-philosopher's deceptions wouldn't do it, and in general wouldn't even know how to go about it. But if you're taking the anti-sophistical stance and you're skeptical of his credentials, authority, or knowledge and experience, then it may be worth some attempts to see if he's being honest about his own background and experience. If you can't find those papers or books he's referred to, or you can't get to them in any way (e.g., online, or through a university library or a common book seller), then your degree of suspicion and skepticism should be heightened, and this ties in with our markers of ⊘ *Misrepresentation*, ⊘ *Exaggerated Claims*, and ⊘ *Misleading Citation*.

Another telltale sign in the same vein is seen in unfounded (and often personal) attacks on philosophers whom the pseudo-philosopher regards as her opponents. Philosophers are, of course, highly critical in their pursuit of wisdom; and they're quite demanding of other philosophers in terms of meeting standards of clarity and rigor. But any attacks should be on a philosopher's *position*, or his *arguments*, or his *principles* and their consequences, or on his *criteria of adequacy*. Instead, since the pseudo-philosopher has no basis in *genuine* philosophy she may attempt to denigrate (through the use of derisive language) or ridicule those she sees as her opponents or competitors. And she may attempt to intimidate you into going along with the picture she's painting. Chapter 11 contains some illustrations of this kind of behavior.

This behavior can go hand in hand with an aggressive variety of self-promotion in which the author diverts your attention away from issues of genuine philosophical relevance and importance, and turns instead to an attempt to undermine the character of her opponent — perhaps by references to his race or ethnicity or where he was educated, or his religious beliefs. At the same time she may inflate the significance of her own accomplishments. In many instances of pseudo-philosophy, what should be discussions pertaining to the pursuit of truth and wisdom instead turn into presentations or contests of personality. Such behavior may be seen to exhibit our markers of ⊘ *Discreditation*, ⊘ *Intimidation*, ⊘ *Discouraging Inquiry*, and ⊘ *Accusations and Excuses*, and to violate principles related to the genuine philosophy markers of Φ *Rationality* and Φ *Objectivity*.

Denigration of opponents and self-promotion are also accompanied by a technique employed by many cults: to make *you* feel special and somehow above others in your abilities to think and understand — particularly under the guidance of the pseudo-philosophical author, speaker, teacher, leader, or guru. This is accomplished by a rather persistent kind of "intellectual flattery" towards the reader or member of the audience, and we'll see some examples in Chapters 10 and 11 as well.

More generally, Guideline #2 is a recommendation to be sensitive to ways in which things don't "match up" with the Philo persona of the genuine philosopher, or ways in which they do match up with the Pseudo persona of the pseudo-philosopher — and then use those observations to guide you in a more detailed assessment in terms of markers. Be particularly sensitive to such issues as deception, obscurantism, anti-rationality, avoidance of dealing with certain questions or issues (e.g., consequences of a position), unexplained or misused jargon, use of common words in odd ways that remain unclear, false claims about credentials and accomplishments, irrelevant citations or "evidence", and the manner in which responses to opponents or critics are made.

Guideline #3
Look for markers

Familiarize yourself with the categories of markers (e.g., Markers of Integrity, Markers of Competence, Markers of Trickery, Markers of Language Abuse, etc.) and then more specifically with the individual markers within those categories such as Φ *Rationality*, Φ *Objectivity*, Φ *Domain Awareness*, ⊘ *Obscurantism*, ⊘ *Exaggerated Claims*, ⊘ *Intimidation*, etc. The more you read and apply these markers and categories, the more easily you'll see instances of them in what you're reading.

Using Guideline #3: In surveying our tools, we see that there are 11 *markers of genuine philosophy* and 19 *markers of pseudo-philosophy*. It's these that you'll be looking for in an article as you read it, and so you need to either know them or be able to refer to them as you make your way through the article. That may seem like a lot to keep in mind, and you should expect developing that ability to take some time and practice; but our treatment of the examples in the following chapters will provide you with that time and practice.

The markers have all been separated into *categories* that are a bit more intuitive and easier to remember than the specific markers themselves. It's easier, for example, as part of your anti-sophistical stance, to suspect that an author is somehow trying to trick you — and then to quickly scan the *Markers of Trickery* to see specifically what sort of trickery the author might be employing — than to try to memorize the *Markers of Trickery* from the beginning.

Guideline #4
Continually review critical questions that you should expect to be answered.

Using Guideline #4: A genuine philosopher will take care to lay out his goals, present the problems he's going to address, and then proceed to address them. This is what such markers as Φ *Problem Orientation*, Φ *Adequacy*, Φ *Clarity*, and Φ *Explanation* are all about. A pseudo-philosopher may make feints in these directions but then veer in a direction characterized by markers such as ⊘ *Obscurantism*, ⊘ *Vagueness and Equivocation*, and ⊘ *Discouraging Inquiry* while redirecting your attention away from clearly stated problems and solutions to them.

An effective way of "auditing" whether you're being presented with genuine philosophy or pseudo-philosophy is to ask yourself several critical questions at intervals as you read through an article or sit through a presentation:

Auditing with critical questions

- What did I expect to learn from this? What was I told I would be learning?

- What have I learned? Can I express this to others in a coherent way so they can understand it as well?

- What have I *not* learned that I was told I would?

- What does the author (presenter, leader, teacher, ...) want me to believe?

- What does he want me to do?

- How does this connect with a pursuit of truth and wisdom?
- What's the nature of any masquerade and what's the goal of any attempts at deception?

In addition to giving you a good overall view of whether what you're reading (and its author) is living up to reasonable and coherent expectations, the answers to these questions can point you to markers that are either present or absent in the source, and to features of the Philo and Pseudo personas that are being exhibited in it.

Guideline #5
Be guided by the degree of conformity to our models

When looking at a specific case, continually compare and contrast the markers that you're seeing, how the case exposes the persona exhibited by the author, and the degree to which this matches each of the models of genuine philosophy and pseudo-philosophy.

Using Guideline #5: These methods are oriented towards distinguishing genuine philosophy from pseudo-philosophy, and the primary goal of applying the methodology is to make a judgment about whether a particular source or author is genuinely philosophical or pseudo-philosophical. By following the first four guidelines you'll gather information necessary to make this decision and to justify it. In making that judgment, be guided by the degree that the source or author you're examining conforms or fails to conform to each of the models.

This is the *preponderance of the evidence* that supports your "inference to the best explanation" (or more accurately in our case, what is most reasonable to believe) concerning whether it's genuine philosophy or pseudo-philosophy with which you've been presented. Again, the overall question you're seeking to answer is "Is it more reasonable to conclude that this source (or author) is involved in genuine philosophy or in pseudo-philosophy?".

For the most part there will be little or no doubt, once you've reached your conclusion; and you'll be able to defend it thoroughly by means of the evidence you've gathered in terms of markers and personas. But there will — on occasion, and owing to both human nature and difficulties inherent in precisely characterizing the nature of any intellectual or academic discipline — be cases where your efforts are inconclusive, where there is no *preponderance* of the evidence, or where there appears to be both some degree of genuine philosophy and some degree of pseudo-philosophy involved.

Chapter 9
Nursing Theory, Knowledge, and Science

> *In this chapter:*
> - Nursing theory: what is it?
> - The role of philosophy in nursing theory
> - Mary Silva's philosophy of nursing knowledge
> - Pseudo-philosophy in the service of autonomy
> - Consequences for nurses and their patients

In our first case study in pseudo-philosophy we'll look at a relatively self-contained example of the use of philosophy in expressing and supporting some fundamental views and positions in Nursing Theory, how these originated, what the motivations for them are, and to what degree pseudo-philosophical elements may be present in them. This will serve as a simple example of applying the models of the philosopher and the pseudo-philosopher that have been developed in previous chapters, of identifying markers of genuine philosophy and pseudo-philosophy, and of arriving at a judgment concerning whether what we're seeing is pseudo-philosophy or something else.

9.1 A brief orientation to Nursing Theory

Nursing Theory refers to a collection of "theories" concerned with the goals, motivations, attitudes, philosophical and scientific perspectives, methods, and techniques of nurses and nursing organizations in their roles in clinical treatment, the overall practice of medicine, and the administration of patient care in private practice, hospitals, clinics, the domain of public health, and the government regulation of health care. Those involved in the development, application, and promulgation of Nursing Theory (and individual nursing theories) draw an analogy, either explicitly or implicitly, to theories in the empirical and social sciences. And foundational arguments are provided — by "nurse scholars", "nurse theorists", "nurse administrators", and others predominantly within a university context — to establish the scientific and epistemic credibility of nursing theories and the authority of those who propound and embrace them.

While some nursing theorists attempt to trace the roots of Nursing Theory back to Florence Nightingale, in fact it was not until at least the 1960s that any glimmer of genuine theorizing or theory creation began to be seen in the nursing community. This appears to be concomitant with a movement to transition nursing education to a more properly *academic* context, treat nursing more as a *profession* than a trade, and to move the production of nurses out of the trade school approach of dedicated (often hospital-based) training programs into *university-based degree programs* (B.S. in Nursing, for example, B.S.N, and M.S.N, etc.) rather than a praxis-oriented training program with the ultimate goal of licensure by a state-supervised bureaucracy. Nurses, it was beginning to be felt, weren't really very much like plumbers and electricians — or at least they shouldn't be.

Even with the glimmerings in the 1960s, what are referred to as attempts at the development of a nursing theory at that time didn't comprise a genuine *theory* (as a unified and clearly explicated set of concepts integrated into principles or laws) but remained more along the lines of a codification of goals and practices intended to distinguish nursing from the common trades in terms of its goals and how those were to be achieved. And it's generally agreed that only with Martha Rogers' 1970 publication of her book *An Introduction to the Theoretical Basis of Nursing* (Rogers 1970) was the first genuine attempt at a theory of nursing seen by nurses and the broader academic and medical communities. Rogers' overall perspective in that book was that nursing (as an activity and as a calling or profession) must be seen as both a science and an art. Out of this arose her *Science of Unitary Human Beings*, and subsequently there was an accelerated pace in the recognition and development of a nursing theory (or theories of nursing), the parallel development of larger and more influential professional nursing organizations that took such theories to form part of their intellectual foundations, the creation and evolution of academic departments in universities (oriented towards both baccalaureate and advanced degrees), and the influence of such organizations on the role of nursing in public health and medical practice.

In an attempt to avoid ambiguity and confusion, I'll use the capitalized "Nursing Theory" to refer to the broad range of nursing theories — including Nursing Metatheory (theory about nursing theories) — and the uncapitalized "nursing theory" to refer to a particular nursing theory (e.g., Rogers' nursing theory, Silva's nursing theory, etc.), at times not being specific about the referent. Owing to the vast range and sheer number of nursing theories at this time, it may be impossible to avoid all ambiguity without excessive pedantry; and so I'll often choose readability over precision when additional precision would not be helpful.

Because of the scope of Nursing Theory and the number, complexity, and variety of nursing theories, we couldn't hope to provide a fair and adequate account here of questions concerning the presence or use of pseudo-philosophy in Nursing Theory. Nor would I want to argue that all Nursing Theory is pseudo-philosophical or that in some way the very project of Nursing Theory requires pseudo-philosophy. Instead — for our first (and simplest) "case study" in applying our models of pseudo-philosophy — we'll focus on a very limited example of Nursing Theory from its early days, closely examine the appeal to philosophy in that example, see what conclusions can be drawn from that, and then suggest other ways that this could be expanded more fully in the broader Nursing Theory domain. Our primary goal here is to illustrate how the view of pseudo-philosophy developed in Part 2 of this book can be applied in a relatively simple real-world case.

9.2 The nursing theory/philosophy controversy

Discussions concerning what roles philosophy does, should, or must play in the development of Nursing Theory — and hence in nursing — are common in the now bewildering number and variety of professional nursing journals, nursing Web sites, and publications of professional nursing and public health organizations. The International Philosophy of Nursing Society, for example, is devoted specifically to research and discussions of philosophy in nursing, and it publishes the journal *Nursing Philosophy*.

None of this, even from the beginning, has proceeded without substantial controversy. And the fundamental controversy swirling in and around Nursing Theory is — quite simply — whether it makes any sense. Of course, most would agree that *parts* of Nursing Theory make sense. It's virtually impossible to make any fully general claims in this regard since there isn't a single universally accepted formulation of Nursing Theory. Indeed, some argue that such diversity and multiplicity of nursing theories is a desirable and necessary feature of an acceptable Nursing Theory. Yet everyone involved would agree that a substantial portion of Nursing Theory (and specific nursing theories) has been aggressively questioned and attacked as being unscientific, anti-scientific, anti-rational, politicized, or nonsensical. Even a brief examination of the pages of such publications as the *Journal of Advanced Nursing*, *Nursing Inquiry*, *Nursing Philosophy*, *The New England Journal of Medicine*, *Nursing and Health*, *Nursing Science Quarterly*, *American Journal of Nursing* — and other journals, conference proceedings, and books too numerous to mention — is sufficient to demonstrate the breadth and depth of the concerns and often acrimonious disputes that result.

Chapter 9: Nursing Theory, Knowledge, and Science

The controversy often involves appeals to philosophy of one sort of another, and this ranges from varieties of logical empiricism to varieties of historicism found in Kuhn, Laudan, Lakatos, and Toulmin, on to varieties of phenomenology and Marxism, and thence to the currently popular perspective of postmodernism. So there is no question in the Nursing Theory community (and in at least much of the broader nursing community itself) that philosophy is important to Nursing Theory and to a proper view of nursing as a calling and profession. But there is no agreement on exactly what roles philosophy should play, what it should be expected to contribute, and exactly *which* philosophy (or which *sort* of philosophy) should be playing those roles.

Three threads that dominate the discussion can be summarized as:

Common threads in Nursing Theory

- In order to accomplish its goals, nursing needs to be regarded as a *profession on the same level as medicine practiced by physicians*, and with its own autonomous rights, privileges, and obligations.

- This requires the creation of an *academic discipline of nursing* and the recognition of "nurse-scholars" to articulate the goals and foundations of the discipline, to perform research on nursing and its nature and application, and to formulate and enact policies appropriate to that professional discipline of nursing.

- In turn, this requires a *theoretical foundation* for that discipline grounded in both science and philosophy.

That theoretical foundation is what the nursing community (or at least a large portion of the academic and educational segment of that community) refers to as *Nursing Theory*. There seems to be broad agreement (at least among nurses) on these three points concerning how nursing should be viewed both by its own scholars and practitioners, and by those in other disciplines. Courses in Nursing Theory (often required) are offered in academic departments of nursing, and outside the university such courses are available for post-graduate nurses to take.

Problems arise when attempts are made to specify the nature of the science (particularly the "nursing science") and the nature of the philosophy that are to serve as the required foundation. At that point a significant number of nurse-scholars and nursing theorists appear anxious to abandon what they regard as the "historical" or "received" view in the history and philosophy of science and turn instead to "alternative" views of science and to philosophical perspectives that can be employed to support those alternative views. The resulting liberalization of criteria for what counts as "good science" then cascades into justifications of "alternative treatments", "alternative therapies", and "alternative medicine". And suddenly nurses are being encouraged (or required) to tolerate, to be trained in, and to apply techniques that don't appear compatible with what they were previously taught was good scientific and nursing practice. Criticisms are then voiced that the conceptual and theoretical foundations of those practices are unsound and amount to the practice of mysticism and pseudo-science.

Suspicions and skepticism

In Chapter 8 we adopted the attitudinal triad of *suspicion*, *skepticism*, and *scrutiny* as comprising our *anti-sophistical stance* that should be brought to the analysis of anything purporting to be philosophy. In the next section we'll have ample opportunity to exercise this in the context of a particular treatment of Nursing Theory; but as something of a lead-in to this, lets look briefly at some suspicions and skepticism that have been expressed by others concerning Nursing Theory and attempts at providing it with a philosophical and intellectual foundation.

Well-known computer and cognitive scientist Jef Raskin offers the following reaction as part of his brief but scathing critique of Rogers' nursing theory:

Raskin's reaction to encountering Nursing Theory

" 'Read this!' my wife said when she came home from the start of a new term at nursing school. The book she handed me was Martha Rogers' *The Science of Unitary Human Beings*. The more I read, the more I thought I was the butt of an elaborate joke she had somehow put together. 'You've got to be kidding,' I said.

'I'm not. This is one of the texts for our Nursing Theory course,' she replied, with a tone of voice and facial expression that showed her disapproval.

It wasn't just the book that was suspect. My wife's Nursing Theory course itself had a number of the hallmarks of a cult indoctrination: Any serious intellectual challenge to the basic ideas was treated as troublemaking, the leader was held in reverent awe and was regarded as having knowledge beyond the current reach of science." (Raskin 2000)

Raskin goes on to offer a number of cogent observations and criticisms of Nursing Theory and its motivations (touching quickly on some issues in the philosophy of science) that we shall return to a bit later below. While many of the most powerful and telling criticisms of Nursing Theory have been brought by members of the broader scientific community, not all has been quiet in this regard within the nursing community itself. And this report of Raskin's indicates how the theory (a product of academics and "nurse scholars") is often received by the nursing rank and file.

A number of the features and consequences of Nursing Theory and its development are critically examined by Alan Sokal, Jean Bricmont, Doug Stalker, and Clark Glymour in such works as *Fashionable Nonsense* (Sokal and Bricmont 1988), *Beyond the Hoax* (Sokal 2008), and *Examining Holistic Medicine* (Stalker and Glymour 1989), where detailed and sustained critiques are advanced against Rogers' and subsequent theories as being pseudo-scientific, devoid of sense, and without rational foundation. Sokal, for example, characterizes Rogers as one of the "intellectual precursors of pseudoscience in nursing," says of her Science of Unitary Human Beings that "From a logical or empirical point of view, there is only one appropriate word: looney," describes her attempts at scientific language and description as "mumbo-jumbo," and sketches in some detail her "devoted cult of followers" as well as some effects that her work and her followers have had on the discipline and practice of nursing. Sokal attributes their endorsement of pseudo-science to their embracing of the philosophical approach of postmodernism (which was itself subjected to a withering critique in his *Fashionable Nonsense*). More broadly, in *Beyond the Hoax*, Sokal accuses Rogers (and illustrates this with a number of examples) of simply not understanding science and of relying — at least in part — on pseudo-philosophy to support her pseudo-science. While Sokal focuses on problems in appealing to postmodernism as an underlying philosophical foundation for Nursing Theory, his observations and criticisms in fact have a broader scope and we'll review them after we've looked at our own example in the next section.

Similarly, in *Examining Holistic Medicine*, Glymour and Stalker have collected a number of different perspectives and critiques on the notion of holism in medicine and nursing. Here there are two dozen papers on the topics of holism, holistic philosophy, holistic methodology, and the holistic practice of nursing and medicine. The authors are scientists, nurses, doctors, and philosophers; and their chapters range from treatments of background and history to detailed criticisms of the very idea of holism and its applications in contemporary medicine and nursing.

Stalker and Glymour remark that "The greatest influence of the holists seems, however, to be in nursing," and for us, the most significant and informative article in *Examining Holistic Medicine* is Susan M. Williams' "Holistic Nursing". Williams is a Registered Nurse with an M.S.N. degree and CCRN (critical care) certification. She provides (from the "trenches") perceptive and clear accounts of why clinical nurses are attracted to such approaches as holism and how Nursing Theory has led them astray in their sincere desire to improve the practice of nursing and the care that's delivered to patients. We'll look at the details of Williams' views in Section 4 below in the context of our example focusing on Mary Silva's approach to using philosophy as a foundation for "nursing knowledge".

9.3 Silva's philosophy of nursing knowledge

Beginning in the late 1970s, Mary Cipriano Silva (RN, PhD, and a Fellow of the American Academy of Nursing) became a vocal proponent of the *necessity* of philosophy in developing a modern intellectual basis to nursing that would support and guide its development in the academic and professional nursing communities. Her early work in this area struck a chord in those communities (at least at the higher levels of nurse scholarship) and continues to be regarded as foundational and iconic. In this work she champions a view of nursing that she describes as "more holistic and less traditional" than one taken by the broader medical community, and she proposes a view of philosophy as providing a foundation for "deriving nursing knowledge" while advancing the even stronger view that "all nursing theory and research is derived from or leads to philosophy." What develops from these ideas is a perspective on nursing, science, and research that requires the adoption of altered concepts of evidence, theory, meaning, knowledge, and scientific validity. This in turn has been at least partly responsible for ushering in a new era of clinical treatment in nursing, educational programs for nurses, the relation of nurses to the broader medical community, and the spread and support of both alternative views of science and "alternative medicine."

Setting a context for pseudo-philosophy

In a 1977 issue of the *Journal of Nursing Scholarship,* Mary Silva published a paper titled *Philosophy, Science, Theory: Interrelationships and Implications for Nursing Research* (Silva 1977) — hereafter, *PST*. The journal's summary line of this paper was "A time to question the singular approach to nursing knowledge." This became an iconic contribution in the early history of Nursing Theory and nursing scholarship, often cited, and reprinted in at least one major Nursing Theory text. In it, Silva presents a case for the "critical use of philosophy in deriving nursing knowledge."

She begins, and then ends, the presentation of her ideas with these thoughts on what she is trying to accomplish:

Silva's announced goals for philosophy in Nursing Theory

"Although many articles have spoken to the nature of theory or science in nursing ..., few have examined the links between them and fewer yet have examined the role of philosophy in the deriving of nursing knowledge. To bridge this gap, I would like to present an overview of the relationships among philosophy, science, and theory, and then describe some implications for the conduct of nursing research." Silva 1977 59)

"In summary, when nurse researchers examine the total philosophy-science-theory triad, they develop a more holistic and less traditional approach to the possibilities of deriving nursing knowledge. They are more open to contributions of other disciplines and less likely to see the research process as though through a glass darkly." (Silva 1977 62)

In these comments, Silva introduces several concepts that reappear throughout the paper (and in subsequent writings both by her and others). The first of these is the concept of *deriving nursing knowledge*, and while this is central to Silva's concerns and recommendations for Nursing Theory and nursing practice, the precise sense of "deriving" remains unclear among such possibilities as "logically inferring" (deducing from other knowledge), "scientifically establishing" (through experimentation and confirmation), and "coming to believe through intuition or introspection." It's also unclear, from the perspective offered by Silva, in what sense nursing knowledge is *knowledge* — as opposed to, say, intuition of some sort, or mystical experience. And a third concept of importance to Silva (following Rogers) is that of holism — and how the methodology being proposed for knowledge acquisition is *holistic*.

Silva's explicit statements of her goals in the introductory and summary paragraphs of *PST* seem quite innocuous and uncontroversial. Who can disagree with the goal of presenting an overview of the potential role of philosophy in Nursing Theory, with suggesting some implications of employing philosophy in nursing research, and with considering various possibilities for broadening the concept of knowledge employed in nursing and Nursing Theory? Surely the goal here is simply to broaden the understanding of nurses and provide a wider context for the discussion of issues important to them.

But it turns out that Silva has much more specific goals in mind than these broad and innocuous ones, and those appear in the final section of her paper where she proposes a radical view of knowledge that has dramatic consequences for how nursing is practiced and how Nursing Theory is to be understood, evaluated, and justified. We'll examine the true motives and goals behind Silva's views and arguments below, after we complete a critical survey of her paper and of her appeals to philosophy in it.

◆ PHILOSOPHY AND SCIENCE: A SUPERFICIAL VIEW

PST is written in three sections that progress towards Silva's final insights into the implications for Nursing Theory and nursing practice of the use of philosophy, ethics, and philosophy of science. In the first section, "Relationships Between Philosophy and Science," Silva presents a brief (approximately two page) overview of the history of philosophy and the emergence during the Industrial Revolution of science from philosophy. This account contains several fundamental distortions or inaccuracies which should trigger some degree of suspicion and skepticism as part of our anti-sophistical stance .

For example, there is the claim that prior to the Industrial Revolution "no real distinctions were made between different kinds of knowledge." But by ignoring the development of science, logic, mathematics, and philosophy in the late middle ages, this misrepresents the status and accomplishments of each (⊘ *Misrepresentation*).

This is followed by a superficial account of the development of early modern science and its separation from "natural philosophy". We're then quickly told that "Science had taken man apart but had not put him back together," and that philosophy was once again required in order to "unify scientific findings that man as a holistic being might emerge."

At that, we must wonder what "holistic being" means and exactly how that view of man had somehow been expunged by science since it would appear that under any normal understanding of "holistic", Aristotle and the medieval philosophers and scientists (or natural philosophers) viewed man as a holistic being — but then somehow once science was no longer *called* "natural philosophy", its view of man changed? This is part of a narrative (often encountered, though infrequently stated explicitly) according to which science is unable to take a perspective of humans other than as "mechanisms", and so we need something in place of science or in addition to science in order to treat people "holistically" (whatever that may turn out to mean). At this point we're definitely seeing some degree of ⊘ *Obscurantism* and ⊘ *Vagueness and Equivocation* in the use of fundamental terms, and our suspicions should be aroused concerning exactly where Silva is going with this.

Silva ends her introductory section with a characterization of the philosopher that she pulls directly from a document created by the 1968 Association for Supervision and Curriculum Development (ASCD) Commission on Instructional

Theory; and she does this in order to provide some justification for claims that "intuition, introspection, and reasoning are some of his [the philosopher's] methodologies". In contrast, she tells us that "The scientist is primarily concerned with causality. Cause and effect, in one way or another are central to his goal of deriving scientific laws. ... His approach to understanding reality is characterized by tentativeness, verifiability, observation, and experience."

In support of these highly simplistic views of science and the philosophy of science Silva quotes repeatedly the work of three educational, social science, and behavioral science researchers — passing up the opportunity to refer to the views of those working in the natural sciences. Aside from a brief (one sentence) reference to Philipp Frank's views on probability in his 1957 book, and a fleeting nod to Israel Scheffler on how mathematics doesn't involve experimentation, Silva makes no reference to any genuine philosophers, and particularly to genuine philosophers of science such as Carl Hempel, Ernest Nagel, Herbert Feigl, and May Brodbeck whose books such as *Philosophy of Natural Science* (Hempel 1966), *Aspects of Scientific Explanation* (Hempel 1965), *The Structure of Science* (Nagel 1961), and *Readings in the Philosophy of Science* (Feigl and Brodbeck 1953) had been widely available and used heavily in philosophy of science courses for the prior 10-20 years. Nor does she mention anything like the widely read *Harvard Case Histories in Experimental Science* by James Bryant Conant (Conant 1948), or the work of Thomas Kuhn, whose *The Structure of Scientific Revolutions* (Kuhn 1962) had been first published in 1962 and was still a raging topic of interest and debate in the philosophy of science community through the 1970s and 1980s.

It's a peculiar approach to insist on the central importance of philosophy in nursing science, and then, in your defense of this thesis, ignore the entire body of contemporary Anglo-American philosophy and history of science that is most relevant to such a view. It suggests ◊ *Ignorance of Prior Work* and ◊ *Inadequate Understanding*. But more specifically, Silva's views on science indicate a lack of familiarity with the central and predominating role of scientific *theory* and its role not only in *prediction*, but also (and even more importantly) in *explanation*. Such a lack of familiarity with the history, nature, and role of theories in the empirical sciences leads Silva to focus on the hypothetico-deductive method as the predominant feature of modern science and results in many of her statements and complaints about science being unjustified and inaccurate.

This apparent ignorance of foundational issues in epistemology and philosophy of science is particularly problematic since Silva accepts uncritically as a representation of scientific meaningfulness (from an empiricist point of view) such views of empirical science as behaviorist Fred Kerlinger's that "If an explanation cannot be formulated in the form of a testable hypothesis, then it can be considered to be a metaphysical explanation and thus not amenable to scientific investigation. As such, it is dismissed by the scientist as being of no interest." At best this is an oversimplification of some very early logical positivist formulations of the verification principle of meaning which, by the 1970s had been highly criticized and rejected among philosophers. Moreover, such a view of explanation, meaning, and testability in science is simply false and ignores the rich accounts of theory construction and acceptance/rejection that had been developed by the late positivists and their successors through the 20 years prior to these publications of both Silva and Kerlinger. While this may be how Kerlinger viewed modern science, it is not an account with which researchers in the natural sciences would have agreed, and not an account with which philosophers of science — from either the empiricist or the historicist perspective — would have agreed. Unfortunately, displays of such ignorance or misinterpretation continue throughout the rest of Silva's paper and repeatedly exhibit such pseudo-philosophy markers as ⊘ *Misrepresentation*, ⊘ *Misuse of Terminology*, ⊘ *Inadequate Understanding*, and ⊘ *Ignorance of Prior Work*.

As the basis of her understanding of philosophy, philosophy of science, and the methodology of science, Silva appeals in this section of her article only to such sources as Kerlinger's *Foundations of Behavioral Research* (Kerlinger 1973), educational theorist G. F. Kneller's *Introduction to the Philosophy of Education* (Kneller 1971), historian Edward McNail Burns' *Western civilizations: Their history and their culture* (Burns 1955), social researchers S. Labovitz's and R. Hagedorn's *Introduction to social research* (Labovitz and Hagedorn 1971), and the Association for Supervision and Curriculum Development. This provides to Silva a severely limited understanding of issues in philosophy and science (about which she makes broad and fundamental claims throughout), and a very narrow perspective on the topics that concern her.

There is no indication in such appeals (or in Silva's discussion) that she has made any effort to learn, first-hand, about the philosophical problems, arguments, and proposed solutions that confront her in pursuing her goals. Instead, she appears content with what are generally second-hand presentations of a narrow spectrum of these. I'll say more about the extent and effect of this attitude later on, but for now we should simply recognize it as incompatible with the Philo persona's focus on truth, knowledge, wisdom, and critical investigation. And it represents an absence of such markers of genuine philosophy as Φ *Inquiry*, Φ *Critical Appraisal*, Φ *Methods*, and Φ *Domain Awareness*.

♦ SCIENCE AND THEORY: A CONFUSING VIEW

In her next section, "Relationships Between Science and Theory", Silva offers a characterization of "science as a system". Her treatment of this injects elements of a humanistic theism into the description of scientific knowledge and its limitations, mischaracterizes the statements that "express" science, and attempts to provide a description of the relation of science to truth that is simultaneously simplistic, narrow, and hopelessly vague in appealing to such concepts as *the nature of things as they are* and *the true nature of things* (which concepts Silva never examines critically). She offers a short list of some "characteristics of science as a system," immediately concedes that these don't distinguish science from either philosophy or "theory," complains that "the many terms used to define theory can be bewildering," and then offers us a brief list of "some common denominators of theory" (these are: set [*sic*], postulates, definitions, and hypotheses).

Throughout this treatment of science and theory Silva conflates a number of fundamental concepts (such as postulates and hypotheses) and employs terminology ("proven", "disproven", "verified", "derived", "deduced") in vague and confusing ways. Her account of definition (based, again, on material from the ASCD Commission on Instructional Theory) does not in fact provide any insight into what a definition might be, and particularly what it might be in the context of a scientific theory. Instead, she discusses the difference between primitive and theoretical terms as a firm and theory-independent distinction (although in fact a primitive term may also be a theoretical term under most construals of these) and then provides examples in which she fails to grasp that a particular term is not theoretical or primitive *simpliciter*, but only relative to a particular theory in which it appears —so that the same term may be a primitive (or theoretical) in one theory but not in another. Why she goes down this confused path of introducing the concepts of primitive and theoretical terms is not immediately clear, but a hint may appear in her statement regarding primitive terms that "They represent entities which one can only intuitively experience" — which, in addition to being untrue, works in a reference to intuition without either justifying this claim or explaining what "intuition" means in the case of intuiting what terms should be chosen to be taken as primitive in a given theory.

This section on the relationships between science and theory is replete with such examples of ⊗ *Obscurantism*, ⊗ *Misrepresentation*, ⊗ *Misuse of Terminology*, ⊗ *Puzzling Terminology*, ⊗ *Inadequate Understanding*, and ⊗ *Ignorance of Prior Work*. At the end of her exposition, Silva tells us that "The process of theory building, therefore, involves the formulation and testing of hypotheses which have been deduced from a set of statements derived from scientific knowledge and philosophical beliefs." Aside from the vague uses of "deduced" and "derived" in it, this is an unobjectionable (if very brief and generally empiricist) characterization of the relationship of hypotheses, testing, and theory in science. But we don't benefit from the two pages of misunderstood and misapplied concepts and terminology that have led up to this. And those misunderstood and misapplied concepts contribute only to a perception that in whatever way philosophy is being employed here, and to whatever degree, the pursuit of knowledge and wisdom — reflected in such markers as Φ *Inquiry*, Φ *Explanation*, Φ *Critical Appraisal*, Φ *Clarity*, and Φ *Domain Awareness* — does not appear to be of significant concern.

◆ **PROBLEMS OF CRITICAL APPRAISAL, DOMAIN AWARENESS, AND COMPETENCE**

Insight into Silva's perspective and the thoroughness of her understanding and treatment of the issues of interest to her can also be gleaned from an examination of the sources that she makes use of in guiding and justifying her views. In her characterization of science, for example, Silva relies entirely on a single philosophical source: *The Philosophy of Science: an introduction to some general aspects of science* by P. Henry van Laer (van Laer 1963), a virtually unknown philosopher who taught at Leiden University and wrote from a Thomistic perspective. This is a peculiar choice on which to base your view of modern science and its philosophy, particularly in the context of the late 1970s where a more refined empiricism had emerged in the prior two decades from logical positivism, and the historicist school of philosophy of science represented by Kuhn, Lakatos, Laudan, *et al.* was receiving intense attention in academic philosophy.

By contrast, Van Laer's work received little attention outside Catholic circles, where it finds occasional citations in Ph.D. dissertations in Catholic universities and is listed as #229 in the *Philosophy* section of the *Catholic Archive* (The Catholic Archive 2020). But three (generally disparaging) reviews were written in peer-reviewed journals of it and its view of science and scientific theory.

In his excellent and comprehensive review (McMullin 1955) in *Revue Philosophique de Louvain* of the original French edition of Van Laer's book, well-known philosopher, priest, and physicist Ernan McMullin was highly critical of Van Laer's account of science, knowledge, and theory. Among other criticisms, McMullin takes Van Laer to task for obscurantism in formulating his positions and principles, for confusing fundamental philosophical concepts such as meaning and reference, for vagueness and equivocation in his use of terminology, for deviating from the standard scientific meanings of critical terms, for confusing definition with proof, for conflating such concepts as *spiritual*, *intangible*, and *non-material*, and for misunderstanding the methods of physics and the nature of "modern abstract mathematics."

In a similar though less aggressive review (Caldin 1958) in the *British Journal for the Philosophy of Science*, E. F. Caldin (a professor of physical chemistry at the University of Kent) finds Van Laer's grasp of the nature of the natural sciences to be wanting, and expresses a concern (as McMullin did) about van Laer's appeal to such notions as *the nature of things* and "the difficulties involved in assessing the status of scientific laws and theories." He more particularly criticizes Van Laer's claims that "we have insight into the nature of things" and that "we know by direct insight" such things as "that nature is deterministic" — a view of *insight* that appears indistinguishable from Silva's notions of *intuition* and *introspection*.

A third review (Kaminski 1958) of Van Laer's book, written by Stansilaw Kaminski in Polish, appeared in *Studia Logica* (a respected international journal in logic and the philosophy of science). It is heavily critical of Van Laer's understanding of science and its philosophy, and substantially more detailed than the reviews of McMullin and Caldin. Kaminski was, like McMullin, a Catholic cleric and was a Professor of Philosophy at the Catholic University of Lublin. He was highly regarded (both within Catholic and Thomistic circles and in the broader international community of philosophy, philosophy of science, and logic) in the areas of Aristotelian-Thomistic philosophy, philosophy of modern science, methodology of modern science, methodology of metaphysics, and philosophy of mathematics.

Kaminski characterizes Van Laer's book as a simplistic and cursory treatment *both* from the perspective of Thomistic philosophy *and* from the perspective of modern science. He views it as out of date regarding the theory and methodology of the natural sciences, and as depending on a vague concept of science which includes in science both philosophy and theology (a flaw that Silva inherits from it in being unable to use it to distinguish philosophy and theory from science). Kaminski in fact offers a detailed negative critique of the very characterization of "science as a system" that Silva later employs (almost *verbatim*), endorses, and attributes to Van Laer.

We'll probably never know exactly how Silva stumbled on Van Laer and his highly criticized (and by 1977, *very* out of date) book, but it almost certainly was through some vector involving Thomistic philosophy, and so possibly through her post-graduate studies in ethics at Georgetown University. Whoever recommended it to her did Silva no service, and her use of the book as her primary philosophy of science source is very puzzling since it's hard to imagine her consulting any genuine philosopher of science and being pointed in that direction.

Can Silva be excused for being unaware of the three published reviews (twenty or more years previously) of Van Laer's book, and how these were unanimous and uniform in their criticisms of it? Perhaps, though at best it indicates a failure of scholarship for a noted nurse-scholar, and exhibits

⊘ *Inadequate understanding*, ⊘ *Ignorance of prior work*, and ⊘ *Lack of rigor*. But it isn't possible to ignore her uncritical attitude towards reading philosophy and attempting to make use of it for her own purposes.

Silva's decision to *employ* Van Laer in the way she does, her wholly *uncritical acceptance* of Van Laer's views, her lack of any attempt to find a genuinely appropriate and coherent view of the nature of science, and her comfort with leaving that goal unrealized, represent an attitude characteristic of Pseudo rather than Philo. In addition to ignoring or violating norms of scholarship, she exhibits an explicit failure to employ Φ *Critical Appraisal* and a complete *indifference to the pursuit of truth and wisdom*. Similar remarks apply to Silva's consistent appeals to the ASCD Commission on Instructional Theory, and to educational and social theorists, as authorities on theory and science.

A pseudo-philosophy of nursing knowledge

In her final section of *PST*, "Implications for Nursing," Silva presents what she believes are three "perspectives" that are "different from the traditional viewpoints about the derivation and significance of nursing knowledge". These three perspectives are:

Silva's "three perspectives" on science, theory, and philosophy

- "Ultimately, all nursing theory and research is derived from or leads to philosophy."

- "Philosophical introspection and intuition are legitimate methods of scientific inquiry."

- "Nursing knowledge arrived at by the scientific method too often sacrifices meaningfulness for rigor."

Silva believes that embracing these three perspectives — which are *substantive* claims about philosophy, knowledge, and science — will result in an opening of the minds of nurses to new "potential avenues which lead to the advancement of nursing knowledge" and free their "thinking and creativity." It will eliminate "too much rigor" in nursing theory, in the testing of nursing theory results, and in nursing practice. And it will result in "a more holistic and less traditional approach to the possibilities of deriving nursing knowledge."

Now in the common sense world, outside of any context of philosophical or abstract academic or intellectual discussion, we would be strongly inclined to regard Silva's statement that *introspection and intuition are legitimate methods of scientific inquiry* as incoherent and representative of a thorough misunderstanding of what science is. But, employing the Principle of Charity, we may realize that this depends on precisely what "inquiry" may mean. Let's see where that takes us.

In support of these perspectives Silva offers the following observations and claims in proposing that intuition be adopted as an epistemic method, *on the same level as scientific method*, to yield knowledge; and that it be recognized as producing *nursing knowledge* and justifying knowledge claims in nursing:

Silva's view of intuitionistic knowledge

- "Historically and traditionally, nurses have been indoctrinated into a singular approach to the derivation of nursing knowledge — the scientific method."
- "[M]any graduate nursing students have been indoctrinated into a methodology of nursing research which excludes anything but strict adherence to the scientific method."
- "Nursing knowledge arrived at by the scientific method too often sacrifices meaningfulness for rigor."
- "This stress on scientific method continues strongly today."
- "The time has come to value truths arrived at by intuition and introspection as much as those arrived at by scientific experimentation."
- "[T]he scientist has no greater claim to truth than does the theoretician or the philosopher."
- "Intuition is not knowledge arrived at out of nothing; it is knowledge arrived at by a deep grasp of a subject."

What we see here is a view expressing two primary points. The first of these is that nurses have historically and traditionally been "indoctrinated" (and even coerced) into taking a view of knowledge that is too restrictive in the context of nursing and the goals of nurses. This view appears with some frequency throughout the literature of Nursing Theory, and it's often coupled with complaints of sexism (since historically most nurses have been female) and elitism (on the part of the scientific research community and doctors, who historically have tended to be male). In the first section of her article *Therapeutic touch and postmodernism in nursing* (Glazer 2001), for example, Sarah Glazer details such complaints and refers to the resentment against doctors as a "male-dominated oppressor group" and to nurse-scholar Patricia Valentine's characterization of nursing as a "female-dominated field and a 'ghettoized', demeaned profession because it is associated with traditional female, domestic values like caring, rather than skill" (Glazer's words). This view then sees nurses — historically — as comprising a disadvantaged social class, dominated by doctors and scientists, constrained to employ methods that are appropriate for the *doctors'* goals and tasks, and lacking the autonomy to make decisions commensurate with *nurses'* responsibilities, goals, and skills. A new approach to nursing knowledge is seen as a way to break this tradition of domination and establish nursing as an autonomous profession.

The second point expressed by Silva in proposing her intuition-based theory of knowledge for nursing is that intuition (and introspection) can provide the basis for this theory, and so separate it from the epistemology of science, which she repeatedly characterizes as overly "rigorous". In fact, it appears that the *only* philosophical argument appearing in this paper of Silva's is an argument she advances in support of her thesis that intuition should be recognized as being as rational and as acceptable a basis for knowledge claims as are the methodologies of science. Let's see how that works out.

Fatal philosophical flaws

Silva's argument for her intuition-based concept of knowledge is quite short — in fact, two brief paragraphs in her final section:

Silva's argument for intuition as a method of achieving knowledge

"Intuition is not knowledge arrived at out of nothing; rather, it is knowledge arrived at by a deep grasp of a subject, although one may not be able to articulate the process by which a conclusion is reached. The derived knowledge may not always be correct, but neither is knowledge arrived at with all the advantages of the scientific method. The large numbers of unsubstantiated hypotheses support this assertion.

In addition, knowledge gained through introspection cannot be overlooked as it constitutes one of the major approaches to the derivation of knowledge-rationalism. The prime example, of course, is mathematics where truth is deduced from reasoning and not contingent on observation or experience. According to [(Scheffler 1965)], mathematicians conduct no experiments, surveys, or statistics, yet 'they arrive at the firmest of all truths, incapable of being overthrown by experience (p. 3)'."

Considered as an exercise in philosophy, as providing philosophical support for a thesis, or as offering an argument for her position, this is simply dreadful.

The first problem with this argument is that it never attempts to provide us with any sense in which intuition can be thought of or practiced as a *method*. Compare this situation to the scientific side of things where we have an abundance of methods and well-documented methodology: which is to say, carefully (rigorously) described procedures, often with carefully described measuring equipment and observational techniques, a step-by-step process for applying such procedure in a particular case, and a carefully described procedure for determining what the result is and whether it is dependable (as an observation, a measurement, etc.).

Now certain philosophers (Bergson and Deleuze come to mind) have discussed intuition "as a method", although it's far from clear whether the concepts of intuition in those cases are even coherent. There is in addition Descartes's notion of intuition which might be pressed into service by Silva, but Descartes appears to be a bit more discouraging about using intuition in the (more empirical) way that Silva desires. He refers, for example, to the problem of actually acquiring an intuition that can be regarded not only as *dependable*, but as something of which "there can be no room for doubt," and the examples he gives are all mathematical or conceptual — and so not at all what Silva seems to need or have in mind for the empirical domain. He specifically excludes "the fluctuating testimony of the senses or the deceptive judgment of the imagination as it botches things together" — which seems almost as though it's a prescient warning to Silva *not* to go in that direction. Silva concedes, in fact, that her notion of intuition fails to yield the certainty that Descartes' does, but she wants only to argue that it produces a kind of knowledge that is *as good as* that yielded by science.

We'll leave aside any possible criticisms of the notions of intuition found in Descartes, Bergson, and Deleuze since Silva neither refers to them nor appears to have them in mind or even to be aware of them. In fact, she seems to have nothing more in mind than the everyday concept of intuition as some sort of *feeling* you have that something is true. She in fact never hints at anything that appears in any way to be a *method* or to be methodical. So throughout her paper, Silva's notion of intuition remains wholly obscure. This presents the most significant problem in evaluating her claims and recommendations concerning the use of intuition in acquiring nursing knowledge: we really have no idea what "intuition" *means*, other than as a reference to a vague feeling, impression, or hypothesis or guess, perhaps loosely linked to some experience or experiences. And this illustrates how such ⊘ *Obscurantism* and ⊘ *Vagueness and Equivocation* can render a philosophical argument or position to be unintelligible and useless. We can't, from the high ground of our anti-sophistical stance, agree with Silva (or even intelligibly disagree with her) because *we don't know what she means*. But this isn't all that's wrong with Silva's argument and view of intuition in nursing knowledge.

Silva needs to convince us that a belief arrived at through intuition is as good as a belief arrived at through the scientific method. Here, we take "as good as" to mean *as reliable as, as dependable as*, or *as useful as*. Remember, Silva's claim is that *the scientist has no greater claim to truth than does the theoretician or the philosopher* and that we must *value truths arrived at by intuition and introspection as much as those arrived at by scientific experimentation*. But *can* we? What reason does she give us the think that we can?

◆ CONFLATIONS, CONFUSIONS, AND BAD LOGIC
⊘ KNOWN FALLACY, ⊘ INADEQUATE UNDERSTANDING

The problem with this view of intuition's being a reliable method for attaining knowledge is that it's not a *method*, it's not *reliable*, and it doesn't result in *knowledge* — at least not in the direct way that Silva needs it to. Her argument that intuition is as reliable as science in representing truth and knowledge is expressed in her statement that

> "The derived knowledge may not always be correct, but neither is knowledge arrived at with all the advantages of the scientific method."

And this is an abbreviated form of the argument:

Silva's fallibility argument that intuition is as reliable as science

- *Premise 1*: Science is not infallible and at times leads to conclusions and beliefs that turn out to be incorrect.

- *Premise 2*: Intuition is not infallible and at times leads to conclusions and beliefs that turn out to be incorrect.

- *Conclusion*: Therefore, we should regard science and intuition as equally reliable with respect to the conclusions they yield, and we should regard the results of each as knowledge (or at least as rationally held belief).

More briefly put: If two events or processes both lead us to adopt beliefs about the world, and if neither yields us *certain knowledge*, then the one provides us with as good grounds for our beliefs as the other does.

But this is an example of a kind of faulty reasoning that would be recognized immediately by any competent philosopher or (one would hope) by any student who had ever taken a course in logic or critical thinking. In fact, there are several different fallacies that it can be seen to illustrate, and I'll leave as an exercise for the reader the task of finding those. But it is perhaps easiest and most natural to see this argument as a ⊘ *Known Fallacy* of the *Weak analogy* type described in Section 7.2.

The problem for Silva in such an argument is the *degree* to which scientific method and reasoning fails to be fallible — or, more to the point, the degree to which scientific method and reasoning is *successful* in producing accurate predictions and beliefs that are borne out in applying them in the real world. As I mentioned previously, no one can dispute the role that science (and so the scientific method) has played in creating the world we live in today — which includes the highly successful treatments of a significant number of diseases and conditions that previously were responsible for the deaths or miserable lives of untold numbers of people. That's a significant record that no one can dispute. How many diseases and medical conditions has intuition treated or cured? How would you make the case that it was *intuition* that *justified* our beliefs and *justified the application* of those beliefs to achieve results in the real world?

By contrast, intuition (whatever you may mean by it) has been shown to be of (at best) unpredictable success and value. Silva attempts to buttress the image of intuition by pointing to mathematics as an area in which it is often used. But this indicates only that she has no idea of what she's talking about. Certainly intuition (in one sense or another) may appear in the generation of hypotheses or ideas to be further pursued. But *the intuition* is not *itself* knowledge or rational belief. And the history of mathematics (and indeed science) is littered with the rubble of dead intuitions that turned out to be false. These include the well-known paradoxes in the theory of sets and the theory of numbers, infinity, and paradoxes involving naming, denotation, and truth.

Then there are the numerous paradoxes and unintuitive phenomena encountered in natural science itself. A lengthy list of paradoxes — all of which involve faulty intuitions that need to be replaced by rigorous thought — can be found in the (Wikipedia 2020g) *List of Paradoxes*. Appealing in any way to mathematical intuition as a paradigm of intuition's being (Silva's exact words) "knowledge arrived at by a deep grasp of a subject" is in fact to choose the worst example of any possible relation of intuition to knowledge. No mathematician regards intuition as *knowledge* or as *justifying* claims to knowledge or to rational belief. Throughout her treatment of intuition and its role in leading to knowledge, Silva has thoroughly conflated *discovery* (in which intuition, suitably characterized, may play a significant role) with justification (in which appeals to intuition are entirely out of place).

Lest we think that these numerous and well-known paradoxes are merely a collection of esoterica illustrating the undependable nature of intuition in the real world, consider this simple test: Ask any class of students (from elementary school through college) "If you drop a 10 lb. weight and a 1 lb. weight from the same height, which will hit the ground first?" A significant number of students in the class will get it wrong. In fact, a majority of students will get it wrong. In general, anyone not having had a course in physics will get it wrong — *because the answer is counter-intuitive*. And this despite the fact that we all have vast experience in dropping and throwing objects of various weights under various conditions. It required scientists (including Galileo and others) to demonstrate the correct answer — by using rigorous scientific method and in addition providing a rigorous logical explanation based on scientific theory — in the 16th century. A version of the experiment was repeated by an Apollo 15 astronaut in 1971, using a feather and a hammer in the airless atmosphere of the moon.

The point of these observations about intuition in mathematics and in empirical contexts is that intuitions cannot be regarded as *sources of knowledge* as Silva wishes. Trying to prop up this view with any amount of philosophy must fail. And Silva's attempts to do so expose her ⊘ *Inadequate Understanding* of the problems that she faces in attempting to use her amorphous concept of intuition as a "method" in justifying knowledge claims.[11]

- ♦ QUESTIONS UNADDRESSED AND UNRESOLVED
  ⊘ SPECIAL PLEADING, ⊘ SUPERFICIAL RESPONSE, ⊘ LACK OF RIGOR

In addition to Silva's failure to provide any clear picture of what she regards as intuition, her failure to indicate how intuition may be used in a *methodical* way, and the fundamental logical error in her argument comparing the reliability of intuition to scientific method, she fails to address — and even to consider — obvious and elementary *counterexamples* to her claims about the role that intuition can play in justifying claims of belief and knowledge:

1. *What happens if the intuition of one nurse differs from the intuition of another nurse — even if both have a deep grasp of the subject involved?*

    How is such a dispute to be resolved? Or is this just regarded as an instance where intuition can't be used in the way envisioned by Silva? This is a genuine conundrum that's a direct result of the subjective nature of intuition (and introspection) — and of the underlying subjective and relativistic concepts of knowledge and truth. And don't we know from our own frequent experience how likely it is for people's intuitions to differ from one another? The history of mathematics, science, and philosophy demonstrates the likelihood of divergent (and often incompatible) intuitions among even the most careful thinkers in those fields. Yes, sometimes our intuitions turn out to be true. But often not. And yes, a group of people may share an intuition; but another group may share an intuition incompatible with that one. This question about resolving conflicts of intuition has no obviously satisfactory (or even coherent) answer, and Silva fails to acknowledge it in any way.

2. *What happens if intuition differs from the results of scientific experimentation and testing?*

    This question is quite problematic. If the answer is that science always wins, then this seems to contradict Silva's claims about the autonomous reliability of intuition and about science having "no greater claim" to truth than does intuition. But if we don't always regard science as representing the more reliable and more rational and better supported choice in such a case, then where is the reasoning and argument that intuition can *ever* provide the better one? And how would this even be determined? Scientifically? Or as a matter of anecdotal reporting? Or faith?

3. *What happens if a nurse's intuition conflicts with other beliefs (perhaps not the result of scientific methodology) that can be argued to be both rational and supported by substantial experiential or anecdotal evidence?*

    This question is similar to 2, but replaces the potential deciding role of science with a less formal approach such as anecdotal evidence. Silva hints in a couple of places that often what she thinks of as intuition is based on such experience and evidence. But we're still left with the possibility of conflict between, for example, a belief supported by widely accepted anecdotal evidence and a particular nurse's intuition.

4. *What legal (e.g., negligence, malpractice) liabilities and consequences may there be in appealing to a nurse's intuition as justification for treatment that deviates from adopted best practices or scientifically established knowledge?*

    Here we envision a situation where a nurse has performed some service to a patient as part of the patient's treatment, but the result has not been what was expected and the patient or his family have sued on grounds of malpractice. Is it expected that the nurse could use her intuition as a legal defense of the malpractice charge?[12]

5. *What distinguishes intuition in its epistemic role of justifying beliefs, actions, and practices from other sources of personal experience (such as religious or mystical experience, the effects of various psychological conditions such as schizophrenia, or the use of psychoactive drugs)?*

If we are to recognize the "nonrational aspects of rationality", where do we draw the line and how do we tell when to do it? Opening the door to one kind of subjective and personal knowledge opens it wide enough for other kinds of knowledge to crowd through it. How can the line be drawn to allow Silva's variety of intuition (whatever that is) to be used as a justification for claims about belief and knowledge, and for treatment by nurses in clinical settings, but forbid other personal and subjective "ways of knowing" to be used in the same way and in the same contexts?

It may not be easy to provide answers to these questions. But the questions themselves are not difficult to state, and they all should spring into the mind of anyone presented with Silva's proposals concerning the role intuition should play in "nursing knowledge". Silva herself cannot be unaware of them and the challenge they represent to the very coherence of those proposals and to her views of nursing knowledge. Not only does she fail to attempt any answers to them, but she never even acknowledges them or the fundamental problems they represent.

These are examples of ⊘ *Special Pleading* (both by ignoring unfavorable consequences to her views and in providing a weak representation of them), ⊘ *Superficial Response*, and ⊘ *Lack of Rigor* (although, given Silva's general lack of respect for rigor, we should perhaps not be surprised that she fails to employ it herself). Acknowledging these questions, and at least presenting them to the reader as issues to be dealt with, would go a long way towards demonstrating that Silva's goals in using philosophy involve the pursuit of truth and wisdom (or at least that she *values* that pursuit). But her failure in mentioning them instead suggests that her goals are more rhetorical and sophistical than philosophical.

Results and motives

As we saw at the beginning of the previous section, Silva's explicitly announced goals in *PST* are fairly vague, and appear to be quite innocuous — seeming only to suggest that an attention to philosophy in Nursing Theory can be beneficial in expanding nurses' understanding of their profession and opening a broader context for discussion. But we've also seen what appears to be Silva's continuing reluctance and failure in devoting the necessary effort to mastering and applying the knowledge and methods required to accomplish these goals on a foundation of genuine philosophy. The result has been a continuous trail of pseudo-philosophy markers and failures to exhibit the fundamental aspects of the Philo persona. This makes a strong case for deeming Silva's paper and proposal to be pseudo-philosophical, but one element of this case is still missing.

In Section 6.2 (*Dimensions of the Pseudo*) I raised the question of whether the pseudo-philosopher is a bumbling fool or an evil genius and proposed, on conceptual and historical grounds, a model of pseudo-philosophy in which both dimensions of *incompetence* and *exploitation* were represented. In Section 7.3 I then asked whether we should be willing to regard someone who was merely incompetent in philosophy as being a pseudo-philosopher, or rather require that the pseudo-philosopher exhibit at least some degree of exploitation or dishonesty. And the view that I adopted there was that a judgment of pseudo-philosophy (for our purposes in this book) would require demonstrating at least some degree of intentional deceit and dishonesty. A strong case for philosophical incompetence has been made for Silva in this instance, but is there a case for exploitation? The answer, I think, is clearly yes.

It's one thing to suggest that attention to, and knowledge of, philosophy may contribute various benefits to the development and understanding of Nursing Theory. That seems uncontroversial and is almost certainly true. But it is quite another for pursuit of that goal to end in the proposal of an approach to knowledge that is intended at least as a competitor to science in certain respects and under certain conditions, and is furthermore a radical proposal to recognize intuition and introspection as sources and justifications for knowledge claims that may in fact conflict with those of science. Yet this is the *only* substantive proposal and application of philosophy to be found in Silva's paper. And this is not the end point of a natural progression of employing philosophy to broaden the discussion of topics in Nursing Theory, to be "more open to contributions of other disciplines," or "to see the research process" in a different way.

◆ SILVA'S UNDERMINING OF SCIENCE WITH PHILOSOPHY

In considering the "Relationships between Science and Theory," Silva begins by advancing a mildly (and not unreasonable) skeptical view of knowledge according to which "Man is no longer able to know all things." But this quickly gives rise to a more concerted attack on the possibility of attaining objective knowledge according to which "What constitutes truth is a vexing epistemological question," man is unable "to know the true nature of things," and (a leap

Section 9.3: Silva's philosophy of nursing knowledge

here) the job of the scientist is to "estimate the truth responsibly." In her "Implications for Nursing", Silva begins to conflate the various concepts of knowledge and belief (along with truth and "truth conditions").

Silva maintains that "By identifying and applying the contributions of epistemology to nursing, nurse researchers can gain further insights into the research process." But by failing to make or acknowledge the fundamental philosophical distinctions among belief, irrational belief, rational belief, justified belief, justified true belief, knowledge, and certain knowledge (which form the core of concepts dealt with in classical epistemology), Silva sets the stage for introducing intuition and introspection as sources of knowledge yielding *truths* which are to be valued "as much as those arrived at by scientific experimentation." And so she arrives at her radical view that "the scientist has no greater claim to truth than does the theoretician or the philosopher" — buttressing this with her specious argument that because both science and intuition are fallible approaches to acquiring knowledge (i.e., neither yields *certainty*), then they are equally successful and reliable.

This progressive undermining of the epistemic power and reliability of science (which forbids intuition and introspection as *justifications* of knowledge claims) results from a blurring of the lines between belief and reasonable/rational belief, reasonable belief and knowledge, and knowledge and certainty. It also makes knowledge claims based on intuition and introspection impervious to scientific criticism — by being a different *kind* of knowledge with its own "truth and belief conditions," and so not being open to criticisms from the research and medical *establishments* with their narrow focus on *scientific* knowledge. Or so the argument goes. And this has been Silva's goal all along: to stake out a territory of "nursing science" which can be defended against the requirements of "rigor" and scientific methodology.

The intentional (and deceptive) blurring of the lines among these critical epistemological concepts and how they function in science (and more generally in evaluating claims to reasonable belief and knowledge) is an *exploitative technique* that renders Silva's analysis and proposals an exercise in rhetoric and sophistry. And additional insight into the motivation behind such an approach can be found in criticisms by a number of authors concerning the misuse of philosophy in the creation and justification of nursing theories.

◆ MOTIVES AND THE BROADER CONTEXT

In addressing the question of why holism enjoys such a success among nurses and nursing theorists, Susan M. Williams, in her article "Holistic Nursing" (Williams 1989), lists the "strong need for a professional identity separate from that of medicine". In turn this is driven by nurses' desires for independent credibility, recognition for their contributions, and achieving a higher degree of control over the practice of nursing. Williams then sees the attraction nurses have to holism not as one based on it's alleged improved or broadened approach to knowledge and epistemology, but as a practical way of differentiating between nursing and medicine — that is, as an instrumental way of getting out from under the onerous demands that the medical establishment imposes in the form of scientific rigor. She attributes the unwillingness of nurses to be more skeptical and critical of holistic approaches to the fact that nurses as a group "lack a rigorous background in traditional science and its criteria for research." And she advocates that nurses resist the "uncritical adoption of unorthodox practices, meaningless and banal jargon, and unsupported claims of efficacy derived from poor data".

In her landmark article "Therapeutic touch and postmodernism in nursing" (Glazer 2001), Sarah Glazer raises the question "How have techniques steeped in mysticism gained such a foothold in the nursing profession?" She refers to "sophisticated philosophical rationales made by nurses for abandoning scientific method" (meaning, particularly, postmodernism) and "misreading philosophy in the service of an antiscientific world-view," which I have argued is exactly what we see in this case of Silva's approach. Glazer specifically mentions epistemology as a term that takes on a meaning often unrecognizable in terms of the theory of knowledge as this is conceived by traditional philosophers.

While in the paper we've just examined, Silva has chosen for her philosophical underlayment the dubious work of P. H. Van Laer, in her later paper with Daniel Rothbart (Silva and Rothbart 1984) she goes all-in with the (then currently popular) Thomas Kuhn and Larry Laudan; and Van Laer has disappeared from view. It is therefore amusing in Glazer's paper to encounter Susan Gortner's complaint that nurse theorists take a "philosopher of the month" approach to choosing a philosophical foundation for their work (Gortner 1993).

This isn't surprising since in 1983 Silva was recommending that nurse theorists update their theories to make use of what are the "current trends in philosophy of science" — although she does acknowledge an annoying problem in following this path since it requires nursing theorists to continually update textbooks they've authored to conform to the new more popular philosophical approach as they throw the old one under the bus.

This approach to what we might think of as *philosophy consumerism* in no way, of course, resembles a pursuit of truth and wisdom, but rather a pursuit of academic fashion since Silva does not recommend *evaluating* the current trends and comparing them to past trends in order to determine which (or which parts) of the new trends may be *better suited* for nursing theory, or even in order to determine if the newer trends are *better in some relevant way* with regard to nursing theory. Instead, she suggests updating to the newer trends *because they are the current trends* and so presumably better (for nursing) because they have become *more popular* (in academic philosophy) — illustrating the appropriateness of Alan Sokal's description of "fashionable nonsense" for such approaches. Quite clearly, her view is that whatever is being served at the philosophy window today (the philosophy *de jour* or *à la mode*) should be accepted uncritically as reflecting newly revealed truth, and so adopted by nursing theorists as authoritative. This may be a path to the height of current intellectual fashion, but it is not the road to knowledge and wisdom.

Glazer later (in her attempt at explaining the attraction of nurses to the philosophies of Heidegger and Husserl), describes the inclination of nurse-theorists to "borrow from" different philosophers in a shallow and haphazard manner (as we've seen Silva do in the case of Van Laer, and later Kuhn and Laudan), with little attempt to understand the material being borrowed. She accurately and succinctly characterizes this behavior among nurse-scholars as "essentially employing fancy code words for the same goal: abandoning scientific research methods". In *Beyond the Hoax* (Sokal 2008), Alan Sokal also says of Martha Rogers (another icon of Nursing Theory) that she *borrows* terms from physics and then throws them around without regard for their meaning. Such behavior of *borrowing terminology* from an established theoretical domain and mixing it indiscriminately and obscurely is a common feature of pseudo-science and pseudo-philosophy (represented by our pseudo-philosophy markers ⊘ *Misrepresentation*, ⊘ *Misuse of Terminology*, and ⊘ *Inadequate Understanding*).

Again, what we see in this is the exploitation of philosophy to fit a predetermined goal of eliminating the rigorous logical and empirical requirements of science (and more broadly, rational epistemology) from being used as criteria in judging the intelligibility of the newly proposed concept of *nursing knowledge* — thereby freeing the Nurse Theorist from this constraint and achieving independence and separation from the dominating methodologies and institutions of science and medicine. From this perspective, Silva's early approach in 1977 can be seen as a precursor to the later use in Nursing Theory of philosophies such as historicism (Kuhn, Laudan, et al.), phenomenology (Heidegger and Husserl), and postmodernism (Derrida, Deleuze, et al.) in the battle for achieving independence of nursing as its own profession, with its own theory, its own research methodology, its own academic discipline, and its own authority.

We must also keep in mind that it's not merely the exploitative use of philosophy in support of these goals that makes that use pseudo-philosophical. Not all use of philosophy in Nursing Theory has amounted to pseudo-philosophy. Using philosophy to achieve a non-philosophical goal does not, in itself, result in pseudo-philosophy. And we should hope not, lest philosophy never be of any practical value. Rather, it is the *uncritical, unreflective*, and *cynical* use of philosophy, incompatible with the pursuit of truth and wisdom, that makes that use pseudo-philosophical.

9.4 Consequences of pseudo-philosophy for Nursing Theory

By following the guidelines of Chapter 8, taking an anti-sophistical stance, looking for markers of pseudo-philosophy and genuine philosophy, and comparing the persona that Silva presents to those of Philo and Pseudo, we see that there's substantial evidence to support a judgment that this work of Silva's is pseudo-philosophical. When we further consider her motives for proposing a radical approach to the concept of knowledge in Nursing Theory and nursing science, see how these lead her to distort and obscure the presentation of critical concepts, to employ faulty reasoning, and to ignore obvious and fundamental questions about her proposals, we see that her approach is a close match to Pseudo's while lacking the features of Philo's required in a pursuit of truth and wisdom. As a consequence, a judgment of pseudo-philosophy in this case appears unavoidable.

But what about other consequences? In such a case of pseudo-philosophy we should expect to see — or at least be able to predict — some consequences of following the views and proposals offered. In Silva's case we're able to do this in part because her recommendations serve as a precursor to later recommendations proposing the use of intuition, introspection, and other "holistic" and obscure methods in Nursing Theory and nursing practice. And so accounts and predictions of such consequences are not purely speculative. We'll now mention some of these; and others are easily found by searching literature in nursing and medical journals.

The primary point for us in our study and models of pseudo-philosophy in cases such as this is that *pseudo-philosophy is used to support concepts and positions in pseudo-science*, and *the application of pseudo-science has direct consequences in the real world*. Particularly in the case of Nursing Theory, if you take away the pseudo-philosophy, then the pseudo-science cannot stand up to any degree of scrutiny at all. It is the pseudo-philosophy that serves to shield the pseudo-science from certain types of criticism by proposing an alternative view of knowledge and reasonable belief.

An argument often given in favor of holistic treatments is "They seem to work for a lot of people in a lot of cases (using informal and 'qualitative' means of assessment such as patients' self-reports of results)." So what's the harm? But in her article on therapeutic touch and postmodernism mentioned above,

Section 9.4: Consequences of pseudo-philosophy for Nursing Theory

Sarah Glazer, reports an example provided by nurse Kevin Courcey (Courcey 2019) which points out that the placebo effect often demonstrated by holistic treatments may result simply in the masking or ignoring of sever underlying causes (as in the case of indigestion caused by gastric ulcer, pain caused by as yet undiagnosed cancer, etc.) until a catastrophic result presents itself. And so employing "non-rigorous" methods and "alternative concepts of knowledge" to justify the use of holistic methods such as healing touch can have disastrous consequences for patients rather than the "no harm" worst-case result envisioned by practitioners of the pseudo-science. This observation is not speculative.

Sarah Glazer (2001) reports an interview in which Linda Rosa describes a malpractice suit resulting from treating a post-surgical patient with healing touch after he had been given a maximum dose of pain medication and still complained of severe pain. The patient became severely disturbed at the treatment (thinking that someone had been called to perform the Last Rites on him), no doctor was ever called, the patient was released, and returned three days later with an infected bladder that had to be removed in a second surgery. If you were the holistic nurse in question, what could you possibly offer the court that might be regarded as a defense of your holistic therapy in such a case — that in "qualitative studies" a "significant proportion" of patients reported "feeling better" as a result of the "therapy?" Or would you prefer to explain to the judge your relativist view of knowledge and how your intuitionistic understanding is as good as science and the scientific method?

In his *"Modern Medicine and the Postmodernist Challenge: Examining the Issues"* (Doyle 2013), Cleveland Clinic Professor of Anesthesiology D. John Doyle points to a significant movement in the HIV/AIDS community that holds — on the basis of pseudo-scientific and pseudo-philosophical arguments — that treating AIDS with antiviral agents is ineffective and inappropriate, that such therapies are excessively toxic, and that AIDS organizations are in bed with the big pharmaceutical companies. And he mentions the effects that such views have had on public policy regarding AIDS treatment, particularly in South Africa. The arguments advanced in favor of such views follow the path that Silva blazed with her and her followers' appeals to alternative ways of knowing, social relativism of truth and knowledge, and multiple realities. Doyle's final line in his article is "How many more cases of AIDS will result from dangerous and false ideas? No one really knows."

Damien Contandriopoulos is a Professor in the School of Nursing at the University of Victoria, and between 2014 and 2019 held a Canadian Institutes of Health Research Chair in Public Health. In his invited commentary "About academic bullshit in nursing" (Contandriopoulos 2019) he offers three brief examples from publications by revered Nursing Theory authors as illustrations of what he calls an "ostensive definition" of bullshit. He then argues (*contra* Silva *et al.*) that appeals to "subjectivist conceptualizations" borrowed from philosophy "weaken the potential for productive intra-disciplinary debates," and that this is "deeply damaging to the field [of nursing] itself."

Contandriopoulos goes on to consider further detrimental effects of bullshit, which in large part he identifies with the influences on Nursing Theory of postmodernism and the type of "subjectivist conceptualizations" we've seen in the case of Silva's pseudo-philosophical appeal to intuition and introspection. His observations about this are that such an approach to nursing and Nursing Theory (1) impedes the understanding of the world, (2) by employing useless and ambiguous language, weakens the connection between participants in discussions, language, and reality, and (3) becomes a "tool to foster obedience." He concludes that what he refers to as "academic bullshit" resulting from appeals to postmodernist and other subjectivist orientations towards knowledge and belief is "actually dangerous for the scientific effort" because it results in a focus on ideological language and philosophical interpretation of meaningless and useless subjectivist theories — rather than on *understanding the world or improving practice* (i.e., pursuit of truth and wisdom).

These remarks indicate the consequences that an approach like Silva's — based on pseudo-philosophy and its support of pseudo-science — can have for nursing, Nursing Theory, and nursing patients. The blurring of the boundaries among belief, justified belief, true belief, and knowledge can result in (and has resulted in) the adoption of treatments that are ineffective, expensive, dangerous to patients, and dishonestly presented. Ironically, this leads to the additional consequence that the very goals claimed by nursing theorists, and for which in some cases the pseudo-philosophical foundations are provided — the goals of making nursing an autonomous and respected profession and academic discipline, along with the integrity and reputations of practicing nurses and professional nursing organizations — will be subverted, damaged, and severely weakened to the degree that philosophical support of its conceptual foundations is seen to be only an exercise in sophistry.

Chapter 10

The Curious Case of Keith Raniere

> *In this chapter:*
> - Keith Raniere, the philosopher
> - Philosophy in Raniere's publications, presentations, and representations
> - Rational Inquiry™ — a patented philosophical technology?
> - Making a judgment
> - The role and effects of pseudo-philosophy

After a five-hour deliberation on Wednesday, June 19, 2019 in a U.S. Federal District Court in Brooklyn, N.Y., Keith Raniere was found guilty by a jury on all counts brought against him. The U.S. Attorney in charge of the case, and the FBI Director in Charge remarked that

> "As found by the jury, Keith Raniere masqueraded as a self-help guru to gain the trust of his followers, and then exploited them for his own financial gain and sexual gratification," — *Richard Donoghue, U.S. Attorney for the Eastern District of New York*
>
> "Nxivm's so called self-help programs did anything but help the women they professed to empower. What's been proven today is that Keith Raniere preyed on the vulnerabilities of his many female victims, sold them lies and other falsehoods, and committed horrifying acts of coercion. This guilty verdict is a welcome end to a case that highlighted the many avenues of criminal activity pursued by a man whose intentions were deplorable beyond belief." — *FBI Assistant Director-in-Charge William F. Sweeney*
>
> ["Jury Finds Nxivm Leader Keith Raniere Guilty of All Counts" (U.S. Department of Justice 2019)]

Chapter 10: The Curious Case of Keith Raniere

After a lengthy delay, on October 27, 2020, and following testimony by 15 victims, Raniere was sentenced to 120 years in prison and ordered to pay a fine of $1.75 million. How did Raniere (and some of his associates who were also convicted) end up like this? And what does it have to do with philosophy and pseudo-philosophy?

Some initial hints can be found in references of the U.S. Attorney to Raniere's claims about being a "savant and a genius" and to the "cult-like organization" he created and maintained. And we should take note of the mention of Raniere's having *masqueraded* as a self-help guru since we know (Section 6.1) that masquerade has been regarded as an essential component of pseudo-philosophy. But Raniere's path to the Brooklyn courtroom was long and twisted.

- Was Raniere acting as a philosopher and presenting himself as a philosopher?
- How was philosophy (and an appeal to the significance of philosophy) used by Raniere?
- What did this accomplish?
- What were the consequences?

10.1 Background

Keith Raniere was born on August 26, 1960 in Brooklyn, New York. His father James worked in the advertising industry and for a period managed the Seagram's account for his firm. At the time, Seagram Company Ltd. was a large multinational conglomerate headquartered in Canada, and one of the major producers of alcoholic beverages in the world. In representing Seagram's, James Raniere met and worked closely with Seagram's Chairman Edgar Bronfman, whose daughters Claire and Sarah would later contribute huge sums of money in support of Keith's companies and legal struggles — and also come to be regarded in the press as two of Raniere's major targets and victims. Keith's mother taught ballroom dancing, but the parents divorced in 1968 when he was 8 years old.

♦ EDUCATION

Raniere spent his elementary school years in the late 1960s at a Waldorf school before transferring at age 12 to another private school (Rockland County Day School) from which he graduated at the age of 17 in 1978 (shortly after the death of his mother). He enrolled in Rensselaer Polytechnic Institute (RPI) at age 18 the following fall, graduating in 1982. These dates — corroborated by a variety of sources and consistency tests — are somewhat at odds with dates claimed by Raniere and his followers who have him "leaving" high school early and also "graduating" early.

Raniere has claimed repeatedly to be a genius student at RPI, and he apparently graduated with a B.S. degree in biology. He and others have made claims about Bachelor's degrees (and minors) in other disciplines that he also received at the time of his graduation, but there appears to be no way to confirm or dispute such claims without seeing a copy of his transcript. Information presented at his 2019 trial, and based on transcripts obtained by the prosecution, indicates that he graduated with a 2.26 Grade Point Average (out of a possible 4.0), having failed or barely passed a number of courses in the sciences and mathematics. This court information includes examples of failing grades in courses such as Advanced Ordinary Differential Equations, Quantum Mechanics, and Theoretical Physics, and a grade of D in Experimental Physics — resulting in an overall performance of barely C level course work.

♦ **EARLY WORK HISTORY**

After graduation, Raniere obtained a job as a computer programmer for the State of New York (ironically, as it now turns out, for the Division of Parole). This mundane commercial programming job is a peculiar career choice for someone claiming to be a genius level student in multiple disciplines with multiple degrees, and having completed and contributed to significant research projects in physics at both RPI and MIT — particularly since science and engineering graduates of RPI are highly sought both in industry and as candidates for graduate programs in academia. As a consequence, Raniere's claims about his university-level education, his degrees, his performance, and his overall comparative intelligence must be regarded with at least some degree of skepticism.

At this point — and assuming that we had taken the trouble to look into some of Raniere's claims about his life and accomplishments — our suspicion concerning Raniere's honesty and attitude towards truth should have been triggered, and we should be well into adopting a skeptical attitude and beginning to increase our degree of scrutiny as described in Section 8.3. But we also have to remember that in the 1980s and 1990s, investigating this sort of information took quite a bit more effort than a simple Web search does today, although even at that time a number of newspaper and magazine articles about Keith Raniere, written by investigative reporters, were appearing.

In the 1980s, through working with the Amway company at a low level, Raniere also became familiar with the idea of a multi-level marketing scheme (MLM). Multi-level marketing is a technique of marketing and selling products

Chapter 10: The Curious Case of Keith Raniere

that's also sometimes referred to as "pyramid selling". It depends on a non-salaried workforce of sales people whose pay, in significant part, depends on recruiting other sales people and then being paid a commission on the sales of those they've recruited — explaining why legal authorities often refer to such sales strategies as *pyramid schemes* since in order to make significant money as a sales agent you have to build a pyramid of others (who in turn build pyramids of others) under you to feed portions of their own sales up the pyramid to you.

♦ RANIERE'S COMPANIES

In 1990 Keith formed his own multi-level marketing company: Consumer's Buyline, Inc. This company came under increasingly severe scrutiny from authorities in 23 states as an MLM scheme. It ultimately was closed in 1993 (in conjunction with Raniere's signing a consent decree) under pressure from those authorities. A year later Raniere formed the National Health Network, another multilevel marketing company (this one selling vitamins), and that failed in 1999.

In its turn, Raniere's National Health Network was succeeded by his Executive Success Programs (ESP: described as a "personal development company") in 1998, which was claimed to "change the way people think, make decisions, react, and perform." It claimed to have a radical new (and patentable!) technology called *Rational Inquiry* that was used to accomplish that goal. This is Raniere's entry into what we might call the "commercial philosophy market", and references to philosophy and to Raniere's understanding and use of it became central to the products and services of ESP. But it was also an MLM scheme in that members were required to "pledge to share and enroll people in ESP" in order to "make the world a better place to live" (and also to make money from it, of course).

ESP then quickly morphed into NXIVM (pronounced as "nexium"), and the corporate relations began to get a little complicated and murky. NXIVM retained ESP as an appendage to manage and run its "seminars" and "training programs" which in turn (according to claims repeatedly made in court documents by Raniere, his representatives, and representatives of NXIVM) were "developed by NXIVM's founder Keith Raniere" and were based on "his Rational Inquiry system."

Also in the mix is First Principles, Inc. — another Raniere company formed at approximately the same time that is sometimes claimed to be what became NXIVM, and sometimes (even in the same legal document) claimed to be a separate corporate entity. As just one example of such claims and relationships, see the opening paragraphs of "NXIVM Corporation et al. v. Estate of Morris Sutton et al." (U.S. District Court 2016).

As things ended up, there was NXIVM + ESP + First Principles operating together to employ Raniere's Rational Inquiry methodology to accomplish the goals of changing "the way people think, make decisions, react, and perform." This was philosophy at work to provide a better life and more successful careers — at least for those who joined Raniere's organizations and paid to take his courses and listen to his lectures. And perhaps more important, to recruit more new members into the pyramid structure. Newspaper and magazine articles were beginning to talk of a "cult" and of peculiar goings-on inside the NXIVM inner circle. If you want a taste of what Raniere's offerings were like at this point, take a break and look at some of the YouTube videos (Raniere *et al.* 2017) that emerged from the NXIVM offerings (and were used as sales and marketing tools to attract members). You won't get the full experience of a paid-up NXIVM member, but these provide some interesting insights that we'll explore below.

10.2 Raniere as a philosopher

To begin, what's the evidence that Keith Raniere — throughout the history of NXIVM, its predecessors, and its associated companies — was involved in any way in philosophy or pseudo-philosophy? Was he acting as (or masquerading as) a philosopher? Did he and others see him as acting as a philosopher? Were they encouraged, or provided with motivations, to see this? These turn out to be easy and straightforward questions to answer, and the answers are all "Yes."

Whenever talking about his educational credentials, Raniere was always concerned to mention that he had a minor in philosophy. He seems to regard this as a mark of distinction and something that others should know in understanding his knowledge and capabilities. His personal Web site (now removed) characterized him as a "scientist, mathematician, philosopher, entrepreneur, educator, inventor and author." He and others have asserted claims in a variety of circumstances that he is a "philosophical leader." And he emphasized on a number of occasions and in promotional materials that he and his organizations were involved in teaching ethics, and that he had created tools for teaching ethics and critical thinking. Of course, these are claims that philosophers (such as Aristotle) and pseudo-philosophers (such as the Sophists) have made through the ages.

Numerous interviews and legal depositions contain accounts by followers, employees, associates, ex-employees, and members of his inner circle that he lectured to them about philosophy for lengthy periods. Journalist Vanessa Grigoriadis, in a 2018 NY Times article (Grigoriadis 2018) reported listening to him talk at length (in an interview with him) about philosophical theories, free will and whether humans have it, whether mysticism is an abused tool of understanding, how to approach a solution to Zeno's Paradox, and whether there is an afterlife. All this was within the context of explaining the nature of his work and the services provided to those taking courses from his companies such as NXIVM.

In the lengthy first part of a deposition on March 11, 2009 (U.S. District Court 2009) concerning a suit brought by NXIVM against several individuals, the Ross Institute, and Wellspring Retreat, Inc., Raniere claims to be "the philosophical founder and the person who answers the questions relating to — the ultimate questions relating to the education, the philosophy" of NXIVM. He goes on to say that he is the "sole creator" of the Rational Inquiry Method employed by NXIVM in its courses, and that Rational Inquiry teaches "A specific ordering of questions, a specific ordering of philosophical concepts; things like that," and that "So with respect to who has, if you will, the most knowledge relating to the ESP [Executive Success Program] philosophy and who has the ultimate authority to explain that philosophy or answer the questions, I am the highest rank." During that deposition he also makes an attempt to explain some basic features of his understanding of ethics, rules, and intent. And he refers to an upcoming series of panels — in conjunction with a visit by the Dalai Lama — involving ethics discussions and the implementation of an "ethical plan."

Ivy Nevares (a long-time NXIVM member, editor/translator for Raniere, and one of the women closest to him) says on her Web site that

Ivy Nevares

> "Ivy co-authored and published numerous articles on science, philosophy and ethics in the Mexican scientific journal, *Conocimiento* (*Knowledge*). A special edition of the journal was dedicated entirely to these literary creations a year later. The articles were then published as books: *Odin and the Sphinx* (2008) with a foreword by former Ambassador and Permanent Representative for Mexico to UNESCO Dr. Luis Eugenio Todd, and *The Sphinx and Thelxiepeia* (2009) with a foreword by His Holiness the 14th Dalai Lama." Ivy Nevares (Nevares 2020).

These facts together with others too numerous to list in detail — including the 43 YouTube videos of Raniere giving scripted "interviews" on such topics as authenticity, ethics, Rational Inquiry, and meaning — are more than sufficient to establish that he was in fact presenting himself as a philosopher and employing philosophy (or pseudo-philosophy) in some way to describe his views, his goals, his teachings, his accomplishments, and the products and services of his commercial ventures.

With this brief account of the evolution of NXIVM, Keith Raniere's careers over a period of approximately thirty-five years, and his determination to be perceived as a philosopher, let's turn our attention to the primary questions that concern us. These are

- Was Raniere involved in using philosophy or pseudo-philosophy in his methods and teachings?
- If he was, was he acting as a genuine philosopher or as a pseudo-philosopher?
- How do our models, scenarios, and personas of the philosopher and the pseudo-philosopher apply in this case; and how do they contribute to an understanding of it?

As we answer these questions, we'll naturally have to look more closely at exactly what Raniere and his associates were doing, but our focus will remain on whether and to what degree Raniere was making use of philosophy or pseudo-philosophy. We'll need to take care not get side-tracked by the many and disturbing salacious aspects of this case or by the tangled web of civil and criminal charges and counter-charges, as well as the very detailed legal maneuvering that took place over the years. Remember that being regarded as some sort of criminal doesn't mean that you're not an exemplary philosopher. Just look at the case of Socrates, who was handed a death sentence because he was found guilty of failing to acknowledge the traditional gods of Athens, introducing new deities, and corrupting the youth — although perhaps comparing Raniere to Socrates will turn out to be a stretch.

10.3 Where is Raniere's philosophy?

One of the difficult aspects of this case is that much of the easily accessible evidence appears in second– or third–hand reports by participants, or in the news media. Much of this is of highly varying quality and reliability. One source of more reliable (and much more direct) evidence appears in thousands of pages of dry, tedious, and often complex court documents that include legal complaint filings, motions, attorneys' responses to filings of various sorts, lengthy depositions, and court decisions and orders.

A second more direct source is a collection of 43 video interviews on the Keith Raniere *Conversations* YouTube channel (Raniere, *et al.* 2017). These are conducted by two of Raniere's employees at the time and have the appearance of a set of well-scripted brief "infomercials" rather than of a serious presentation of Raniere's scientific and philosophical views, or even how such views apply to his overall goals.

Finally, perhaps the most direct and accurate presentation of Raniere's philosophical views and his intended application of them is to be found in a series of articles authored by him and published over a period of several years in a magazine. Unfortunately, the magazine was a fairly obscure Mexican publication. It is no longer published, and the articles in it (including Raniere's) are in Spanish. Ivy Nevares remarks (in the quotation above) that these articles were later collected into two books, and I presume she means to say that the English versions of the articles comprise those books since the books have English titles. But the books are essentially unavailable.

◆ Evidence of ⊘ Discouraging Inquiry

Despite these difficulties with "source material", we'll make use of each of these direct sources of Raniere's thoughts in our analysis and assessment of his use of philosophy. And one advantage of looking at this case is that it illustrates the lengths to which you may sometimes need to go in order to demonstrate, or even to be reasonably confident of, a judgment concerning pseudo-philosophy.

As part of our own methodology here, we would normally expect to look at an author's or speaker's corpus (his collected works, or at least some significant subset of these), identify specific instances of genuine philosophy and pseudo-philosophy markers occurring in those works, fit those to our models and personas, and make a judgment about the presence and degree of pseudo-philosophy present in those works. So we'd be looking at published papers in professional (usually peer-reviewed) journals, magazines, PowerPoint (and similar) presentations available in electronic form, and books, theses, and dissertations. In the case of Keith Raniere, we won't get very far because the *only* explicit statements of his philosophical views occur in inaccessible books published by a NXIVM company, internal NXIVM documents, YouTube videos that are very brief, shallow and expose little philosophy, and court documents that are tedious to piece through and also expose little philosophical content. This is an early red flag in itself and it exhibits our pseudo-philosophy marker of ⊘ *Discouraging Inquiry*.

Certainly most philosophers and pseudo-philosophers want to reach a broad public audience, or at least *some* public audience, in order to influence as many people as possible with their "philosophy". Academic philosophers write scholarly papers for publication in peer-reviewed journals, and they give presentations at universities and meetings of professional philosophical associations. Non-academics also seek to publish articles and books of various sorts, or more recently they seek to contribute to online forums, in order to make their philosophical principles and views known; and there are now quite a number of such opportunities. But what we quickly discover about Keith Raniere is that over a period of decades while he was claiming to be a philosopher — while others were claiming that he was a philosopher and was delivering philosophical teachings, and while he would talk (in public, on YouTube, and during legal testimony) *about* his philosophy — the *details* of that philosophy, its *principles*, and its *concepts* were never exposed to public scrutiny in any accessible publications authored by him.

We know that Raniere is said to have published two books that — in part and to at least some degree — express the fundamentals of his philosophical thinking. *Odin & the Sphinx* was published in 2007 and *The Sphinx & Thelxiepeia* was published in 2009 — both by Ethical Publishing LLC (one of Raniere's companies that seems to exist no longer). Although both are listed on Amazon, neither is readily available either there or from other book dealers. Two used copies of *The Sphinx & Thelxiepeia* are (as of this writing) offered on Amazon for approximately $1,300 each, and copies of *Odin & the Sphinx* may be available from some booksellers for about $250 — pretty pricey for paperbacks in the area of philosophy or personal development. However, in all cases it's unclear that if you ordered a copy of one of these books you would ever receive it. I cannot find a copy of either book in any library system — *anywhere*.

Since Ivy Nevares has said that the articles published by Raniere and her in the Mexican "scientific journal" *Conocimiento* were later collected into these books and "published" for the use of NXIVM members and in NXIVM and ESP courses and "trainings", we can take it that those *Conocimiento* articles provide us with the basis and core of Raniere's philosophizing and use of philosophy in his companies. So we can use them as our primary sources in making a determination of whether his work is genuine philosophy or pseudo-philosophy. We'll take a quick look at the nature of these articles, and then do a deep and detailed dive into one of them as an example of just how Raniere uses philosophy and what the quality of his philosophy is like. Then we'll look more briefly in some of the others in order to show how pervasive Raniere's approach is throughout his writings.

10.4 The *Conocimiento* corpus

As soon as we focus on these *Conocimiento* articles, we're faced with several questions and suspicions. First, it's difficult even to find the articles and to find the remains of this now defunct publication. However, a *Conocimiento* Web site still exists (Conocimiento 2020) where back issues of the publication are readily accessible — in Spanish, of course. The full title of *Conocimiento* (*Knowledge*) is *Ciencia Conocimiento Tecnologia (Science Knowledge Technology)*, and it was a purely Spanish language publication. It's plain to see that this is a relatively obscure publication since its editorial page proclaims that it's a "monthly magazine, with a circulation of 10,000 copies." Compare this to a magazine like *Discover* which in 2012 had well over half a million subscribers, or to *Scientific American* which claims a print circulation of well over 150,000.

Conocimiento is not what can properly be referred to as a *journal* in the normal sense this word is used in the sciences, engineering, philosophy, or academia. While it has an editorial board, it's unclear what the submission and acceptance processes amount to, it doesn't appear to employ a system of referees (recognized experts in the required fields) to evaluate submissions, and it's published on a monthly schedule, which is much more frequent than professional journals publish their issues (in large part because of the time required by the professional review process). Describing *Conocimiento* as a "scientific journal" (as Ivy Nevares does, and as it's also described in other NEXIVM literature) is at best a distortion, and certainly an example of ⊘ *Exaggerated Claims*.

Raniere's articles and books
⊘ Misrepresentation and ⊘ Exaggerated claims

Keith Raniere's articles are always designated as "special" or "special for *Conocimiento*" and are often relegated to the back pages of an issue. Each of them is only a few pages long and ends with a stylized and highlighted box titled *About Executive Success Programs, Inc.* which is a brief advertisement for ESP training programs, saying in part (my English translation)

> "All ESP programs use a state-of-the-art patent pending technology called Rational Inquiry™, a science based on the belief that the more consistent an individual's beliefs and behavior patterns are, the more successful he will be in everything he does. Rational Inquiry™ allows people to re-examine and incorporate perceptions that may be the basis of self-imposed limitations. For more information: info @nxivm.com."

Together with the designation of the articles as "special," this makes each Raniere article appear to be much more akin to what in an American magazine would be labeled as an "Advertisement" rather than a genuine technical contribution. At best they appear to be infomercials of one sort or another, and whatever the acceptance criteria normally were for articles in *Conocimiento*, it's very clear that those were held to a higher standard than Raniere's "special" articles.

Going beyond that appearance, *Conocimiento* certainly doesn't approach the level of a scientific research journal as Keith Raniere, Ivy Nevares, and other

NXIVM and ESP representatives and followers have claimed. A more accurate characterization of *Conocimiento* is that it was a *magazine*, published on a common monthly magazine schedule for local/regional distribution in Mexico, that contained articles summarizing, describing, and illustrating the results of research in areas of science (including the social sciences), technology, manufacturing, and medicine. It was not a research journal, did not present results of new research to the research community, and did not pretend to. Instead, it was targeted more towards a broad community of business people, investors, managers, and others who have an interest in remaining up to date on their knowledge of these areas. No one (including its publisher) would mistake *Conocimiento* for a professional scientific or philosophical research journal.

Along these lines, an Albany *Times Union* article in 2012 (Odato and Gish 2019) also characterizes *Conocimiento* as a magazine and remarks that

> "Raniere directly markets in Mexico, frequently contributing to the magazine *Conocimiento* (*Knowledge*) with plugs for NXIVM, or Executive Success Programs."

Even within that context, Raniere's articles appear peculiar. Virtually all other articles in *Conocimiento* are — to at least some degree — documented with careful references to the relevant research literature and prior work that they discuss, collected together in a section typically labeled *References*. This provides pointers to genuine scientific research literature that readers can use to follow up on the topics covered in the more popularized types of articles that appear in *Conocimiento* itself.

Raniere's articles contain nothing of the sort. While other articles contain substantial detail about scientific theory, methods, and technology, Raniere's do not. His first appearance in *Conocimiento* is in the September-October issue of 2005, and he has the two lead articles — each on the topic of justice — which we'll look into in some detail in a later section. Shortly after that he embarks on a program of the frequent, often monthly, publication of short articles usually 2-4 pages, but some up to 6 pages, in length. These differ substantially from other articles in the magazine (which are much more detailed and technical) and have the appearance of a monthly editorial or "thought" column more than of anything resembling a scientific contribution or philosophical analysis or presentation. This train of Raniere's articles continues through the magazine's last publication in 2012. Raniere appears to have published nothing else in any other magazine or journal, although as Ivy Nevares has testified, these *Conocimiento* articles were collected into two books published by Raniere's own publishing company.

What we're seeing here, of course, are clear examples of the markers ⊘ *Misrepresentation* and ⊘ *Exaggerated Claims*. It's easy to see this when we contrast the remarks of Ivy Nevares, Keith Raniere, and others in the NXIVM camp about the publication of Raniere's philosophy in a "scientific journal" with the reality of its publication in an obscure (and for most potential readers in the US and elsewhere, inaccessible) monthly Mexican popular science and technology magazine of very limited circulation. And this is before we look at the *content* of those articles, which we'll do below.

Why publish in Conocimiento?

Why had Raniere decided to publish explanations and illustrations of his thoughts, concepts, and methods in a rather out-of-the-way Mexican magazine with low circulation, and in Spanish? How likely were these articles to be read, or even found, by the public at large? How likely were they to read by potential clients? If *you* were a genius scientist, mathematician, and philosopher (as Raniere proclaimed himself to be) who had invented an *innovative technology* and supporting science and philosophy that you felt could help many people across the globe to lead better lives, and (as Raniere suggests in several articles) you had an obligation to make such a contribution, and you were now running a company whose purpose was to disseminate that technology and methodology ... well ... then ... would you find some magazine of severely limited distribution in northern Mexico as the conduit to publish aspects of your invention and discoveries as short "special" articles? Probably not.

Who would you be hoping to reach in this way? What would your potential customers in the U.S. and elsewhere be expected to think? It would appear that the only benefit to such an approach is that you'd then be able to claim that you had published a number of "scientific" papers in a "scientific journal." This is what Raniere and his employees and followers at NXIVM and ESP subsequently did: these *Conocimiento* "special articles" (referred to as articles in a "scientific journal") were continually offered as evidence for the meaningfulness, usefulness, and acceptance of Raniere's philosophical and scientific ideas, even though none of the *contents* of the articles were (even in part) described or made use of in any other venue accessible to public view.

Philo, in the spirit of Φ *Inquiry* and Φ *Critical appraisal*, would be seeking the attention of other philosophers to expand on and provide critical analysis of her work. Raniere instead appears to do his best to hide his work from anyone outside of a highly constrained environment within which he has control.

Section 10.4: The Conocimiento corpus

An initial impression: philosophy or pseudo-philosophy?

At this early stage of investigating his thought, we can't help noticing that:

- Raniere has failed to exhibit the marker of Φ *Domain Awareness* in an expected way by failing to link his work to prior relevant work in any way. But we'll need to review the significance of this later since by itself it may not be very important if his work is truly new and innovative.

- Raniere has acted in a way incompatible with the Philo persona by failing to work towards sharing his wisdom with others in an effective way and making it available for critical review. His manner of publication has made it appear that he's doing his best to make it difficult for people to examine the details, justifications, and consequences of his concepts, arguments, and theories. And of course, inaccessibility of the sources prohibits anyone from criticizing the ideas expressed in them — a clear example of ⊘ *Discouraging Inquiry*.

- Raniere has acted in a way incompatible with the Philo persona by appearing to be knowingly and intentionally deceptive concerning the nature of his publications and claims made about them — by trying to make it appear that his writings were examined and accepted by the scientific and broader research community in a way in which they were not. This is an example of ⊘ *Misrepresentation* and ⊘ *Exaggerated Claims*.

- Raniere *may* have exhibited the ⊘ *Ignorance of Prior Work* pseudo-philosophy marker (in seemingly being unaware of related significant work).

- While there are citations to relevant and related thinking and literature in almost all other *Conocimiento* articles -- there are none in any of Raniere's. This makes it appear as though his articles are being treated in a way different from other articles in the magazine, and this is further suggested by the labeling of his articles as "special" contributions. We should note also that in several places in issues of *Conocimiento*, Ivy Nevares is listed as an editor of the magazine and this appears to introduce the possibility of a conflict of interest in the objectivity of the editorial board and the regular and frequent publication of Raniere's articles. It's especially peculiar for what's supposed to be a "scientific journal." Again, this appears to be an example of ⊘ *Misrepresentation*.

These observations should incline us at this point to adopt a stance in which we're alert to other signs of pseudo-philosophy as we look more closely into Raniere's views and his presentations of them.

Digging in: "When the Justice of Man Meets the Justice of God"

Let's now take a close look at one of Raniere's articles that addresses some important questions and issues in science and philosophy. We'll use this as a concrete example of applying our models and methods, and of the quality of Raniere's philosophical thought, how he presents his ideas, and what his goals and motives appear to be. I'll then leave it to you — if you're inclined at that point, and can access and read additional articles (*Conocimiento* 2020) — to apply our methods to other examples of Raniere's writings.

The article I'll select for this exercise is "When the Justice of Man Meets the Justice of God" ("Cuando la justicia del hombre toca la justicia de Dios"). This is the introductory article in the September-October 2005 issue of *Conocimiento*, and the theme for that issue is *The Science of Law* ("La Ciencia del Derecho"). It contains articles on the problems and effects of the use of genetics in legal contexts, DNA testing and criminal investigations, the "teaching of legal science" in the 21st century, modernizing justice with technology, the concepts of knowledge and truth in legal science, approaches to dealing with domestic violence, etc. The second article in this issue is also authored by Raniere and titled "Ultimate justice" ("Justicia última"), but for the sake of brevity we'll ignore that one here. It offers no more insight into Raniere's philosophical thought or method.

As an example of Raniere's use of philosophy, "When the Justice of Man Meets the Justice of God" is a particularly good representative in several respects. First, it's the very first article that Raniere wrote for *Conocimiento*, and it's absolutely clear that the writing is his: the by-line is "Keith Raniere and Ivy Nevares, translated by Ivy Nevares and Farouk Rojas"; and so while Nevares acted as an editor and translator, Raniere is first author and the content of the article is unquestionably his own work.

Second, this article has a heavy dose of philosophy (and some theology) in it, and it's a clear case where Raniere is both dealing with fundamental philosophical concepts and applying them to address certain puzzles or problems he sees and describes. He clearly takes some philosophical positions in this article, advances philosophical arguments, and uses these to justify his views. We'll look through the article (it's only three pages in the magazine!), see what philosophy and pseudo-philosophy markers it exhibits, and get a sense of the degree to which the author is exemplifying either the Philo or the Pseudo persona.

We look at a work like this with the purpose of understanding it, evaluating its content, deciding whether to accept or reject the views expressed in it, and coming to a view about the reliability and integrity of its author. And when we do this, we should have some initial questions in mind that we expect to have answered at the end of our evaluation. These include

- What is the author's point? What does he or she want us to believe or to learn?
- What concepts, evidence, and arguments (logic and rational support) does the author provide in making this point?
- Are these clearly and intelligibly introduced?
- What are the successes and failures?
- Are there outright errors or deceptions that detract from the points being made?
- What specifically *philosophical* concepts, positions, and arguments appear — and are these used in genuinely philosophical or in pseudo-philosophical ways?

Additionally, as we move ahead with these questions in mind, we also look for markers of genuine philosophy and of pseudo-philosophy that we developed as part of our models in Chapters 4-7.

To introduce or illustrate his important points, Raniere uses four very brief dialogs between "A theologian" and "A scientist." All but one consist of only two or three statements. Each dialog is followed by a discussion of what the dialog illustrates. In general, throughout his writings in *Conocimiento*, he uses contrived examples that we're to accept as factual representations of situations, and these serve as foils for his views and positions. This is an acceptable rhetorical technique, but in the context of genuine philosophy it's regarded as a very weak approach — because you can always cook up a fictitious example that meets your needs to illustrate or support a point. In itself, then we may regard this as an indication of the ⊘ *Misrepresentation* or the ⊘ *Lack of Rigor* marker. This is particularly bothersome in Raniere's writings since he frequently introduces a story as though it were true and uses it to illustrate or support a point he's making, but when you go to find any details of that story (e.g., a company mentioned in it, actions taken by individuals, etc.) you discover that it's entirely made up.

Chapter 10: The Curious Case of Keith Raniere

Raniere's views on science vs. religion
⊘ Obscurantism, ⊘ Lack of Rigor, ⊘ Vagueness and Equivocation

In "When the Justice of Man Meets the Justice of God," the primary point Raniere wants to address involves the natures of science and religion: whether there's a strict dichotomy involving these (as he feels most people believe, though he gives no evidence for this), or whether this "diametrical opposition" is "reconcilable." This is a worthy question that's attracted significant attention in the history of philosophy and of religion. It would be good to know what sorts of things might count as answers to this question. It would be good to have some fairly clear understanding of the nature of this *diametrical opposition*: for instance, some clear examples of precisely how science and religion are felt to be *opposed*, exactly how that opposition is *diametrical* (and whether there are non-diametrical oppositions in play), and what a *reconciliation* might look like. These are the kinds of Φ *Critical Appraisal* questions that are also suggested in our discussions of *Skepticism* and *Scrutiny* in Section 8.3, and in Guidelines #1 and #4 in Section 8.7.

They are also exactly the sorts of questions that philosophers worry about, and to be sure, the literature of philosophy is replete with discussions and proposed arguments and solutions to these questions. But Raniere doesn't pause to clarify the problem, and certainly not to adopt any criteria of adequacy (Φ *Adequacy*) that might serve us as a goal, a guide, and a determination of whether we succeed or fail at the (pretty vague) task he's set. Instead, he moves ahead.

Raniere begins by observing that religion is a belief system based on "articles of faith," and that it has a further code of conduct based on that belief system:

> **Raniere:** "Religion, it can be said, is a belief system that has articles or points of faith on which it is based. It also has a code of conduct that is based on the belief system. These two components - principles and doctrine - are essential."

He doesn't explore or suggest what a belief system is, in what sense it's a system, or what a belief is and how it might be distinguished from other things (such as a fact, an emotion, an article of faith, or knowledge). That is, he takes belief to be a *primitive concept* in whatever philosophical theory he's building about religion. Each reader has to imagine that he or she understands what Raniere means by "belief" in this context. Incautious readers may assume they understand what's being said and what the consequences of that may be, and they may *assume* that other readers have the same understanding of what Raniere is saying; but the likelihood of this being true is remote — owing simply to the vagueness of the concepts with which Raniere has left us.

210

Already it looks as though we're seeing examples of the pseudo-philosophy markers ⊘ *Obscurantism*, ⊘ *Lack of Rigor*, and ⊘ *Vagueness and Equivocation*. And keep in mind that the audience Raniere is addressing in these articles (and *knows* that he's addressing) is comprised of people who in general have no familiarity with philosophy. So his failure to spend any time in introducing the fundamental concepts he's employing is a violation of Philo's goal of Φ *Clarity*.

Raniere then moves on to a characterization of science. His first observation is:

> **Raniere:** "Science is knowledge and knowing. It is both content and process. As content, science is organized knowledge, where the organization is consistent and reproducible; Therefore, verifiable. We validate this knowledge with the assumption that if something happens a thousand times, it will happen again."

This may sound to you like a good, if brief, characterization of science and how it's distinguished from other disciplines. But it exposes some fundamental misunderstandings of the history, philosophy, and nature of science (oddly similar in some respects to that of Silva that we examined in Chapter 9).

♦ TWO ASPECTS OF SCIENCE

By saying that science is both knowledge *and* knowing, Raniere means to point to the fact that there are two important parts to what we refer to as "science". First, science is a *body of knowledge*: things we have come to know about the world and how it works. We know all kinds of things about fluids and how they behave through changes in temperature, for example. We know a lot about gases and how they behave under different pressures. We know a great deal about light and how to make things like electric lights and lasers. We know about planets and their orbits. We even know about stars and stellar evolution, and biology and organisms and species. And on and on. That's the *body of scientific knowledge*. It's the *content* of science.

But second, in science we *know how to know* — how to become knowledgeable about these things — and then how to use that knowledge to accomplish a huge variety of goals to make our lives better. This is *scientific methodology* (or the epistemology of science, or the theory of knowledge employed in science) that provides us with the body of science and makes it reliable and useful. This is what answers the question "*How* do we know what things are true according to science?" And this is (in Raniere's words) the *process of science*, or at least it's a very significant part of that process.

The distinction that Raniere makes here is a good and important one for a philosopher of science to make, but then he starts to wander off in less reliable directions.

It's misleading (⊘ *Misrepresentation*, ⊘ *Inadequate Understanding?*, ⊘ *Ignorance of Prior Work?*) to say that the content of science is organized knowledge. This gives the impression that science is just a set of facts or observations (perhaps including a large number of generalizations relating what we observe in the world), and that these are somehow organized in a way that's consistent and reproducible. Even to the degree that this is accurate, however, it ignores what makes science so much more (and so much more powerful and reliable) than just a set of what David Hume referred to as "constant conjunctions" where (in Raniere's words) "something happens a thousand times."

What's ignored is the nature of a *scientific theory* as a system of *scientific laws* that are related to one another in complex ways and, equally importantly, are related to *other scientific theories*. The unit of *scientific* knowledge isn't — as Raniere leads us to believe — the isolated *fact* or *generalization* that we've seen happen "a thousand times."[13] It's the scientific theory such as Pasteur's *Germ Theory of Disease*, Lavoisier's *Oxidation Theory of Combustion*, Newton's *Laws of Motion* (sometimes referred to as *Newtonian Mechanics*), Einstein's *Special Theory of Relativity* (which essentially replaced Newton's theory or rendered Newton's a special case of Einstein's more general theory), Darwin's *Theory of Evolution*, and all of the other theories that make up or have led to what is our contemporary scientific knowledge.

It's the processes of *theory* testing, *theory* confirmation, and *theory* acceptance and rejection that truly constitute the (Raniere's word) "process" of science. When you take a course in biology or physics or chemistry or some other science, you may study some "facts," but most of your effort goes into understanding *theories*, how they're applied, and how they work with other theories.

My point in dwelling on this somewhat extended analysis of science is that Raniere's remarks seem to expose a high degree of ignorance or misunderstanding of critical aspects of science now agreed upon by philosophers and historians of science (⊘ *Inadequate Understanding*, ⊘ *Ignorance of Prior Work*). This whole part of science has either escaped Raniere in getting the degrees he claims, or else he's trying to mislead us for some reason by ignoring it. For example, paying it the attention it deserves would make clear that there are some fundamental aspects of science not shared by religion.

Raniere also tells us that what makes scientific knowledge acceptable and valuable to us is that its consistency and reproducibility renders it *verifiable*. But no knowledgeable philosopher of science, and no one even moderately familiar with the history of the philosophy of science in the 20th century would choose to use the term "verifiable" in this context and in this way.[14]

Arguments raged at great length in the 20th century about both the meaning and proper (or even intelligible) role of what philosophers called *verification* in science and epistemology, and indeed the position (or school) of Logical Empiricism (or Logical Positivism) was built on the concept of verification and its role in knowledge. Carl Popper argued against verification as establishing scientific knowledge and in favor of falsification (though falsification then turned out to have its own problems). And to a significant degree, Thomas Kuhn's *The Structure of Scientific Revolutions* (Kuhn 1962) is an extended argument against the view Raniere appears to casually take for granted concerning the role of verification in scientific knowledge.

These two facets of Raniere's characterization of science (his appeal to verifiability and his apparent ignorance of the critical nature and role of theories) indicate that Raniere's philosophical characterization of science, its relation to knowledge, and how it enables us to achieve knowledge, has to be seen as naive, simplistic, and incompatible with currently accepted views that philosophers hold on these topics. Either he's intentionally misleading us by presenting an account of science that he knows to be inaccurate in fundamental ways (in which case his he's exhibiting the pseudo-philosophy marker of ⊘ *Misrepresentation*), or he's instead exhibiting the markers of ⊘ *Inadequate Understanding* and ⊘ *Ignorance of Prior Work*. In either case he's failing to exhibit the genuine philosophy marker of Φ *Domain Awareness*.

Unfortunately, Raniere isn't satisfied with providing us this incoherent characterization of science as "knowledge and knowing," and he almost immediately switches gears and moves on to talking about how to define reality.

◆ **CHEATING WITH PERCEPTION TO DEFINE REALITY**

> **Raniere:** "There is a certain irony in trying to define this term. However, perhaps we can agree that reality can be defined as what our perception acts on, including, of course, our perception itself. No matter how much we try to remove the human interpretation of science - by means of double blind and crossover tests, for example - it never ceases to be an effect of our perception."

But this isn't a definition of reality, and it violates several principles (going back to Aristotle) for providing a definition for a term or concept. It's also pretty confusing — which is what happens when you violate those principles: Is reality what our perception *acts on*, including that perception itself? So is reality just perceptions? Perceptions *of what*? Perceptions *of reality*? That seems circular, doesn't it? Then is reality just the perception of itself — which is itself a perception? What are we supposed to do with this prime example of ⊘ *Obscurantism*? This is the kind of thing that can give philosophy a bad name.

What Raniere does is to immediately leap from it to another claim that "the human interpretation of science ... never ceases to be an effect of our perception." What does this mean? What are the consequences of it?

Well, there's a well-published and thoroughly debated philosophical theory that's probably what Raniere has in mind and which he would have encountered in an introductory philosophy of science course, or perhaps an introductory course in epistemology. It's called "the theory-ladenness of observation" (Bogen 2020) and in its well-known versions doesn't devolve into circular incoherence. However, it seems that Raniere has picked up the jargon without understanding the fundamental concepts, the theory, and the consequences. For good measure he tosses in references to "double blind and crossover tests" — presumably because he thinks his particular audience is familiar with pharmaceutical trials, or medical, or perhaps sociological contexts. And because such terms sound ... well ... scientific and important. But in the basic sciences such as chemistry, physics, and biology, these tests play no role.

There's a word for what Raniere is doing here and it's *"gobbletygook"* — which the *Cambridge Dictionary* defines as "language that sounds important and official but is difficult to understand." It seems tailor-made for use in contexts where an author is attempting to be misleading and obscure, and we'll be using it a lot. Of course, it goes hand in hand with our markers of ⊘ *Obscurantism*, ⊘ *Misuse of Terminology*, and ⊘ *Puzzling Terminology*.

We also might wonder — and this fits in with our question of "What is the author's point?" — *why* Raniere wants to "define reality." What's the point of this? How is it connected to the topic of the journal issue which is *The Science of Justice*? How will an abstract definition of reality (which Raniere never really provides in any event) help with this? We'll return to this puzzling question in a later section below. But first, Raniere wants to sort some things out about perception.

> **Raniere:** "Our very awareness of our perception comes from science, and as our science improves, our effective perception improves and *vice versa*. Although science allows us to improve our perception, we must not forget that everything remains our best guess of what could really be happening 'out there.'"

Section 10.4: The Conocimiento corpus

This example of gobbletygook falls under our marker of ⊘ *Vagueness and Equivocation* for equivocating on the term "perception". And it's a perfect example of equivocation in pseudo-philosophical use.

In the first use of the word "perception" ("Our very awareness of perception *comes from science*"), it refers to our *direct perceiving of things* in the world. This does not "come from science". This is part of our capabilities as humans and mammals. We don't need science in order to perceive things in the world — we just do it. Let's call this "immediate perception" or "direct perception". Also beware not to conflate a perception with your "awareness" of (i.e., your noticing or thinking about the perception) — because this is exactly where Raniere wants to lead us.

What *comes from science* (what science makes us *aware of*) is an *understanding* of *how this process works*, what sensory organs (eyes, ears, etc.) are involved, how these interact with our neural systems and our brains, etc. This *scientific understanding of perception* is what science contributes to our knowledge. It's the *scientific sense* of the word "perception" and is both *abstract* and connected to our *concepts* in ways that immediate perception is not.

In the second use of the word ("as our science improves, our *effective perception* improves"), it's not at all clear what "perception" is supposed to mean or refer to — but it seems to have acquired a meaning closer to *understanding* than to (immediate) *perception*. A clue that something funny is going on in this assertion is that the modifier "effective" has been added. But what does *it* mean? How is *effective* perception different from perception — if it is? We don't know. It's a rhetorical trick to avoid the more transparent statement that "As our science improves, our perception improves," because *this* statement will strike pretty much anyone as wrong (or at least as *ambiguous*). Science gives us *knowledge about* perception, or provides an *interpretation of* our perceptions. It doesn't make our *actual perception* any better.[15] But the phrase "*effective* perception" is used to forestall us from advancing this criticism, and encourage us to continue on without worrying about Raniere's equivocation and how it may be misleading us.

In this passage, Raniere is attempting to claim — at least in part — that our scientific knowledge *of* perception somehow has the result of our actually *perceiving* things better, more accurately, or more efficiently. But that's ridiculous! It's like saying that scientific knowledge (just the *knowledge*!) that I gain in my course in anatomy and physiology makes my muscles function better and makes me stronger — which is absurd. Otherwise, my fastest path to success in the NFL as a professional athlete would be to take a bunch of science courses and not waste time on all the weight-lifting. This appears to be an example of either ⊘ *Special Pleading* or ⊘ *Inadequate Understanding* in Raniere's failure to

Chapter 10: The Curious Case of Keith Raniere

anticipate or acknowledge rather obvious difficulties and counterexamples in the view of perception that he wants us to adopt.

But then things get worse because Raniere tells us that even after our use of perception and our scientific knowledge of perception, we still have only a "guess of what could really be happening" in the world of reality! Really? Is that what we're being asked to believe? That science gives us just another *guess* at what reality is and how it works? This guess has allowed us to save untold lives through the development of medications and medical and surgical treatments. This guess has allowed us to improve agricultural and food production and distribution to feed millions of people who otherwise would have starved. And this guess has provided the very material or screen on which you're reading these words — along with your digital phone, your smart TV, your car, and any number of other things that you use every day.

This view of Raniere's that science provides us only with a best guess is also incompatible with one he expresses in the paragraph immediately after it, where he says

> **Raniere:** "Science is knowledge and consistency. Indeed, we have categorized trillions and trillions of human observations into knowledge. Our science is correct because of the vast information on which it is based and its excellence in predicting correctly."

So now we're told that science is quite a bit more than a best guess. It's knowledge (which requires it to be *true*), it's consistent (which includes being consistent with our perception since he takes science to include all the "trillions and trillions of human observations" that we get via our perceptions), and it's correct (i.e., again, *true*). But this directly violates Φ *Consistency*. Also, of course, he has it backwards: science isn't correct because it predicts correctly; it predicts correctly because it's correct. It's the *correctness* of science that *results* in the accurate predictions, and not the other way around. While we don't have a specific marker for this type of simplistic logical/conceptual blunder, at the very least it exemplifies ⊘ *Inadequate Understanding*.

Prior to these confused claims about the consistency and correctness of science, Raniere had just taken us through an argument (however faulty it may be) that what science gives us is just a "best guess." Are we now expected to forget this and embrace his new conclusion that science is *correct*? At this point we have to concede that any hope of seeing Φ *Rationality*, Φ *Clarity*, and Φ *Consistency* have flown out the windows of incoherence and nonsense that Raniere has forced open with ⊘ *Obscurantism*, ⊘ *Vagueness and Equivocation*, and ⊘ *Lack of Rigor*.

The conclusion that Raniere wants us to endorse about science being only a "best guess" just doesn't follow from the facts and arguments he's using to prop it up. But he's done his best with equivocation to trick us into believing what he wants. Why? There are two related answers to this. The first is that he has an ulterior motive, and this is to lead us to believe that *there is no fundamental difference between the reliability of beliefs that we come to through science* (which he acknowledges yield consistent and correct knowledge) and *the reliability of belief that we come to through religion* (which he never describes as being either consistent, correct, or yielding knowledge).[16] This lack of a difference in the reliability between what science provides us and what religion provides us would make science out to be like religion in a fundamental sense and would support the view that Raniere is working towards in this article — which is that science and religion are "compatible" with one another.

But there's more than compatibility at issue here. Many would agree that science and religion can be seen, at least in certain ways, as being compatible. This article of Raniere's goes in a completely different direction:

Raniere: "Like reality, the existence or non-existence of God is merely a perception."

Why does Raniere want to persuade us that reality is "merely a perception" and that science and religion are just two different (yet compatible) ways of looking at it? This is an extreme approach if all you're out to do is to show that science and religion can be compatible with one another. It's difficult to say — in the context of just this one article — why he pursues such a radical epistemological position. But it should raise our level of suspicion and incline us towards a heightened degree of scrutiny.

Raniere may be doing this in order to impress the *Conocimiento* readership with his philosophical prowess — to convince them that he's capable of the kind of careful thought on abstract and complex subjects required of the philosopher, and that he has genuine knowledge and skills in that domain. In that case, as we've seen, he's not doing a very good job of it. In fact, Raniere's talk of reality being *merely a perception* is strikingly similar to George Berkeley's well-known argument for the existence of God based on his principle that "to be is to be perceived," and Raniere appears to be (in the manner of a pseudo-philosopher) "borrowing" this for his own murky purposes.[17] Certainly if he minored in philosophy he would be well aware of this aspect of Berkeley's philosophy, although where Berkeley's approach is carefully and cleverly done, Raniere's is incoherent. And Raniere's borrowing without mentioning Berkeley would be an example of ⊘ *Misappropriation*.

A second, and more focused, goal of Raniere's approach here appears to be similar to what Silva does in attempting to blur the distinction between science and intuition. Why would anyone want us to believe that there's basically no difference between what science (i.e., rational thought and analysis) can provide us in the way of reliable knowledge and what a non-rational (or potentially irrational or mystical) approach can provide us?

The answer to this question is that if you can get people to lose confidence in (or abandon) a critical and rational approach to evaluating knowledge claims (i.e., abandon an anti-sophistical stance) then it's much easier to lead them in directions where they otherwise wouldn't go. This is what happened for decades within the NXIVM and ESP environment in which Raniere was the self-proclaimed and acknowledged guru, leader, and philosopher who had (in his exact words) "the most knowledge relating to the ESP philosophy," who had "the ultimate authority to explain that philosophy," and who, in that organization, had "the highest rank."

Pitching both religion and science as *merely perceptions* opens the door for Raniere to propose his own (equally competitive and "correct") perception in the form of his NXIVM "philosophy", and this is reinforced by his observation that "All types of faith exist and are valid because they are faith, and in the act of accepting any of them, we blind ourselves to other types of faith." At the very least, this kind of argument that Raniere subjects us to is a clear example of his *masquerading* as a philosopher, and he leaves us with a totally muddled account of the fundamental concept of perception and its relation to both science and religion.

♦ WHERE DID GOD GO?

Didn't Raniere just get done telling us that science (not religion) gives us an insight into reality that is consistent and correct knowledge? That would mean that reality isn't *merely* a perception wouldn't it? We're now left in total confusion concerning the relation of reality to science and the nature of science in contributing to our understanding of reality. This is obscurantism and anti-rationalism being practiced at their highest levels.

Moreover, nothing he says in the article establishes that God is *any kind of perception* at all — as opposed, for example, to being an incoherent concept, a theoretical construct, or simply a mystical idea of some sort. And so what kind of *perception* are we supposed to believe that God is?

For Raniere, is God supposed to be some kind of immediate perception — in the sense of a *revelation* or *immediate experience* of God? Does God appear to us personally so that we can see and hear (or at least experience) Him? Or is

He the kind of theory-laden perception that we get through science — so that it's really science that presents God to us as a perception? But then, as Raniere has told us, that would be just a "best guess". On that account, God would turn out to be a "best guess" somehow revealed to us through our science? We have no clue as to what the answers to these questions might be because Raniere is simply throwing unexplained and meaningless statements like this at us.

In fact, he's left us in a position that's worse than that, since in the end he offers us the final insight that

> **Raniere:** "If there were an answer to the question 'Why?' That answer might be 'God'. Here the term 'God' is freely used and is not intended to supplant a more particular symbol to which you could ascribe, be it a Judeo-Christian God, a divine principle or reality beyond the mask of human perception. Your article of faith, if you are an atheist physicist, a Catholic scholar, a Hindu monk, etc., will naturally give a more particular shape to this universal concept."

So God has now become such an amorphous "universal concept" that the word "God" has no particular sense (is not a "particular symbol") — which is another way of saying that to Raniere the word is meaningless. It takes on a sense only through the tenents of a given religion or dogma. So "God" means what you want it to, and you can impose on the term "God" any meaning you like. Okay — but how is this remotely like science? Well, *it's like science only if what science provides to us in terms of our understanding of the world is no better than what an arbitrarily chosen religion does*. But by Raniere's own admission, science gives a *knowledge* about the world that allows us to *accomplish* things in the world in an *effective and predictable way*. And so he's once again spiraled into incoherence in trying to make religion appear to be fundamentally similar to science.

If we do our best to apply the Principle of Charity, all this sounds like material that Raniere may have come across in an introductory philosophy course, but not understood very well. It might be some sort of indirect appeal to the *Argument from Design* (or *Teleological Argument* (Wikipedia 2020n)) where we're told that we can infer God's existence from the high level of complexity and intricate functioning we see in the everyday natural world. In fact Einstein says something along these lines in a 1955 letter to a Jewish philosopher, suggesting that "God reveals Himself in the harmony of the world" — which of course, particularly for Einstein, is what science describes. But Raniere's presentation of this thought — whatever he intends — is just more meaningless gobbletygook and another example of ⊘ *Obscurantism* and ⊘ *Inadequate Understanding*.

Chapter 10: The Curious Case of Keith Raniere

◆ WHAT HAPPENED TO THE *SCIENCE OF JUSTICE*?

Seemingly because the topic of the issue of *Conocimiento* in which this article appears is *The Science of Justice*, Raniere offers us insights such as:

> **Raniere:** "Of course, from the scientific point of view, there is amazement of the ultimate justice system that appears in an orderly universe.
>
> You could say that science is a justice system that attempts to elucidate God's justice system."

"Of course"? Again, this is complete gobbletygook, and Raniere hasn't bothered anywhere to mention this "ultimate justice system" previously, nor does he make any attempt to explain or describe it or to indicate in what sense it is a system of *justice*. So sure, you could *say* that "science is a justice system" — in about the same way that you can say that a square has only three sides, that 3 is less than 2, or that a camel can pass through the eye of a needle. But there's no hint of what it *means*, and it serves as an excellent example of ⊘ *Obscurantism* and of each of our pseudo-philosophy Markers of Language Abuse. This is the kind of thing that a student might throw into a philosophy assignment in an attempt to sound insightful and profound. It is neither.

And then,

> **Raniere:** "As we examine our perception more deeply through science, we find a deeper sense of justice in the external world — it could be called 'God' — and a deeper sense of purpose and complexity in the universe.
> ...
> It is also true, from an already stated perspective, that science adapts to the definition of a religion and we, as scientists, hypothesize about the future with faith."

Certainly this is more obscurantism through the use of vague terms and unexplained statements using them. What, for example, is this "deeper sense of justice" he's talking about? And how does it come to us through a better scientific understanding of *perception*? And why would we want to call a *sense of justice* "God"? At best this is metaphor run wild — and not philosophy.

What about the view that "science adapts to the definition of a religion"? Again (⊘ *Puzzling Terminology*), he's made no attempt to explain the nature of this *adapting* or to point to examples of it. And (⊘ *Misrepresentation*) in fact science does no such thing. Rather, it goes about its scientific business without regard for religion.

Scientists can "hypothesize about the future with faith"? If this is to make any sense at all, it rests on yet another equivocation since the faith it refers to can't be the religious faith he's been talking about.

There's no way to regard this as anything more than nonsense that results from just stringing words together. But this gibberish has had what might be one of it's intended functions: it's distracted us from the fact that in this entire article Raniere hasn't discussed the *science* of justice at all!

In this article, Raniere has talked about science, he's talked about religion, he's talked about perception and knowledge, and he's mentioned justice in fleeting and poetic ways. But nowhere has he taken any time to talk about how justice can be scientific, whether there is or could be a *science of justice* (as there is a science of biology, anthropology, or sociology), or even how contemporary science may be *applied* to issues in justice. This is very odd because the rest of the articles in this issue of *Conocimiento* deal with those questions — and you'd expect the introductory article in such an issue to at least mention them, to make some genuine contribution, or at least perhaps to set the agenda for further discussion. Raniere dodges all of those opportunities, and so we have to wonder exactly what his point was in crafting this particular article. We'll return to this question shortly.

Two more samples from Conocimiento

We've just looked in detail at a single article from the collection that comprises Raniere's philosophical views and the application of these to problems in the world. Of course, it's dangerous and unfair to generalize from a single example, but we're using this example here only as an illustration of what's found throughout Raniere's writings and how our markers and models apply to this kind of material. The rest of these *Conocimiento* articles fare no better.

There are — so far as I've been able to determine — at least 32 of these articles that span the period from September of 2005 through May of 2012. In terms of the quality of content, the approach, the style of writing, and the philosophical skill, they're all on the same level. Here are summaries of a couple more of these articles just to illustrate and enforce conclusions we've been moving towards at this point. We'll then bring our examination of Raniere's *Conocimiento* articles to a close.

♦ "NEGLIGENCE IN COMMUNICATION RESULTS IN MULTIPLE DEATHS"

This very brief article (Raniere 2005) addresses problems in determining which news reports we read are reliable and likely to be true and accurate as opposed to articles that are "fake news". It proposed to do this by answering such questions as "How should the news data be presented?" "When are the opinions and interpretations of the news data appropriate?" and "What makes an opinion or interpretation of news data honorable or dishonorable?" The overall goal is stated as "the ethical management of data."

The article offers nothing more than mundane observations about difficulties in interpreting information you find on the Web, and it contains a short list of ways in which information can be distorted by authors and publishers. As part of this, Raniere seems to repeat some basic concepts that he learned in an elementary informal logic course or a critical thinking course, but using unusual jargon to do so.

The motivation for the article is exposed in the final paragraph where Raniere makes the pitch that

> "We have developed a complete set of tools and a consistent and reproducible methodology to analyze communications and common media. Our corporation has a complete division dedicated to the creation of a communication data source without bias, honorable, scientific. Help take this next step in human development, please join us."

This is then followed by the usual boilerplate paragraph describing Raniere as "the scientist, mathematician, philosopher and entrepreneur Keith Raniere" and providing contact information for ESP through a NXIVM email address. One other piece of information related to this article is that at the point it was published Raniere was in the process of creating yet another of his companies. This was "The Knife of Aristotle" and its logo employed the universal and existential quantifier symbols from formal logic. It became "The Knife Media" and was dedicated to "change the way news is reported and history is preserved." It had (of course) "a unique process of analysis." But its Web site and social network accounts seemed to become inactive, and its Facebook page announces that it ceased publishing in August of 2018.

♦ "Microhumanity" and replacing conventional ethics

The focus of this article (Nevares and Raniere 2005) is on rules and ethics — although no clear characterization or analysis is ever provided for the concept of rule, and the view of ethics that emerges is murky indeed. Rules are then talked about in relation to games, teams, relations of dependence, interdependence, and independence, the advantage of cooperation for mutual benefit, and a concept of "competing against" which appears to be what many would refer to as a "zero sum game."

This article is quite difficult to follow, but in it Raniere sees himself as creating a new kind of system for guiding behavior that he calls an "interdependent system." This will replace traditional systems of ethics. It will be "based on ethics," but not on rules. All this is explicitly in the realm of a system of morality as a guide to decision and action — and in fact this is an explicit selling point for the educational and training services provided by Raniere's ESP company. And it's bold in seeking to replace "conventional ethics" with something new, rational, and more effective.

The precise nature and functioning of an "interdependent system" are never made clear and are left at a murky and partly emotional level, although some examples (confusing and not altogether coherent) are given. If I were forced to guess, I'd speculate that Raniere has some sort of self-interest ethical system (or "ethical egoism" (Shaver 2019)) in mind. And this speculation is compatible with some fleeting references that Raniere makes to Ayn Rand (see Chapter 11) — in which case the approach would appear not to be particularly new and innovative. But he never provides enough detail to understand what he's really getting at. As a result, any attempt to get a grip on what he's proposing is lost in his systemic ⊘ *Obscurantism* arising from ⊘ *Misuse of Terminology* and ⊘ *Puzzling Terminology*, and augmented with ⊘ *Misrepresentation*.

In the end it becomes clear that the real purpose of this article is to pitch the services of ESP in providing training in the use of Rational Inquiry to ensure that students will be able to adopt "more consistent ... belief patterns" and create within their companies an environment that allows them "to reach their full potential." The message seems to be that by taking the ESP courses you can put the whole idea of ethical *rules* behind you and instead employ innovative techniques to create and work within an interdependent system that will guide your thoughts and actions in an ethical (though not rule-based) way. Unfortunately, given what Raniere has provided us as insight into his thinking, this appears to require stripping the word "ethics" of any coherent meaning that it's ever had — never mind how your thoughts will be "guided" without an appeal to rules of some sort.

A fundamental part of the problem here is that even as he's talking about his new and innovative approach, he wants to use the concept of ethics to characterize it. So he says things like

> "... This is possible because the interdependent system is based on ethics, not rules, so no resources are lost due to unnecessary irrational fears, defenses or repression. ...
>
> Only in interdependence are we able to recognize that the successes of others benefit us and, likewise, our personal successes benefit them.

> From this recognition comes an honorable desire to compete ethically with others to improve all of humanity. ...
>
> Rational Inquiry allows individuals and groups to create ethical and goal-based interdependent systems, compared to more traditional and rule-based dependent or independent hierarchies."

So ethics (traditional? rule-based?) isn't good. But an "interdependent system" is good because it avoids the problems of traditional ethics (which somehow makes you feel bad or anxious or stressed). Furthermore, an interdependent system is *ethical*! And it's *based on ethics*! But what can this mean? What does "based on" mean, and what can Raniere mean by "ethics" in this article? It can't be a system of rules for guiding behavior. It can't be a system of moral laws. But then what's left? If you take the rules out of ethics, what do you have left?

What we're left with is one word ("ethics") whose meaning appears to have been abandoned and lost, and one new phrase ("interdependent system") for which we don't yet have a meaning. We don't know what the components are of an interdependent system — although we do know they aren't rules! And we're told that ethics and interdependent systems are somehow related, but we don't know how. The result appears to be a paradigm of pseudo-philosophy — based on ⊘ *Obscurantism* and a lack of Φ *Clarity*.

The Conocimiento corpus: a summary

This collection of articles that appeared over a period of years in the magazine *Conocimiento* is the best and most complete representation of Raniere's philosophical thought and use of philosophy that we have. It exhibits — repeatedly and quite uniformly — a number of pseudo-philosophy markers and aspects of the Pseudo persona. And at the same time it fails to exhibit several critical markers of genuine philosophy and aspects of the Philo persona of the genuine philosopher: Φ *Explanation*, Φ *Rationality*, Φ *Clarity*, Φ *Consistency*, and Φ *Domain Awareness*. Before moving on to a final judgment, however, there are two more sources and aspects of Raniere's philosophy that we should examine for the sake of fairness and completeness.

10.5 The YouTube performances

While the set of articles Raniere published in *Conocimiento* comprises the core of his writings, there is another wealth of information available in video form, and this is the set of YouTube videos that were posted during the period of December 2016 through April 2017 (Raniere 2017d). These were clearly

Section 10.5: The YouTube performances

meant to be informative, at least at a superficial level, to potential clients of ESP services, to present Raniere himself in an appealing manner, in part as a thoughtful philosopher, and to act as a marketing vehicle for ESP courses and services. They show Raniere being "interviewed" on a number of topics of interest to him that are dealt with in the ESP offerings. We'll look briefly at a couple of these just to highlight some of the features of Raniere's approach and goals, and compare these to our models of the genuine philosopher and pseudo-philosopher.

First, let's look at some broader features of these videos. In the title of this section I've called the videos "performances", and that's because that's exactly what they are. They're not Raniere speaking to an audience or class, or even speaking directly to the viewer. Instead, they're contrived as interviews of Raniere by two of his close associates and subordinates in NXIVM.

Allison Mack is an actress who had starred in the television series *Smallville* prior to joining Raniere's organizations, becoming one of his closest confidantes, and participating in recruiting women into what she later came to regard as a secret NXIVM cult. Allison entered acting at a young age and, in a blog, once described herself as not having "a proper education". In April of 2019 she pled guilty to federal conspiracy and racketeering charges involving the abuse, torture, and enslavement of women within NXIVM. As of this writing, she is awaiting sentencing.

Marc Elliot is an author and inspirational speaker with a very challenging medical history. He believes that he was cured of Tourette's Syndrome by Keith Raniere and NXIVM. Following Raniere's convictions he announced a talk in defense of Raniere and NXIVM, but this was later canceled. Marc has a Bachelor's degree in biology from Washington University in St. Louis and was originally planning on becoming a medical doctor. He's described as having been a NXIVM "coach" and "inspirational speaker." He was named as an unindicted co-conspirator in the criminal case against Keith Raniere, and despite Raniere's conviction and the exposure of the details of life inside the NXIVM empire, he continues to "support" whatever is left of that:

> "Marc completely overcame his Tourette's in 2013, drawing from innovations from courses in emotional intelligence (NXIVM), using only mind over body, and sheer will. ... Even with the recent events with NXIVM, Marc continues be a proud supporter in their current battle against hate, something Marc has always stood for." (from the Marc Elliot Web site (Elliot 2020))

Of course the "recent events" include the convictions of Raniere and some of his closest NXIVM associates on horrendous charges of mistreating and abusing a number of women. But in the title of his canceled talk in 2019, Elliot chose to characterize these prosecutions and convictions as "character assassination"; and he has reportedly declined to be interviewed about his NXIVM experiences.

As a consequence, what we see in these videos isn't designed with the primary purpose of communication or information or the pursuit of truth and wisdom in mind, but with presenting an impression under the guise of philosophical discussion. Let's see what that impression is.

◆ "UNDERSTANDING LABELS AS TOOLS"

This short 3 minute video (Raniere and Elliot 2017b) is about labeling of individuals as being of a certain *type*, or being in a certain class, or falling under a certain description as a result of some property or condition they have. The main focus begins in terms of people being "labeled" as Tourette's Syndrome patients (or sufferers). Marc Elliot introduces the topic and tries to express his concern about what he clearly feels is a kind of unfair labeling that can be detrimental to people with Tourette's Syndrome. But he's quickly prevented by Raniere from stating a clear problem or asking a well-phrased question. Instead Raniere interrupts him and launches into an initial broad discussion of what labels are.

Raniere begins by saying that "labels are a system," "labeling is a tool," and there are both "benefits and downsides" to it. He insists that all labels are "approximate,"[18] and then gives examples of difficulties in making some particular labels precise — as though this demonstrates that all labels are approximate. This begins Raniere's venture into philosophy of language in the area of what philosophers normally refer to as "reference and meaning", and which you can regard as a core competency in the philosophy of language.

In the process of giving some simplistic remarks about how getting the meaning of a label to do the job you want it to do is difficult, he raises the question of "How is the exact way that you should label labels?" and says that this is a problem because it's "self-referential". Now self-reference can be a serious problem in logic and philosophy as illustrated by a variety of paradoxes including the well-known Liar Paradox: "This sentence is false." That sentence *is* self-referential since it refers ("this sentence") to itself (Beall and Ripley 2016). And because of that, it has the consequence that it's both false (if it's true) and true (if it's false).

But asking how a label should be labeled or how a group of labels should be labeled *isn't self-referential* — it's just a normal problem in labeling (for a particular purpose, for example). Even if we want to raise the question of what general principles are to be followed in labeling labels (which, oddly, Raniere doesn't bother to consider), it's still not self-referential. There's just no *self-reference* there.

Raniere's introduction of the notion of self-reference in this example is simply out of place. It's *irrelevant* to the original problem he introduces concerning the precise characterization of a particular label, it's *unhelpful and unenlightening* concerning how labels work, and it's *wrong* in a most fundamental way. It exhibits our markers of ⊘ *Misrepresentation* (in this case, misrepresenting one problem as another) and ⊘ *Misuse of Terminology* (in this case, the term "self-reference").

Additionally, Raniere avoids introducing the distinction between a label acting as a *name* (of a set of people, for example) and the label acting as a *description* (attributing properties to the members of the set). This is a fundamental distinction in the philosophy of language and would help to address the concern that Marc Elliot is trying to express — which is that using the label as a *name* (simple designator) can have unfortunate consequences because of an incorrect or misleading *description* (meaning) associated with it.

Raniere simply misses this opportunity to state a genuine problem clearly and to use genuine philosophy to address it. Nor does he approach even more helpful questions (also hinted at in Elliot's concerns) about what principles and techniques might be employed to make the use of labels more effective and reasonable, to reduce the risk in using them, and to increase the benefits. And this is something that a philosopher ought to be able to help us with. Instead, Raniere rattles off a few quick banal, unhelpful, or incorrect remarks about labels, and this isn't at all what we should expect from a genuine philosopher.

♦ "EVOLVING SOCIETAL VALUES TO TRANSFORM ARTS AND MEDIA"

Allison Mack opens this discussion (Raniere and Mack 2017) by saying that in general, news media are becoming less responsible and moral in their reporting. She then asks "How do you work in a commercialized field and make the impact you want to make and yet still have it be something viable?" This question itself is a bit vague since it's not at all obvious what she means by "viable", and that's an odd choice of terminology in the context. But it's clear from other things she says that she's asking how to get along in a job environment where you're sometimes (if not frequently) faced with a choice between what your employer wants you to do and what you think is right or wrong.

Raniere responds with

Chapter 10: The Curious Case of Keith Raniere

> **Raniere:** "Well, it's a system. ... The problem right now with society is that it's not self-reflective. We don't have a strong community structure, a strong national structure, and down to the strong family structure and individual structure. These things are not reflective of really a specific type of morality."

But *what's* a system? This seems to be another case where he uses one of his favorite words ("system") to refer vaguely to some situation or thing that exhibits some degree of complexity — without making an effort to indicate exactly what he's talking about. Might he mean that business or commerce is a system? Yes, he might mean that. But how does that help us respond to Allison's question?

He then immediately employs another favorite term ("structure") in saying that the problem with society is a result of the absence of structure in communities, the nation, families, and individuals. But what sort of structure is he talking about? And what are the signs of this absence, and what should we expect in its place? We don't know. Moreover, although it might make sense to talk about structure (organizational structure?) missing from communities and the nation, these in fact seem to have a lot of structure. Many people would say they have *too much* structure!

In terms of family structure, he might mean to refer to the shift in contemporary society away from either the nuclear family or the extended family, but we just don't know what he means. And it's even less clear what he might mean in saying that *individuals* in our society don't have a strong structure. That can't mean something like *skeletal structure* (which at least is a kind of structure that an individual has). But then what could it mean? At this point we seem to be in a pretty deep well of ⊘ *Obscurantism*.

There's also, Raniere says, a problem of "reflectivity." That is, our society isn't "self-reflective," and the structures of our communities, our nation, our families, and our individuals aren't reflective of a "specific type of morality." You may immediately notice an equivocal use of "reflective" here, but that's the least of our worries right now. So let's let it pass. Also the phrase *specific type of morality* is equivocal. Does he mean that there's a particular type of morality (among a range of possibilities) that isn't reflected in our society? Which one is that? Or does he mean that there isn't *any* identifiable type of morality that's reflected in our society? These are two quite different things. (⊘ *Vagueness and Equivocation*, ⊘ *Puzzling Terminology*, lack of Φ *Clarity*)

This response of Raniere's seems to be simply bewildering. But it seems okay to Allison since she doesn't ask him to clarify it, and in fact looks at him and nods like he's just said something *brilliant*. So according to Raniere the problem must be a lack of structure. Let's see where that leads us.

Raniere shifts gears and suggests that the problem (or *a* problem) is that people don't have a real definition for good and bad. So they can't justify and depend on their moral judgments. Now we seem to be getting somewhere.[19] This seems to go in the direction of an answer to Allison's original question, which was about how to get along in a job environment where you're seemingly being asked to do things that you think aren't right. How can that problem be addressed? Well, Raniere's answer is

> **Raniere:** "Society in itself, if it continues the way it's going will end up where it's headed. ... But humans have the capacity to actually sit and think about where we want it to be, think about how we'd like it to change. And that contemplation has to be something that becomes understood in society. ... that the different ethical issues that come up are discussed."
>
> *[He refers to his company's* "ethicist curriculum," *and then ...]*
>
> "Being an ethicist will be as much of a foundation to society as being a business person. ... Right now that doesn't exist so much."

Raniere then wanders off into a discussion of rock music *vs.* classical music and the different rewards in those domains, talks about sports as a trivial though lucrative part of society, employs a confusing analogy of how learning to be ethical is similar to going to a health club to exercise and become healthy, and ends with

> **Raniere:** "If you want to be involved in transforming people, educating people, moving them forward, unless people are aware of they're paying money [sic] for where they are at as opposed to where they want to be, you'll become less viable commercially. So it's an interesting problem."

Well, there *was* an interesting and genuinely philosophical (and also practical) problem that started this discussion, but the answer to it seems to be that society needs to be changed by training people as ethicists to be dispersed throughout all of its "structures." Somehow, any diagnosis of what the structures are, what's wrong with them, and exactly how this will be fixed by taking Raniere's courses in ethics didn't make it into the conversation.

What to conclude from the YouTube videos

Although we'll look into a couple more of the YouTube videos in the next section, the two we've considered here are sufficient to provide examples of how our models can be used to analyze potential cases of pseudo-philosophy in this particular body of Raniere's thinking. What can we conclude and take away from this experience?

♦ PSEUDO-PHILOSOPHICAL PROBLEMS EXHIBITED IN THE VIDEOS

First, the videos demonstrate that Raniere doesn't like clearly stated questions or problems — and our examples are representative of the entire set of the videos. He has a pronounced aversion to Φ *Problem Orientation* and Φ *Clarity*. Whenever confronted with a clearly stated question he turns his response into a vague and obscurantist reply that doesn't address that problem. Instead, he replaces the original problem with a vague one that he addresses using a variety of jargon while trying to leave you with the impression that he's devoted significant thought to your problem and produced an answer for you — if only you're capable of understanding it.

There appear to be two main goals in these videos, and the videos are obviously highly scripted to pursue those goals. First, the ultimate goal is to convince people that Raniere personally, and his companies programmatically, have something to offer that will *help* you and *make you a better person* (a more thoughtful and more intelligent person). You just need to take the courses he offers. Second, the videos are designed to provide you with a certain impression of Raniere and confidence in him. Here's a thoughtful philosopher and scientist dealing with important problems in an innovative manner, and getting results from which you can benefit. And an important part of communicating this impression lies in Raniere's demonstrating his capabilities as a *philosopher*. Raniere is striving to appear as a competent philosopher who is moral, concerned about important problems in society, in control of understanding these problems, and even noble in his pursuit of solutions which he can provide to you.

But there seems to be a high degree of dissonance in how this picture gets painted. Raniere makes elementary mistakes when he tries to get specific about some aspects of philosophy or to provide a philosophical account of critical topics. This raises red flags in terms of a number of our pseudo-philosophy markers — especially the *Markers of Trickery, Markers of Language Use,* and *Markers of Competence.*

◆ WHAT'S MISSING FROM THE VIDEOS?

More broadly we have to ask some questions about what's *missing* from these videos: what's missing that we would *expect* to be there if they were being produced by a genuine philosopher:

- Where are specific responses to the questions or issues that these videos purportedly deal with?
  (Φ *Clarity*, Φ *Methods*)

- In fact, where are specific questions and goals articulated in any clear and understandable way?
  (Φ *Problem Orientation*, Φ *Clarity*, Φ *Adequacy*)

- Shouldn't we expect to see Raniere explaining what he *does* in his training courses — instead of just saying that the courses exist and will help us, or that they'll somehow teach us an innovative approach to ethics that will help us in our careers? Shouldn't he provide at least some examples?
  (Φ *Explanation*)

- Shouldn't we expect to see Raniere describing what we're going to learn in those courses, and what their goals and content are?
  (Φ *Explanation*, Φ *Adequacy*, Φ *Methods*)

Without answers to these questions, the image that Raniere is trying to paint in his YouTube videos can't be seen as being compatible with the Philo persona. Together with the various red flags in these videos represented by our pseudo-philosophy markers, and his appeal to philosophy in recruiting new customers and NXIVM members, this tilts us further in the direction of viewing Raniere's overall approach as pseudo-philosophical.

10.6 It's all about Rational Inquiry™

One point that quickly becomes clear in looking at any of Raniere's videos, the *Conocimiento* articles, public statements, or court documents is that Raniere's "technology" of Rational Inquiry is central both to his own philosophy and approach to life, and to the products, programs, training, and experiences that his companies (NXIVM, ESP, Ethical First Principles, and the bizarrely inappropriately named Ethical Science Foundation) were producing and offering over a period of years. All these sources make clear that Raniere views Rational Inquiry as his fundamental innovation and invention, and that everything else rests on it, its principles, and its applications. Rational Inquiry is Raniere's *philosophical methodology* and *the core of his philosophy* — used to justify and to accomplish everything else.

The Rational Inquiry videos

Let's see what Rational Inquiry is and how it works. We can begin by looking at two of his YouTube videos that appear to be intended to answer the critical questions "What is Rational Inquiry?" and "How does Rational Inquiry work?" In fact, those are the titles of those videos.

♦ "WHAT IS RATIONAL INQUIRY?"

Marc Elliot begins this 2.5 minute interview (Raniere and Elliot 2016) by asking

> **Marc Elliot:** "Why do you call Rational Inquiry a technology, and then how do you see that works? Or how does the methodology work and help people with Tourette?"

Finally we have a straight and simple question put to Raniere about what his primary approach is and how it works to accomplish all the things he's said it has. His response is

> **Raniere:** "You could call it a *method*ology too, but "technology" fits more tightly.
>
> We have a series of theoretical understandings that have procedures and methodologies with them. That we apply to different situations to get certain types of results.
>
> You could say "methodologies" or "knowledge base" or things like that.
>
> It is based on certain types of understandings and assumptions. We can challenge those assumptions and understand what it does to the thing itself. It is in itself the knowledge base, is like an object. And we apply it in different ways. So it's not just one methodology. It's not a single step by step thing. It's based on guiding principles that are understandings."

Marc nods thoughtfully, apparently grateful for this answer to his questions, and the presentation is over. What have we learned about Raniere's technology/methodology/knowledge base of Rational Inquiry (which is, by the way, always trademarked™ by him)?

We've learned nothing. Instead we've been subjected to meaningless and unexplained jargon ("understandings", "knowledge base"), and while we've been told that Rational Inquiry is based on understandings and assumptions, we haven't seen a single example of one of these, and "understanding" is a peculiar term to make use of here. What's being understood? And what *is* an understanding? Is it like a *belief*? We have no clue. We've also not seen any examples of the "different situations" that Rational Inquiry is applied to or what the "certain types of results" might be.

So this has been another paradigm case of ⊘ *Obscurantism* and ⊘ *Puzzling Terminology*. Well, maybe things will be clarified in ...

♦ "How Rational Inquiry Works"

In this video (Raniere and Elliot 2017a) Marc Elliot is very excited about how successful Rational Inquiry is. He describes it as sounding "too good to be true." But Marc asks Keith *how the methodology works*.

We get treated to another round of talk about "understandings." This time they're described as "innovations" and vague references are made to patents that are "being pursued." This sounds good because if a process or technique is patentable, then there has to be at least a clear description of it. That's required by the patent office.

Raniere compares Rational Inquiry (as a new technology) to an "ox-dragged cart" introduced to farmers who previously were only able to use hand tools to till their fields. And the cart allows them to plow their field in a single day. Unfortunately for Raniere, this is a ludicrous example which makes him look embarrassingly ignorant — since fields aren't plowed with *carts*. Carts can be used to put things in and haul them around whereas plowing a field requires ... well ... a *plow*. Nonetheless, Marc smiles and nods happily, knowing that he's been let in on a truly fundamental insight.

Raniere moves on to say that his tools are "unique" and that using these tools "gets results where other tools don't get results." No examples are provided, but he modestly denies that there's anything miraculous about these tools and that *"everything is straightforward and explainable."* By means of explanation he then starts to flood the conversation with new unexplained jargon: a "conversational type of technology," an "understanding" that is "outside of those patterns" of previous "human performance technologies." A return to gobbletygook.

As the video draws to a close, we realize that we never did get the account of Rational Inquiry that Raniere assured us was "straightforward and explainable." Just more examples of ⊘ *Obscurantism*, ⊘ *Exaggerated Claims*, and ⊘ *Puzzling Terminology*. But not a flicker of Φ *Explanation*, Φ *Adequacy*, or Φ *Clarity*.

The Rational Inquiry patent

We've seen that Rational Inquiry isn't explained in the YouTube videos. It's also not explained in the *Conocimiento* articles, which is more puzzling since we know from Ivy Nevares that (in book form) these served as the handbook for Raniere's coaches, courses, and "trainings". But there are two other sources in which we might finally come to an understanding of what Rational Inquiry is: the patent that was filed on this technology, and court documents in which Raniere responds to questions concerning the nature and use of Rational Inquiry. And these also expose additional aspects of his claims to make use of philosophy.

Raniere made his initial filing for a Rational Inquiry patent in (Raniere 2000). The patent was filed internationally and has been rejected or abandoned in every country where it was filed except possibly for the World Intellectual Property Organization and South Africa where its current status is unclear but appears to be suspended (which means that it's languishing indefinitely). The U.S. Patent Office rejected the patent in 2004, Germany rejected the patent application in 2013, China in 2008, Japan in 2009. Australia rejected the patent in 2011, in part with the observation that

> **Australian patent examiner:** "While dressed up in somewhat convoluted terminology, what appears from the description is that the claims are directed to very common processes of counseling and therapy or personal motivation that are described in the documents cited and these would clearly form part of the common general knowledge of those practicing in the relevant art."

In short, in so far as the patent application could be understood in spite of its ⊘ *Obscurantism* and ⊘ *Puzzling Terminology*, it did not offer anything approaching a patentable technology, appeared to describe common techniques of therapeutic and motivational programs, and exhibited ⊘ *Exaggerated Claims*.

Section 10.6: It's all about Rational Inquiry™

◆ **RATIONAL INQUIRY™ = THE SOCRATIC METHOD?**

From another perspective, we have a November 14, 2018 letter signed by attorney Mark Agnifilo, requesting bail for Keith Raniere in his federal court case, and in which Agnifilo describes Rational Inquiry as

> **Raniere attorney Mark Agnifilo:** "Rational Inquiry is a complex, essential concept to the Nxivm teachings. However, in the simplest terms, it is the Socratic Method of pointed questioning. As any law student knows, a law professor may call upon him or her during a lesson and ask well-placed questions to determine what the student believes about a certain topic and where, if anywhere, that belief comes from. What the law professor does in a law school classroom, Nxivm does elsewhere regarding how we view ourselves, form relationships and make decisions for ourselves and others." (Agnifilo 2018, 2-3)

Agnifilo's concession to the Court that Rational Inquiry is simply an embroidered version of the Socratic Method is fascinating since it means that Raniere's own attorney is admitting that the logical and epistemological basis for what Raniere claimed to be the innovative foundation of his philosophical method isn't novel and isn't — and could never have been — patentable. And it points to pseudo-philosophy markers such as ⊗ *Exaggerated Claims* and ⊗ *Misappropriation* since Raniere (in his own written materials, in his YouTube videos, and in court depositions) claimed that Rational Inquiry was original and not borrowed from others.

Agnifilo's letter then goes on to draw a parallel (later ridiculed by federal prosecutors) between Socrates and Keith Raniere. But in it he again makes a strong argument that what Raniere was doing was *philosophy*. He goes so far in his letter as to include footnotes to Bertrand Russell's *A History of Western Philosophy* and to Kierkegaard, Sartre, and Nietzsche. It's important to note, however, that in Agnifilo's praise for Raniere's work here, he concedes that Rational Inquiry is not a technology, and that the only methodology involved in it amounts to classroom teaching and the Socratic method (which, however, if you watch many of the YouTube videos, you'll see isn't remotely what Raniere practices). As a consequence, Agnifilo presents to the court the view that Raniere was *acting as a philosopher* and as a *philosophy teacher* in a classical manner. From an objective viewpoint, Raniere was *masquerading as a philosopher*.

◆ **THE ROLE OF RATIONAL INQUIRY**

An excellent and detailed article on the history of Raniere's many patent applications (among which some — often humorous ones — were granted) is

Kenzie Bryant's *Vanity Fair* article "How NXIVM Used the Strange Power of Patents to Build Its 'Sex Cult'" (Bryant 2018). In it, Daniel Nazer, who is *Mark Cuban Chair to Eliminate Stupid Patents* at the Electronic Frontier Foundation explains why Raniere spent so much time and effort in developing his Rational Inquiry patent applications and promoting Rational Inquiry as a "patent-pending technology":

> **Daniel Nazer:** "If your whole shtick is going around and convincing people that you're this genius, then the patent system is a way to buttress that. Because [the United States Patent and Trademark Office] will hand out nonsense to people like Keith Raniere."

In a March 11, 2009 sworn deposition in a civil suit by NXIVM, ESP, and First Principles against The Ross Institute and others (US District Court 2009), the Ross attorneys were doing their best to get Raniere to provide them with a clear picture of what exactly comprised Rational Inquiry and how it was used. Raniere testified that he was the "sole creator" of the Rational Inquiry Method and that he didn't "consult with any source materials" in creating the method. But when questioned about whether he made use of ideas from the Church of Scientology and neurolinguistic programming, he says things like "No, I don't think so," "None specific that I can think of," "I don't know if that's a part of the method"; and then contradicts himself about having learned or used concepts from Scientology.

Next, one of the attorneys presses him about having made use of any of Ayn Rand's works in developing the Rational Inquiry Method: "Did you incorporate any of her philosophy into Rational Inquiry Method?" Raniere's response is an evasive and equivocating "Not in the method, but some of the patterns within her philosophy — some of the things within her philosophy I think are very good." He then concedes that "Certain things within the Money module are a tribute to her work." Sensing the presence of our pseudo-philosophy markers ⊘ *Misrepresentation*, ⊘ *Exaggerated Claims*, and ⊘ *Misappropriation*, the attorney leaps on this admission; but he just can't get Raniere to be specific about more details of Rational Inquiry and what ideas and work of others may have gone into it.

Changing direction slightly, the attorney then starts to quiz Raniere about exactly what's in the patent application. But Raniere denies knowledge of this! He's then asked if he's aware that in 2004 the (U.S.) Patent Office issued a final denial of the patent application. This could be a bit of a problem since the NXIVM and ESP people continued well past 2009 to refer (e.g., in the YouTube videos) to the innovative "patent-pending technology" they were using in their courses. Of course, the patent had been filed in quite a number of countries, and some of those were still "pending" (though really in more of a state of limbo).

Raniere stumbles in his answer and asks if he can take a break before answering, but the attorneys press on. Raniere says that he's "not sure" if he's seen the Patent Office document rejecting the application — that was all done by his attorney — and that with respect to the patent documents, "I don't read them. There are a lot of them." He also says that he doesn't know the exact status of the patent or what the last time was that his attorney contacted the Patent Office. The deposition continues, throughout that day and the next, and things don't get better. NXIVM ultimately lost the case.

All of this provides both insight into what the true role of Rational Inquiry was for Raniere and an explanation of why he never seemed able to articulate exactly what Rational Inquiry is or how it works: there's (literally) nothing to it. It's just pseudo-philosophical jargon based on obscurantism, equivocation, and misuse of language for the purpose of convincing people that Raniere is a philosophical and technical genius in whom they can have faith. But Rational Inquiry wasn't even a house of cards. It was never more than a mere allusion to a house of cards that hadn't been built. It was, indeed, in Marc Elliot's confused glimpse of reality, "too good to be true."

10.7 Making a judgment

We've spent quite a bit of time and effort in this example following the guidelines laid out in Chapter 8, looking carefully through the lenses of our models at what Keith Raniere has said in his writings, his videos, and in court documents, and looking at what others have said about him and his philosophy. It's quite apparent that Raniere falls firmly into the characterization of the pseudo-philosopher that our models provide.

No portion of his work matches the Philo persona, and there are continual and explicit failures to exhibit the markers of genuine philosophy. There is no evidence that Raniere ever produced anything like a coherent philosophical theory in his attempts to deal with questions in religion vs. science, ethics, epistemology, or perception — or even that he managed to produce a coherent and intelligible set of concepts to address the issues he raises. At the same time, his work and behavior strongly conform to the Pseudo persona and repeatedly exhibit examples of the markers of pseudo-philosophy. And we can provide a bit more perspective on this by considering the critical questions with which we began this chapter — slightly rephrased to reflect the view of Raniere as a pseudo-philosopher.

Chapter 10: The Curious Case of Keith Raniere

◆ **WAS RANIERE ACTING AS A PHILOSOPHER AND PRESENTING HIMSELF AS A PHILOSOPHER?**

This question is important because it wouldn't be fair (and wouldn't fit our models) to cast Raniere as pseudo-philosophical if he wasn't acting in the role of a philosopher or claiming to be presenting us with philosophical insight and results. In this case it's abundantly clear. From what Raniere has said about himself and his philosophical training and skills, from what his followers and supporters have said about his philosophical leadership and contributions to NXIVM and other organizations, from what appears in his YouTube videos, *Conocimiento* articles, and court documents, it's explicit that he was acting as a philosopher and intended to be taken to be acting in this role. Moreover, his appearance in the role of a philosopher had a profound effect on members of NXIVM and his followers, what beliefs they were willing to adopt, and what actions they were willing to take.

◆ **HOW WAS PSEUDO-PHILOSOPHY USED BY RANIERE?**

Raniere used an appeal to philosophy — and his claim to be a philosopher — to provide the appearance of establishing a foundation for what he claimed to be his innovative methodologies and services, to assure people that he was a genuine intellectual (in fact, a genius), that he cared about problems they were facing, and that he had a deep understanding of these problems and their solutions. He employed pseudo-philosophy as a tool to provide his clients and prospective clients with a level of confidence and faith in what he was telling them, and in the value of what he could provide to them. This is one of the fundamental techniques of pseudo-philosophers in which they *masquerade* as philosophers and *borrow* the respectability of genuine philosophy and its contributions.

We may wonder whether Raniere's appeal to philosophy and philosophical questions, concepts, and theories is merely a trivial part of his approach or a central one. But it would appear that it's beyond being a trivial component of Raniere's strategy and tactics. A good test of this is to ask "If we look at Raniere's writings and videos (some of which formed the core of the ESP courses and 'trainings'), and we take out all of the sections (e.g., in the discussions of ethics, labels, social philosophy, metaphysics, and knowledge) employing the use of pseudo-philosophical jargon and concepts, what's left?"

The answer to this question has to be "Not much." There are frequent references to science, but he doesn't offer science. He offers interpretations of science based on pseudo-philosophical views he adopts in areas such as ethics, epistemology, and the philosophy of science. What's left is some story telling, some attempts at analogy and allegory, and made-up examples. But removing the pseudo-philosophical material leaves a big hole, and the result doesn't hang together in any way. If we take away Rational Inquiry and the ever-present references and appeals to it, there's hardly much left at all. Pseudo-philosophy is the glue that binds together all that Raniere was offering.

◆ **WHY DID RANIERE USE PSEUDO-PHILOSOPHY IN THIS WAY?**

There are two facets to this question: what were Raniere's motivations and ultimate goals; and what was gained by his use of pseudo-philosophy in pursuit of them? In either case, I don't think we can do better than the description provided by the U.S. Attorney and the FBI in describing these goals as "financial gain and sexual gratification" — which, we may observe, are a long way from the pursuit of truth and wisdom as traditionally practiced by the genuine philosopher. Raniere's use of pseudo-philosophy was a masquerade (and the U.S. Attorney uses this word in describing Raniere's actions) employed to conceal his goals and distract from his pursuit of them.

◆ **WHAT WERE THE CONSEQUENCES?**

As a startling number of news reports, interviews, court documents, and trial transcripts demonstrate, the consequences in this case were dire and the effects on the lives of a number of women were appalling. People were treated as — and allowed themselves to be treated as — slaves, both physically and psychologically. They were even *called* slaves and called *themselves* slaves. Lives were ruined, families were destroyed, fortunes were lost (or mostly, at least, given away). And yet some of the followers still follow.

How could so many people, for so long, have missed what was happening? How could so many people have fallen under the spell that was woven? The answers to those questions have to be deferred to the psychologists, psychiatrists, and the behavioral scientists. But whatever their answers turn out to be, I think we have to acknowledge that pseudo-philosophy played an important role in providing a part of the conceptual framework within which those tragedies took place.

10.8 A final appraisal

We can go a little further and ask what kind of pseudo-philosopher Raniere is. That is, where does he stand in the pantheon of the great pseudo-philosophers? Does he have a distinctive style or flair? Surely even among scoundrels we can provide some sort of ranking. Alas, I'm afraid that Raniere isn't going to make it into the *Pseudo-philosophy Hall of Fame*. He's a pseudo-philosopher, but he just isn't very good at it. In terms of both effort and quality he has to get pretty low marks, although in practice he got far with what he had.

In Chapter 6, and particularly in Section 6.2, we saw that the practice of pseudo-philosophy can be viewed as taking place in a space defined by dimensions of *Incompetence* (which is to say the quality or lack of quality of the philosophical techniques and knowledge that are employed) and *Exploitation* (the use of that knowledge and methodology to achieve goals incompatible with truth and wisdom). Where does Raniere end up in this pseudo-philosophical space?

We have to give Raniere high marks for achieving his goals through the use of pseudo-philosophy. He appears to have been careful and selective in choosing his targets — focusing often on women (and some men) from one or another area of the "entertainment arts", from people involved in (or attracted to) certain "soft" (and in some cases at least somewhat pseudo-scientific) areas of behavioral modification, personal improvement, or counseling, and from people having little or no experience with genuine science or philosophy. In short, his congregation was recruited or self-selected from a population of people seeking some improvement in their lives, but without any particular interests or skills in critical thinking, and without much sense of caution for someone's providing what on the face of it are at best obscure visions of the promised land. These were people whose thoughts could be molded, and who in fact were anxious for the molding.

Regarding his financial backers (some of whom stuck with him throughout his trial and continue to support him in one manner or another today), he seemed to favor the children of wealthy families, who had not found it necessary to be a part of the workforce, and who had sufficient financial resources and time that they could lead independent lives and contribute to a variety of causes and projects. Given that perspective, it may not be so much of a mystery that no one on the inside noticed (or cared) what was actually taking place in Raniere's organizations over two decades. They had faith, and (as we know from a number of testimonials) the faith was bolstered by doses of pseudo-philosophy on a regular basis. So on the *Exploitation* axis, Raniere is pretty far to the right.

In the area of philosophical skill and competence, he doesn't do as well. At best, Raniere's philosophical competence (as demonstrated in the *Conocimiento* articles, the YouTube videos, and the court documents) is at about the level of a C student at the sophomore or perhaps junior university level. In fact, on the axis of *Incompetence* he seems to be at its furthest reach. In our chart in Section 6.2 we don't have a label for this position which is in the upper right corner at the maximum value of *Incompetence* and the maximum value of *Exploitation*.

This is why we can view Raniere as a highly successful pseudo-philosopher, but not a good one: his pseudo-philosophy was very successful, but of low quality. It wasn't just philosophy gone bad. It was bad philosophy gone bad, but bad philosophy with a purpose and with carefully selected targets. And it worked. For a bit more insight, now that we've examined this specific case of pseudo-philosophy, go back and re-read Chapter 6 — especially the section on Quine and Ullian, and the one on Nicholas Rescher. You'll see some striking similarities between those characterizations and this case.

Ironically, for a particular and carefully chosen audience, Raniere really was a kind of genius and savant — though not the kind he claimed to be. So as a one-sentence summary of the quality and success of Raniere's pseudo-philosophy, it's accurate to say that he is a low-functioning but highly successful pseudo-philosopher. In the next chapter, we'll see something quite different.

Chapter 11
Ayn Rand: Mostly Borrowed, Nothing New?

In this chapter:
- Personal and intellectual history
- Attitudes towards Rand
- Difficulties of interpretation and understanding
- Rand's view of philosophy
- Rand's ethical theory
- Determinations and explanations

It appears undeniable that the most well-known, influential, and hotly debated non-academic philosopher of the 20th (and now 21st) century has been Ayn Rand. But as I've pointed out in earlier chapters, the history of philosophy is littered with great philosophers who didn't fit what we now take to be the paradigm of the professional or academic philosopher. While Rand continues to have (and attract) a loyal group of staunch supporters and defenders, she has often been called a pseudo-philosopher, and her views have been characterized as being confused, misleading, dishonest, and dangerous. So it's now time to see how Rand comes out on the account of pseudo-philosophy developed here: genuine philosopher, pseudo-philosopher, neither, or somewhere in between?

11.1 Background

It will be helpful in understanding what follows if we first take a bit of time to set some context in which Ayn Rand pursued her approach to philosophy. Some perspective of the influences on her in this and related domains, as well as her goals and experiences, will contribute to an understanding of her approach and the way in which she presents philosophical problems, concepts, positions and arguments. This is particularly important since followers of Rand will frequently say that her approach is either unique, or is at least unusual to some degree, and either lies outside the range of common academic philosophy or is related to it in only tenuous ways — and hence that Rand's philosophy should be judged by other standards.

Although true philosophical insight and originality may be characterized by innovation and uniqueness of approach or methodology, employing claims to these as a defense against charges of pseudo-philosophy always involves some risk since it can be used by pseudo-philosophers or their followers to excuse or conceal such markers as ⊘ *Obscurantism,* ⊘ *Discouraging Inquiry,* ⊘ *Inadequate Understanding,* ⊘ *Ignorance of Prior Work,* and ⊘ *Lack of Rigor.* As a consequence, understanding Rand's approach to philosophical method — and how this may be related to her literary method — is crucial in evaluating her work as genuinely philosophical or pseudo-philosophical.

Ayn Rand was born Alissa Zinovievna Rosenbaum in St. Petersburg Russia on February 2, 1905. Her parents were Jewish, and her father owned and operated a pharmacy in Petrograd until it was confiscated in the Russian Revolution of 1917. They then moved to the Crimea (at that point untouched by the Revolution) in order to start anew financially and to escape other consequences of the Revolution. They returned to Petrograd (the renamed St. Petersburg) in 1921, after the Revolution had reached the Crimea and when Rand was 16 years old.

From an early age, Rand was fascinated with stories, the telling of stories, and how stories could and should be told; and her focus tended to be on myth and metaphor. A concise expression of her own views of writing (both literary and philosophical) is found in "The Goal of my Writing" (Rand 1963b), an essay originally published in 1963 and later included in her book *The Romantic Manifesto: A Philosophy of Literature* (Rand 1971). This article is explicit in revealing that Rand considered herself to be primarily an *artist* whose goal is to communicate *ideals* (not ideas) and emotive feelings. "The Goal of my Writing" was published after both *For the New Intellectual* and *The Virtue of Selfishness,* and so must be taken to inform any understanding of what Rand regards as her method in each of these philosophical works as well.

Rand sees herself as a "creator," which she disdainfully distinguishes from "a recording secretary." For Rand, a *creator,* in the case of writing, creates *stories* (not *descriptions*) and the *characters* that act in those stories according to a fanciful *plot* that the story follows. All of these are *invented* rather than (merely) *reported.* The motive and purpose of her writing, Rand says, is "the projection of an ideal man." The author, *as creator,* paints a picture of an *ideal* scene, and without the constraints imposed on the "recording secretary" to describe, with accuracy, current reality. She emphasizes the heroism (and heroic stature) of her primary characters as heroes to be admired and emulated.

Rand also says at this point that "Art does not teach," and that teaching is not the purpose of an art work. Again, art (and so her *writing*) for Rand isn't descriptive, but rather inspirational and evocative — it's the writer as visionary poet rather than as historian or analyst. The purpose of art (and her writing) is to *move* people — to make them *feel* (in a certain way about something) and so to *act* (in accord with that feeling).

Thinking back to Chapter 1 and Sections 5.4 and 5.7, we can't avoid seeing Rand's attitude in "The Goal of my Writing" as representative of a perspective more compatible with sophistry, rhetoric, and literature than with philosophy. We'll return to this issue below, but for the moment remain content with Rand's view of writing as being based on stories in which strong character development, ideals, and heroes play critical roles while what she regards as mundane description of everyday reality has no place.

After the family returned to Petrograd in 1921, Rand enrolled in Petrograd State University and graduated in 1924, majoring in history. Several reports have her doing a minor in philosophy, but it's not clear how accurate this is, what that would mean within the newly Soviet university system at that time, and whether it's true.

After Rand's death in 1982, and following many years of effort, tribulation, misdirection, and deception, Chris Sciabarra was able to track down Rand's university transcript. A translation of the transcript and his summary/analysis of this, along with the intriguing details of his quest, are described in his 2013 second edition of *Ayn Rand: The Russian Radical* (Sciabarra 2013), his 1999 article "The Rand Transcript" (Sciabarra 1999b), on his Web page "Investigative Report: In Search of the Rand Transcript" (Sciabarra 1999a), and in a number of other articles and Web sites. Sciabarra's rendition of the transcript includes brief descriptions of the courses Rand took in the area of philosophy as well as a number of speculations concerning both the content of those courses and their influence on Rand's thinking and approach to philosophy.

Unfortunately, copies of the original transcript (in Russian and unedited) have never been made available to the public. You might wonder *why* this is so if it's critical to establishing Rand's *bona fides* in genuine philosophy, but as a consequence we have only reports, summaries, or "translations" of the transcript. Purely as a matter of practical expediency, we'll assume that these are mostly accurate, although there are good reasons (see the "Filtering out commentaries" part of Section 3 below) to be cautious and not to feel overly confident in this assumption. For our purposes here, it likely doesn't matter; but this situation of the inaccessibility of Rand's transcript appears to exhibit aspects of ⊘ *Discouraging Inquiry* — not on Rand's part, but in the actions of some of her followers.

After graduating from Petrograd State University, Rand briefly took a job as a museum guide and also became a student at the State Institute for Cinema Arts in order to concentrate on the study of screenwriting. An opportunity presented itself for her to visit relatives in Chicago, she received permission from the Soviet authorities to do this, and in 1926 she left the Soviet Union for the United States, embarked on her career, and never returned to the Soviet Union or Russia.

This brief summary of Rand's early life provides us with a skeleton view of her goals and her education and formal training in areas related to philosophy. We'll return to it in later sections and add more detail at that time as well.

11.2 The hurling of epithets

One of the major problems with a great deal of what passes for Ayn Rand "criticism", "analysis", or "scholarship" is that it's heavily partisan and quickly turns into something more closely resembling a playground fight, a food fight, or trash-talking. The critics (or often detractors) and the defenders (or often zealots) retreat to their own respective circles of wagons and hurl verbal missiles at each other with abandon. A good time is had by all, but what then?

If you search the Web for information pertaining to Rand's philosophy and to criticisms of it, you discover an amazing number of references to articles, news stories, lectures, articles, and books critical of Rand, but virtually none that are supportive of Rand or even neutral in what they say about her. There are reasons for this that don't require a conspiracy theory to explain it; but I won't go into the details of that here.[20] In fact the desired search results *do* appear in searches — just not on the first page, or the first five pages. But if you look far enough down in the returned results, you'll find what we would normally think of as "pro-Rand content".

If you really want to find views expressed by Randians (or followers or defenders of Rand's views and work, or serious interpreters of it), you need to look on sites that are devoted to these, such as *Objectivist Living*, *The Journal of Ayn Rand Studies*, *The Ayn Rand Institute*, *The Atlas Society*, and *The Harry Binswanger Letter*. Beyond those, in 2003 "A Randian Roundup: A Review of the Objectivist Literature" (Ryan 2003) was published in the *Transactions of the Charles S. Peirce Society* by Scott Ryan, and this contains (at least as of 2003) a fairly complete list of pro- and anti-Rand sources and commentaries presented in a neutral manner (even though Ryan himself is inclined towards a generally critical stance regarding Rand, her supporters, and her views).

Typical of epithets hurled at Rand, her followers, and admirers are:

- The Wikipedia entry on *Pseudophilosophy* (Wikipedia 2020l) contains a separate section on Objectivism which consists of a short list of brief derogatory remarks referring to Ayn Rand and her approach to philosophy as amateurish, unfamiliar with the body of recognized philosophy, mercenary, and cultish.

- In his article "Ayn Rand's Pseudo-Philosophy" (Chait 2011) in *The New Republic*, Johnathan Chait offers such remarks as
    - "It isn't so much a philosophy as what someone who has never actually encountered philosophy imagines a philosophy might look like."
    - "One of the many hilarious things about Rand is her philosophical crankery."
    - "[H]er fraudulence in this realm is pretty striking. She was a true amateur who insisted on seeing herself as the greatest human being who ever lived because she was almost completely unfamiliar with the entire philosophical canon. A pulp screenwriter who had read a tiny bit of philosophy — about as much as an average undergrad at a liberal arts college — she developed wild delusions about her place in intellectual history, delusions that managed to seduce the members of her cult."
- While reflecting on her earlier fascination with Rand, Victoria Bekiempis, in "Confessions of a recovering Objectivist" (Bekiempis 2012), refers to Rand's writings as "atrocious tomes" and "pop philosophy," and offers such comments as
    - "She championed integrity, but bastardized Nietzsche's best ideas."
    - "The kernel of this belief system is nothing more than a philosophically hollow shell."

For the most part, such observations are delivered without any significant or specific support, are emotive or polemical in nature, and don't approach what we would think of as careful criticism or analysis. In addition, some of them are just outrightly false. Of course, this is because the "debate" takes place in what are most charitably referred to as "opinion magazines" or "editorial contexts", and so the result is often a semi-sophisticated version of name calling. One of the goals of the theory of pseudo-philosophy developed in Part 2 of this book is precisely to avoid such a perspective in applying the term "pseudo-philosophy" to a writer or her work.

The hurling of epithets may result in at least some of the members of two opposing sides feeling good (and righteous!). But what does it *accomplish*? It's good theater. It rallies the *believers* (or the *non*-believers). But, since it's being guided on both sides by mobs with intellectual torches and pitchforks, it's not an intellectual, analytic, or knowledge-oriented exercise. And it's definitely not a *philosophical* exercise. It's not an exercise in the pursuit of truth and wisdom. It's an exercise in cheerleading (or maybe campaigning for views you embrace) and is, in itself, often a *pseudo*-philosophical exercise. We need to turn away from that path and focus instead on the question "What does it accomplish to classify someone as a pseudo-philosopher?" And moreover, what is that *intended* to accomplish? And then "Is Rand a genuine philosopher or a pseudo-philosopher?"

An alternative

Parts 1 and 2 of this book allow us to provide answers to these questions — and so provide an alternative to the hurling of epithets. They propose a theory of pseudo-philosophy that's detailed, conformant to the history of philosophy and how philosophers traditionally have viewed pseudo-philosophy, and applicable to philosophers and their works in the real world. Largely by way of contrast, that theory also addresses the questions "What is a pseudo-philosopher?", "What is a philosopher?", and "Why is that distinction important?" What I've provided is a theoretical answer to those theoretical questions (i.e., questions that are about the theory or metatheory of philosophy). That's primarily a *semantic exercise*: it establishes a *meaning* for "pseudo-philosophy" that's *intelligible*, *informative*, and *useful*.

But an inextricably related question about the *use* of the term "pseudo-philosophy" is "What should a careful and reasoned characterization of someone, either as a genuine philosopher or as a pseudo-philosopher, *accomplish*?" Or "What do statements like 'Aristotle was a genuine philosopher', and 'Keith Raniere was a pseudo-philosopher' *mean in practice*?". And *"How does answering those questions help us in any way?"* These are *pragmatic* questions, and answering them is an exercise in *pragmatics* (how we *do* things and what the *results* are).

The answer that I've provided to these pragmatic questions (and am now illustrating in this part of the book) is that classifying someone as a pseudo-philosopher acts as a warning similar to "Bridge freezes before roadway," "Soft shoulder," "Objects in the mirror are closer than they appear," "Falling rock zone," and "Beware of rip tides." These are all warnings (having both supportive evidence and predictive power) *not to trust* something — not to assume that what you're being presented with is dependable and beneficial (or even just harmless). They are warnings of deception or illusion, and of the possibility of subsequent or consequent harm. And they are warnings to adopt a cautious and skeptical stance in order to avoid that harm.

11.3 Simplifying our investigation

We're going to be concerned with two fundamental questions regarding Ayn Rand's philosophy and her approach to it:

Fundamental questions about Ayn Rand's philosophy

- What difficulties confront us in understanding and evaluating Rand's philosophy?
- What do these difficulties expose about Rand's philosophy or pseudo-philosophy?

To address these questions, and to make use of Ayn Rand as an illustration of our models and methods in approaching the philosophy/pseudo-philosophy distinction, we're going to have to simplify our approach in certain quite specific ways. This section provides an explanation and justification for doing so.

The approach we'll be taking in this case is a bit different from the one we followed in the previous case. While Keith Raniere made use of pseudo-philosophy and was a pseudo-philosopher, he wasn't a very good one. His philosophical ideas, theories, and arguments didn't exhibit a high degree of complexity or sophistication; and in fact he devoted some effort to making the details of those quite difficult to find — and obscuring them once they were found. Raniere was what we might think of as a *minor league pseudo-philosopher*.

But Ayn Rand is something quite different. If she's a genuine philosopher, then she's a significant genuine philosopher; and if she's a pseudo-philosopher, then she's a *major league pseudo-philosopher*. She doesn't hide her work or conceal its details. To the contrary, she attempts to make it as widely available as possible. And there's a lot of it. Even just her primary works relevant to the areas of philosophy amount to well over 3,000 pages — compared to the roughly 2,500 pages in the collected works of Plato, and the similarly sized complete works of Aristotle and of Immanuel Kant.

In evaluating Rand's work and applying our models to it, we can't — in a single chapter and for the purposes of simply illustrating our approach to pseudo-philosophy — hope to cover all of the material in that size corpus, or even all of the material in a tenth of it. Nor do we need to — because our goal here is to provide an *illustration* of how our methods are to be applied. In order to achieve that, we need only deal with a *representative sample* of Rand's work, and by doing that show how our methods can be applied to the rest. That's how we'll proceed. We need only ensure that it *is* representative and of sufficient depth and significance. However, even then we're faced with quite a choice.

Rand's writings in the area of philosophy span various sub-areas of that discipline. In particular, her works address issues in metaphysics, epistemology, logic, aesthetics, and moral and political philosophy. For readers without fairly extensive experience in philosophy, and without a certain level of formal study, some of these areas are much more daunting to deal with than others. Let's face it: philosophy can be difficult to understand. Philosophers typically adopt at least some level of new terminology (often seemingly arcane or bizarre) to represent their ideas, and then devote a great deal of time expressing their ideas, theories, and arguments using that terminology.

Often learning even the basics of a philosopher's views includes essentially learning a new language while struggling with the ideas that the new language is being used to express. It can be difficult to tell if the ideas being expressed are nutty, or if you just haven't understood them correctly because of the new jargon. This is particularly true in the area of metaphysics, which tends to be dense with new terminology (universal, particular, persistent, essence, ontology) or common words used in uncommon ways (individual, part, whole, constituent, being, concept, perception, form, instance, cause). To accomplish our purpose here (of illustrating the use of our models and methods), we need to avoid this kind of highly distracting complication — at least to the degree that we can. And we also need to limit the scope of the examples we investigate in Rand's work, simply in order to make an understanding of what we're doing manageable and achievable within this context.

Limiting the scope

As a consequence, we're going to avoid any direct confrontation of Rand's often complex and bewildering metaphysics and related theories of psychology, philosophy of mind, and epistemology based on it. This means avoiding any detailed consideration of such works as her *Introduction to Objectivist Epistemology* (Rand 1990) in which she lays out her theories of perception, cognition, measurement, concept formation, consciousness, identity, and various notions related to logic and the philosophy of language. However, although we'll avoid any detailed and direct approach to the topics covered in this and related work, we will need to refer to some specific points raised in it on occasion.

We're also going to avoid any direct consideration of her novels and other works of literature. The primary reason for this is that these are in fact *works of literature*, and only at best indirectly works of philosophy — even though it's common to encounter the claim that Rand's philosophy is presented and illustrated in her novels and other literary works. It's both difficult and also unfair to treat such works as philosophical works for the purposes of criticism (consider Rand's own assessment of her goals and methods in *The Goal of My Writing*). It's difficult enough to understand and interpret someone's genuinely philosophical writing when the author is explicitly and conscientiously presenting it as such. But problems of interpretation and understanding are complicated substantially when a level of literary interpretation, literary criticism, and indirect expression of ideas through story telling, metaphor, and polemic employed by fictional characters is introduced. Since Rand does provide us with explicitly *non-literary* philosophical works, we'll restrict our attention to these and divorce, so far as we can, Rand's philosophy from her literature, polemic, and ideology.

Filtering out commentaries

An additional problem with analyzing and interpreting Rand's philosophical works is that they don't come to us in a pure form — that is, in a form that contains only Rand's own expression, explanation, and defense of her ideas in a straightforward way. Instead, contributions of hers (usually in the form of articles or chapters) are mixed with contributions of others whom she regarded as her followers. For example, in *The Virtue of Selfishness* (Rand 1964), 5 of the 19 chapters are written by Nathaniel Brandon.

Introduction to Objectivist Epistemology contains 87 pages by Rand. But it also includes a 37-page article by Leonard Peikoff, 7 pages of introductory material by Peikoff and Harry Binswanger, and a 178-page transcript of some "Epistemology Workshops" that include Rand and others as participants, and the accuracy and completeness of which has been seriously questioned even (or especially) by Rand acolytes. The result is a book in which only a bit less than 30% is Rand's own contribution and her explicit and intended statement of the concepts, principles, and arguments central to Objectivist epistemology. All of the rest, in fact, was *added in subsequent editions*, and this is made clear on the title pages of Peikoff's (stunningly inept) "The Analytic-Synthetic Dichotomy" and the Appendix ("Excerpts from the Epistemology Workshops"), which the editors admit is a *modified transcript* of some of Rand's workshops.

That lengthy "Excerpts" transcript is peculiar in several important respects. First, aside from Rand herself, the participants are not identified anywhere in the transcript or in the book. Instead, they're referred to only by the single letters "A" – "E". Whatever possible reasons there may be for this anonymity, none is given. It's difficult to see what's gained by this intentional omission, and it seems to be directly incompatible with Objectivist principles — particularly since the workshop participants are said (in Peikoff's "Foreword to the Second

Edition") to include "a dozen professionals in philosophy, plus a few in physics and mathematics." Including their names and professional credentials would have gone far towards enhancing the credibility and legitimacy of both Rand and the workshops (not to mention Peikoff and Binswanger, who decided to include this workshop section). As it is, this presentation of the excerpts leaves us with another example of what appears to be ⊘ *Discouraging Inquiry* and perhaps ⊘ *Exaggerated Claims*. The excerpts, and descriptions of the participants as "professionals in philosophy," are offered to us at least in part to substantiate the view that Rand was being taken seriously by academic philosophers and academics in other disciplines. But then their names are withheld, which is especially peculiar in an academic context. It hints at a lack of integrity incompatible with the Philo persona. However, we shouldn't blame Rand for this impression since the decision was that of Peikoff and Binswanger.

In January of 2020 — 50 years after the workshops were held and the "Workshops" section included in the book — Harry Binswanger posted an article (Binswanger 2020) in *The Harry Binswanger Letter*, offering an excuse for not identifying the participants (which in the interim had been identified by others), and then saying that "There were only five full participants," while the rest were "auditors" or "guests." He then admits that of the full participants, only three were genuine *professors*, a couple were "instructors," and the rest were graduate students — conceding that his use of the "Prof. designation" was a "device ... rather than a description of their academic titles."

A *device*? What kind of *device* is *that*? What, exactly, is the *purpose* of a "device" by means of which you knowingly — in a university context — falsely communicate to your reader that multiple participants in an academic workshop, created and administered by academics, are *professors* when they're nothing of the sort? And then fifty years later say, roughly, "Oops.": it apparently somehow merely happened without anyone's thinking about it, although the "Prof. designation" (Binswanger's) phrase appears to have been a studied decision at the time of publication. It seems inescapable here that "device" means "deception", particularly since the workshop and reporting of it took place fully in a university context where such titles are of *extreme* importance.

In his 2020 article Binswanger then identifies eight of the participants referenced in the "Excerpts" section as, at that time, graduate students (including himself and Allan Gotthelf). Of the remainder, Leonard Peikoff had received his Ph.D. in philosophy from NYU in 1964 and at the time of the workshops was apparently an Assistant Professor of Philosophy at The Polytechnic Institute of Brooklyn, John Nelson was on the philosophy faculty at the University of Colorado in Boulder, and George Walsh was in the philosophy department at Hobart and William Smith. So Peikoff's "dozen professionals in philosophy" shrinks down to three professors and a bunch of students (who are difficult to count as *professionals*, although "professional hopefuls" might be accurate).

Once past this problem of what appears to be outright deception by the workshop organizers and editors, Peikoff's characterization of the participants in the workshops, his own "Forward to the Second Edition" and Harry Binswanger's "Preface" make it clear that their presentation of the workshops in this edition of *Introduction to Objectivist Epistemology* — that is, the very text of this Appendix in the book — is not at all reliable as an accurate representation of what happened in the workshops, or of Rand's views, positions, and arguments. Peikoff demurs explicitly and at length from the accuracy of the content of the "Excerpts", saying that Rand would have edited it extensively prior to publishing it herself, that it can't be taken as "official Objectivist doctrine," and that Rand's theory of Objectivism is to be found "in the book she herself published, i.e., the present edition minus the appendix" (which is just the 87 pages that constitute approximately the first 30% of the book).

Binswanger concedes that the Appendix created by him and Peikoff "is not a verbatim transcript of the workshops," that Ayn Rand never reviewed this material, and that the editing consisted of "cutting, reorganizing and line-editing." He then goes on to describe the details of these transformational operations (some of which were severe and required great effort and time), and points out that in cases where he and Peikoff agreed that some of Rand's material "might be confusing or misleading," they either simply *deleted* it (!) or stuck in their own "clarifying term or remark" (in square brackets).

This sort of "scholarship" doesn't inspire confidence in the material being offered as representative of Rand's thought. It definitely exhibits the pseudo-philosophy markers of ⊘ *Misrepresentation* and ⊘ *Lack of Rigor*, and at least treads in the direction of ⊘ *Misleading Citation* since it reformulates Rand's work into something else. But we shouldn't allow it to taint our view of material that genuinely is Rand's own thinking and presentation.

I belabor this point about the accuracy and dependability of these kinds of secondary sources affixed to Rand's primary works in part to justify our ignoring them in our current context — since *they can't be taken to be reliable representations of Rand's ideas*, and may in fact introduce significant distortions. But also I want to point out that this kind of thing appears in the case of certain philosophers who tend towards pervasive levels of obscurantism and to attract cadres of committed followers who view their own role as "interpreting the word of the Master." Often this is without overly much regard to *what the Master actually said*, and the focus instead is on rehabilitating or enhancing the Master's image or reputation through some degree of reconstruction, reinterpretation, or "improvement."

In the relatively recent history of philosophy, examples such as Heidegger and Wittgenstein come to mind, and in such cases there is also frequently the presence of some kind of "personality cult." Without characterizing Rand and her followers as a cult (which has been done quite enough elsewhere), I think it's undeniable that there's a Randian personality cult in just the same way that there exists a Wittgenstein personality cult and a Heidegger personality cult, openly recognized by Wittgenstein and Heidegger scholars.

As an example of what we might call "Rand revisionism" or "Rand rehabilitation" we can look at an article (Bubb 2006) by Frank Bubb in which he attempts to dodge a criticism of Rand's philosophy by providing a *supportive interpretation* of a brief portion lifted from one of John Galt's emotional and polemical speeches in *Atlas Shrugged*. In his abstract, Bubb says this demonstrates that Rand was not committing a philosophical error, but "was instead *operating on the basis of* premises *implicit* in the *theme* of Atlas Shrugged and in her other writings" (emphasis mine).

While it may be *possible*, as Bubb suggests, to provide a "context" like this (fictional though it is) in which what Rand says *might* make sense, in fact Rand did not do this, and so this effort at improving Rand's work is not Rand's, but Bubb's — whether or not it is successful. Since our focus here is on *Rand* and *her* presentation of *her* philosophy (and not Rand*ians* or Objectivists more generally), we'll eschew any serious consideration of these secondary sources and attempts at rehabilitation. In short, we cannot (and should not attempt to) judge Rand's work through the work of her followers. If we were to do this, then we should have to take the bad with the good, and in that direction there is much that is not good, and Rand and her legacy should not be saddled with it.

Rand quoting Rand

This leads us to the classic Randian behavior of quoting at substantial length from the speeches of fictional characters in her own novels. *For the New Intellectual* (Rand 1963a) contains an initial 56-page section by Rand dealing directly with her philosophical views, followed by 193 pages of direct quotations from her novels *We the Living, Anthem, The Fountainhead*, and *Atlas Shrugged* — so that over 75% of *For the New Intellectual* is simply reprinted excerpts from Rand's novels! And only about 25% of it is a direct expression of her philosophical thought and reasoning. While many of her followers take this to be an attempt by Rand to explain or elucidate her philosophy through the content of her fictional literature, or to make it more "accessible" to the reader in literary form, Rand herself is careful to point out that this isn't at all what her intention was:

Chapter 11: Ayn Rand: Mostly Borrowed, Nothing New?

Why Rand quotes from Rand, according to Rand

"The full system is implicit in these excerpts (particularly in Galt's speech), but its fundamentals are indicated only in the widest terms and require a detailed, systematic presentation in a philosophical treatise. I am working on such a treatise at present; it will deal predominantly with the issue which is barely touched upon in Galt's speech: epistemology, and will present a new theory of the nature, source and validation of concepts.

...

For those who may be interested in the chronological development of my thinking, I have included excerpts from all four of my novels. They may observe the progression from a political theme in *We the Living* to a metaphysical theme in *Atlas Shrugged*.

These excerpts are necessarily condensed summaries, because the full statement of the subjects involved is presented, in each novel, by means of the events of the story. The events are the concretes and the particulars, of which the speeches are the abstract summations.

When I say that these excerpts are merely an outline, I do not mean to imply that my full system is still to be defined or discovered; I had to define it before I could start writing Atlas Shrugged. Galt's speech is its briefest summary.

Until I complete the presentation of my philosophy in a fully detailed form, this present book may serve as an outline or a program or a manifesto."

Ayn Rand, preface to *For the New Intellectual*.

From this we learn that Rand's system of philosophy is *implicit* in her characters' speeches, but the fundamentals and details are elsewhere; and even then, the speeches are only *condensed summaries* and form *merely an outline*. We also learn that Rand knew that a *philosophical treatise* (and not a work of fiction) was required for the genuinely philosophical presentation of her views.

Here Rand makes it clear that the excerpts from her fiction are included for those who might be interested in how her thought evolved over the years — apparently to provide some insight into her intellectual development. And, consistent with this, the AynRand.org Web site (AynRand.org 2020) remarks that "Rand viewed the book [*For the New Intellectual*] as a 'cultural commercial' for her novels" — and so she very likely didn't consider the inclusion of the self-quotations to function in any way as fundamental "presentations" of her philosophy or as an explanation or exegesis of it, but rather as fictionalized accounts of how people *might* express or exemplify that philosophy. That is, these count as *illustrations* (and even then, fictional ones involving — recall — *idealized* actors) rather than as explanatory and analytical presentations of the fundamental philosophy.

Rand goes on to emphasize that the excerpts are only summaries of portions of her "full system" and how that system applies to the specific events ("concretes and particulars") portrayed in the novels. What this means is that the excerpts from her literary works are summaries of thinking and arguments *developed elsewhere*, and with some significant detail absent. It's not at all clear from her remarks exactly *where* this detail has been (or will be) developed, or even what it is, but she does say that the "presentation" of it isn't yet "complete" and that *For the New Intellectual* itself may serve only as an outline of it. She may be referring to what became *The Virtue of Selfishness*, *Introduction to Objectivist Epistemology*, and similar essays.

This confusion aside, what's important here — and I think this is often missed by her followers and interpreters — is that Rand seems to recognize the difference between a careful, direct, and explicit presentation of her philosophical thought (in the manner of Aristotle, whom she idolized and sought to emulate, Plato, and Nietzsche) and a "novelization", "fictionalization", "popularization", or folktale version of it for popular ("cultural commercial") consumption and polemical purposes. And she apparently doesn't want her readers to think that she was offering the one as though it were the other. In addition, even this brief analysis of Rand's remarks on quoting from her own literary works illustrates that she was well aware of the problems of understanding and interpretation that such works — being detached from a careful presentation of philosophy (and reality!) — can present. For her, this seems to be an ongoing struggle between her desire to be a *creator*, on the one hand, and, on the other, the need (in order to be taken seriously as a philosopher) to exhibit some of the commitment to accuracy and detail of the *recording secretary*. And in this, she may feel caught at times in a false dichotomy of her own making.

Guidelines for appraising Rand's philosophy

As a consequence of these considerations, and by way of brief summary, we'll adopt these policies in assessing Rand's philosophical writings for our purposes here:

Chapter 11: Ayn Rand: Mostly Borrowed, Nothing New?

Focus, constraints, and strategy in appraising Rand's philosophy

- Focus on explicitly philosophical works written by Rand herself.

- Avoid any consideration of Rand's literary/fictional works.

- Avoid becoming involved in the details of secondary sources by "Randians" or "neo-Randians", commentaries, and add-ons to her own writings (such as articles not authored by Rand, or "enhanced" source materials edited or massaged by others and later published together with Rand's original works).

- Restrict our primary focus to Rand's *For the New Intellectual* and *The Virtue of Selfishness* as sufficiently representative of her philosophical methodology, principles, and techniques to judge her work as being either genuinely philosophical or pseudo-philosophical.

- Avoid delving into Rand's treatment of metaphysical and epistemological topics unless specifically necessary or immediately helpful. In particular, while acknowledging its position in Rand's philosophical corpus, we won't become involved in any significant appraisal of Rand's *Introduction to Objectivist Epistemology*.

- Avoid spending time on any criticisms of Rand that are largely political/ideological responses to her views and aren't directly relevant to her underlying philosophy or whether what she's doing is philosophy.

- So far as possible, divorce Rand's philosophy, philosophical positions, and philosophical methods from ideology, polemic, and literary interpretation.

Our overall goal is to look at a fair and manageable representation of Ayn Rand's philosophy through the lens of our models of genuine philosophy and pseudo-philosophy in order to come to an objective judgment regarding which of those models Rand best fits. As we did in the previous chapter, we'll employ our Simple Principle of Abduction of Section 8.6, our models and personas of Chapters 4 and 7, and a reasonable sampling of Rand's philosophical work to form our conclusion and to justify it.

This may leave us with some disputable points that a broader and deeper look into Rand's writings might resolve — or might not. But at that point we'll have provided the context within which such a discussion can take place in a rational and principled manner (avoiding the mere hurling of epithets), we'll have stripped the dispute of ideological and polemical argumentation, and we'll have clarified fundamental issues and eliminated conflations and confusions that afflict less careful approaches. The choice we make of the representative material drawn from Rand should provide us with a strong argument and strong evidence for our conclusions. And the result will be a judgment possessing a high degree of clarity and reliability based on those grounds and our methods.

We must keep in mind that our goal here isn't to determine (or to argue) that Rand's philosophy is "right" or that it's "wrong", or that it should be accepted or rejected. Our goal is to determine whether — in the coherent and useful sense provided by our models — it counts as *philosophy* or instead as some *imitation* or *masquerade* of philosophy (pseudo-philosophy).

11.4 *For the New Intellectual*

This 1961 book (truly, only a moderately long article: (Rand 1963a)) is universally acknowledged to be Rand's first venture away from her novels and fiction into a straightforward approach to philosophical topics and content. While published in book form, most of the book is lengthy quotes from those novels, the title section itself makes up only about 25% (about 60 pages) of the book, and it's based on a 1960 speech that Rand delivered at Yale University.

The Randian view of intellectualism

Rand begins the book by declaring that America is culturally bankrupt and its leadership by "professional intellectuals" has collapsed. She addresses her remarks to the "new intellectuals" whom she intends to take over the intellectual guidance of the nation. She doesn't pause to indicate what an intellectual is, what are the capabilities, skills, or training of intellectuals, or how they come to be burdened with retrieving American culture from (intellectual) bankruptcy. But she does refer vaguely to "modern intellectuals," attributes a number of deplorable views and attitudes to them, and mentions "intellectual professions" without either providing examples or telling us in what way those professions are "intellectual" while others are not.

Quite likely, since this was originally a speech delivered at Yale University, Rand realized that everyone in the audience would already believe that they were part of the new intelligencia of which she was speaking. This wouldn't be especially problematic in a newspaper article or a rousing political speech; but in what's conceded and intended to be a book on the principles of your philosophy, failing to be clear about the fundamental concepts may trigger the reader's skepticism and begin to give an impression of ⊘ *Obscurantism*, ⊘ *Puzzling*

Terminology, ⊘ *Vagueness and Equivocation,* and ⊘ *Lack of Rigor*. Certainly Rand had the time to remedy this problem in rewriting the speech into a printed article about the foundations of a part of her philosophy, though she didn't take the opportunity to do this.

What we see here is an example of one of Rand's presentational techniques in which she'll introduce a concept or term central to her discussion, but without providing a clear account of it, and then make extensive use of it in fundamental and significant claims about problems, goals, and potential solutions to problems. In this way she rather habitually and systematically employs an approach involving ⊘ *Obscurantism* and ⊘ *Puzzling Terminology* that puts the reader in a position where he's inclined or required (in the interest of fairness) to suspend any judgment or critical analysis of Rand's claims pending further clarification — and thereby to take a stance of *provisional acceptance* of what she's saying. This has the effect of staving off skepticism on the part of the reader, and it provides some inhibition (⊘ *Discouraging Inquiry*) to adopting an anti-sophistical stance. In effect, it encourages the reader to *suspend* adoption of a critical attitude by leveraging the Principle of Charity. Rand's supporters, on the other hand, tend to view it as simply a part of her characteristic method, or perhaps as one or another variant of dialectic (of which more later).

Rand goes on to contrast intellectualism with "Zen Buddhism and its equivalents," by which she apparently means to include Existentialism; but she gives us no clue as to why and how Zen Buddhism and Existentialism are anti-intellectual or resemble one another, other than to suggest vaguely that it has something to do with mysticism. She then launches into a lightning attack on what seems to be all of Western philosophy since Aristotle, and at that point we need to stop short, catch our breath, and assess the situation with a bit more care because the view Rand presents of history and philosophy seems simply incorrect in fundamental factual respects that trigger our skepticism, encourage adoption of our anti-sophistical stance, and demand a degree of scrutiny even at this early stage.

The picture that Rand paints is of a world in which fundamentally nothing good happened in philosophy or intellectual thought since Aristotle's contributions in ancient times, and where anti-rationalism and anti-intellectualism ran rampant throughout the Middle Ages, supported and encouraged by the Roman Catholic Church and its religious orders on the one hand, and by anti-intellectual and bullying monarchists and aristocrats on the other. But this isn't exactly the historical world of philosophy that most people familiar with philosophy in the Middle Ages will recognize — and for good reason.

Rand makes sweeping claims that philosophy teaches us that "reality is unknowable" and "knowledge is an illusion." But *which philosophy* teaches this?

Which philosophers are teaching us this? She offers no citations, nor initially any clues. But she shortly says that in the "pre-capitalist societies" (which according to her never existed until significantly after the post-Renaissance period) there were "no makers of knowledge." So for her, the spectrum of philosophy in the post-Aristotle period through the Middle Ages and the Renaissance was one in which nothing good or useful was done, at least in philosophy. And later (from her perspective, writing in 1961) she complains that the "pragmatist, positivist, and anti-conceptual mentality" of the 20th Century not only provided an anti-intellectual approach in philosophy but "had to lead in practice to the torrent of blood and brute, non-human horror of such socialist societies as Nazi Germany and Soviet Russia."

This is pretty scary, and a broad condemnation of the work of philosophers over a period exceeding 1,700 years — including a significant number of Jewish philosophers (persecuted by the Nazis rather than aiding their rise) who were in either the highly productive logical positivist movement or the Polish Schools of logic and philosophy of the 1920s and 1930s. Unfortunately we can't know the exact dates, the length of the period involved, and exactly who (according to Rand) is at fault — though it seems that everyone was — because *Rand isn't telling us these things*. However, beyond that void of information, and from the perspective of the history of Western philosophy in the late 19th and early-to-mid 20th centuries, her view seems to be utterly false. And it appears to reveal either a shocking ignorance (⊘ *Inadequate Understanding*, ⊘ *Ignorance of Prior Work*) of someone masquerading as a philosopher, or an intent to distort and deceive (⊘ *Misrepresentation*, ⊘ *Special Pleading*). This isn't merely a matter of perspective, opinion, or interpretation. It's a matter of well-known facts about philosophy and its history. Let's consider just a few of the views Rand expresses in *For the New Intellectual* about philosophy, knowledge, and the history of ideas.

♦ **PLATO'S PHILOSOPHER-KING?**

On the first page of *For a New Intellectual*, Rand casually employs the term "professional intellectual" — without any indication of what it means. Again, no examples are provided to help us understand how professional intellectuals are to be distinguished from other intellectuals (who would be ... *amateur* intellectuals?). But a few pages later she says that professional intellectuals don't exist in "primitive, savage societies," that "the professional intellectual is a very recent phenomenon" which dates only from the industrial revolution, that "The professional businessman and the professional intellectual came into existence together" and were both products of capitalism and the industrial revolution. Still, we have no idea of what a professional intellectual *is*. But finally she contrasts the professional intellectual with others:

Ayn Rand (1961) on the "professional intellectual"

"The professional intellectual is the field agent of the army whose commander-in-chief is the philosopher. The intellectual carries the application of philosophical principles to every field of human endeavor. He sets a society's course by transmitting ideas from the "ivory tower" of the philosopher to the university professor—to the writer—to the artist—to the newspaperman—to the politician—to the movie maker—to the night-club singer—to the man in the street. The intellectual's specific professions are in the field of the sciences that study man, the so-called "humanities," but for that very reason his influence extends to all other professions. Those who deal with the sciences studying nature have to rely on the intellectual for philosophical guidance and information: for moral values, for social theories, for political premises, for psychological tenets and, above all, for the principles of epistemology, that crucial branch of philosophy which studies man's means of knowledge and makes all other sciences possible. The intellectual is the eyes, ears and voice of a free society: it is his job to observe the events of the world, to evaluate their meaning and to inform the men in all the other fields." (Rand 1963a 26-27)

Alas, this fanciful and heroic portrayal of the professional intellectual is still quite puzzling.

Try to draw a diagram of the relations between the philosopher, the professional intellectual, the university professor, writers, artists, and the others mentioned — and you'll immediately see the difficulty. One glaring problem is that aside from the philosopher and the professional intellectual, each of the others is classified by her *job* — that is, what she gets *paid* to do: how she *makes a living*. Initially you might think that the philosopher is a university professor in a philosophy department (being paid to teach and produce research in philosophy). But that can't be true since Rand distinguishes him from the professor (and sets him *above* both the professor and the professional intellectual in this hierarchy).

It's all very well to say that the job of the professional intellectual is to "observe the events of the world, to evaluate their meaning and to inform the men in all the other fields," but what can this *mean*? It doesn't seem as though there's any real *job* here. Who *pays* the professional intellectual for doing this — thereby making him or her a *professional* intellectual? And who pays the philosopher to be the commander-in-chief? And how many commanders-in-chief can you have? Perhaps she envisions a kind of free market of professional intellectuals, each vying for influence and offering their services competitively. But that starts to sound a lot like the existing situation of professional writers,

Section 11.4: For the New Intellectual

newscasters, reporters, university professors, and political consultants. What's new about Rand's proposal and vision? This is Rand at her story-telling best: weaving a story that *almost* makes sense until you think about it and try to see how the details work out — because critical details are missing.

What does the professional intellectual's workday look like? How does he "carry" these ideas from the philosopher to all of these other people? The professional intellectual can't be a university professor since the professional intellectual is a *conduit of ideas from the philosopher to the professor*. Likewise, he can't be a writer, an artist, a newspaperman, a politician, a movie maker, a nightclub singer, or a man in the street — since these are all *recipients* of the work of the philosopher and the professional intellectual. So it turns out that these hypotheses about the professional intellectual can't be right either — and things are even more confusing and incoherent than they first appear.

Maybe the professional intellectual is a businessman? No — because at the same time we're told that the professional intellectual's "specific profession" isn't actually intellectualism (after all, how could that be a profession in any reasonable sense?), but lies in the area of the humanities or social sciences — and that those in the natural sciences need his guidance for unspecified purposes involving moral values, social theories, politics, psychology, and for the principles of epistemology (i.e., knowledge). But this makes the professional intellectual sound a lot like a philosopher (which we already know he's not because he's the *field agent* of the philosopher — right?). And by the way, does this really mean that a scientist (such as Charles Darwin, Albert Einstein, E. O. Wilson, or Alan Sokal) couldn't be a professional intellectual? But someone who has some job (?) in the *humanities* can? That not only sounds silly. It sounds dangerous.

At this point we realize that not only have we failed to understand what a professional intellectual is, or what exactly she does, or how exactly she does it, and how she makes a living and spends her workday — but that the answers to these questions seem even further from us than they did before. Rand seems to have created a concept and a picture of the professional intellectual — an "ideal" as she's described it in *The Goal of My Writing* — that's not only incomplete, but hopelessly incoherent as it rests on ⊘ *Obscurantism*, ⊘ *Puzzling Terminology*, and ⊘ *Lack of Rigor*. But maybe there's help, from the history of genuine philosophy, for Rand's vision — even if she'd be inclined to dismiss it.

In fact, what Rand seems to be suggesting about the roles (or maybe the role?) of the philosopher and the intellectual — in so far as it appears coherent at all — is nothing new. And some of it certainly isn't new to her. Consider what Plato says in *The Republic* about the *philosopher-king*:

Chapter 11: Ayn Rand: Mostly Borrowed, Nothing New?

Plato (circa 375 BC) on the philosopher-king

(452) "The guardians of our State are to be watch-dogs, as we have already said."

(473) "Until philosophers are kings, or the kings and princes of this world have the spirit and power of philosophy, and political greatness and wisdom meet in one, and those commoner natures who pursue either to the exclusion of the other are compelled to stand aside, cities will never have rest from their evils — nor the human race, as I believe — and then only will this our State have a possibility of life and behold the light of day."

(503) "I hesitated to make the assertion which I now hazard — that our guardians must be philosophers. You remember all the contradictory elements, which met in the philosopher — how difficult to find them all in a single person! Intelligence and spirit are not often combined with steadiness; the stolid, fearless, nature is averse to intellectual toil. And yet these opposite elements are all necessary, and therefore, as we were saying before, the aspirant must be tested in pleasures and dangers; and also, as we must now further add, in the highest branches of knowledge."

(541) "And you will admit that our State is not a mere aspiration, but may really come into being when there shall arise philosopher-kings, one or more, who will despise earthly vanities, and will be the servants of justice only."

The Republic of Plato (Plato 2016)

It's difficult to see much of a gap between this and what Rand is saying about philosophers and professional intellectuals, isn't it? And it also strikes a tone similar to Rand's in deploring the current state of society and how that can be changed — by the philosopher-king in Plato's case and the professional intellectual in Rand's.

We're told by Rand historians that while Rand violently disagreed with Plato in terms of his metaphysics, epistemology, and ethics, she did at least study Plato in her university courses and undoubtedly read *The Republic* quite closely. And we know this in part because she so explicitly disagrees, on multiple occasions, with views Plato expresses in *The Republic*. So Rand's failure to mention

Plato here in conjunction with the professional intellectual can't be an example of ⊘ *Ignorance of Prior Work*.

Sure, Rand has (though not coherently at this point) introduced the professional intellectual and distinguished him (in a murky way) from the philosopher, but clearly she *borrows* this idea from Plato's work that preceded her own by about 2,300 years. Yet, apparently swept up in the novelty of her own ideas, she neglects to mention this connection — providing a pretty clear example of ⊘ *Misappropriation*. And the undeniable fact that Rand then applies some tweaks to the idea of the philosopher-king in order to fit it into her own world order can't make this any less an appropriation of ideas previously expressed by someone else. Rand insists on credit for what she sees as her own contributions to philosophy. Shouldn't she render the same courtesy to Plato as well — especially for material she borrows from him and makes a fundamental part of one of her few explicitly philosophical publications? This does not appear to be the Philo persona (Section 4.2) being expressed in Rand's work.

◆ **THE ONLY TRUE INTELLECTUALS: THE AMERICAN FOUNDING FATHERS**

Rand's views also seem in line with Plato's concerning the position of the philosopher (or in her case intellectual?) in society as a ruler, or at least a powerful member of government, when she says that

America's first and only intellectuals (as of 1961)

> "The Founding Fathers were America's first intellectuals and, so far, her last. It is their basic political line that the New Intellectuals have to continue."

In fact, the *only* examples of American intellectuals that Rand produces for us in *For the New Intellectual* appear to conflict in direct ways with the paradigm that she otherwise wants to provide us of the (idealized) "new" intellectual. All were male, all white, all but Franklin from wealthy and entitled families. Most were devoutly religious (and even Franklin looked favorably on religion). All but Franklin and Washington attended and graduated from prestigious colleges; and Washington was well trained as a surveyor — which in itself placed him in an upper stratum of society. All of the Founding Fathers but Adams and Hamilton owned slaves at some times in their lives, and most owned slaves (sometimes many) throughout most of their adult lives. While Hamilton didn't personally own slaves, close members of his family did.

Why do these facts matter? They matter because they demonstrate quite directly that Rand has presented an account of the professional intellectual (and in fact, her *ideal* intellectual in general) that is simply incoherent and incompatible with the basic concepts and principles she's telling us we *must* accept in order to avoid incoherence and irrationalism ourselves.

Slavery, for example, was certainly part of the "basic political line" of the Founding Fathers, and yet Rand herself is adamantly opposed to slavery and finds it to be *fundamentally incompatible* with Objectivism and its basic morality. Likewise, the devotion to — or tolerance and encouragement of — *religious belief* by the Founding Fathers is *fundamentally incompatible* with Objectivist principles, and Rand was explicit about this at every opportunity throughout her life. But religion was a part of the Founding Fathers' "basic political line"; and it found its way explicitly into a number of places in our Constitution.

How are the Founding Fathers to serve as exemplars if they fail in these two fundamental respects to exemplify Rand's vision? How are we to understand what Rand is saying about the fundamental concept of the professional intellectual in her philosophy if it appears incoherent in this way? These direct and explicit clashes of the basic principles Rand is enunciating with those individuals she holds up as exemplars (and not only exemplars, but the *only* American exemplars) illustrate how Rand's approach is incompatible with the Philo persona, exhibits features of the Pseudo persona, and displays such markers as ⊘ *Obscurantism*, ⊘ *Vagueness and Equivocation*, ⊘ *Inadequate Understanding*, and ⊘ *Lack of Rigor*. There appears to be a fundamental problem with coherence in her thinking that she simply doesn't recognize — or that she's willing to tolerate for some more important goal.[21]

♦ HUME'S VIEW ON THE PHILOSOPHER'S EFFECT IN SOCIETY

As Plato's philosopher-king provides us with some insight into the nature and function of the professional intellectual, so does a brief remark of David Hume's in *An Enquiry Concerning Human Understanding* (Hume 2008). Hume is another philosopher that Rand loves to hate. Further along in *For the New Intellectual*, Rand complains at length about Hume's treatment of the notion of causation (which appears in the *Enquiry*), characterizes Hume's approach to philosophy as that of Attila (see below), and accuses him of declaring that philosophical speculation is "a game, like chess or hunting" (he never did say this, of course — this is her pejorative rhetorical characterization of Hume).

So it would seem that Rand must have read some of Hume, and must have read the *Enquiry*, although the accuracy of her interpretations are certainly questionable. But then it's at least a bit surprising to recall Hume's account of the role of the philosopher in society that appears in the *Enquiry*, and to compare this to Rand's comments about the professional intellectual:

David Hume (1748) on philosophy affecting society

"Besides, we may observe, in every art or profession, even those which most concern life or action, that a spirit of accuracy, however acquired, carries all of them nearer their perfection, and renders them more subservient to the interests of society. And though a philosopher may live remote from business, the genius of philosophy, if carefully cultivated by several, must gradually diffuse itself throughout the whole society, and bestow a similar correctness on every art and calling. The politician will acquire greater foresight and subtility, in the subdividing and balancing of power; the lawyer more method and finer principles in his reasonings; and the general more regularity in his discipline, and more caution in his plans and operations. The stability of modern governments above the ancient, and the accuracy of modern philosophy, have improved, and probably will still improve, by similar gradations." (Hume 2008 6-7)

Hume offers a slightly different perspective from Plato's in not desiring to place the philosopher in a position of political power over society, and in this he and Rand seem to agree. He begins by stating the importance of *accuracy* (which is to say clarity and precision of expression) in the philosopher's work. He then describes the way in which philosophy and the philosopher's work will — *"if carefully cultivated by several"* — have beneficial effects on every aspect of society. This includes effects on the politician, the lawyer, and the general.

More striking, Hume says that the philosopher and his work will "bestow a similar correctness on every art and calling" in the same manner that Rand says "his influence extends to all other professions." There's such a degree of similarity between this account of Hume's and Rand's conception of the new intellectual and role of the philosopher that it's difficult not to see Rand's description as a rephrasing of Hume's. And again, her lack of any mention of Hume, in the continuing context of her claim to be proposing a new and innovative view, must make us wonder whether this is an example of either ⊘ *Ignorance of Prior Work* or ⊘ *Misrepresentation* (in the form of an uncredited misappropriation of ideas). But in any event, there seems little particularly new or innovative about Rand's "professional intellectual" proposal, other than the new jargon in which she chooses to phrase it, and a rather pervasive lack of clarity in terms of details.

A perspective on Rand's style

On page 14 of the *For the New Intellectual*, Rand introduces an elaborate metaphor — *Attila and the Witch Doctor* — that then occupies every subsequent page as it's used to frame Rand's own positions and to attack those she sees as her antagonists. This is another example of Rand's creation of a *story* which she presents as an accurate reflection of reality that can be used to justify her own views and criticize those of others. Her approach may appear similar to our use of the Philo and Pseudo personas, but in Rand's case she makes no attempt to establish that these personas genuinely represent the people to which she attributes them, and so they end up being caricatures rather than reliably established representatives. It's a dramatic, but risky, technique.

In Section 2 above we saw something of Rand's own view of her approach to writing: how she saw herself as a creator rather than as a "recording secretary," how the crafting of a story, its characters, and especially its heroes and their tasks are used to create an emotive idealization meant to inspire her readers into admiring and emulating those heroes. How does this technique appear in *For the New Intellectual?* How is it used by Rand to communicate her philosophical concepts and principles? How does our knowledge of Rand's understanding of story-telling and her view of writing help us form a clearer view of what she's doing in *For the New Intellectual*? And how does that help us in fitting what Rand is doing to either our Philo or Pseudo persona, and to our models of the genuine philosopher and pseudo-philosopher? The fable (and it is a *fable*) of *Attila and the Witch Doctor* provides us with insight into all these questions.

Ayn Rand was born and raised in a culture with a long tradition of fairy tales or folktales, and it turns out that the Russian folktale is a highly stylized form of writing. In fact, the structure of the Russian folktale was carefully analyzed and described by Vladimir Propp in his 1928 book *Morphology of the Folktale* (Propp 1968). In that book, Propp created a formal model of the folktale in which he identified all of its essential components (such as the Hero, the Hero's tasks, Villains and their sub-types, a mistake or error that allows the Villain to act, the Hero's actions against the Villain, the Hero's rewards, etc.). Interestingly, Propp and Rand both attended Petrograd State University — Propp in 1913-1918 and Rand in 1921-1924. Propp remained in Petrograd, teaching in lower schools (while Rand was attending the university and then the State Institute for Cinema Arts). He returned to the university as a faculty member in 1932, became Chairman of the Department of Folklore in 1938, and later (until his death in 1970) a professor in the Department of Russian Literature.

While there's no evidence that Rand ever met Propp or attended any of his classes or lectures while both were in Petrograd, Propp's book on folktales is a scholarly account and formal analysis of precisely the Russian folktale/fantasy literature familiar to Rand from her childhood and which also would have been studied to some degree in school courses in Russian history and literature. It was precisely this genre and its history and structure that Propp analyzed and documented so thoroughly.

It should then come as no surprise that when we read *For the New Intellectual* (particularly in the context of Rand's "The Goal of My Writing") and come upon the story of Attila and the Witch Doctor, we discover that we're reading (in form and content) a simplified Russian folktale cast as an allegory for the struggle between Rand's philosophical views and the views of traditional philosophers. Both Attila and the Witch Doctor are *villains*. The new intellectual is the *hero* who will thwart their evil intentions against humanity. Indeed, Anne Conover Heller, in her book *Ayn Rand and the World She Made* (Heller 2010), characterizes *For the New Intellectual* as "a mixture of historical parable and madcap fairy tale," and points out that the weapon with which Rand arms her hero (who in fact is intended to be *you — the reader* — as a new intellectual) is a "new morality" of which Rand has often described herself as "the architect".

Rand obviously feels well at home in writing dialog and stories, and much less comfortable in writing expository philosophy that may need to deviate (as a matter of philosophical analysis or history) from a story line she can control. Her goal, from childhood, was to become a screen writer, and she oriented her education specifically towards this end.

One point to keep in mind, as part of the anti-sophistical stance, is that a metaphor employed to clarify or explain is only as good as its correspondence to reality — and surely an Objectivist should agree with this. The danger in Rand's constant substitution of metaphors and tales for exposition lies in crafting the story, associating parts of reality with elements (features, events, relations, and characters) inside the story, making inferences *within* the context of the story about those features and characters, and then accepting (or proposing) the results of those inferences as *accurately representing reality outside the story*. In the warning of ancient and medieval map-makers — whose works could have disastrous results if their representations deviated far from reality — "*Hic Sunt Leones*": *Here there are lions.*

From the perspective of our models, the danger of employing this story-telling technique in presenting philosophical concepts, views, positions, and arguments is that it may result in the creation of a cluster of occurrences of the ⊘ *Known Fallacy* marker (including *False dichotomy*, *Straw man*, *Ad hominem*, and *Appeal to fear*), ⊘ *Misrepresentation*, and ⊘ *Special Pleading*. Some of these dangers are described in Whittaker Chambers' *National Review* article "Big Sister is Watching You" (Chambers 1957). Although Chambers doesn't mention the history of Russian folktales and their structure, his appraisal of Rand's method in *Atlas Shrugged* echoes the Russian folktale author's playbook as written by Vladimir Propp.

Chambers describes *Atlas Shrugged* as a "somewhat ferro-concrete fairy tale," managing to capture some of the Soviet-era literary and artistic style Rand absorbed in Petrograd. And he refers to her characters as "operatic caricatures" whose heroes are all "geniuses" and "breathtakingly beautiful," unrelated in significant ways to the real world they're intended to represent. This in turn, he suggests, results in Rand's avoiding the difficult work ("plaguey business of performing the one service that her fiction might have performed") of providing a detailed and objective account of principled differences between her heroes and her villains, rather than merely polemically extolling the virtues of the caricatured heroes and the depravity of the caricatured villains as they work their ways through the folktale plot.

Chambers also warns of being tricked by the "mischief" that Rand makes in "dodging into fiction" that she knows isn't an accurate representation of "political reality." And, referring to her technique in *Atlas Shrugged* as "primitive story-telling," he warns the reader not to allow these oversimplified caricatures and contrived situations to distract "the eye that seeks to probe [reality] fully." This, of course, is a warning for the reader not to be distracted from the goals of truth and wisdom to which the genuine philosopher is committed.

Now I said, in the subsection "Limiting the scope" in Section 3 above, that we're going to avoid any direct consideration of Rand's novels precisely *because* they're works of literature and so shouldn't be judged by criteria appropriate to works of philosophy. And I won't violate that decision here. But when Rand's fiction and tales intrude into works that she offers to us as explaining the principles of her philosophy, they're fair game.

This brief consideration of Whittaker Chambers' literary review of *Atlas Shrugged* serves to focus attention on what we'll see are certain recurring aspects of Rand's style of presentation, and it will be helpful to have this example, and its historical background in terms of Russian folktales, as we move forward in examining Rand's philosophical works. Were we to view Chambers' review as a critique of a philosophical work, we'd see immediately that he's pointing out occurrences of such markers as ⊘ *Misrepresentation*, ⊘ *Special Pleading*, ⊘ *Intimidation*, and ⊘ *Known Fallacy* — and that, from his perspective, Rand's style presents itself as more characteristic of the sophist and rhetorician than of the philosopher.

Fiction writers can control the story and make it as fanciful as they like, and still remain safe. Explorers, philosophers pursuing truth and wisdom, and those concerned with objective reality — as Rand supposes herself to be — must have a primary concern about what the story *represents* and how *accurately* it does this. And thus Hume's reference to a "spirit of accuracy" as a requirement for the genuine philosopher. Small flaws in the story may have dire consequences when applying it to the real world. And significant flaws in relating a real-world individual to a character in the story (and then back in the other direction) can render the story useless for illustrating claims about the real world — giving rise to what we might call the *Fallacy of Caricature* (which would be a version of the Straw Man argument). Unfortunately, one thing that Rand does *not* borrow from Hume (as we'll see in more detail as we proceed) is the spirit of accuracy.

With this additional insight into Rand's method of presenting her views, we proceed to a consideration of her philosophical presentation in *For the New Intellectual*.

Attila, the Witch Doctor, and the conjuring of demons

The two stars in the particular drama constructed in *For the New Intellectual* are *Attila* ("the man who rules by brute force") and *The Witch Doctor* ("the man who dreads physical reality", or alternatively, "the man of faith"). They are, according to Rand, "philosophical archetypes" who embody "two variants of a certain view of man and of existence." That is, Attila and the Witch Doctor are an "*artist's conceptions*", and not real people.

Rand spends fully 10 pages on developing these caricatures in a lengthy, emotive, and polemical soliloquy that mirrors the style of speeches by the heroic characters in her novels. This section in *For the New Intellectual* is not a philosophical presentation — in which concepts and principals are carefully introduced and explained — but rather it's a repetitive rhetorical tirade, using pejorative language, that resembles a propaganda speech. However, again, its purpose is to "paint a picture" or "sketch an image". It resembles nothing so much as a "character development" or two "character sketches" that would be done for a screen play. At this, Rand has substantial training and experience.

The rhetoric of Attila and The Witch Doctor also has another goal: to make us *feel* a certain way about Attila and The Witch Doctor, and so to make us *feel* a certain way about those people (such as other philosophers) whom Rand will *label* by means of these caricatures. So when Rand says, a few pages later, that "Attila's soul" spoke through Hume, then we know how we should *feel* about Hume and his philosophy, don't we? And we should *feel* this way even if Rand hasn't in fact advanced any coherent response to the problems Hume confronts in his epistemology (⊘ *Superficial Response*), and doesn't advance any compelling (or even detailed and intelligible) alternative position to Hume's that addresses those same problems. This, again, is not philosophy. It's rhetoric and sophistry of the highest order as it exhibits such examples of the ⊘ *Known Fallacy* marker as the *Ad hominem* and *Appeals to fear* arguments.

Here are brief summaries of these two caricatures. Most of the phrasing in them is taken directly from Rand, but you should look at the original section yourself for the details and full effect.

The Attila caricature

Attila exists without concepts or understanding, acting only on his "urges". He's a beast of prey who survives by the physical conquest of men. He never thinks of creating anything, but only taking over things that others have created. Attila is a coercer rather than a producer. His values are provided to him by The Witch Doctor, and he extorts obedience by means of a club. His brain is a jumble of concretes unintegrated by abstractions, and he feels that The Witch Doctor can give him what he lacks, which is a long range view and a code of moral values. Attila is a tribal chief or absolute monarch.

The Witch Doctor caricature

The Witch Doctor dreads physical reality and the necessity of practical action. He escapes into his emotions and visions of a mystic realm where he enjoys a supernatural power not limited by nature. Emotions are tools of cognition, and wishes take precedence over facts. The Witch Doctor obliterates the distinction between the perceiver and the perceived. He believes that contradictions are possible and A is non-A. The Witch Doctor is a religious leader or logical positivist.

In the history of myths and fairy tales, Attila would be recognized as a villain, and in fact a specific sub-type of villain seen as *The Beast*. Rand's description of Attila is beastly — inhuman — and the image it conjures for us is a slovenly and animalistic sub-human driven by base urges who wants only to dominate and to destroy heroes and any sign of rationality and civility in society. This caricature does not, in any way, appear to describe David Hume.

Just to seal the image, Rand refers to Attila as a "beast of prey," and in a highly unusual gesture for Rand she refers to another philosopher (Nietzsche) as her inspiration for using this phrase. Nietzsche did indeed employ the "beast of prey" image with regard to his "superman" in *On the Genealogy of Morals* (Nietzsche 1996). But as always, Rand omits any specific citation which would allow us to examine Nietzsche's use of these terms in context, and so perhaps either enhance our understanding, or indicate how Rand's own use of the term might deviate from Nietzsche's. Rather than Rand's animosity towards "the beast," Nietzsche does seem more sympathetic towards it — referring to "the splendid blond beast." He seemingly has in mind the African lion, and accords it some degree of (his word) "admiration." But for her purpose, Rand borrows the phrase and image of Nietzsche's character and strips it of any possible redeeming value. It takes some degree of charity not to see this as at least a minor example of ⊘ *Misleading Citation*, ⊘ *Lack of Rigor*, or ⊘ *Misappropriation*. Again, what we see here is Rand as the *creative writer* and rhetorician rather than the *philosopher* — painting a picture intended to elicit emotion rather than reason.

Of course most of Rand's philosophical essays are reworked, edited, or simply reprinted versions of speeches she gave in front of audiences. And we therefore shouldn't expect to see the details and care for accuracy that we would in a philosophical article prepared for publication (and certainly not one for submission to a refereed journal). But the fact remains that for each of these speeches-turned-into-articles, Rand had all the time she would need and want to add those details to the written version in order to turn it into a complete, readable, informative, and careful *philosophical* presentation of her views — resembling the work of Philo rather than of Pseudo.

Uniformly, however, in these cases Rand simply doesn't do that, thereby exhibiting a ⊘ *Lack of Rigor* and overall superficial philosophical treatment of her subject. And this case of a missing (and possibly quite informative) citation — a citation that she takes the trouble of making (vaguely and indirectly) in the speech — is just one example. In the same context where she drops this vague reference to Nietzsche (pp. 33-37 of *For the New Intellectual*) she also offers brief (more like hit-and-run) criticisms of the philosophers Immanuel Kant, G. W. F. Hegel, August Comte, Jeremy Bentham, Herbert Spencer, and Karl Marx — with *no* evidence offered that these criticisms are reasonable or accurate, *no* specific attributions to specific individuals, and not a single citation to even point the reader to where these philosophers commit the sins of which she accuses them (thus ⊘ *Failure to Give Fair Hearing* and ⊘ *Discouraging Inquiry*). Yet on the basis of these brief and unjustified criticisms (Rand's own version of the hurling of epithets) she moves quickly on to make sweeping statements about "[t]he failure of philosophers" and "[t]he great treason of the philosophers from the Middle Ages through modern times" (⊘ *Exaggerated Claims*).

This is not the behavior of a philosopher who's pursuing truth and wisdom. It's appropriate, perhaps, for a reporter of some newspaper, news magazine, or news blog — who may have space limitations, editorial constraints, little editorial supervision, and who isn't pretending to be a philosopher writing a book on her fundamental philosophy. But it wouldn't be acceptable, for example, as a submission to the *Journal of Ayn Rand Studies*, whose submission guidelines are clear about the level of scholarship required by its standard peer review process. You can see the difference between those articles and Rand's own books and articles by looking through some of its current or back issues in the *(The Journal of Ayn Rand Studies* 2020), though issues more recent than about 6 years require access through a library or university system, or by fee or subscription. Ironically, however, it's difficult to see how Rand's own writings would be found acceptable for publication by the editorial staff of the journal named in her honor and focused on that very work.

This is not a trivial issue of Rand's failing to "play the academic game" and sprinkle her articles and books with citations to other philosophers. First, *she* is the one who introduces these references to philosophers, makes (totally unsubstantiated) claims about them, and does so as part of the process of explicating her own philosophy and the importance, significance, and innovation of it. So these claims about other philosophers are *fundamental* both in illustrating *their* misguided views and demonstrating how those contrast with *hers*. But towards this end, these claims can't be left at the level of vague statements and generalities that Rand offers.

Conjuring the logical positivist demon

When Rand boldly says of the logical positivists that

Rand on the Logical Positivists

"Knowledge, they said, consists, not of facts, but of words, words unrelated to objects, words of an arbitrary social convention, as an irreducible primary; knowledge is merely a matter of manipulating language."

we have to ask "*Which* logical positivist said this?"[22] *Where* did he say this?" *But no logical positivist ever said that knowledge consists of words*. Rand is complaining about a view that *all* meaning and truth is conventional (i.e., merely a matter of social convention about the meanings of words, agreed upon by language users), and so not linked in any way to *reality*. The positivists, of course did not hold such a view, but a much more sophisticated one regarding whether there is any *single* or "preferred" *language* for describing reality.[23]

It's a mystery how Rand arrived at this grotesque misinterpretation of Logical Positivism, although it reflects a view I've seen before, always in a context of some sort of Aristotelian perspective filtered through one or another slant on Thomism — always in the case where the person holding the view had never actually read logical positivists themselves, or possibly read (and misinterpreted) only A. J. Ayer's *Language, Truth, and Logic* (Ayer 1952), and took it to be an accurate representation of Logical Positivism.

Rand's wildly mytho-poetic description of the Witch Doctor becomes less and less coherent as it proceeds. I've provided only a brief summary of it (using her own words and phrases). At least the description of Attila is coherent (if crude), but her description of the Witch Doctor spirals quickly into a jumble of jargon that has the sound and fervor of a possessed fundamentalist minister preaching in an overheated tent revival. There is no philosophy in it — only invective.

By the time Rand winds down the sermon, she has (on p. 12) cast the logical positivist as a Witch Doctor, but also (on pp. 34 and 43) pinned him to the Attila caricature as well. And she's done this not by careful analysis, argument, and demonstration, as befitting a philosopher, but simply with rhetorical condemnations.

Rand decides to tar the logical positivists with the brush of mysticism in claiming that they held "that such concepts as metaphysics or existence or reality or thing or matter or mind are meaningless" (though how this would be mystical is unclear, particularly since it was the positivists' goal to be anti-mystical). However, although Carnap, in his early writings, quite explicitly held that metaphysics (as practiced primarily by the German Idealists such as Fichte, Schelling, and Hegel) was meaningless, there was a more general dispute among the positivists about how broadly this claim could be made.[24]

In the years prior to Rand's writing of *For the New Intellectual*, Carnap had also gone beyond his own early works and positions and broadened his view on the nature of metaphysics and whether certain variants or interpretations or understandings of it could be accommodated. *In no case*, however, did the positivists hold that the concepts of existence, reality, thing, matter, or mind were *meaningless*. Rand uses this ⊘ *Misrepresentation* to cast herself as the hero in her own fable against the villainous (and entirely abstract and unidentified) Positivist. The idealized Objectivist hero confronts the idealized evil Positivist, and a battle of idealized Titans ensues, with the idealized Objectivist hero proclaiming the necessity for conformance to objective reality. As rhetoric and sophistry, it's wonderful. As philosophy and the pursuit of wisdom, not so much.

And recall that Rand says of the Witch Doctor that "He believes that contradictions are possible and A is non-A. The Witch Doctor is a religious leader or logical positivist." This is one of those circumstances where on the basis of certain similarities Rand perceives, she associates the logical positivist with her Witch Doctor caricature. Then she subsequently takes the step of attributing other properties of the Witch Doctor to the logical positivist: in this case the belief that "contradictions are possible." But *no logical positivist believed that contradictions were possible or that A is non-A*. And of course she offers no evidence that any logical positivist did, and so she offers us another helping of ⊘ *Misrepresentation* with a side dish of ⊘ *Known Fallacy* in the form of a *Straw man*.

How Rand would have picked up this view of logical positivism is anyone's guess, I suppose. But at best it can only be seen as a serious and incoherent distortion of some of the views of Carnap and others (possibly including Quine) concerning the role of language in scientific theories, whether there's a single correct language of science, how the abstract/theoretical terms (Rand would

Chapter 11: Ayn Rand: Mostly Borrowed, Nothing New?

prefer "concepts") of science get their meanings, and what roles they play in the construction and application of scientific theories. But as a characterization of any logical positivist, it's downright *wrong*, and we have to regard it unquestionably as an example of ⊘ *Misrepresentation,* ⊘ *Inadequate Understanding,* and ⊘ *Lack of Rigor.*

From our perspective as a reader of what's claimed to be a philosophical work, we must also ask *how* (and in fact *whether*) Rand makes any direct response to these offensive theses of logical positivism to which she refers. Quite simply, she makes no such response at all — and of course any response is precluded by her complete failure to characterize the logical positivist position with any specificity or accuracy. All we get is a condemnation of the logical positivist's "combined neo-mystic Witch-doctory and Attila-ism," and a statement that

Rand on what logical positivism says

"They assured [the scientist] that the task of theoretical science is the manipulation of symbols, and scientists are the special elite whose symbols have the magic power of making reality conform to their will ('matter is that which fits mathematical equations')." (Rand 1963a 34).

Notice that in this passage Rand has explicitly quoted the phrase "matter is that which fits mathematical equations" — indicating that it's from the writings of one or another logical positivist. *But it's not! It's not anything that any logical positivist ever said. And it's not anything that a logical positivist ever meant.* So this is yet another blatant example of ⊘ *Misinterpretation,* ⊘ *Misleading Citation,* and ⊘ *Lack of Rigor* (although in this case the lack of rigor seems to result from an intent to deceive). But the real point here is that in *For the New Intellectual* Rand does not either clearly characterize the positions of her opponents or offer us any clear response to the positions that she so vociferously condemns. And this counts as systematic ⊘ *Obscurantism* and ⊘ *Superficial Response* on a broad scale, in the pursuit of persuasion rather than truth and wisdom.

♦ WHAT DID THE VILLAIN CARNAP REALLY SAY?

What, by way of contrast, do we find when we turn from Rand to Carnap and look at what he actually says in his paper "The Elimination of Metaphysics Through Logical Analysis of Language" (Carnap 1959)? Carnap begins with

Rudolph Carnap: from "The Elimination of Metaphysics Through Logical Analysis of Language" (1932)

"There have been many opponents of metaphysics from the Greek skeptics to the empiricists of the 19th century. Criticisms of very diverse kinds have been set forth. Many have declared that the doctrine of metaphysics is false, since it contradicts our empirical knowledge. Others have believed it to be uncertain, on the ground that its problems transcend the limits of human knowledge. Many anti-metaphysicians have declared that occupation with metaphysical questions is sterile. Whether or not these questions can be answered, it is at any rate unnecessary to worry about them; let us devote ourselves entirely to the practical tasks which confront active men every day of their lives!

The development of modern logic has made it possible to give a new and sharper answer to the question of the validity and justification of metaphysics. The researches of applied logic or the theory of knowledge, which aim at clarifying the cognitive content of scientific statements and thereby the meanings of the terms that occur in the statements, by means of logical analysis, lead to a positive and to a negative result. The positive result is worked out in the domain of empirical science; the various concepts of the various branches of science are clarified; their formal-logical and epistemological connections are made explicit. In the domain of metaphysics, including all philosophy of value and normative theory, logical analysis yields the negative result that the alleged statements in this domain are entirely meaningless. Therewith a radical elimination of metaphysics is attained, which was not yet possible from the earlier anti-metaphysical standpoints. It is true that related ideas may be found already in several earlier trains of thought (e.g., those of a nominalistic kind); but it is only now when the development of logic during recent decades provides us with a sufficiently sharp tool that the decisive step can be taken."

This doesn't seem crazy or a threat to Western civilization, does it? There's nothing in it — or in this entire paper of Carnap's, or in any of his writings — about "magical power" or "making reality conform to their will." It sets out a problem and establishes it within the history of philosophy. It's clear and succinct. Carnap goes on to suggest that the development of modern logic (of which Rand, by the way, seems totally ignorant) may contribute to a solution to this problem. Moreover, he offers the very Objectivist-sounding and sincere appeal to "let us devote ourselves entirely to the practical tasks which confront active men every day of their lives!"

Now, after reading Carnap's paper, you may decide that Carnap is right or that he's wrong. Many have thought that Carnap was wrong — or at least unconvincing — while others have been inclined to follow his lead and attempt to repair any flaws in his approach. But you can't do any of this unless you actually read the paper, understand his arguments, and evaluate what he has to say. That is, you need to do the work of the genuine philosopher in pursuing truth and wisdom. Rand gives us no hint that she's done this (with Carnap or any other positivist). Instead, she caricatures a well-thought-out philosophical position and argument, and quickly casts it aside as "neo-mystic" — without any attempt at justifying *that* evaluation either! Exactly what makes it neo-mystic? We're not told. There's no talk of mysticism or of the mystical experience in Carnap's paper or in the other positivists — except for their viewing any such talk (being of a metaphysical nature) as meaningless.

Harking back to our discussion in Section 3.1 of what it means to be a genuine astronomer, we have to see Rand's treatment of Carnap and the logical positivists as akin to an astronomer who criticizes Copernicus without reading his work or understanding his theory, and who confuses him with Ptolemy. That's not a competent astronomer. It's someone trying to *masquerade* as an astronomer and offering us crackpot ideas about astronomy. This isn't just a matter of Rand's being *wrong* about details of Carnap's approach. It's a matter of not caring to devote attention to being accurate and pursuing the truth — because that would conflict with the broader *story* that Rand wants to tell and wants us to believe. It's fiction in the service of persuasion.

For Rand, this is not remotely a match to the Philo persona, but a very close match to Pseudo. Rand could have — at least briefly — provided a cogent account of what the logical positivist attack on metaphysics was and what errors, weaknesses, or unacceptable consequences might be seen in this. That's what a philosopher would do. But she does not, leaving us instead with only caricature and unfounded condemnation. The rest of *For the New Intellectual* continues in this style.

What should we have expected?

As Scott Ryan points out in "A Randian Roundup: A Review of the Objectivist Literature" (Ryan 2003), Rand's primary goal in *For the New Intellectual* was to castigate philosophers throughout history for having failed to solve problems (such as "the problem of universals") to which she believes she brings unique and successful solutions. But as we've seen, she seems only able to do this by distorting and misrepresenting that history and those philosophers; and attempting to replace their work with rhetoric rather than philosophy.

While I've provided a clear example of such distortions and misrepresentations in the case of logical positivism, and hinted at them in the direction of Hume, in fact the technique is pervasive and a continuing example of using rhetorical techniques of story-telling in place of the careful conceptual work and clearly stated and explicated principles required of the genuine philosopher. Other examples in *For the New Intellectual* include Rand's overstatement of Aristotle's contribution to the development of science and so to the industrial revolution (though he had a lasting influence in certain areas of classical biology — which some argue continues to deter advancement in areas of biological taxonomy), and any influence in such areas as the structure of English and the history of logic.

In fact, much of the work of the late Medieval philosophers (such as Jean Buridan), 19th century American philosophers (especially C. S. Peirce), and the logical positivists was in logic, semantics, and philosophy of language (of which Rand seems almost entirely ignorant or stubbornly resistant) — and this was a reaction to known weaknesses and limitations in Aristotle's logic and his simplistic and parochial views on language. Yet it's the developments of these improvements and replacements of Aristotle's logic that led to what we have today in terms of rich formal logical/semantic/pragmatic systems yielding practical consequences in the real world of computer science, cognitive science, artificial intelligence, computational linguistics, inferential systems in medicine, self-driving cars, autonomous robots, sophisticated drones, and automated production — to name just a few examples.

In short, it's not Aristotle who's responsible for your cell phone's working. And to the contrary, it is very *non*-Aristotelian advances in the areas of logic, language, metaphysics, and epistemology that are responsible. That's something an Objectivist should realize and applaud — rather than dismissing the entire Medieval period and philosophy through the 20th century as valueless and "traitorous."

Even looking back further into history, Rand should have known — or taken the time to learn — that the course of science and philosophy was inexorably altered by the replacement of Aristotle's views on matter in motion with Newton's views *that better corresponded to objective reality*. This was hardly a secret during the time that Rand was being educated in Russia, and indeed it's common for instructors to begin courses in modern philosophy with a detailed consideration of Newton because of the resounding effect he had on overcoming the Aristotelian perspective in both science and philosophy. But certainly a major weakness of Rand's is her almost total ignorance of the philosophy of language and the history and philosophy of science, and it's this ignorance that allows her to cling to an antiquated perspective of philosophy anchored in the ancient world.

Yes, Aristotle was the "inventor of logic" (more precisely, the inventor of *formal deductive logic*). We should acknowledge this and be grateful for it. But clinging to that narrow metaphysical basis and origin is clinging to an intellectual anchor that's not at all in the spirit of the pursuit of wisdom that Aristotle himself saw as the primary goal of the philosopher. Rand's own treatment of philosophical problems, and her presentations of attempted solutions, is hobbled by her ignorance and narrow understanding.

In Section 3.1 I pointed out the obligations that anyone has who purports to be a philosopher or to be doing work of a genuinely philosophical nature. And part of that (in analogy to a genuine astronomer) is to be familiar with a certain *body of work*. The level at which you want to play the game determines the degree of familiarity (and scope) required of you regarding that body of work. Rand wants to play the game at the highest level. She in fact says repeatedly that she *is* playing it at the highest level, and in fact at a higher level than virtually all others in the history of philosophy. But she woefully fails to meet the bar in terms of her command of the required domain of knowledge. This, at least to a significant degree, is what turns her attempts at philosophy into pseudo-philosophy.

But it's not just a matter of Rand's getting a few things (or even quite a number of things) wrong about the history of philosophy and the views of philosophers she sees as antagonists. It's a matter of her *using* these misinterpretations and distortions to *craft a story* and paint a picture in which she promotes her own work as providing solutions where none have been provided before. This takes her along both dimensions of the pseudo (*Incompetence* and *Exploitation*) that are described in Section 6.2, and it puts her at least on the edge of appearing to be a crackpot.

None of this is to say that various fundamental views expressed by Rand, or concepts that she employs, or principles that she enunciates and applies, are without value or are incorrect. That's not part of the job we're doing here. But it is to say that her *presentations* of these — and the philosophical theories and positions she develops and offers us — are *not philosophical*, but are *pseudo*-philosophical. As Whittaker Chambers remarks in his review of *Atlas Shrugged*, "[A] great many of us dislike much that Miss Rand dislikes, quite as heartily as she does"; but this shouldn't incline us to "take her at her word." And it shouldn't incline us to see her pseudo-philosophy, rhetoric, and sophistry as any kind of genuine philosophy. It is not.

We began Section 3 above by saying that one of our primary questions would be to ask what difficulties confront us in understanding and evaluating Ayn Rand's philosophy. Our examination of Rand's *For the New Intellectual* has now provided a partial answer to this question, and we can identify these difficulties as including

Difficulties in evaluating Rand's philosophy

- Presentation of philosophical concepts/views/theories/principles through the use of *metaphor* and *allegory* in the form of folk tales whose characters (or caricatures) represent philosophical heroes and villains.

- Persistent use of *significant distortions* and *misrepresentations* of philosophers throughout history, their views, the problems they were addressing, and what they proposed as solutions to those problems.

- *Misleading* (or entirely *fictitious*) *citations* in support of such misinterpretations and distortions; and a determined *avoidance of being specific* about precisely what is being criticized in the work of others.

- A high degree of *obscurantism* in Rand's presentation of her own concepts, principles, and views, resulting in part from an *avoidance of an expository presentation* in favor of a rhetorical, allegorical, and polemical one.

- A *fundamental methodological failure* on Rand's part — resulting in or exacerbating all of the above difficulties — to convert what was originally intended as an inspirational speech into a more careful expository presentation of critical philosophical concepts, principles, views, and arguments. Essentially, this can be seen as a failure to convert a rhetorical and polemical work into a philosophical work — but continuing to offer the rhetoric as philosophy.

These difficulties in turn have exposed how Rand — in *For the New Intellectual* — has repeatedly exhibited a number of pseudo-philosophy markers and demonstrated a much closer match to the Pseudo persona than to Philo. And so at this point we have to be tilting strongly in the direction of considering Rand's work as pseudo-philosophical.

For the New Intellectual is full of rhetoric, invective, and sweeping claims. But it's also full of obscurantism, distortion, misrepresentation, misleading citations, misappropriation, special pleading, unexplained or insufficiently explained terminology, appeals to fear and emotion, and an almost total lack of evidence or argument to support those principles and theses that, in an unending stream, we're expected to accept and follow. This isn't the work of a philosopher. It doesn't begin to provide us with what we need in pursuing wisdom, it fails the tests of genuine philosophy, and in the end is just a masquerade.

But *For the New Intellectual* is Rand's very first attempt at venturing away from fiction into the realm of expository philosophy, and we should continue to look further at more of her philosophical work. This brings us to *The Virtue of Selfishness*.

11.5 *The Virtue of Selfishness*

According to *The Ayn Rand Lexicon*,

"The *Virtue of Selfishness* is a collection of essays presenting Ayn Rand's radical moral code of rational selfishness and its opposition to the prevailing morality of altruism — i.e., to the duty to sacrifice for the sake of others."

"*The Virtue of Selfishness* is indispensable reading for anyone who wants to understand the crucial ethical issues at the root at [*sic*] so many of our cultural debates today—who wants to understand the revolutionary ideas that guide the lives of Ayn Rand's fictional heroes—who wants to lead an existence that is both moral and practical—who wants to discover why, in the words of one of the heroes of *Atlas Shrugged*, 'the purpose of morality is to teach you, not to suffer and die, but to enjoy yourself and live.'" (The Ayn Rand Institute 2020)

Our review of *For the New Intellectual*, has demonstrated that Rand's style is conducive to a complex and confusing presentation which can be difficult to untangle by the average reader. *The Virtue of Selfishness* presents an even greater challenge in that regard since, unlike the largely polemical *For the New Intellectual*, it contains lengthy and detailed arguments, involving a number of critical concepts, and in support of Rand's theory of ethics. Because our goal in this chapter is not to provide an exhaustive analysis of Rand's philosophy, but rather to demonstrate how our models of the genuine philosopher and pseudo-philosopher may be applied in practice, it behooves us to forgo a lengthy and detailed analysis of *The Virtue of Selfishness* in favor of a more focused review that highlights Rand's presentation and justification of her ethical theory.

Towards that end, we'll be guided in part by Eric Mack's careful analysis of Rand's ethics in his paper "Problematic Arguments in Randian Ethics" (Mack 2003), hereafter *Problematic Arguments*. I'll make use of Mack's insights and critiques of Rand's writings to focus our attention on those portions of her thought that are most pertinent to our own evaluation of her ethical theory as being genuinely philosophical or pseudo-philosophical.

An introductory look at Rand's ethical principles and concepts

Mack devotes 65 pages of his article in *The Ayn Rand Journal* to carefully documenting, analyzing, and criticizing the concepts, views, and arguments that comprise Rand's "egoist" ethical theory. Finding some serious faults in Rand's approach, he then attempts what he calls a "rescue operation" in order to see if that theory can be rescued from what he sees as Rand's faulty formulation and defense of it. Such an intense effort is outside the scope of what we can hope to review here, and goes far beyond our needs in illustrating how our view of pseudo-philosophy applies to real-world cases. But the core of Mack's critique, and his insights into Rand's reasoning can cogently guide our own assessment of whether she's involved in doing genuine philosophy or pseudo-philosophy. Following that thread, what I'll do is first to simplify and distill some of Mack's observations and criticisms, and then explore how our models of the philosopher and pseudo-philosopher apply to this view of Rand's work in *The Virtue of Selfishness* (hereafter, *Virtue*).

In *Problematic Arguments* Mack makes the case that Rand expresses and argues for her ethical theory in the form of a complex presentation that he calls the Shuffle. This consists of multiple ambiguities and equivocations that are used to "shift" among different interpretations of Rand's fundamental ethical principle, which we'll call the Principle of Survival.

We'll approach an understanding and critique of the Shuffle by first, in this section, taking a preliminary look at the Principle of Survival, briefly introducing some of the fundamental concepts it employs (*ultimate good, parasitism, rationality*), and seeing two different ways in which it can be understood. In the next section (*Ambiguities and equivocations*) we'll look more carefully at these, at the *components* that go into making up the Shuffle (the concepts involved in it, the principles set forth for consideration, the logic) and problems that arise from these components and their use. The following section (*Prelude to the Shuffle*) will present an overview of the Shuffle, and then in *The Shuffle* we look at the details of each shift, how Rand attempts to achieve her goal, and what the result of that is.

Mack is not in any way concerned with assessing Rand's positions and arguments as being pseudo-philosophical or potentially pseudo-philosophical. Indeed, throughout *Problematic Arguments* he makes every effort to treat Rand as a serious professional philosopher and contributor to ethical thought.

Nonetheless, he does make some remarks that rather explicitly describe the dangers and potential consequences of pseudo-philosophy as we've discussed these in earlier sections of this chapter, in previous chapters, and in our models:

Eric Mack:
Objectively approaching Rand's ethical thought

"Before proceeding further, I should state for the record my own overall view of Rand as an ethical thinker. I think that Rand has offered us some very deep ethical insights, e.g. regarding the essential relationship between valuing and the human good and about the relationship of affirming the ultimate separate value of each individual's good and affirming each individual's possession of moral rights. Beyond that, Rand is simply without peer as an insightful, powerful, and heroic ethical crusader on behalf of individualism, individual freedom, and a free social and economic order. Unfortunately, I also think that line-by-line many of Rand's ethical arguments are just awful. It is not merely that she does not bother with fine distinctions and academic niceties. Rather, her arguments all too often consist of gross misrepresentations of her opponent's views, conflations of importantly distinct doctrines, crucial equivocations, and massive beggings of the questions at hand. And the awfulness of these arguments is compounded by the arrogance, contempt, and hostility with which they are usually expressed. ...

As long as those who appreciate Rand's deep insights and who want to sustain and expand her ethical crusade do not break free of these really bad arguments and their characteristic tone, they will fail in their own attempts to make Rand's insights and crusade attractive to a wider, intellectually discriminating, audience." (Mack 2003 3-4)

While acknowledging the importance of Rand's ethical attitude and "crusade," Mack also offers a warning (similar to one we offered above in our discussion of Attila and the Witch Doctor) that Rand's errors can't simply be passed off (as many of her supporters are inclined to do) as an idiosyncrasy of style, a different "method of argumentation," or a failure in conforming to common academic conventions. Her errors are much more fundamental than this. Mack then observes that a *consequence* of clinging to her grossly flawed presentations and arguments is that a broader and "intellectually discriminating" audience (i.e., an audience not previously committed or ideologically bound to Rand's views) will be turned away from what he sees as Rand's fundamentally important insights.

From our own perspective, these are observations that pseudo-philosophy may have the effect of inhibiting or discrediting valuable insights that *could* otherwise be proffered effectively through the medium of genuine philosophy — and welcomed (or at least seriously debated) by that broader audience. Ironically, such discussion and debate (and acceptance) is what Rand herself was seeking — at least within the more discriminating intellectual community, as she attempted to characterize that in *For the New Intellectual*.

As an illustration of Rand's approach to the expression of her philosophy and the defense of her ethical principles, Mack then focuses on one example which he treats in excruciating detail. We can't duplicate that degree of detail here, and instead I'll provide a much-simplified and compressed version of Mack's critique. This will be sufficient to represent accurately both Rand's treatment and Mack's critique of it, to enable you to retrace the arguments in both *Problematic Arguments* and *Virtue*, and to illustrate how our models of genuine philosophy and pseudo-philosophy apply in Rand's exposition of her ethical philosophy.

♦ THE RELATION BETWEEN ULTIMATE GOOD AND PARASITISM

We begin by considering a typical principle that Rand wants us to accept:

An individual's ultimate good requires that the individual avoid parasitism.

Here, "individual" of course refers to an *individual human*, and Rand will typically use such terms as "survival", "life" or "happiness" in place of "ultimate good". "Parasitism" refers to parasitic behavior, and this includes dependence on others, failure to be productive, wanting "handouts" (typically from government sources), etc. One of the first things that Rand does in talking about the *ultimate good* of a human is to identify this with the *survival* (continued life) of that human, largely because Rand wants to argue to such conclusions as "An individual who participates in parasitic behavior will die (or have a shortened life)." In order to make things a bit clearer and easier for us in what follows, we'll transform our principle into this acceptable Randian version which we'll call the *Principle of Survival*:

Rand's Principle of Survival

An individual's survival requires that the individual avoid parasitism, act rationally in achieving his goals, and be productive.

Rand seems nowhere to attempt a definition of "parasite," "parasitism," or "parasitic behavior," but instead provides a number of examples or negative characterizations of these, or caricatures them in ways similar to the manner in which she characterizes her villains. So in *Virtue*, for example, a parasite is characterized as a moocher, a looter, not an individualist, not independent, not a producer, etc. A parasite is someone who goes through life dependent on the labor and production of others, and whose dependence on those others degrades (and reduces the good in, and the length of) *his own* life. The obvious analogy is to biological parasites which infect a host, and the Principle of Survival relates the concepts (and phenomena) of survival, parasitism, rationality, productivity, and (human) goals.

Avoiding parasitism means being productive, and the consequences of the Principle of Survival for Rand include that an individual's survival *requires* being productive and hence non-parasitic. In fact, Rand is concerned to defend several principles and assertions related to the Principle of Survival in one way or another. Some we might regard as *rephrasings* of the Principle of Survival (saying the same thing, but in a slightly different way), some we might regard as being *consequences* of the Principle of Survival (so that they *follow from* the Principle of Survival, some we might regard as more basic principles *from which* the Principle of Survival *follows*, and some we might see as logically or factually *related to* the Principle of Survival *in more or less indirect ways* or as either *supporting* the Principle of Survival or *being supported by* the Principle of Survival. Rand is often not clear about exactly what the relationship is in each case. Here are some examples:

Examples of principles and declarations related to the Principle of Survival

1. An individual's *ultimate value* requires that the individual avoid parasitism.

2. An individual's *pursuit of happiness* requires that the individual avoid parasitism.

3. One's life is one's ultimate value. "These are two aspects of the same achievement." (*Virtue*, p. 17)

4. "The standard of value of the Objectivist ethics [is] that which is required for man's survival *qua* man." (*Virtue*. p.23)

5. The meaning of the *definition* of man's survival *qua* man is that: "'Man's survival *qua* man' means the terms, methods, conditions and goals required for the survival of a rational being through the whole of his lifespan—in all those aspects of existence which are open to his choice." (*Virtue*, p. 24)

6. A human's *ultimate value* is his own life and *requires* rationality, productiveness, and pride. (*Virtue*, p. 25)

7. "Rationality is man's basic virtue: the source of all his other virtues. ... Irrationality is the rejection of man's means of survival and, therefore, a commitment to a course of blind destruction; that which is anti-mind, is anti-life." (*Virtue*, p. 25)

8. The achievement of his own happiness is man's highest moral purpose. (*Virtue*. p. 27)

Considered together, there appear to be some potential problems of ⊘ *Vagueness and Equivocation* among these declarations.

♦ UNCLARITY INVOLVING CAUSATION AND MEANING

Some of these appear clearly to be intended as *conceptual statements*, where their *meanings* and truth or falsity depend solely on the concepts that are appealed to and the relations among those concepts. For example, it's difficult to see how any degree of empirical investigation could contribute to understanding or to accepting or rejecting any of 3, 5, and 8.

Others seem to imply that a *causal* (empirical, factual) interpretation is intended. For example, (6) appears to be suggesting that the ultimate value of your life can be achieved (brought about or *caused*) only through the exercise of rationality, productivity, and pride. Likewise (7) suggests that rejecting rationality will *cause* (result in) your destruction. But it's two pages later (p. 27) before Rand makes clear that "destruction" in this case doesn't mean destruction in the sense of *the end of your life*, but in terms of your survival *qua* man. That is, it's your "*humanness*" that ends: your *human* life; your life *as a human*)[25] However, in other places Rand wants to say that failure to exercise such virtues as rationality and productivity will end in *death*, and not (merely) loss of your humanity.

Many readers may be surprised and puzzled at Rand's insistence that failure to follow her ethical prescriptions of independence, rationality, and productivity will result in *death* rather than, say, discomfort, depression, unhappiness, or other similar states. This may seem to be a needlessly extreme consequence for Rand to saddle herself with demonstrating to her potential converts. Why not instead argue that in general adopting her ethical principles will lead you to a happier, more fulfilling, and more rewarding life — but drop the death threat?

Although Rand never seems to be particularly explicit about this, there may be a couple of reasons for her commitment to such an extreme view. One is ideological/philosophical, and one is practical. First, Rand may feel that this requirement is compelled by her understanding of Aristotle's metaphysics — in particular his theory of human nature and whether, for example, rationality is part of the *essence* of being human. Rand clearly feels it is, though there is some dispute about this in Aristotle scholarship.[26] But the second reason is the more practical one.

Rand sees herself as proposing an ethical theory that simply can't be denied. This is Rand's triumph (well, one of them) over philosophers throughout history: the formulation of an ethical theory whose validity can be *proven* and from which we *cannot deviate* on *pain of death*. Given that goal, it is simply not sufficient or acceptable for her to conjure up an ethical theory that may be argued simply to be *better* than others in certain ways or to be an *acceptable*, or even *preferable*, alternative. Better isn't good enough. *Necessary* is the only acceptable result.

I think it's likely that in fact both of these considerations are driving Rand's formulation and argumentation in this case. But, as Mack has made very clear in *Problematic Arguments*, there's no question about the extreme interpretation that Rand wants to impose on her own principle, and it can't be dismissed as hyperbole.

♦ CONFUSION AND COUNTEREXAMPLES INVOLVING RATIONALITY AND CHOICE

This raises another confusion that points to a potentially fundamental problem Rand faces. At various points Rand says clearly that being rational or irrational is a *choice* that we can make. Rationality is a *virtue* and she want's us to *choose to be virtuous* — that's the point of having an ethics and ethical principles that *guide our choices*. Her whole project (through the fictional and philosophical writings) is to convince us to act in certain ways by *choosing* to act in accord with certain principles which *she* is providing us. But if rationality is a *part* of being human — part of what *makes* us human, which Rand repeatedly urges us to believe in the strongest language — then where is the *choice*? Where is the *possibility* of choice to act *irrationally*?

A way out of this conundrum (and the way Rand follows) is to first recognize that including rationality in man's nature (making rationality *constitutive* of the concept of man) doesn't mean or imply that man will always or for the most part *exercise* that rationality. It means that man has the *capability* of exercising it — the capability of being rational. And this leaves open the question of how (and in how many ways) rationality can be exercised in a given situation or context. Although Rand tends to think and talk of rationality as being binary (it's either there or not, either on or off), we need to beware of thinking that an injunction (a moral guideline or ethical requirement) of acting rationally means that in any particular choice there is only *one* rational alternative. Such an attitude may be buried in Rand's principles and declarations only to be exposed by inconsistencies and counter-examples. But this will be difficult to determine if those principles and declarations are obscure or ambiguous.

As an example, can't I *rationally* choose to be unproductive and live a lazy life (figuratively, if not literally) on a tropical beach? Or can't I choose rationally to live a life of crime as a high-end jewel or art thief? That also doesn't seem immediately implausible. Certainly someone could point out to me that there are risks to doing that (getting caught, being physically harmed or killed, incarceration). But there are risks in choosing any career or working in any job, and probably being an international jewel thief has substantially less risk than being a member of a SEAL team or a firefighter or a salvage diver. So if someone tries to tell me that my decision to pursue the unproductive life on the beach or the (admittedly glorified) criminal life of the "high-class" jewel thief is *irrational*, then it seems quite rational to regard that person as nutty and unrealistic. Is the concept of the *successful human parasite* really *incoherent*? It doesn't seem so.

These kinds of considerations are in fact *counterexamples* to the foundation for the ethical theory that Rand is proposing. They should occur to any reasonable (rational) person and make us skeptical of Rand's attempts to chain the notion of rationality (or the very *concept* of *being human*) to such principles as the Principle of Survival and to these other concepts of productivity and various forms of what she thinks of as parasitism. But let's see how she attempts to shore up the ethical foundation she's trying to build.

Mack sees Rand's arguments as taking place in the form of an elaborate set of ambiguities and equivocations that he calls "the Shuffle" and that attempts to circumvent these counterexamples. But in order to say what the Shuffle is, and then to describe some of its details, we first have to get through some preliminaries involving Rand's reasoning and terminology.

Ambiguities and equivocations

To take us where she wants to lead, Rand must convince us that we should accept the Principle of Survival. This is critical for her ethics since it will form part of the foundation for adopting a number of moral rules that *prescribe* (require) certain types of conduct (individualism, self-reliance, independence from government "handouts") and *proscribe* (forbid) others (mooching, looting, parasitism, socialism). Ultimately it will support claims about *laissez-faire* capitalism being the only proper economic basis of society, it will discourage or prohibit certain types of social programs (that would support or encourage parasitism and dependence on government), it will cast all forms of *collectivism* (which includes socialism, communism, and Marxism) as destructive sources of evil in society, and it will exalt the decisions and behaviors exhibited by the heroes of Rand's novels.

Rand needs to convince us that the Principle of Survival is *true*, or at the very least that it *makes sense* and *is plausible*. Without this, there's no reason for us to accept the Principle of Survival and follow Rand's other ideas about ethics and society. And there's no reason to believe that all of what she's portrayed for us in her novels and other fictional works is anything other than that: plain fiction with little or no connection to reality.

Convincing us of this requires producing evidence or argument in support of the Principle of Survival in order to answer such questions as "Why should we believe that the Principle of Survival is a good principle to adopt?" or "Why should we believe that the Principle of Survival is true?" More broadly, Mack asks the question (*Problematic Arguments*, p. 13) "How can Rand ... move [from her views of survival and ultimate good] to the sort of ethics of human well-being that is exemplified in the lives and choices of her fictional heroes?"

Much of what's found in *Virtue* is devoted first, to attempts at supporting the Principle of Survival, and then to an exploration of its consequences for individual behavior, society, and politics. Rand's first chapter in the book — "The Objectivist Ethics" — is where the primary arguments in favor of the Principle of Survival take place, and this is the focus of Mack's critique and our own attention here: Can Rand accomplish these goals in a genuinely philosophical (and hence believable and reliable) way?

The answer to this question turns out to be that while it's very likely *possible* for Rand to have succeeded in achieving these goals (Mack indicates how), *in fact she did not*. And her failure to do this exposes fundamental aspects of her pseudo-philosophy and illustrates how the pseudo-philosophy results in failure to establish her goals. As we'll see, the problems with Rand's presentation of her ideas in this case center around several critical examples of ⊘ *Vagueness and Equivocation*, and we'll be examining each of these in turn:

- An ambiguity in interpreting the Principle of Survival itself.
- An ambiguity concerning the meaning of "*survival*".
- An ambiguity concerning Rand's use of the critical phrase "*proper to*" as she uses this in understanding the Principle of Survival and its consequences.

◆ ONE AMBIGUITY: CONCEPTUAL VS. CAUSAL INTERPRETATIONS OF PRINCIPLES

As Mack points out, there are two ways in which this principle can be understood — basically two ways of understanding what the Principle of Survival is *about* — and that therefore there's some ambiguity in the principle and some possibility of equivocation when evaluating, justifying, or applying it.

The first of these interpretations of the Principle of Survival we'll call the *conceptual understanding* of the Principle of Survival. According to this interpretation, we take the Principle of Survival to be making a statement about the *concepts* of survival and parasitism, and how these concepts are related — for example whether the *concept* of survival *excludes* (is *incompatible with*) the *concept* of parasitism. So, under this interpretation of the Principle of Survival, it's *about concepts*; and determining whether it's true or plausible will depend on how we understand those concepts.

The second interpretation of the Principle of Survival we'll call the *causal understanding* of the Principle of Survival. This recasts the sense of the principle along the lines of its saying that parasitism *causes* a lack of survival and that non-parasitism is *causally related* to an individual human's survival. If we read the Principle of Survival according to this causal understanding, then the Principle of Survival is *about the observable world* (and perhaps empirical or theoretical laws that govern it). And so the truth or plausibility of the Principle of Survival depends on *facts that we can observe in the world* — for example, whether we see that parasitism exhibited by a human is always associated with the shortening or termination of his life (so we have *empirical evidence* that parasitism is causally related to death of the human). According to this interpretation, we would have to regard the Principle of Survival as false if we found *counterexamples to it*: examples of parasitic people who survived and lived.

The important logical point here is that if we employ the conceptual understanding of the Principle of Survival, there *cannot be counterexamples to it* since it's a statement about what we *mean* by "survival" and by "parasitism". But if we employ the causal interpretation of the Principle of Survival, then when we look at the world around us *we may discover counterexamples* to the principle.

Ambiguity:
two interpretations of the Principle of Survival

The Principle of Survival: *An individual's survival requires that the individual avoid parasitism, act rationally in achieving his goals, and be productive.*

Conceptual Interpretation
(The Principle of Survival is about the *concepts* of survival and parasitism)

The Principle of Survival is about what we *mean* by *survival* and *parasitism*. Observing things in the world plays no role in determining the acceptability of the Principle of Survival. It's a stipulation about how we understand the concepts of survival and parasitism, and so there *cannot* be counterexamples to it.

Causal interpretation[27]
(The Principle of Survival is about *what happens in the world* regarding parasitism and survival: that parasitism in humans results in their deaths.)

The Principle of Survival is about facts and relationships (involving parasitism and survival) in the world — whether instances of parasitism are always associated with lack of survival. Its plausibility depends on our making observations in the world concerning instances of parasitism, non-parasitism, survival, and non-survival — and so there *may be* counterexamples to it in our observations of events in the world.

We then see that the Principle of Survival suffers from ambiguity because we can *either* take the principle to be a *conceptual claim* (similar to definitions of the terms of "survival" and "parasitism" as Rand suggests in (5) above), or some kind of "conceptual truth" about how we *understand* the claim), *or* we can take the Principle of Survival to be a *factual/causal claim* (about what *actually happens in the real world* that we can observe). One consequence of this is that when we're reading what Rand says about the Principle of Survival, we need to be sure we understand whether it's the conceptual or the causal interpretation we're supposed to be applying to it since that will change what the Principle of Survival *means* and how we determine if it's plausible or true. The danger is that Rand's interpretation can change from one context to another, and it may not always (or ever) be made explicit to us.[28]

That, unfortunately, is just *one* way in which the Principle of Survival is ambiguous in how Rand would have us understand and use it. It has a second dimension of ambiguity that centers on what the term "survival" means in it.

♦ A SECOND AMBIGUITY: TWO SENSES OF "SURVIVAL"

Mack points out (through the use of several examples and references within *Virtue*) that Rand switches between two senses of "survival" in her attempts to justify the Principle of Survival. According to the first sense (which he calls "bare survival" or "unrefined survival"), survival is simply the *continuation of life*: the avoidance of death — no matter what the quality or details of that life may be. In this sense survival is survival in its basest form: if you're in a permanent coma, you're surviving. So this is about the lowest level of survival to be imagined. But according to the second sense of "survival" employed by Rand (which Mack calls "refined survival"), survival for a human is *survival qua man* — what most of us would think of as *life worth living*.

Ambiguity: two senses of "survival"

Unrefined survival: survival = continuation of life

Refined survival: survival = continuation of life *qua* **man**

The word "*qua*" is a preposition from Latin that's usually taken to have the meaning of "as", "in so far as", "in its capacity as", "as being", "considered under the aspect of" etc. It's a translation from a Greek word that Aristotle used in a similar capacity — and he certainly popularized this use within philosophy. Its use is intended to focus your attention on a certain *aspect* of what's being referred to, or to constrain the meaning of a term to a specific context. And it often changes the *meaning* of the term to which it's applied by eliminating a broader meaning that might be more commonly presumed. In this case it changes the meaning of "survival" from "physically alive in the most rudimentary biological sense" to "alive in the sense of having and experiencing human life as we know it".

For Rand to refer to "man's survival *qua* man" rather than simply to "man's survival" means that she's talking about a man (or human) surviving *as a human* (or in the *manner* of a man) — and not, for example, as a vegetable-like creature on life support, no brain function, and unable to see, speak, or interact with the world. Similarly, of course, what she has in mind is that a mere animal such as an amoeba or a wolf cannot exist *qua man* — cannot *be a man*. And we must keep in mind that under the conceptual interpretation of the Principle of Survival, "survival *qua* man" has *as part of its meaning* for Rand the use of rationality, productivity, and the absence of parasitism.

Rand herself tends to distinguish bare survival from refined survival in murky and inexplicit ways. Often when she uses the unadorned term "survival" she means bare survival — as when she speaks of "men who survive by imitating and repeating," "the survival of such mental parasites," those "who survive by brute force," when "survival is made possible only by their victims," "men who attempt to survive, not by means of reason," etc. In other cases her use of the unadorned "survival" term refers to the conceptually loaded sense of "survival *qua* man," "survival as a human," "survival proper to a rational being," etc.

And so in a number of cases it's not immediately clear what Rand means by "survival" and whether she's switching (shuffling) from one sense to another without clarifying this to the reader — for example, when she says that "men cannot survive by attempting the method of animals, by rejecting reason, and counting on productive men to serve as their prey." Does this mean that they can't survive *at all* (bare survival) or that they can't *survive qua man* (refined survival)?

The answer to this question isn't clear (even in the broad context), and it's important because, of course, it's possible for someone to *survive in the bare sense* while at the same time *not surviving in the "qua man" sense*. And at the same time that Rand seems to be focusing on the connection between refined survival (survival *qua* man) and her principles, she wants to maintain that it's *bare survival* that's put at risk and lost by failure to abide by requirements for employing rationality, achieving productivity, and avoiding parasitism:

Man's *bare* survival (*avoidance of death*) requires him to be rational and productive

"But just as animals would not be able to survive by attempting the method of plants, by rejecting locomotion and waiting for the soil to feed them—so men cannot survive by attempting the method of animals, by rejecting reason and counting on productive men to serve as their prey. Such looters may achieve their goals for the range of a moment, at the price of destruction: the destruction of their victims and their own." (*Virtue*, p. 23)

which can only mean that just as an animal attempting to survive as a plant does will *die*, so a man attempting to survive by rejecting the use of reason and the pursuit of productivity, and exhibiting parasitic behavior, will also *die*. (There's a serious question as to whether the scenario of an animal acting as a plant is even coherent and makes any sense at all. But let's not enter that labyrinth here.) An animal attempting to survive as a plant cannot survive *at all* (bare survival). It can't even achieve some sub-optimal form of animal life. It will just die. And so this analogy is introduced to demonstrate that similarly a man attempting to survive as an animal does (i.e., *sans* rationality and productivity, and without parasitism) will likewise not even be able to maintain a sub-optimal form of life, but will not be able to survive at all.

The distinction that Mack makes between *refined* and *unrefined* (or *bare*) survival is introduced to make explicit Rand's often implicit (or worse, indeterminate) distinction between the unadorned use of "survival" (which as we've seen is ambiguous) and her use of such terms as "survival *qua* man" and "human survival" (which *generally* seem to be used synonymously). In turn, this is important because this ambiguity afflicts our understanding of such principles as the Principle of Survival and arguments involving such declarations as 1-8 above.[29]

♦ A THIRD AMBIGUITY: "PROPER TO"

There is, alas, a third ambiguity lurking in the conceptual shrubbery of Rand's exposition and argumentation. This involves the phrase "proper to" and its use in characterizing the relation between man's (or an individual man's) survival and his rationality. Within *Virtue*, Rand makes use of this phrase five times in "The Objectivist Ethics" (Chapter 1), and once each in "The Ethics of Emergencies" (Chapter 3), "The Nature of Government" (Chapter 14), and "Racism" (Chapter 17). Nathaniel Brandon uses it in "Isn't Everyone Selfish" (Chapter 5). What does it mean, how does Rand use it, how is it ambiguous, and how does that matter?

To begin, the choice of "proper to" doesn't seem proper to a context in which clarity and precision is required. See? As I've just used it, "proper to" seems to mean *appropriate to* because its choice appears not to be best for the goal at hand (clarity and precision). But its range of commonly encountered meanings is surprisingly broad, and its use can imply anything from a very loose connection equivalent to "compatible with" to a very close (or even *necessary*) connection. It is often, though not always, associated with some rule, habit, common behavior, or social norm.

The senses of "proper to" in, for example, "A handshake is proper to greeting someone," (permitted and not unexpected) and "Repayment of the loan is proper to the contract," (required) are quite different in the type and strength of the relations to which they're referring. And recognized equivalents or synonyms of "proper to" include "appropriate to", "suited to", "correct with respect to", "correct for", "belonging to", "required for", "characteristic of", "right for", "results in", "fitting to", "compatible with", and "consistent with". If you *wanted* to choose a phrase with a high degree of ambiguity, you could hardly do better than "proper to".

Mack is concerned with Rand's ambiguous use of "proper to" in her attempt to shuffle from the *bare sense* of survival in her arguments to the *refined sense*. We'll look at more details of this below, but for now we'll just note that the problem with the ambiguity of "proper to" can be seen where Rand says

Rand's ambiguous use of "proper to"

"Since reason is man's basic means of survival, that which is proper to the life of a rational being is the good; that which negates, opposes or destroys it is the evil.

Since everything man needs has to be discovered by his own mind and produced by his own effort, the two essentials of the method of survival proper to a rational being are: thinking and productive work." (*Virtue*, p. 23)

and then how Rand moves from these statements to a conclusion that *reason is required for man's survival* by means of an argument which in highly abbreviated form looks like:

Rand's equivocal shift from
"Reason is the *typical* means of man's survival"
to
"Reason is the *necessary* means of man's survival"

1. Reason *is* man's basic *means* of survival.
2. Therefore, reason is *proper to* man's survival.
3. Therefore, *only* survival that results from man's reason is *proper to* man.
4. And so the *only* survival that is *properly human* survival (survival proper to man) is survival that results from *man's use of reason to achieve that survival*.

This argument — were it valid and convincing — would then allow Rand to shift in a plausible way to reinterpret statements like the Principle of Survival from being about *bare* survival to those same statements being about *refined* survival (possibly avoiding some of the most obvious and embarrassing counter-examples in the process) and so allow her to claim support for her view that man's very (bare) survival requires his *use of* (and not just his *capacity for*) rationality. And in this way Rand might hope to use *observations* about refined survival to support the *conceptual* understanding of the Principle of Survival that includes its sense of survival as bare survival.

But note that this argument is essentially an inference from "x is *typically* true" (or "x is true *as a matter of fact*") to "x is *necessarily* true" — or alternatively, from "Man *can* do x (use his rational capacity to survive)" to "Man *must* do x (in order to *be man*)". The apparent plausibility of that "logical" (actually *illogical*) move hinges on using the same phrase — "proper to" — with two different meanings as that shift takes place from step 2 to step 4 in her argument: a classic rhetorical example of ⊘ *Vagueness and Equivocation*.

It's far from clear that Rand was thinking through all of the logical connections and details in this argument, and no more clear whether she was aware of the ⊘ *Vagueness and Equivocation*. Mack is inclined to think that her use of ambiguity in these circumstances may be uncontrived but opportunistic — and so more in the direction of Incompetence than Exploitation (Section 6.2). But in any event, Rand's use of equivocation with "proper to" represents a fundamental flaw in her methodology (⊘ *Known Fallacy*, ⊘ *Lack of Rigor*, ⊘ *Inadequate Understanding*) since she attempts to make an inference from the *fact* that man *typically or frequently employs reason to survive* (first meaning of "proper to") to the conclusion that that there is a *conceptual or logical connection* (second meaning of "proper to") between a man's use of reason and his successful survival.[30]

With these several examples of pseudo-philosophy markers in hand, we can now turn our attention to the Shuffle itself.

Prelude to the Shuffle

Mack points to this paragraph from "The Objectivist Ethics" — and more specifically to its first sentence — as embodying the core of the Shuffle:

The core of the Shuffle

> "Man cannot survive as anything but man. He can abandon his means of survival, his mind, he can turn himself into a subhuman creature and he can turn his life into a brief span of agony—just as his body can exist for a while in the process of disintegration by disease. But he cannot succeed, as a subhuman, in achieving anything but the subhuman—as the ugly horror of the antirational periods of mankind's history can demonstrate. Man has to be man by choice—and it is the task of ethics to teach him how to live like man." *Virtue*, pp. 24-25.

And he points to the equivocation between the *conceptual interpretation* of "Man cannot survive as anything but man.":

(Conceptual interpretation)

Man's staying alive *by means of* (his basic means of survival) his rationality requires him to employ that means of survival in order to stay alive.

and the *causal interpretation* of "Man cannot survive as anything but man.":

(Causal interpretation)

Man's staying alive *requires (can be achieved only by)* the use of his rationality.

The first of these is simply a rephrasing/rearrangement of the *tautology* that "In order for someone to stay alive by a certain means he is required to use that means to stay alive." In this case the means in question is the use of rationality. But the second makes a *causal claim* about *what is necessary in order for a man to stay alive in the real world*: that use of rationality is the *cause* of staying alive — and in fact, for Rand, is the *only* cause that humans can invoke to ensure their survival.

The *conceptual* interpretation can't be false: it's just a statement that establishes part of the *meaning* of "staying alive" (*qua* man). It requires no justification by appeal to the real world since it's true based on how the concepts of staying-alive-as-a-man and man's-survival are related to one another (i.e., since the concept staying-alive-as-a-man has as part of its meaning, in Rand's view, the concept using-rationality-to-stay-alive). In a sense, this statement (which is intended to appear to be an informative and meaningful claim about how humans survive in the world) is in fact an exercise in reformulating a definition in which staying-alive-as-a-man is related to man's-survival. It's a version of "*A man must do A because doing A is part of being a man.*"[31] But the *causal* interpretation is a statement about what can or cannot be achieved *in the real world*, and so we can look in the real world and see if it's true (or at least plausible). If we find counterexamples to it, then we must regard it as *false*, or at least in need of clarification and perhaps modification.

In her 1957 interview with Mike Wallace, Rand is explicit about how her ethical principles are to be seen as *necessary* (logical or conceptual) *truths* when she says that her morality is one (the *only* one) "that can be proved by means of logic which can be demonstrated to be true and necessary" (Rand and Wallace 1957). As in the case of any ethicist who wants to claim that the ethical principles they're setting forth for us to follow aren't simply "good ideas" or beneficial "guidelines" that will for the most part provide the basis for a good (or better) society and for people's lives — but that the principles are *necessary* or *required* in some absolute sense — Rand faces a difficult task: How do you establish the *necessity* of the principles that you're trying to get people to recognize and adopt? Rand clearly wants to do this, her ethical writings are full of claims about how certain behavior (individuality, productivity, non-parasitism, rationality) is *required*, and that it's required of man by his very nature.

In addition, Mack thoroughly documents this goal of Rand's throughout *Problematic Arguments*. Rand isn't saying "If you follow my ethical guidelines, then your life is *more likely to be happy and successful*." She's saying (quite literally in a number of places) "If you don't follow these ethical guidelines, then *you will die* as a result of that failure." But then an immediate problem is: Where do you get the *force* of that kind of pronouncement from? Whence comes that *necessity* and that *requirement*? How does failure to heed Rand *cause* your death? One way of looking at the problem that Rand has constructed for herself is to see that she needs to demonstrate a *convergence* between the conceptual and causal interpretations of her *Principal of Survival* in some way that supports both interpretations. The Shuffle can be seen as an attempt to get each of those to support the other.

Someone proposing a theistic ethics has what is at least what appears to be a relatively simple answer to this problem: an appeal to the will of God (or perhaps to "the gods"). And then the answer to all your ethical problems devolves to determining what the will of God/gods is. Of course, there is a cascade of problems from this approach, including a number of thorny issues such as the *Problem of Evil* (Wikipedia 2020i). At least a theistic approach gives your ethical principals a hefty punch and a strong sense of being requirements rather than just recommendations for the good life. Rand, of course, can't go in this direction since she strongly rejects any religious appeal as irrational.

But Rand is enamored of both Aristotle and Aquinas (which seem to be the only philosophers prior to herself whom she regards as not being complete charlatans), and so is also enamored of a *natural law* approach to ethics (Murphy 2019). Her problem is to find a version of that approach that provides her ethical views with what she wants in terms of necessity, but without the religion (or other form of irrationality or mysticism). This is not an easy row to hoe. But it is easy to see her arguments in *Virtue* as attempting to accomplish just that by an appeal to a kind of Aristotelian/Thomistic natural law approach in which the religious elements are somehow factored out. Enter the Shuffle.

Rand needs a principle such as the Principle of Survival to be interpreted in the *conceptual* sense in order to have the force (similar to natural law) that *requires* man to behave in certain ways. For Rand, this force comes from divorcing our understanding of the principle from the phenomena we encounter in the everyday real (empirical) world and understanding it purely on the basis of the concepts to which it refers: survival, parasitism, rationality, and productivity. But then how do we know that these are the *correct* concepts? And how do we remove the *definitional* character of the Principle of Survival in order to (in Mack's words) "evade the emptiness of a conceptual defense that is purely stipulative?"

In the final analysis, the answers to these questions involve Rand's theory of concepts as this is expressed in *Introduction to Objectivist Epistemology*, but our purposes here (and Mack's in *Problematic Arguments*) neither require nor benefit from entering that thicket. The simple answer to these questions is that you have to look in the empirical real world in order to see if your concepts are correct by observing that (a) the real world is *consistent* with your principle when applied to the real world, and (b) the application of the principle validates it in terms of demonstrating its *truth*, or at least its *plausibility*. And at least initially, a shifting by Rand from a conceptual interpretation of the Principle of Survival to a causal interpretation makes methodological sense and appears appropriate. But it's what happens after this initial shift where the trouble starts.

In addition to needing the *conceptual interpretation* of the Principle of Survival to be regarded as true, Rand also needs the *causal interpretation* to be true (or at least plausible) in order to maintain her primary goal of establishing that (*in the real world*) failure of man to use his rationality to survive will result in death. This is critical because it's only the causal interpretation that can establish a connection in the real world between a human's staying alive and using his rationality. Without that, the conceptual interpretation leaves us only in the world of defining our concepts and can't be used by Rand to justify the moral rules (regarding rationality, productivity, and non-parasitism) that she holds are *necessary* for man to follow in order to survive *in the real world*. She at least appears to know that she can't simply make her ethical principles come out to be true of the real world by playing with definitions.

To summarize the relationship between the conceptual interpretation of the Principle of Survival and the causal interpretation of the Principle of Survival that Rand needs to establish,

Roles of conceptual and causal interpretations

- The *conceptual interpretation* of a principle (such as the Principle of Survival) provides that version (interpretation) of the principle with a force beyond its being a mere recommendation or suggestion.

The principle asserts a *necessary connection* among the concepts employed in the principle in virtue of some of those concepts' being *constitutive of* (included in) the others. For example, Rand takes such concepts as rationality and productivity to be *constitutive of* the concept of human survival.

The conceptual interpretation of a principle such as the Principle of Survival, if it employs the "correct" concepts, is akin to what philosophers have referred to as a "natural law" although the law-like force to it comes from the conceptual relationships it expresses rather than (for example) the will of God. But conceptual interpretations are of no value unless they are meaningful and *applicable in the real world* in support of requirements of behavior and action. There must be a "bridge" from the conceptual principle to the real world in order for it to apply to the real world rather than only to our (otherwise completely abstract) concepts.

- The *causal interpretation* of the Principle of Survival provides that version (interpretation) of the principle with an *empirical* meaning and application to the real world of actions and events in which people are involved.

A causal interpretation can provide *support* for a principle (*if* its application results in a *validating* instance of it) or it can provide grounds for *rejecting* the principle (if its application results in a *counterexample* to it). The causal interpretation of the principle provides the necessary "bridge" from our concepts to reality.

Rand wants (and for her purposes, needs) her principle to be demonstrably true in both the conceptual and causal senses — or else she loses either its necessity or its applicability. With these observations in hand we can now look at the details of the Shuffle and assess its consequences.

The Shuffle

Mack characterizes the Shuffle as:

Eric Mack's characterization of the Shuffle.

"What then is the Shuffle? The Shuffle is some combination of: (a) shifting from a *causal to a conceptual defense* without recognizing what one is doing; (b) merely *stipulating or not arguing adequately* for the conceptual revision that one is employing within one's conceptual defense; (c) not recognizing that the conclusion which is supported by one's conceptual defense is *not the same as* the conclusion that would be vindicated by looking at the world were it not for those pesky counterexamples; and (d) shifting (back) from the conclusion of the conceptual defense to the conclusion of the causal defense. The Shuffle is most egregious when an author simply scampers back and forth between causal and conceptual understandings of a given proclamation—*scampering to the conceptual understanding when the real world counterexamples cannot be denied* and *scampering to the causal understanding when the author seeks to evade the emptiness of a conceptual defense that is purely stipulative.*" (*Problematic Arguments*, p. 22, emphasis added)

The Shuffle, then, is a series of *shifts* in how Rand *interprets* a principle that she's attempting to both justify and apply. And Mack's description of it also exposes the *reasons* and *motivations* for these shifts. There are several slightly different ways in which we can look at the Shuffle and the individual "moves" or shifts that make it up. In what follows I'll present a view that may appear to be slightly different from Mack's although this difference is (I believe) only a matter of emphasis while offering some clarity and simplicity for the non-expert reader.

It's not unreasonable to view the Shuffle as a logical and conceptual version of the venerated *shell game* (also known as *the swindle*) where the "sharp" or

"operator" (that would be Rand) diverts the attention of the "mark" (that would be you) while one thing is switched for another precisely where the mark's attention *should* remain focused. Whether Rand is performing the Shuffle knowingly or unwittingly isn't, perhaps, a decision we can hope to come to here. But she puts herself directly on the horns of a dilemma since (a) if she's intentionally shuffling, then she's along the Exploitation axis in the plane of the pseudo described in Section 6.2; but if she's unwittingly shuffling (and unwittingly employing those multiple interpretations, ambiguities, and fallacies repeatedly in the way she does), then she's out along the other axis of Incompetence.

Rand wants to hold that certain *virtues* (such as independence, individual responsibility, rationality, and productivity) are *required* for *staying alive* (*bare survival*). People who lack those virtues will simply *die*. Much of Eric Mack's *Problematic Arguments* (particularly the earlier sections) is devoted to demonstrating that this is in fact the stance Rand takes and intends to take. In order to show that conformance to her ethical principles will result in avoiding this consequence, Rand needs to project the conceptual understanding of the principle

Section 11.5: The Virtue of Selfishness

into the real world where we can observe its consequences and thereby *validate* her claims.

This process is carried out through several steps that we'll refer to (following Mack) as *shifts* from one version (interpretation) of the Principle of Survival to another, and the Shuffle emerges as the sequence of these shifts. For the sake of brevity and clarity, I'll present each shift in a stylized summary form that makes explicit the *change in interpretation* that takes place in the shift (from conceptual to causal, and from causal to conceptual), indicates what *equivocations* are involved in the shift, and describes Rand's *reasons and motivations* for making the shift as well as the *result* of that particular shift in contributing to Rand's support of the principle.

◆ THE FIRST SHIFT

Shift: from the *conceptual* to the *causal* interpretation and from an unspecified sense of "survival" to the *unrefined* sense.
Reason: Make the principle testable in the real world.

Rand begins with a principle that we can express as

> **Version 1.** An individual's **survival** requires that the individual avoid parasitism, act rationally in achieving his goals, and be productive.

Version 1 is of course just the Principle of Survival that we've stated above. But Version 1 is *ambiguous* in terms of the sense of "survival" and also in how it's to be interpreted as a conceptual or causal principle. In order for us to be convinced of it as a guide to our actions we need to be assured that it's not just offered as having a purely conceptual interpretation in which Rand is basically *defining* survival to mean rationality, the avoidance of parasitism, and productivity. We need to be able to *apply* this principle in the real world in order to see if it's true or false when we look at the *facts* of human behavior and the *consequences* of these. So to enable us to test this principle, Rand makes it more specific and shifts from Version 1 and its conceptual interpretation to a modified version of it that has a causal interpretation:

> **Version 2.** An individual's **unrefined survival** requires that the individual avoid parasitism, act rationally in achieving his goals, and be productive.

Here, the idea is that that using rationality, being productive, achieving goals, and avoiding parasitism *causes* us to be able to continue living while *not* doing these things will result in (*causes*) our deaths. So we can view Version 2 as a disambiguation and change of interpretation of Version 1 that allows us to test it in the real world.

But an alarming problem (for Rand) with this is that there are obvious *counterexamples* to it: just too many cases of people surviving for long periods or entire lifetimes under miserable circumstances as parasites of one sort or another (prisoners, invalids, victims of circumstance, wards of the state, etc.), dependent upon the support of others and without being productive. The world's literature is full of examples of such lives, and each of us probably is familiar with such a case.

Mack considers a number of these counterexamples in sections VI, VII, and VIII of *Problematic Arguments*. A particularly troublesome and obvious counterexample for Rand is the case of the *rational parasite* in which the individual uses her rationality specifically to manipulate and take advantage of others in supporting her life.[32] Here a person is using rationality and parasitism precisely to gain a more successful and pleasant life. Examples of this likewise can't be denied. As a result, Rand hasn't managed to provide us with a principle we can endorse, although she's at least one step closer by making her principle be about events in the real world. So she moves to ...

♦ THE SECOND SHIFT

Shift: from the *unrefined* sense to the *refined* sense of survival, retaining the *causal* interpretation.
Reason: Avoid counterexamples.

Here, Rand shifts from Version 2 to

> **Version 3.** An individual's **refined survival** requires that the individual avoid parasitism, act rationally in achieving his goals, and be productive.

This is a shift from one *causal* principle to another one that's weaker and won't be subject to the counterexamples that Version 2 encountered. It achieves this by shifting from the *unrefined* sense of survival to the *refined* sense (survival *qua* man) where previous counterexamples are ruled out since they no longer count as examples of the *genuine* survival of a human *living in the manner of a human (*qua *man)*.

Unfortunately for Rand, this simply doesn't work. While some of the crudest of the counterexamples are now excluded by focusing only on cases of refined survival, others remain. These include the rational parasite (which is simply never addressed by Rand in a non-question-begging manner). And it also includes examples where rationality and productivity *don't* result in refined survival.[33]

Additionally, it is in this shift where Rand appeals to her equivocal notion(s) of what is "proper to" man's survival, and tries to weave some magic from that particular equivocation. (See again the discussion above regarding the ambiguity of "proper to".) This appears to be the way in which Rand attempts to support her move from unrefined to refined survival without having to give up the claim that the exercise of rationality is *required* for man's survival. But because of the equivocations on which it rests, and the counterexamples that remain for it, this doesn't succeed.

Not to be deterred by (or perhaps oblivious to) her abject failure to provide empirical support for the *causal* interpretation under the *refined* concept of survival, Rand next skips on by shifting *back* to the *conceptual* interpretation while retaining the *refined* concept of survival. She appears to think that this (failed) attempt to support the causal interpretation has provided logical support and empirical content to the conceptual interpretation:

◆ THE THIRD SHIFT

Shift: Back from the causal interpretation to the *conceptual* interpretation while retaining the *refined* sense of survival.
Reason: Needed to reassert the conceptual version of the principle in order to establish the *conceptual* relationship (of *necessity*) between survival and the virtues — and so provide grounds for claiming that survival *requires* the use of rationality and productivity, and the avoidance of parasitism.

This is another failure based on equivocation. It appears that Rand may have satisfied herself that by use of the "proper to" equivocation in the previous shift she's demonstrated the validity of shifting back to the conceptual interpretation while preserving some sort of mixed conceptual and strong causal relationship (under the causal interpretation) between (a) what is "proper to" man in terms of the virtues and (b) man's survival *qua* man. But any illusion of this result rests firmly on faulty inferences she presents to us that critically employ that equivocation — which, again, conflates "proper to" in its *appropriate to* or *advantageous to* sense with "proper to" in its *required by* sense.[34]

◆ WHAT HAS THE SHUFFLE ACCOMPLISHED?

What has Rand accomplished with the Shuffle? Nothing ends up being unequivocally supported, and each shift in the Shuffle involves ... well ... a shifty bit of logic and linguistic slight of hand. As Mack exposes in some detail, the trick here is to make us *think* that it's a single principle (which we've called the Principle of Survival) that's being reasoned about and for which arguments and support are offered. But in fact all three of what we've been calling *Versions* of the principle are *different principles* — with different interpretations, different meanings, different conditions for their truth, and different consequences. So the apparent logic to Rand's argument is illusory.

Although she tries to first reach some defensible formulations of her principle by refining concepts, changing from conceptual to causal interpretations, and then "circling back" to her (then refined) principle, that path is littered with gaps of logic, disguised shifts in meaning that render it a chain of multiple equivocations, and counterexamples to which no responses are offered. And (as Mack points out) even if a lot of that faulty logic and equivocation could be repaired, she still doesn't end up with the principle she started out with, and doesn't end up with her goal (and persistent claim) that failure to conform to her principles will end in *death*. This entire approach of Rand's in attempting to establish the very foundation of her ethical system is a storm of ⊘ *Vagueness and Equivocation,* ⊘ *Special Pleading,* ⊘ *Superficial Response,* ⊘ *Known Fallacy,* ⊘ *Inadequate Understanding,* and ⊘ *Lack of Rigor.* And it illustrates what Mack refers to in saying that "line-by-line many of Rand's ethical arguments are just awful."

As the Shuffle goes, so goes the presentation and coherence of what Rand is offering as an ethical theory in *Virtue.* Initially, it appeared as though the strategy of starting from the conceptual interpretation of a principle, moving to validate that in the real world, revising concepts in response to difficulties encountered (such as lack of clarity, inconsistencies, and counterexamples), reformulating the original principle in accord with those revisions, and attempting to validate the revision could result in a principle that possessed the force of a *correct conceptual relationship* between survival and Rand's virtues, but also a *meaningful and verifiable (or at least plausibly arguable) application in the real world.* But this hope fell apart in the multiple equivocations, fallacious reasoning, shifting interpretations, and failures to handle (or even to acknowledge) counterexamples.

The result is a presentation and process that exhibits repetitive occurrences of our pseudo-philosophy markers while failing to exhibit such markers of genuine philosophy as Φ *Inquiry,* Φ *Rationality,* Φ *Objectivity,* Φ *Clarity,* Φ *Consistency,* and Φ *Domain Awareness.* And throughout, Rand remains a much closer match to the Pseudo persona than to Philo.

What's important in this example and the assessment of it is that Rand is not appearing to be a pseudo-philosopher because she's *wrong* in her basic beliefs concerning the nature of humans and such virtues as rationality, productivity, and non-parasitism. Nor is it even because she's *wrong* in her view that selfishness (under one construal or another) may be a virtue. She may in fact be right about these things (at least broadly stated), and other (genuine) philosophers have held such views and defended them. Rand manifests as a pseudo-philosopher because of *how* she expresses these views and *how* she attempts to justify them and the principles on which they're based. She may be expressing some correct (or approximately correct) *opinions* about man's nature and certain virtues and behaviors. But that doesn't make what she's doing count as philosophy, and that doesn't make her a philosopher.

11.6 Determinations and explanations

What we've seen in our examination of *For the New Intellectual* and *The Virtue of Selfishness* is a number of persistent threads throughout Rand's work that are incompatible with genuine philosophy as characterized in earlier chapters, and which instead are compatible with, and symptomatic of, pseudo-philosophy and the Pseudo persona. These threads include:

- *Misrepresentations* of the views and arguments of philosophers throughout the history of philosophy from the ancient Greeks through the mid-20th century, including the misuse of terminology, leading to *failures to give fair hearings* to alternative positions, and indicative of *inadequate understanding and ignorance of prior work*.

- *Failure to clarify fundamental concepts*, resulting in *obscurantism* and *special pleading*.

- *Appropriation of ideas* from well-known philosophers and sources, without mention and possibly without awareness.

- *Emotive and polemical caricaturing* of a wide variety of individual philosophers or "schools" of philosophy without specific criticisms of (undistorted) positions, principles, or arguments, and instead employing sweeping and unsubstantiated derogatory assertions.

- *Commission of elementary fallacies* of logic and epistemology.

- *Failure to recognize, acknowledge, or respond to counterexamples*.

- *Pervasive uses of equivocation* in the introduction of fundamental concepts, in principles, and in attempts to provide support for principles and declarations generally.

- *Failure to meet basic standards of scholarship*.

Each of these threads exhibits incompatibilities with the Philo persona (Section 4.2) and the associated markers of genuine philosophy while at the same time exhibiting the markers of pseudo-philosophy and a high degree of correspondence to features of the Pseudo persona. The final one — failure to meet basic standards of scholarship — deserves some special attention, in part because it is phrased so broadly, and in part because it always provides an opening for a particular defense of the pseudo-philosopher. Let's call this defense the *anti-sectarian response*.

♦ A QUESTION OF STANDARDS, SECTARIANISM, AND PREJUDICE

The anti-sectarian response says that the list of our criticisms and the accusation of pseudo-philosophy are advanced only from a particular, and particularly narrow, and so generally indefensible, perspective. These criticisms, so it is claimed, assume that there is only one correct way of approaching philosophy (e.g., the perspective of analytic philosophy, the perspective of existentialism, the perspective of phenomenology, etc.); and the anti-sectarian responder says that the criticisms being advanced are not valid (or even meaningful) because their target (Rand in this case) is not of that assumed perspective or tradition and is approaching things in a "novel" way: a different kind of philosophy, a different kind of argumentation, etc.

Thus, the anti-sectarian argues, it's improper to judge her by those (sectarian, parochial) criteria. Note that this is *not* a variant of the "anything goes" school of "I can say anything I like is philosophy because there are no objective criteria for distinguishing philosophy from non-philosophy." The anti-sectarian response doesn't want to deny a distinction — a border — between philosophy and pseudo-philosophy or non-philosophy. Instead it wants to argue that the border has been drawn in the wrong place and for a reason that itself violates the spirit and requirements of genuine philosophy.

It isn't difficult to find such a defense of Rand against criticisms of the sort offered here; and in the Randian literature you may encounter the claim that Rand's approach doesn't conform to the usual canons of logic, exegesis, and epistemology because it's "dialectical" or "hermeneutic" or some such. This, of course, is nonsense. Rand's apparent errors aren't a consequence of her employing either some well-known *alternative* to normal logic (she aggressively embraces Aristotle in that regard — nothing new there!) or some other "mode" of acceptable presentation.

Rand's errors are not merely *apparent* errors: they're *real* errors. Moreover, what she's doing isn't dialectic in any normal and intelligible sense of that term. Not only would Rand not be caught dead employing anything like Fichtian,

Hegelian or Marxist dialectic, but her presentation is not remotely *dia*lectical, instead being (pardon the neologism) *mono*lectical since, as we've seen, it proceeds not on the basis of *dia*log but on the basis of monolog in the form a single-source polemic. Even her fictional heroes aren't inclined towards dialectic but towards lengthy polemical monologs.

Similarly, Rand's argumentation has nothing to do with hermeneutics. Her mistakes can't be excused by trying to perceive them through the lens of some alternative philosophical correctness. They're just mistakes, even (or especially) based on her own understanding of rationality and reasoning.

Eric Mack ends *Problematic Arguments* with a good short response to attempts like the anti-sectarian defense which seek to deflect attention from, to excuse, or to explain away the fundamental flaws in Rand's presentations and arguments:

> "I ask readers to look at those arguments again in light of normal demands upon an author to be precise about what she is asserting and about what the non-questionbegging bases for those assertions are supposed to be.
>
> Another part of my response is to agree that I have foisted alien categories of analysis upon Rand's arguments. Unfortunately, those alien categories are the basic norms of rational advocacy—clarity about what one's conclusions are, consistency in which conclusions one is arguing for, clarity about just what the premises for those conclusions are supposed to be, and avoidance of rhetorical flourishes that substitute for reason and evidence.
>
> ...
>
> And when one begins to see that hostility and contempt are not an appropriate response to people's failure to be convinced by these arguments, one may both get on with the task of identifying better arguments and with distancing oneself from the hostility and contempt that so deeply color Rand's own argumentation." (Mack 2003 59)

Rand's pseudo-philosophy: origins, impetus, and irony

The characteristic flaws and errors we've seen in *For the New Intellectual* and *The Virtue of Selfishness* are not merely occasional, but are pervasive throughout Rand's work. What explains this? How can this happen in the case of someone who thinks of herself as not only a philosopher, but one of the great and innovative philosophers of the ages? How can this happen in the case of someone who has such a large and committed following? There are answers to these questions, and an explanation — though it isn't one which committed Rand followers are likely to welcome.

♦ THE QUESTION OF RAND'S EDUCATION

Much is made at times — by what were Rand's closest associates and fellow travelers during her active years, and by others continuing on through the present — of Rand's own philosophical education in Petrograd. Clearly this is an attempt both to provide her with some degree of academic respectability and to enhance our perception of her as an educated and knowledgeable thinker in a philosophical tradition. But the evidence for this view of Rand is meager, highly speculative, and without verifiable substance. And in addition the view clashes with the evidence in her own writings and with her own testimony, as in her 1959 interview with Mike Wallace (Rand and Wallace 1959) when Wallace asks her where her philosophy comes from and she responds "Out of my own mind, with the sole acknowledgment of a debt to Aristotle, who is the only philosopher that ever influenced me. I devised the rest of my philosophy myself." And then in addition:

> "I am primarily the creator of a new code of morality which has so far been believed impossible, namely a morality not based on faith, not on arbitrary whim, not on emotion, not on arbitrary edict, mystical or social, but on reason; a morality that can be proved by means of logic which can be demonstrated to be true and necessary."

Ayn Rand in (Rand and Wallace 1959)

These statements are revealing and can explain a great deal about Rand's understanding (or lack of it) of philosophers throughout history, as well as her own self-perception as a philosopher. The second of the statements appears to be a clear example of the sort of ◊ *Exaggerated Claims* that Rand was inclined to make about both the uniqueness of her approach and the degree she had demonstrated it to be not only acceptable, but logically *necessary*. It is at least clear that the *only* philosopher whose work she is willing to acknowledge as having *influenced* her is Aristotle. Perhaps this is because he is the only philosopher that she studied to any significant degree.

We *know* that there is good reason to view Rand as an aspiring (and later highly successful) writer of screenplays, scripts, and novels. We *know* that this is a direction that she pursued from childhood, and we *know* that much of her schooling was oriented towards this. But the view that she studied and was well-trained as a philosophy student — even at the undergraduate level — we do *not* know. It is at best speculative and based on what appears to be manufactured and highly interpreted "support", in large part resting on evidence which (to the degree that it exists) has never been made available for public scrutiny. Requests for such evidence are met with either silence or diversion.

In addition, there's the testimony of Rand's own writing, which shows no sign of being written by someone whose work had ever been subjected to standards of philosophical rigor, had ever been reviewed by a competent philosopher or philosophy instructor, had ever been subjected to critical review and required revision as a result, and had ever been held to standards in accurately interpreting the work of others. Rand's work is not the work of someone who has been competently instructed in philosophy, its methodologies, and its standards — and then been held to those standards as part of that educational and training process. It isn't the work of someone who has ever *practiced* philosophy in an instructional setting.

Instead, Rand's philosophical work shows every sign of someone who, in philosophy, was self-taught rather than being educated by means of a formal curriculum, class work, or tutoring and critical evaluation by a knowledgeable instructor. This is particularly true of any 19th or 20th century philosophy outside some narrow areas of German Idealism (specifically Nietzsche), but it seems also to be true of most areas of what would be regarded in a curriculum as *modern philosophy*, including study of the usual rationalists and empiricists. And her ignorance and misunderstanding of logic and philosophy of language, across centuries, is remarkable. In short, it appears that Rand failed to conform to the standards of genuine philosophy because she didn't know what those standards were, had never been compelled to conform to them, and had never practiced them. As a consequence, her domain knowledge was largely constrained by her undergraduate coursework and readings which provided her with a perspective from a particular cultural and political orientation. And recall that whatever else may be said of Rand's formal university education, she was a major in *history* within that environment, not in philosophy, and there is no credible evidence that she "minored" in philosophy in any meaningful sense of that term.

Turning to what we know of Rand's university education, we're presented with more evidence that's compatible with this view. The best account we have of Rand's study at the university in Petrograd is Chris Sciabarra's summary of her academic transcript in his article "The Rand Transcript" (Sciabarra 1999b and 2013). But this article is an *interpretation* of a *translation* of the original Russian transcript (not available for independent examination) and is dense with groundless speculation. Even so, let's assume that the translation is competent and accurate, and that the list of courses Sciabarra provides is accurate and complete. What do we see in this transcript, and how does that correspond to claims about Rand's university experience in philosophy and that she "minored" in the subject?

The (Sciabarra-rendered) transcript contains 26 courses of which 15 are straightforward history courses (from history of the ancient world through medieval history and modern history). Of the remaining 11 courses, 3 are in the area of social science, 1 is in the area of natural science (biology), 1 is in foreign language (French), and 4 are in what is best referred to as "ideology" (political, economic, and social theory from a Soviet perspective). The remaining 2 are the only courses whose titles and descriptions suggest that they would have significant philosophical content: Logic (which appears to be a mixed course in Aristotelian syllogistic, informal logic, and what today we would call "critical reasoning"), and Political Economy (which appears to be a heavily ideological course focused on Marxist theory of economics and value). Perhaps it was in the logic course where Rand learned about Aristotle, in conjunction with some treatment of him and Aquinas in her courses in ancient and medieval history.

This definitely is *not* a picture of someone "minoring" in philosophy, and it's at best disingenuous to suggest that it is.[35] Where are the courses devoted to the history of philosophy? Where are the courses in the empiricists and rationalists? Where are the courses in metaphysics and epistemology? In Kant? In Nietzsche? They are, quite simply, absent. Yes, some of those history and social science courses are likely to have dealt with the thoughts of some philosophers in passing, but this would have been from perspectives other than a critical philosophical one — as discussed in Chapter 5. They would not have provided Rand with *philosophical* training. Keith Raniere has much more of a credible claim to having "minored" in philosophy than Ayn Rand has. In addition, the single course in biology (taught in a Soviet university in the 1920s) goes some way towards accounting for Rand's virtually total ignorance of empirical science and mathematics.

Tilting at his windmill to establish Rand's use of "dialectical" methods, Sciabarra does his best to convince us that it was in this collection of history, social science, and ideology courses that Rand received significant and valuable philosophical training. But he just can't make his argument even remotely convincing, and this is primarily because he seems to have too much integrity to make the strong (though certainly false) claims necessary to support this view. Instead, his descriptions of the courses, their content, and the roles of various professors and their influence on Rand's understanding of philosophy is littered with speculations about which instructor "probably" or "likely" taught a course that Rand took — and then even more speculative suggestions and implications are made about what areas or topics or approaches in philosophy would have been covered in the course *on the assumption* that the speculation concerning its instructor is true!

Sciabarra continually refers vaguely to philosophers with whom various instructors — who *may* have been Rand's professors — were (or *may* have been) familiar. Then there are statements like "it is entirely possible that Rand studied progressive pedagogy closely" from which we are invited to infer that Rand *may have been* introduced to the recently published works of John Dewey to the degree that this "may have left an impression, since she remained deeply critical of the progressive approach." In fact, however, even under the most congenial assumptions about the accuracy of Rand's transcript and of Sciabarra's speculative interpretation of it, there is *no evidence* that Rand received even a moderately good education in philosophy during her time at the university in Petrograd. And at the end of that time she rushed to enroll in the State Institute of Cinema Arts to pursue a career in script writing.

Sciabarra's greatest hope had been to link Rand, as a student, to Nikolay (N. O.) Lossky — a fairly well-known Russian philosopher whom Sciabarra hoped to establish as the intellectual influence for what he sees (though few others do) as a dialectical approach in Rand. But in the end, as documented in his Web page "Investigative Report: In Search of the Rand Transcript" (Sciabarra 1999a), the attempt to link Rand to Lossky was a house of cards. In fact Rand herself seems to have had only a fairly vague memory of encountering him in her freshman year, after which the Soviets terminated Lossky's position in Petrograd, packed him on one of their Philosopher's ships and exiled him. Again, there is no evidence that Rand "studied" with Lossky in any sense.

Now returning to our attempt to find some explanation of the prevalence of fundamental and elementary errors in Rand's philosophical works: If we begin with the stance that, in a spirit of the pursuit of truth and objectivity, we don't want to explain away Rand's lack of philosophical skill and acumen as demonstrated in such works as *For the New Intellectual* and *The Virtue of Selfishness*, then what better explains Rand's pervasive philosophical errors, misinterpretations, and (often misplaced) animosity than simple ignorance, unfamiliarity with the domain and methods of philosophy itself, and lack of skill and experience? What is more consistent with the facts that we actually know? What must an Objectivist epistemologist say to this?

Coming to see that, while Rand had some university-level education in history and in script writing, she had no comparable training and education in *philosophy*, provides a simple explanation of the pervasive fundamental errors we see in Rand's philosophical writings. Certainly she would have seen "chunks" of philosophy and the works of philosophers in her history, social science, and ideology courses. And these would have been used in explaining and justifying points being made in those courses (and in the service of other disciplines or ideologies), as mentioned in Chapter 5. But she was not, during her educational period at the university, exposed to the techniques, criticisms, writing of philosophy papers and assignments, and the feedback on them from qualified faculty that is critical in learning how to *do* philosophy and how to avoid errors in philosophy. This is a core part of the "body of knowledge" requirement discussed in Section 3.1, and of learning the philosopher's trade as described in Section 3.2. You can't be a genuine philosopher without meeting these requirements, and our markers of genuine philosophy and pseudo-philosophy reflect this. There is, undeniably, a strong component of incompetence in Rand's attempts at philosophy — in part resulting from lack of education and training, and the weakness of her domain knowledge — that pushes those attempts in the direction of the pseudo.

♦ MOTIVES, GOALS, AND REWARDS

Our look into Rand's education and actual experience in studying and learning philosophy addresses, in terms of the "Dimensions of the pseudo" discussion of Section 6.2, the issue of philosophical competence in Rand's works. But the other primary component of pseudo-philosophy discussed in that section is exploitation. Where does Rand's work stand in this respect? An answer to that question requires an examination of Rand's motives, goals, and rewards.

Rand did not seek to be a foundational thinker in philosophy. If she had, the choice of an academic career would have been much more appropriate and effective in pursuing that goal. And, during her education in Petrograd, she became familiar enough with that alternative to understand what it would require and what it would mean — though certainly the context of post-revolution Soviet education, ideology, and treatment of intellectuals and academics could not have been very encouraging about such a path. But I don't think that there's anything to suggest that Rand would have failed to succeed in taking that path. She chose not to, and, from the evidence of her actions, apparently never considered it, instead remaining focused on her fascination with the film industry and the role of creating stories for presentation in that genre. In later years, as evidenced by comments in interviews and similar contexts, she in fact shied away from the descriptions of her as a "philosopher," saying that she was a writer who had been driven to philosophy in order to get her message out, and to awaken and influence people.

Nonetheless, Rand did have, as a primary goal, swaying (even compelling) how people thought about theoretical issues and practical decisions in the areas of politics, government, law, and the underlying ethics that support those. At times (unfortunately, as we've seen, at a lot of times) she was willing to sacrifice careful reasoning and philosophical soundness and rigor on the altar of emotive effect and polemic. That is the way of the rhetorician and sophist, and not the philosopher. But I think there is no evidence to suggest that her motives were impure in this pursuit — as compared, for example, to the case of Keith Raniere.

In previous chapters we saw some of the intellectual and rhetorical gains that pseudo-philosophers frequently hope to achieve, and even the ancients were quick to accuse the pseudo-philosopher of pursuing personal gain, as we've seen in Xenophon's condemnation of the Sophists and rhetoricians quoted in Section 5.4.

In Section 7.3 I raised the question of whether dishonesty was an essential characteristic of pseudo-philosophy, deciding it most reasonable to regard some degree of dishonesty or knowing deception as being necessary in order to distinguish pseudo-philosophy from merely incompetently done philosophy — but conceding this to be a matter of decision in one's analysis and methodology rather than a matter of discovery about the "objective nature" of pseudo-philosophy. It is appropriate, then, to ask the question "Does Rand's approach to philosophy involve elements of deceit and dishonesty?"

I think the answer to this question is that yes, it does, but that these elements are not, for Rand herself, in the service of personal gain (at least not in any direct or significant sense in which this is normally understood). The conceptual and argumentative phenomena that we've seen repeated throughout both *For the New Intellectual* and *The Virtue of Selfishness* include too many examples of failures of interpretation, failures to give fair hearing to criticisms and alternative views, failures to avoid obscurantism when easily possible by removing equivocations and conflations of concepts, failures to confront and respond to obvious counterexamples, and failures to revise works that contained these errors prior to publishing or re-publishing them. But what was the benefit for Rand?

Benefits undeniably included recognition, fame, and fortune. Yes, of course in some way Rand benefited from the sales of her philosophical works (and certainly the Rand industry has benefited *much* more since her death), but that was incidental compared to similar benefits that accrued from her fictional works and film projects; and it seems highly doubtful that this was ever a consideration for her. And certainly Rand sought (and felt that she fully deserved) recognition as one of the world's great philosophers who had solved problems that the great minds in philosophy had failed at. Rand's motivation was the motivation of the zealot and committed ideologue: the righteous indignation that people believe something that is *wrong* and *harmful*, and that only she (and those who would follow her) could set things straight and (as she expressed quite literally on many occasions) save society. In this respect she also conforms to the profile of the pseudo-philosopher by Rescher (Section 6.1) in which, in terms of motive, he ascribes to the pseudo-philosopher "the fostering of power interests or ideological influence or literary *éclat* or some such."

♦ A FINAL JUDGMENT

In the end, and for all of these reasons, it is accurate and justifiable to call Rand a pseudo-philosopher, and not to view her as a genuine philosopher in virtue of either methodology, domain understanding, or accomplishments in the philosophical realm. The *pseudo-philosopher* label should serve as a warning to read the philosophical work of Rand carefully, with a high degree of critical attention, and from an anti-sophistical stance — in order to escape from significant errors in thought and reason while benefiting from any genuine insights Rand may have had but failed to explore in a genuinely philosophical, well-founded, and dependable manner.

Regarding where we think Rand may be placed on the plane of pseudo-philosophy as described in Section 6.2, such a decision invites substantial debate. But demonstrably, her degree of Incompetence was quite high. This is exposed in (1) her grasp of the history of philosophy, (2) her understanding of a broad variety of philosophical concepts, positions, arguments, and counterexamples, (3) her baseless and misguided attacks on philosophers from the Ancient Greeks through the logical positivists of the 20th century, and (4) her "just awful" (Eric Mack) methods of analysis and argumentation.

When it comes to Exploitation, it appears unfair and unreasonable to attribute to Rand any particularly nefarious motives. But we must recognize her ready willingness to subvert genuine philosophy and to abandon the genuine philosopher's commitment to truth and wisdom in favor of strongly held personal beliefs and ideological goals. As a consequence, she must be placed in the *Dimensions of the Pseudo* in the upper right quadrant of high Incompetence and high Exploitation. Yet she was neither a Bumbling Fool nor an Evil Genius. And this demonstrates that while the *Dimensions of the Pseudo* may present us with a useful, quick, and simple representation of a pseudo-philosopher, it is neither complete nor precise. The finer details reside in our models of the genuine philosopher, the pseudo-philosopher, markers of genuine philosophy and pseudo-philosophy, and the Philo and Pseudo personas. Within those models, finer distinctions can be made, and reasonable arguments formulated and debated.

Ironically, Rand's own values required of her the sort of rationality and support (rather than the spinning of folktales, heroic stories, and flawed arguments) that only genuine philosophy could provide. And so — at least somewhat reluctantly, it would seem — she was driven in the direction of attempting to provide that. In the case of fundamental philosophical details, this was, for her, a goal too far.

A Concluding Metaphilosophical Postscript

It is not enough to know, we must also apply; it is not enough to will, we must also do.

Johannes Goethe, Maxim #324

For centuries (indeed for millennia) philosophers have complained about pseudo-philosophy being practiced by others claiming to be philosophers — and about people being taken in and suffering in one way or another from the mimicry, exploitation, and fakery of the pseudo-philosophers. But no attempt at a careful, comprehensive, and useful characterization of pseudo-philosophy has emerged. I suspect this is because most philosophers simply don't see pseudo-philosophy as presenting a philosophical problem or a philosophically interesting target for thought and investigation.[36] Pseudo-philosophy, after all, is not philosophy.

Philosophers are often happy to *call* other people pseudo-philosophers, but they don't think (and haven't thought) that the concept of pseudo-philosophy can be given anything more than an amorphous and pejorative sense. And however irritating pseudo-philosophy and pseudo-philosophers may be, genuine philosophers have more important problems to address.

But to treat the concept of pseudo-philosophy as a kind of pseudo concept — as merely a cognitively meaningless epithet hurled by some philosophers at others, or by philosophers at members of other disciplines — is simply facile. And it does a disservice to those from ancient times to the present who have at least attempted to provide objective and substantive characterizations of pseudo-philosophy, who have been concerned about its effects, and who have, to whatever degree of precision, tried to draw a line between what is genuine philosophy and what is not, to warn of the harm that pseudo-philosophy can cause, and to explain how it does this.

So while "pseudo-philosophy" often appears as a handy term for pushing people whose ideas or manners you don't care for off the philosophical stage, I think it is more than that. Or perhaps a better way of putting this is to say that it is philosophically and methodologically better to view it as more than that because a serious and more cogent view of pseudo-philosophy has a number of benefits, both conceptual and pragmatic.

The Pragmatic Model of pseudo-philosophy

This book provides a comprehensive account — a theory, or a model — of pseudo-philosophy and the pseudo-philosopher that distinguishes these from genuine philosophy and the genuine philosopher in an objective, defensible, informative, and useful way. That account places pseudo-philosophy in its *historical context*, will be *acceptable* to the preponderance of professional philosophers and philosophy students, is *applicable* to real-world cases, and is straightforwardly *useful* in distinguishing the genuine from the pseudo in the domain of philosophy, and in identifying both the flaws and the dangers of pseudo-philosophy where it is found.

This theory has deep roots and firm grounding in the history of philosophy and in a number of careful conceptual and methodological distinctions between genuine philosophy and pseudo-philosophy, and between the genuine philosopher and the pseudo-philosopher. The criteria of adequacy concerning these are described in Sections 3 and 4 of Chapter 1, and subsequent chapters demonstrate how they have been met.

Unlike prior attempts at capturing the nature and distinctive character of pseudo-philosophy, the theory developed in Part 2 of this book does not seek to provide a *definition* of pseudo-philosophy nor to provide a quick encapsulated characterization of it through the use of vague or generic concepts and features it exhibits and which may vary across different instances of pseudo-philosophy. But it does lay claim to being the most complete, detailed, and objectively applicable approach to date. And while its conceptual and theoretical underpinnings are strong, we should also recognize that it is to a significant degree a *pragmatic* approach to capturing the nature of pseudo-philosophy and its relation to genuine philosophy and other disciplines. Accordingly, I'll refer to it as the *Pragmatic Model* of pseudo-philosophy. This is especially appropriate given its original goals and the manner in which a substantial part of its usefulness and adequacy has been demonstrated in the examples of Part 3. What is the value, we should wonder, of such an account?

The Pragmatic Model clarifies the nature of philosophy itself by drawing the distinction between it and pseudo-philosophy in ways that are both more comprehensive and granular than previous attempts which remained at a more abstract level and failed to be specific in dealing with purported cases and precisely how an accusation of pseudo-philosophy could be identified and resolved in any principled and systematic manner. By providing this degree of specificity and a clear contrast between the genuine philosopher and pseudo-philosopher, particularly in the context of real-world examples, the model aids us in understanding the natures of both genuine philosophy and pseudo-philosophy.

By focusing in part on the natures of the *philosopher* and pseudo-*philosopher* (rather than on only the discipline of philosophy itself) we come to understand that there are significant components of pseudo-philosophy that involve goals, motivations, and behaviors — and that it can be viewed as a character flaw or a moral weakness as much as a purely intellectual failing. This is consistent with characterizations of pseudo-philosophers, accusations of them, and the animosity directed towards them from Plato, Xenophon, and Isocrates onwards. But the Pragmatic Model exposes this more explicitly, in part by replacing polemic and invective with an objective and neutral conceptual framework in which to make and debate such observations and their relevance.

In a similar way, the Pragmatic Model clarifies what our reaction should be to pseudo-philosophy when we encounter it, *why* that reaction is reasonable, and indeed why it is *required* on the basis of fundamental principles embraced by the genuine philosopher. This is supported by the manner in which the Pragmatic Model provides us with a formal basis (codified in the markers, personas, and models of the philosopher and pseudo-philosopher), rather than leaving us with an emotive, purely abstract, or merely intuitive one, for judging a writer, a work, or a portion of a work as pseudo-philosophical. Again, in making an accusation and judgment of pseudo-philosophy, this moves us beyond the historically common approach of invective and polemic, and removes (or at least reduces) the danger that an accusation of pseudo-philosophy may itself be pseudo-philosophical. In the case of particular accusations or judgments, the Pragmatic Model provides a clear and principled basis on which such accusations and judgments may be expressed, evaluated, and disputed.

This leads to the somewhat ironic result that the Pragmatic Model may be of benefit even to the purported pseudo-philosopher. Rather than returning invective for invective and polemic for polemic, the accused may use the Pragmatic Model to mount a defense against accusations — disputing in explicit ways, for example, the degree to which her work matches the persona and model of the pseudo-philosopher. Or she may choose to attack some of the features or assumptions of the Pragmatic Model itself. But at least she is provided with an opportunity and method for responding to the accusation in principled ways and within a framework which provides sufficient clarity for a meaningful dispute to take place.

Philosophy is often about models — models of moral behavior, models of science, models of the person, models of knowledge and rational belief, models of reasoning, models of perception, models of the human condition, models of government, etc. And so it shouldn't be surprising to find both conceptual and practical value in applying such an approach to pseudo-philosophy where less formal and systematic approaches have yielded little insight and failed to produce edifying results. Some insights are to be found in the Pragmatic Model itself, within the models of the genuine philosopher and pseudo-philosopher. But other insights arise in the details of developing those models. And some of these can be represented by "lessons learned" in working through that development.

Lessons learned

Many, if not most, attributions of pseudo-philosophy include accusations of some degree of dishonesty or exploitation, or of an ulterior motive incompatible with the pursuit of truth and wisdom. We see examples of this going back at least as far as the ancient Greeks' complaints about the sophists and rhetoricians, and also appearing in discussions of pseudo-philosophy by modern and contemporary philosophers such as Collingwood, Rescher, Frankfurt, and Moberger.[37] In Section 7.3 I've argued that a concept of pseudo-philosophy which includes dishonesty or exploitation as a critical component is best in terms of historical senses of pseudo-philosophy and of its intended *uses* — and that it avoids confusion and unnecessary handwringing over handling cases that otherwise become borderline or problematic to resolve in purely abstract and conceptual ways. But the real lesson to be learned here is that we can of course mean anything we like by *pseudo-philosophy*, and that it's simply misguided to think that our job as philosophers is to *discover* what pseudo-philosophy is. The nature of pseudo-philosophy is not lurking behind a fog bank or screen of conceptual complexity, waiting for us to penetrate the veil and discover its essence.[38]

Adopting an adequate, informative, and useful concept of pseudo-philosophy — and a philosophical analysis and applications of this — is at least to some degree, a matter of *decision*. It is in part a matter of deciding what sense of pseudo-philosophy is the most helpful and reasonable to adopt for particular goals, and then not creating pseudo-problems for ourselves by trying to construct a single concept to do multiple jobs that are either incompatible with one another, or are at cross purposes and so introduce confusions and conflicts in pursuing solutions to the very real problems with which pseudo-philosophers have confronted us for centuries.[39]

This doesn't mean that we can't find a core of generally agreeable goals, characteristics, and criteria that any reasonable and useful notion of pseudo-philosophy should satisfy. And this has been done in previous chapters. I think that as a brief characterization, we can regard pseudo-philosophy as a certain kind of fraudulent analysis or teaching that uses established techniques of philosophy (or mimics of these) to render itself attractive and plausible. It is this high-level and broad view of pseudo-philosophy that has been provided with detail and precision in Part 2 of this book and whose practical use and value has been demonstrated in Part 3. Given that, then how should making a judgment of pseudo-philosophy affect us, and how should we respond to it? What are the specific lessons we should take away from this analysis and from the Pragmatic Model? There are several:

> While a judgment of pseudo-philosophy can (and arguably *should*) be interpreted as a moral judgment combined with criticisms of pervasive logical, epistemic, and metaphysical errors or distortions, we should see its pragmatic value as a *warning* to potential consumers about what is being offered by the pseudo-philosopher and what the consequences of accepting that may be. This goes beyond a warning of "Beware! There is sloppy thinking here!" and includes a warning of fakery and deceit.

> Because an informative, useful, and adequate account of pseudo-philosophy naturally depends on the particular details of the concept of pseudo-philosophy (and more generally, on the concept of *the pseudo*) that we adopt, there will always be some room to disagree with that account. And within the account, there will be ample opportunity to debate whether and how it may apply in a specific real-world case. But a theory of pseudo-philosophy rigorous and specific enough to satisfy clear historical, conceptual, and pragmatic criteria of adequacy can provide a valuable and useful alternative to the view that the concept of pseudo-philosophy is hopelessly amorphous and suitable only as a basis for rhetoric and polemic.

> Pseudo-philosophy isn't bad or dangerous because it's *wrong* (though most often, it *is* wrong in fundamental ways). It's not bad merely because it involves *mistakes* in reasoning or in the support of positions taken or views expressed by the pseudo-philosopher. The history of genuine philosophy itself is littered with such mistakes. The pseudo-philosopher is bad because he seeks to persuade his intended victims to adopt beliefs or to take actions independent of (and often incompatible with) a pursuit of truth and wisdom, because he does this by *mimicking* or *masquerading as* the genuine philosopher through the pervasive use and distortion of philosophical methods, and because adopting those beliefs or taking those actions may quite directly result in *harm* to the victim. And often he *intends* that harm. In other cases she may have failed to anticipate or recognize that harm even though she *should*

have done so. We've seen detailed examples of this in Chapters 9 and 10.

➢ In addition to being harmful, the pseudo-philosopher can also be *inspiring*. And in fact it's the inspirational part that often conceals the harm lurking behind the masquerade. These two conflicting aspects of pseudo-philosophy have been remarked on by both Eric Mack and Robert Nozick in the case of Rand's work. They can be seen as well in the case of Mary Silva's (and others') effects on Nursing Theory. And members of NXIVM and followers of Keith Raniere were enthusiastically inspired by the "philosophy" he offered to them.

➢ There's a genuine difference between pseudo-philosophy and poorly done or merely inept philosophy; and enforcing this distinction is one of the goals of the Pragmatic Model. Often, sloppy philosophy is just sloppy philosophy, and is devoid of *masquerade* and *exploitation* — as in the case of a student who's in the process of learning but hasn't yet mastered the concepts, techniques, and skills, and who doesn't yet possess the required *body of knowledge* as described in Chapter 3. In such cases it is typically easy — even for a non-expert — to detect that something is amiss in the philosophical presentation.

It might be argued that Mary Silva's appeal to philosophy and to philosophical concepts and arguments (Chapter 9) falls under such a description of innocuous *inept philosophy* — except that it's not innocuous and she demonstrates, over a period of decades, an aggressive determination to employ philosophy for her specific practical goals independent of any concern for such niceties as truth, coherence, accuracy, and wisdom. Her degree of conformance to the Pseudo persona is simply too striking to allow her to escape entirely the charge of pseudo-philosophy along the Incompetence arm of the Dimensions of the Pseudo described in Section 6.2.

But in cases of pseudo-philosophy perpetrated by more skilled practitioners, it can be much more difficult to detect both the ineptness and the masquerade. Such a case is presented by Ayn Rand who (I think) might have been a philosophically serious contender in the areas of ethics, value theory, and political philosophy — if only she had worked at acquiring the necessary skills and knowledge required of the genuine philosopher instead of thoughtlessly relegating all of that to the realm of Attila and the Witch Doctor.[40]

In Rand's case it's not unreasonable to raise the question "But if Rand's treatment is so complex that it requires a highly trained philosopher to see the problems in it and expose them through lengthy and careful analysis and argument, doesn't that mean that in fact it's *not* pseudo-philosophy? That instead it's genuine philosophy which simply contains some errors — as virtually all philosophy is inclined to?" The answer to this, however, is "No, it doesn't mean that."

The lesson instead is that while it's not difficult to do philosophy in a sloppy way that gives the *appearance* of deep consideration and careful thought, this *appearance* is in fact simply an *illusion*. And the fact that the illusion is difficult to penetrate doesn't make it any less an illusion.

A skilled magician may successfully deceive some very skilled investigators — at least for a period until the investigators can piece through the components and details of his trick. And of course he uses those components and details precisely to obscure the nature of the trick and deflect our attention (as Rand does with the Shuffle identified by Mack). Such cases can be difficult to untangle in order to demonstrate how their vagueries and equivocations result only in nonsense. This is one of the difficulties in exposing pseudo-philosophy and its consequences, particularly to an audience inexperienced or untrained in some of the methods required to do that untangling. And this is why I said (Section 11.3) that if Ayn Rand was a pseudo-philosopher, then she was a major league pseudo-philosopher.

The kind of intensive analyses that Mack and Nozick performed in order to expose the pseudo-philosophical aspects of Rand's presentations is beyond the skill of most readers. But as the examples of Chapters 9-11 demonstrate, the Pragmatic Model of pseudo-philosophy provides a relatively compact tool set and an understandable approach and method for detecting pseudo-philosophical elements where they occur. It accomplishes this through the personas of the genuine philosopher and pseudo-philosopher, the markers of genuine philosophy and pseudo-philosophy, the *anti-sophistical stance*, and the *Practical Guidelines* for applying the models of the genuine philosopher and pseudo-philosopher to specific cases. The best defense against pseudo-philosophy is the anti-sophistical stance and practical guidelines described in Chapter 8.

Finally, there is the question of how to respond to pseudo-philosophy. I discussed this briefly in Chapter 8, but a more meaningful answer can be given now that we've seen the Practical Model applied in three real-world cases. Deciding that we've encountered the work of a pseudo-philosopher should result, foremost, in the withdrawal of any degree of *trust* that we might have — however provisionally — accorded his work, ideas, conclusions, and recommendations. Indeed, this should now be replaced with an explicit attitude of *distrust*.

It should be accompanied by heightened degrees of skepticism and scrutiny in evaluating anything that has been claimed or argued by the suspect author. If we have previously found his work (perhaps in other forms or contexts) to be valuable, we should review our confidence in that on the basis of our new realization of his use of pseudo-philosophy.

We may not (as Eric Mack and Robert Nozick point out in the case of Ayn Rand) be required to give up fundamental attitudes or beliefs *inspired* by the pseudo-philosopher. But we may need to give up any confidence that she has provided us with a sound (and so *pragmatically reliable*) justification for those beliefs. Alternatively, we may be compelled to the realization that we've been duped and manipulated into believing things that are false and dangerous, and that we've consequently made decisions and performed actions that have been harmful to ourselves or to others. The Raniere case is an especially poignant example of this, although it appears in the case of Nursing Theory as well — in the form of ineffective or harmful treatments delivered to patients on the basis of "theory" justified in part by pseudo-philosophy, and in broader effects it may have on the scope and delivery of nursing services as well.

The theory of pseudo-philosophy presented in this book has been designed specifically not only to be amenable to classic historical notions of pseudo-philosophy and to enable a deeper understanding of those, but to provide methods for identifying and dealing with pseudo-philosophy and pseudo-philosophers as we may encounter these "in the wild." It can't pretend to be the only cogent and applicable account of pseudo-philosophy that may be developed. It almost certainly is not. But it meets a broad range of criteria of adequacy that any such theory should satisfy, and so may constitute a kind of standard to serve as a measure for competing accounts. Understanding pseudo-philosophy, its goals, methods, characteristics, consequences, and dangers is a genuinely philosophical task. The Pragmatic Model is one approach to acknowledging and completing that task.

Notes

1. While this is certainly true in general, it is not universally true; and there are now a number of philosophers working outside the area of academic philosophy, particularly in the area of formal ontology as this is used in the empirical sciences. For details of this sort of work and its importance, see (Merrill 2011).

2. A word or phrase is *ambiguous* if it has two or more senses. For example, the word "law", used without qualification, is ambiguous among (1) a meaning of "legal requirement" (such as a statute, criminal law, civil law, etc.) and meanings of (2) "scientific law", (3) "logical law", (3) "mathematical law", or (4) "divine law". But things that are true of laws in the legal sense of this term are not true of laws in the other senses, and things that are true of mathematical laws (e.g., that they are subject to assumption as basic principles or to proof derived from basic principles), divine laws, scientific laws, etc. are not true of statutory laws.

    An *equivocation* is the use of a word in two or more senses within the same context. This may be intentional (as part of a rhetorical attempt to convince us of something in a dishonest way) or accidental in one way or another (resulting from ignorance or inattention to the specific meaning that's intended). As we'll see in later chapters, equivocation is one of the most common errors in argumentation and stating philosophical views and theories, and it's one of the most common weapons of pseudo-philosophers.

3. Rules like this that tell us when things are the same or different are called "principles of individuation" by philosophers, and they play a critical role in the metaphysics or ontology of any philosophical theory. One consequence of the Ship of Theseus problem is the realization that there may be multiple principles of individuation for a given kind of object (such as a ship), depending on *why* we want to make the individuation. And these principles may conflict in determining sameness in particular cases. Does this mean that there isn't a *real* Ship of Theseus? No, of course it doesn't. But we can't delve in the complexities of that argument right now.

4. The *ontology* for any philosophical theory or domain is the set of things (or kinds of things) that *exist* according to that theory or in that domain. For example, in simple arithmetic the ontology consists of 0 and all of the positive and negative whole numbers. In Plato's metaphysics the ontology includes not only material things (including people) in the world, but also *Forms* in which those more worldly things *participate*. And the ontology of a religion will typically include a God, or multiple gods.

5. If you look closely at what Emerson is doing here, you'll be able to detect a variety of equivocation being used. His "foolish consistency" term (to the degree that it can have any sense at all) employs a different and more informal sense of "consistency" than the logico-epistemic one we're discussing. Otherwise, a foolish consistency is like a round square: we can construct that phrase and attempt to refer to round squares, but there aren't (and can't be) any. This is why he's avoiding any details in his examples of Galileo, Copernicus, and Newton — since that would expose the equivocation, and so his deception and fakery. As we'll see later, this is an excellent and very brief example of pseudo-philosophy.

6. For details, see (The University of Western Australia 2015a and c).

7. This looks a lot like what I'm doing and saying in this book! Pay careful attention to how that's *not* pseudo-philosophy. Philosophers often make claims to innovative solutions to problems or to treatments that are different and original in one way or another. In fact, this is a requirement for publishing in the peer-reviewed literature and for (as an academic) being awarded tenure and promotion. Such a claim is not pseudo-philosophical. But exaggerated claims of this sort may be a clue that pseudo-philosophy is taking place (or is about to). The real pseudo-philosophy isn't in this sort of claim, but in how the pseudo-philosopher attempts to persuade you that she has accomplished what's been promised. And if the claim is not only exaggerated, but distorted or misleading, this hints even more strongly at pseudo-philosophy. We'll look at details of such a case in Chapter 11.

8. Philosophers are generally quite reasonable about the number of works they cite, and keep these down to just what's required in order to establish the necessary context and support their claims. On the other hand, I've personally refereed at least one paper in the biosciences which devoted more pages to its reference list than to the body of the paper. This can be a strong clue in itself that the paper may not be of much interest or significance.

9. But compare this to (Moberger 2020) which I believe leaves the philosophy/pseudo-philosophy distinction in a state of unremitting and useless murkiness as a result of the alternative reductionist approach taken there.

10. We may also, at least in a number of cases, see what our markers *represent* as being *constitutive* of genuine philosophy or of pseudo-philosophy (see Section 4.4). For example, not only are *persistent* equivocation, misrepresentation, intimidation, known fallacies, inadequate understanding, etc. *signs* of pseudo-philosophy, but they are also *constituents* of pseudo-philosophy — components of what makes pseudo-philosophy pseudo.

11. However, intuition *may* result in *hunches* or *hypotheses* that can *become* justified belief (or knowledge) if a genuine methodology is used to *justify* them.

Prior to that justification step, there is no *knowledge* to be found in the intuition. A fundamental flaw in Silva's thinking and reasoning resides in her insensitivity to this distinction between how an idea or hypothesis may *occur* to you and how you come (and how others can come) to have a *rational belief and confidence* in it. And she ignores (an example of ⊘ *Special Pleading*) the myriad examples and scenarios in which intuition so easily leads us astray in the absence of such subsequent justification. This is basic epistemology which Silva seems stubbornly intent on ignoring. Silva also seems intent on ignoring different *sources* of intuition and the difficulties of distinguishing these both generally and in each specific case.

12. For more details of such consequences and liability problems, see the section titled "What's the harm?" in (Glazer 2001).

13. You don't have to be a *scientist* to make all those observations and make generalizations from them. People have been doing that for millennia, and yet science is a relatively recent phenomenon in our epistemic world. Gathering the observations and making simple generalizations from them is just gathering data and making speculations based on it. There's nothing *scientific* going on there — except that the information you gather is helpful to what the scientist does, and may be thought of as part of the scientific process if it's guided or used in a certain way. Seeing something a thousand times doesn't make your description of that into a scientific law. And it doesn't make you a scientist. Science occurs at the level of *theory creation* and the criteria and processes employed for *theory acceptance* and *theory rejection*. This is where the scientist steps on top of Hume's constant conjunctions, ascends a level of abstraction, and arrives at *scientific* (theory-based) *knowledge*. Anyone who has had a course in the philosophy of science (and certainly anyone who has minored in philosophy) should be very sensitive to these distinctions.

14. We saw the same error in the case of Silva's notion of science and verification in Chapter 9.

15. Except in the sense that science may provide us with technology such as reading glasses or medical treatments (e.g., eye surgery) that genuinely improve our immediate perception. But that's not at all what Raniere means to refer to here.

16. Notice how Raniere's incongruous suggestion that scientific knowledge is only a *guess* is similar to Silva's attempt to undermine the reliability of science by urging us to believe that it is no more reliable than *intuition*. Silva at least attempts to offer an argument for her view, however specious it may be. Raniere, on the other hand, attempts to base his claim on vague and equivocal notions of perception, and then quickly contradicts himself by saying that "Our science is correct because ..." But both want to lead us towards a view that science (and

the *knowledge* it provides) is no more reliable than *belief* (or faith) we may come to through some alternative and non-rational "way of knowing."

17. See (Downing 2011), but note that Berkeley's notion of perception anchors both it and reality in the mind of God, and this avoids Raniere's conclusion that reality is *merely a perception* (and so there are any number of perceptions that may have, in Silva's words, an "equal claim" to representing reality). But if Raniere is borrowing Berkeley's approach to perception, then either he doesn't understand Berkeley (incompetence) or is distorting Berkeley's treatment for his own use (exploitation). In any event Raniere's approach suffers from an incoherence that Berkeley's does not.

18. Really? Is the label "positive integer" approximate? Or is that not a label? How about "Tetralogy of Fallot"? How are labels different from names in general? Are all *names* approximate in terms of their referents? Is your name approximate? Does "approximate" mean the same as "ambiguous" for Raniere? Are descriptions (e.g., "the current President of the U.S.") approximate? Are descriptions labels? If not, why not? What theory of semantics (meaning and reference) would support the sort of general claims that Raniere so casually makes about labels? None of these questions are even acknowledged in Raniere's discussion of labels. No matter. The interviewer just nods, appreciative of the insight that's been provided to him.

19. But contrast this with his previously expressed view in "Understanding Labels as Tools" (Raniere and Elliot 2017b) about the "approximate" nature of labels. And wonder in what way moral terms such as "good" and "bad" aren't labels according to that view. But if they are, then (since they're approximate) it seems we couldn't hope to achieve the clear distinguishing definitions he says we need. This is certainly a ⊘ *Lack of Rigor* and an apparent failure of Φ *Rationality* and Φ *Consistency*.

20. Such an apparently skewed result of Web searches can often turn out to be a consequence of the algorithms and heuristics that search engines use, coupled with the specific words or phrases you use in the search — and so it can be simply a reflection of the proportion of *anti*-Rand articles that appear in the most widely read and accessed sources on the Web. That is, what appears to be the result of a "slanted" search engine can instead be merely an artifact of the preponderance of anti-Rand articles in the most widely read and popular sources themselves — so not a matter of how the search is conducted, but rather a matter of what there is to be searched.

21. The point I'm making here is *not* that the Founding Fathers are not (or could not be) used as exemplars in the way that Rand wants; but rather that the way in which *she* attempts to do this renders that use incoherent. Certain attributes of the Founding Fathers — such as their practice of religion and slavery — are

fundamentally incompatible with the *ideal* of the professional intellectual that Rand has painted, and with her own expressly stated views on such practices. This can be seen as a particularly egregious example of a *weak analogy* in which Rand renders her own attempt at elucidating the notion of the professional intellectual to be incoherent. Yes, what she is doing here *can* be rescued by a competent philosopher. But she never attempts to rescue it and, in fact, never seems to sense the incoherence of her example within her own views — instead exhibiting a failure of Φ *Critical Appraisal* with respect to her own work.

22. There is some possibility here that Rand is merely being excessively sloppy with her reference to "logical positivists" and intends this to be a criticism of Wittgenstein's "meaning is use" doctrine. In that case it's not an unreasonable criticism, but trying to paint *logical positivists* with that brush then turns out to be an example of one or more of ⊘ *Misrepresentation*, ⊘ *Inadequate Understanding*, or ⊘ *Ignorance of Prior Work*; and it underscores the shallowness of Rand's familiarity with centuries of philosophy, the problems addressed, criticisms offered, and solutions proposed — and illustrates her failure to meet the standard of Φ *Domain Awareness* discussed in Sections 3.1 and 4.6. Again, however, since Rand continues to be careful in offering only the vaguest reference to "logical positivists" as the target of her criticisms, it's not possible for us to be sure of precisely what's at stake here. But it has every appearance of Rand's having another axe to grind and not wanting facts to get in her way.

23. This attack of Rand's on logical positivism is all the more off-target since it was the logical positivists and their predecessors who began to treat semantics and the philosophy of language with rigor and who developed fully detailed theories of meaning that are of use not only in philosophy but in science as well. This includes Frege (whom Rand seems to detest for reasons that are unclear) and the late Medieval nominalists (whom Rand ignores).

Rand (see particularly (Rand 1990)) wants to divorce concepts and truth from language — apparently overlooking the *fact* that it's only through language that we can express or discuss truths about the world. Aristotle had no philosophy of language, and Rand chooses to have none as well. This cripples her philosophy and leaves her unable to advance beyond Aristotle, but apparently (at least in part from ignorance) she seems content with this.

In this context it is ironic to read both *Introduction to Objectivist Epistemology* and Peikoff's "The Analytic-Synthetic Dichotomy" grafted to it since in both of these, references (through the usual use of quotation) to *words and phrases* abound (and of course are different in different translations of these works). And yet there is a thoroughgoing conflation of those linguistic entities with *concepts* — which of course Rand and Peikoff take to be *extralinguistic* and independent of language. It apparently escapes both Rand and Peikoff that in all their talk about concepts, they manage to refer to concepts (if at all) only through the medium of language — and that what they say can make sense (if it does) only because of this use of language. And neither Rand nor Peikoff reflects for a moment on the assumptions underlying these views. To Rand and Peikoff, it is not a word or phrase (or more generally language) that has *meaning*, but *concepts* (whatever these are). This approach (inherited to a significant degree from Plato and Aristotle) makes one wonder why we need language at all, and what its use is to us. And so it leads directly to a kind of fundamental ⊘ *Obscurantism* that infects Rand's theory of knowledge.

24. And note that Rand also deplored the philosophy of these same German Idealists *for the same reasons that Carnap did*.

25. "*Qua*" is a Latin word meaning *as*. Used in philosophy, it has the meaning of "*as x* rather than *as y*" (where often the y is understood in context). In Rand's case, part of the point is that while indeed man is an animal (or humans are animals), there are times when we want to focus on the particularly *human* qualities of humans — that distinguish them from the *other* animals. So in these contexts, and as Rand employs it, "*qua* man" means "considered specifically as a *human*". This technique is used extensively by Aristotle in his metaphysics, and we'll get a better understanding here as we proceed.

26. There are perhaps some interesting side roads in Rand scholarship to go down from this point. For example, what *is* Aristotle's theory of human nature, does Rand understand it correctly, does it apply to Rand's Principle of Survival and her use of this, and can it stand up to the use Rand makes of it without being subject itself to counterexamples or incoherence? We cannot, however, be tempted down such a path at the moment.

27. It might be thought better to call this "the *empirical* interpretation" or "the *factual* interpretation" in order to emphasize that its critical difference from the conceptual interpretation is its empirical content — and so the possibility of testing it in the empirical world and rejecting it on the basis of counterexamples. Referring to it as *causal* might be taken to imply that the principle, so conceived, exhibits a kind of *necessity*. And indeed there is an historically significant notion of cause (appropriate within Aristotelian and Thomistic contexts in which Rand is comfortable) where establishing a *causal* relation thereby establishes a relation of some sort of necessity. But for our purposes this subtle distinction turns out not to matter so long as it remains clear that under what Mack calls the *causal interpretation* it's acknowledged that the principle can be falsified by counterexamples. A primary goal of the Shuffle is to avoid the counterexamples that the causal interpretation as described by Mack (whatever we choose to call it) invites. I will, however, emphasize the factual/empirical nature of the Principle conceived in this way by also referring to it at times as "factual" or "empirical".

28. Note that these two interpretations don't necessarily conflict — and so it's *possible* to have an interpretation of the Principle that's acceptable to Rand on *conceptual* grounds, have a causal/factual interpretation of the principle that's *supported* by empirical observation, and have the result that the two interpretations are consistent with one another (don't produce a paradox or contradiction when considered and applied jointly). In fact, this is just the result that Rand needs. But as we'll see, she appears to become confused by her own equivocations in attempting to justify and employ the Principle of Survival, and so she doesn't produce the coherent and empirically accurate understanding of the Principle needed as the foundation for her ethics.

29. Mack sees one of Rand's most fundamental philosophical and conceptual errors to be her focus on *survival* as the fundamental concept on which to ground her ethical principles, and in her identifying *human good* with *survival*, which he takes to be a "too narrow, too stark conception of the ultimate human good" (Mack 2003 Section IV). It is this that spins Rand into the consequent logical and conceptual morass of ⊘ *Vagueness and Equivocation* we are seeing here. Mack proposes, instead, that Rand's use of survival in this way be replaced with an appropriate notion of *well-being*, and provides a sketch of how this might be done. However acceptable and successful such an alternative might be (even to "Randians"), I am skeptical that it would be acceptable to Rand, given her own goals and commitment to her idiosyncratic understanding of Aristotle's metaphysics upon which she otherwise depends heavily.

30. Note the similarity of this equivocation to that in the conceptual and causal interpretations of the Principle of Survival. This approach of attempting to move from a factual claim to a conceptual claim, or alternatively from a conceptual claim to a factual claim — and to use the one sort of claim to justify the other — is at the heart of what Mack calls "the Shuffle".

31. If you look closely at what's going on here, you should see a striking similarity to attempts throughout Rand's fictional writings to use the tautologies "A is A" and "Man is man" to start with a logical truth (having no empirical content) and then infer from it various factual, causal, or modal statements about the empirical world. This sort of "argumentation" is scattered heavily throughout the self-quotations that Rand includes in *For the New Intellectual*, and it involves its own kind of shuffle as it moves back and forth between different interpretations of the "is" in these statements.

There are complex issues here, and we can't pursue them in this book. Nor can we take a side path and investigate the degree of Rand's understanding of Aristotle or of various fallacies that may arise in being careless in inferences involving "is", such tautologous statements as "A is A", and how your metaphysics may influence your view of those. If you are interested in going down that path, an excellent and very complete guide to it and related literature can be found in Jaakko Hintikka's "The Unambiguity of Aristotelian Being" (Hintikka 1981).

32. See (Mack 2003 42-43 and 48), and note 45 on p. 65.

33. See (Mack 2003 40-53) for details.

34. See particularly (Mack 2003 38) for additional clarity on this point.

35. This exhibits an ambiance resembling Harry Binswanger's reference to "a dozen professionals in philosophy" attending the Rand "Epistemology Workshops" when this was — to be charitable — a wildly distorted description of those events. See *Filtering out commentaries* in Section 11.3.

36. A notable exception to this is the recent (Moberger 2020). While I heartily approve of Moberger's desire to take pseudo-philosophy seriously and provide a clear characterization of it and its practical consequences, I nonetheless feel that his particular reductionist approach is fundamentally flawed. Essentially, Moberger seeks to subsume pseudo-philosophy as a category of "bullshit" as described in Harry Frankfurt's renowned (Frankfurt 1986) — thus "outsourcing" the heavy lifting in the characterization to Frankfurt. But there are serious problems with this approach, and while I can't devote the time here to a thorough critique, I will mention some of these in other notes below.

37. See the sections on Collingwood and Rescher in Chapter 6. For the remarks of Frankfurt (related to the concept of bullshit), see (Frankfurt 1986); and for Moberger's discussion, see (Moberger 2020). Moberger seems to feel a need to deviate from this tradition for reasons that are unclear but may be bound up in the broadness of his central concept of "epistemic unconscientiousness."

I think that casting pseudo-philosophy, as Moberger does, as a "kind of bullshit" is not particularly enlightening, that it leaves out much of the detail, conceptual richness, and usefulness of the approach presented here, and thereby leaves a number of questions open about what is pseudo-philosophy and what is not — as Moberger seems to concede. This is, I would argue, because Moberger's approach — in attempting to provide a reductionist "unification" of pseudo-philosophy with Frankfurt's notion of bullshit — lacks sufficiently rich theories or models of both philosophy and pseudo-philosophy to fully satisfy some of his criteria of adequacy.

Making the concept of pseudo-philosophy parasitic on that of bullshit cannot result in such a theory, although Frankfurt's insights on bullshit undeniably are helpful in understanding certain facets of pseudo-philosophical behavior. While bullshit overlaps pseudo-philosophy, at least in many instances, there is more to pseudo-philosophy than bullshit; and the reductionist approach misses this.

38. A particularly puzzling aspect of Moberger's treatment is that although it's offered as an exercise and contribution in the area of "practical philosophy," and

although he develops several criteria of adequacy for the success of his approach, *no* specific example of pseudo-philosophy is ever brought forward in the paper and dealt with from Moberger's perspective. Mention of any real-world issues involving pseudo-philosophy appear only fleetingly and are confined to postmodernism as treated by Sokal and others. And even in his concluding remarks, the focus remains on pseudo-*science*. Some attention to the historical accusations of pseudo-philosophy, together with an examination of real-world cases of pseudo-philosophy, would have helped Moberger in dealing with such issues as "taking a stand" as a philosopher and as *posing* as philosophy — both of which have straightforward and common sense pragmatic solutions.

As well, the paper is almost entirely devoid of any review of the millennia-long history of attacks on pseudo-philosophy and different characterizations of it by philosophers. It seems clear that from the point of view of Plato onwards, the rhetoricians, sophists, and pseudo-philosophers don't in fact appear to suffer from a high degree of "epistemic unconscientiousness" in any intelligible sense of this term. Indeed, in the eyes of genuine philosophers complaining about them, the pseudo-philosophers know perfectly well what they're doing and are quite focused on pursuing their sophistical goals. It is not *indifference* to the truth that characterizes these pseudo-philosophical actions, but *manipulation* and *distortion* of it — and, following Rescher (2005), active and intentional *mimicry* of the genuine philosopher. This is illustrated as well by the case studies covered in our Chapters 9-11.

39. Problems of this sort arise in (Moberger 2020). Most of Moberger's paper focuses on pseudo-*science* as a subcategory of bullshit, and the subsumption of pseudo-philosophy becomes a secondary concern. The fundamental feature of pseudo-philosophy that Moberger identifies is what he calls "epistemic unconscientiousness." The Pragmatic Model recognizes the epistemic state of the philosopher/pseudo-philosopher in maintaining that distinction, but in a much more detailed and meaningful manner through the Philo and Pseudo personas and the markers of genuine philosophy and pseudo-philosophy, and without appeal to esoteric philosophical jargon. Moberger's treatment devolves into a plethora of distinctions and broader vs. narrower senses of different terms as he attempts to slice and dice (at times in a handwringing manner) different possible concepts of pseudo-philosophy and nuances of epistemic unconscientiousness. A number of questions and problems are raised, though these often appear to be artifacts of this approach itself.

It is difficult to see how our understanding of pseudo-philosophy — in either a fundamental conceptual sense, the historical sense, or the practical sense — has been improved through the attempted collapse of pseudo-philosophy into bullshit (though a practical example might be helpful in that context). A big part of the problem here is the attempt to force the complex concept of pseudo-philosophy into an inclusion/subsumption relationship with the notion of bullshit. This is simply a mistake because a number of important edges and corners get knocked off of a useful and coherent concept of pseudo-philosophy in that process of "unification" (Moberger's term).

40. There are passages in (Nozick 1971) and (Mack 2003) which I believe hint at a similar attitude toward Rand's work.

References

Agnifilo, Mark (2018), Letter to Judge Nicholas G. Garaufis, Document 191, "Re United States v. Keith Raniere, et al., Crim. No. 18-204 (NGG)", United States District Court, Eastern District of New York, filed November 14, 2018.

American Chemical Society (2016), "Academic Professional Guidelines", www.acs.org/content/acs/en/careers/career-services/ethics/academic-profesional-guidelines.html (accessed September 14, 2020).

American Philosophical Association (2017), "Statement on valuing public philosophy", www.apaonline.org/page/publicphilosophy (accessed September 14, 2020).

Ayer, Alfred J. (1952), *Language, Truth and Logic*, 2nd ed., New York: Dover Publications.

The Ayn Rand Institute (2020), "The Virtue of Selfishness", http://aynrandlexicon.com/ayn-rand-works/the-virtue-of-selfishness.html (accessed October 20, 2020).

AynRand.org (2020), "For the New Intellectual: Overview", aynrand.org/novels/for-the-new-intellectual/ (accessed September 18, 2020),.

Baggini, Julian, and Peter S. Fosl (2010), *The Philosopher's Toolkit: A Compendium of Philosophical Concepts and Methods*, Chichester: John Wiley & Sons.

Beall, Jc, Michael Glanzberg, and David Ripley (2016), "Liar Paradox", *The Stanford Encyclopedia of Philosophy* (Fall 2020 Edition), Edward N. Zalta (ed.), plato.stanford.edu/archives/fall2020/entries/liar-paradox/ (accessed September 14, 2020).

Bekiempis, Victoria (2012), "Confessions of a recovering Objectivist", *The Guardian*, www.theguardian.com/commentisfree/2012/jun/10/confessions-recovering-objectivist-ayn-rand (accessed September 18, 2020).

Binswanger, Harry (2020), "Objectivist Workshop Participants Identified", *The Harry Binswanger Letter*, hbletter.com/objectivist-workshop-participants-identified/?doing_wp_cron=1590333164.5472009181976318359375 (accessed September 18, 2020).

Bobzien, Susanne (2010), "Ancient Logic", *The Stanford Encyclopedia of Philosophy* (Summer 2020 Edition), Edward N. Zalta (ed.), plato.stanford.edu/archives/sum2020/entries/logic-ancient (accessed September 14, 2020).

References

Bogen, James (2020), "Theory and Observation in Science", *The Stanford Encyclopedia of Philosophy* (Summer 2020 Edition), Edward N. Zalta (ed.), plato.stanford.edu/archives/sum2020/entries/science-theory-observation/.

Booth, Wayne C. (1983), *The Rhetoric of Fiction*, 2nd ed., Chicago: The University of Chicago Press.

Bryant, Kenzie (2018), "How NXIVM Used the Strange Power of Patents to Build Its 'Sex Cult'", Vanity Fair, www.vanityfair.com/style/2018/06/keith-raniere-nxivm-patents-luciferian (accessed September 17, 2020).

Bubb, Frank (2006), "Reply to Eric Mack", 'Problematic Arguments in Randian Ethics'", *The Journal of Ayn Rand Studies*, 7 (2): 275-286.

Burns, Edward McNail (1955). *Western civilization: Their history and their culture*, 4th ed., New York: W. W. Norton.

Caldin, E. F. (1958), "*The Philosophy of Science* by P. Henry van Laer", *The British Journal for the Philosophy of Science,* 9 (35): 245-46, http://www.jstor.org/stable/685656 (accessed September 16, 2020).

Carnap, Rudolf (1958), "The Elimination of Metaphysics through the Logical Analysis of Language", trans. Arthur Pap, in *Logical Positivism*, ed. A. J. Ayer, 60-81,New York: Free Press, www.scribd.com/document/7301062/Rudolf-Carnap-The-Elimination-of-Metaphysics-Through-Logical-Analysis-of-Language-1957.

The Catholic Archive (2020), http://thecatholicarchive.com/ (accessed September 14, 2020).

Chait, Jonathan (2011), "Ayn Rand's Pseudo-Philosophy", newrepublic.com/article/87328/ayn-rands-pseudo-philosophy (accessed September 18, 2020).

Chambers, Whittaker (1957), "Big Sister Is Watching You", *National Review*, December 28, 1957.

Chasteen, Stephanie (2008), "Crackpot Science", *The New Republic*, sciencegeekgirl.wordpress.com/2008/07/12/crackpot-science/ (accessed September 14, 2020).

Collingwood, Robin George (1958), *The Principles of Art*, Oxford: Oxford University Press.

Colton, Charles Caleb (2017), *Lacon: Or, Many Things in Few Words*, Whitefish: Kessinger.

Conant, James Bryant (1948), *Harvard Case Histories in Experimental Science* (2 vols), Cambridge: Harvard University Press.

References

Conocimiento (2020), *Conocimiento*, issues 1(March 2005)-126(April 2014), http://www.conocimientoenlinea.com/?paged=11 , (accessed October 12, 2020).

Contandriopoulos, Damien (2019), "About academic bullshit in nursing", *Nursing Inquiry*, 26: e12277, doi.org/10.1111/nin.12277 (accessed September 16, 2020).

Cooper, Alan (2004), *The Inmates are Running the Asylum*, Indianapolis: Sams Publishing.

Cooper, Alan and David Cronin (2014), *About Face: The Essentials of Interaction Design*, 4th ed., Indianapolis: John Wiley & Sons, Inc.

Courcey, Kevin (2019), "Therapeutic Touch: Further Notes", *Quackwatch*, quackwatch.org/related/tt2/ (accessed September 16, 2020).

Diamond, Jared M. (2017), *Guns, Germs, and Steel: The Fates of Human Societies*, New York: W. W. Norton & Company.

Downing, Lisa (2011), "George Berkeley", *The Stanford Encyclopedia of Philosophy* (Fall 2020 Edition), Edward N. Zalta (ed.), plato.stanford.edu/entries/berkeley/ (accessed September 14, 2020).

Doyle, D. John (2013), "Modern Medicine and the Postmodernist Challenge", *Ethics in Biology, Engineering & Medicine – An International Journal*, 4 (3): 185-197.

Driver, Julia (2014), "The History of Utilitarianism", *The Stanford Encyclopedia of Philosophy* (Winter 2014 Edition), Edward N. Zalta (ed.), plato.stanford.edu/archives/win2014/entries/utilitarianism-history/ (accessed September 14, 2020).

Dudley, Underwood (1992), *Mathematical Cranks*, Washington: American Mathematical Society.

Emerson, Ralph Waldo (2016), *Self Reliance: and Other Essays*, .

Elliot, Marc (2020), MarcElliot.com, www.marcelliot.com/ (accessed September17, 2020).

Feigl, Herbert and May Brodbeck (1953), *Readings in the Philosophy of Science*, New York: Appleton-Century-Crofts.

Frankfurt, Harry (1986) "On Bullshit", *Raritan Quarterly Review*, 6 (2): 81–100.

Glanzberg, Michael (2018), "Truth", *The Stanford Encyclopedia of Philosophy* (Fall 2018 Edition), Edward N. Zalta (ed.), plato.stanford.edu/archives/fall2018/entries/truth/ (accessed September 14, 2020).

Glazer, Sarah (2001), "Therapeutic touch and postmodernism in nursing", *Nursing Philosophy*, 2 (3): 196-212.

Gortner, Susan (1993), "Nursing's syntax revisited: a critique of philosophies said to influence nursing theories", *International Journal of Nursing Studies*, 30 (6): 477-488.

Grigoriadis, Vanessa (2018), "Inside Nxivm, the 'Sex Cult' That Preached Empowerment", *The New York Times Magazine*, www.nytimes.com/2018/05/30/magazine/sex-cult-empowerment-nxivm-keith-raniere.html (accessed September 17, 2020).

Grünbaum, Adolph (2005), "Chapter 8" in *Formal Philosophy*, Vincent F. Hendricks and John Symons (eds), 2005, 75, Automatic Press.

Haack, Susan (1974), *Deviant logic: some philosophical issues*, Cambridge: Cambridge University Press.

Hall, Ned (2020), "The Natural/Non-Natural Distinction", *Stanford Encyclopedia of Philosophy*, plato.stanford.edu/entries/lewis-metaphysics/natural-distinction.html.

Heller, Anne Conover (2010), *Ayn Rand and the World She Made*, New York: Anchor Books.

Hempel, Carl (1965), *Aspects of Scientific Explanation*, New York, NY: Free Press.

Hempel, Carl (1966), *Philosophy of Natural Science*, Englewood Cliffs, NJ: Prentice-Hall.

Hintikka, Jaakko (1981), "The Unambiguity of Aristotelian Being", *The Society for Ancient Greek Philosophy Newsletter*, 238, online in *The Open Repository @ Binghamton (The ORB)*, orb.binghamton.edu/sagp/238 (accessed October 25, 2020).

Hoffman, Joshua and Gary Rosenkrantz (2017), "Omnipotence", *The Stanford Encyclopedia of Philosophy* (Spring 2020 Edition), Edward N. Zalta (ed.), plato.stanford.edu/archives/spr2020/entries/omnipotence/ (accessed September 14, 2020).

Hofweber, Thomas (2009), "Ambitious, yet modest, metaphysics", in John Chalmers, David Manley, and Ryan Wasserman (eds), 2009, *Metametaphysics: New Essays on the Foundations of Ontology*, 260-289, Oxford: Oxford University Press.

Holland, Nancy J., Scott A. Anderson, Leslie P. Francis, Ned Markosian, Diane Michelfelder, Julinna Oxley, Sally Scholz, and Yolonda Y. Wilson (2016), *Code of Conduct*, www.apaonline.org/page/codeofconduct (accessed September 14, 2020).

Hume, David (2008), *An Enquiry Concerning Human Understanding*, Oxford World's Classics, Oxford: Oxford University Press.

The Journal of Ayn Rand Studies (2020), Penn State University Press, www.jstor.org/journal/jaynrandstud.

Kalish, Donald and Richard Montague (1980), *Logic: Techniques of Formal Reasoning*, 2nd ed., Oxford: Oxford University Press.

Kaminski, Stansilaw (1958), "P. Henry van Laer: *Philosophico-Scientific Problems*", *Studia Logica*, T (8): 328-331.

Kerlinger, Fred N. (1973), *Foundations of Behavioral Research*, 2nd ed., New York: Holt, Rinehart & Winston.

Kneller, George F. (1971) *Introduction to the philosophy of education*, 2nd ed., New York: John Wiley & Sons.

Krauss, Lawrence M. (2007), *The Physics of Star Trek*, Philadelphia: Basic Books.

Kuhn, Thomas (1962), *The Structure of Scientific Revolutions*, Chicago: University of Chicago Press.

Labovitz, Sanford and Robert Hagedorn (1971), *Introduction to social research*, 2nd ed., New York: McGraw-Hill.

Mack, Eric (2003), "Problematic Arguments in Randian Ethics", *The Journal of Ayn Rand Studies*, 5 (1): 1-66.

McInerny, Ralph and John O'Callaghan (2014), "Saint Thomas Aquinas", *The Stanford Encyclopedia of Philosophy* (Summer 2018 Edition), Edward N. Zalta (ed.), plato.stanford.edu/archives/sum2018/entries/aquinas/ (accessed September 14, 2020).

McMullin, Ernan (1955), "Henry Van Laer, Philosophico-scientific problems", *Revue Philosophique de Louvain*, 53 (39): 453-457.

Merrill, Gary H. (2011), "Ontology, ontologies, and science", *Topoi*, 30: 71-83.

Miller, Alexander (2019), "Realism", *The Stanford Encyclopedia of Philosophy* (Winter 2019 Edition), Edward N. Zalta (ed.), plato.stanford.edu/archives/win2019/entries/realism/ (accessed September 14, 2020).

Moberger, Victor (2020), "Bullshit, Pseudoscience and Pseudophilosophy", *Theoria*, 86 (5): 595-611, doi.org/10.1111/theo.12271 (accessed October 31, 2020).

Murphy, Mark (2019), "The Natural Law Tradition in Ethics", *The Stanford Encyclopedia of Philosophy* (Summer 2019 Edition), Edward N. Zalta (ed.), plato.stanford.edu/archives/sum2019/entries/natural-law-ethics (accessed September 18, 2020).

Nagel, Ernest (1961), *The Structure of Science: Problems in the Logic of Scientific Explanation*, New York: Harcourt, Brace & World.

Nevares, Ivy (2020), "My story, thus far.", ivynevares.com (accessed September 17, 2020).

Nevares, Ivy, and Keith Raniere (2005), "Microhumanidad"["Microhumanity"], *Conocimiento*, 31: 13-17, issuu.com/rodrigosotomoreno/docs/revista_conocimiento_31 (accessed September 17, 2020).

Nietzsche, Friedrich (1996), *On the Genealogy of Morals*, trans. Douglas Smith, Oxford: Oxford University Press.

Nozick, Robert (1971), "On the Randian Argument", *The Personalist*, 52 (2):282-304, doi.org/10.1111/j.1468-0114.1971.tb08926.x (accessed October 28, 2020).

Odato, James and Jennifer Gish (2019), "Secrets of NXIVM", *Times Union*, Feb 11, 2012, updated April 17, 2019, www.timesunion.com/local/article/Secrets-of-NXIVM-2880885.php#photo-2238738 (accessed September 17, 2020).

Plato (2016), *The Republic*, trans. B. Jovett, www.gutenberg.org/files/1497/1497-h/1497-h.htm, Project Gutenberg.

Plutarch (2013), *Theseus*, trans. John Dryden, CreateSpace.

Propp, Vladimir (1968), *Morphology of the Folktale*, trans. Lawrence Scott, revised ed., 1968, Austin: University of Texas Press.

Quine, W. V. (1986), *Philosophy of Logic*, 2nd ed., Boston: Harvard University Press.

Quine, W. V. and J. S. Ullian (1978), *The Web of Belief*, 2nd ed., New York: McGraw-Hill.

Railton, Peter, Mi-Kyoung Lee, Diane Michelfelder, Robin Zheng (eds), 2020, *American Philosophical Association Good Practices Guide*, Newark: American Philosophical Association.

Rand, Ayn (1963a), *For the New Intellectual*, New York: Signet.

Rand, Ayn (1963b), "The Goal of My Writing", courses.aynrand.org/works/the-goal-of-my-writing/ (accessed September 18, 2020).

Rand, Ayn (1964), *The Virtue of Selfishness*, New York: Signet.

Rand, Ayn (1971), *The Romantic Manifesto: A Philosophy of Literature*, 2nd revised ed., New York: Signet.

Rand, Ayn (1990), *Introduction to Objectivist Epistemology*, expanded 2nd ed., Harry Binswanger and Leonard Peikoff (eds), 1990, New York: Meridian.

Rand, Ayn, and Mike Wallace (1959), "Glamour and Discourse (or: Optics and Atmospherics")", interview: www.youtube.com/watch?v=1ooKsv_SX4Y (accessed September 18, 2020), transcript: glamour-and-discourse

.blogspot.com/p/mike-wallace-interviews-ayn-rand.html (accessed September 18, 2020).

Raniere, Keith (2000), "Rational inquiry method", patents.google.com/patent/WO2002021481A1/en (accessed September 17, 2020).

Raniere, Keith (2005), "Negligencia en la Comunicación Resulta en Múltiples Muertes"["Negligence in Communication Results in Multiple Deaths"], *Conocimiento*, 20: 54-57, issuu.com/rodrigosotomoreno/docs/revista_conocimiento_20 (accessed September 17, 2020).

Raniere, Keith and Marc Elliot (2016), "What is Rational Inquiry", www.youtube.com/watch?v=KT7H93MBUwA (accessed September 17, 2020).

Raniere, Keith and Marc Elliot (2017a), "How Rational Inquiry Works", www.youtube.com/watch?v=e4i03j2XBxU (accessed September 17, 2020).

Raniere, Keith and Marc Elliot (2017b), "Understanding Labels as Tools", www.youtube.com/watch?v=8ZC2M2t4sMk (accessed September 17, 2020).

Raniere, Keith, and Allison Mack (2017), "Evolving Societal Values to Transform Arts and Media", www.youtube.com/watch?v=YVQaIUTPDI8 (accessed September 17, 2020).

Raniere, Keith, *et al.* (2017), "Keith Raniere Conversations", www.youtube.com/channel/UCMWvfA27XqQFsqQXAFIJnmQ (accessed September 17, 2020).

Raskin, Jef (2000), "Rogerian Nursing Theory: A Humbug in the Halls of Higher Learning", *Skeptical Inquirer* 2000 (24) 5: 30-36.

Rational Wiki contributors (2020), "Cold fusion", *RationalWiki*, rationalwiki.org/wiki/Cold_fusion (accessed September 14, 2020).

Rescher, Nicholas (2005), "Pseudo-philosophy", in Ted Honderich (ed.), *The Oxford Companion to Philosophy*, 2nd ed., Oxford: Oxford University Press.

Rickless, Samuel (2015), "Plato and Parmenides", *The Stanford Encyclopedia of Philosophy* (Spring 2020 Edition), Edward N. Zalta (ed.), plato.stanford.edu/archives/spr2020/entries/plato-parmenides/ (accessed September 14, 2020).

Rodriguez-Pereyra, Gonzalo (2015), "Nominalism in Metaphysics", *The Stanford Encyclopedia of Philosophy* (Summer 2019 Edition), Edward N. Zalta (ed.), plato.stanford.edu/archives/sum2019/entries/nominalism-metaphysics/ (accessed: September 20, 2020).

Rogers, Martha E. (1970), *An introduction to the theoretical basis of nursing*, Philadelphia: F. A. Davis Co., out of print but available in the Open Library: openlibrary.org/books/OL5755455M/An_introduction_to_the_theoretical_basis_of_nursing (accessed September 14, 2020).

Roig, Miguel (2015), "Avoiding Plagiarism, Self-plagiarism, and Other Questionable Writing Practices: A Guide to Ethical Writing", ori.hhs.gov/avoiding-plagiarism-self-plagiarism-and-other-questionable-writing-practices-guide-ethical-writing (accessed September 14 2020).

Russell, Bertrand (1946), "Philosophy for Laymen", *Universities Quarterly*, 1946 (1): 38-49. available online: users.drew.edu/jlenz/br-lay-philosophy.html#nstar (accessed September 14, 2020).

Russell, Bertrand (1996), *The Principles of Mathematics*, New York: W. W. Norton & Co.

Russell, Bertrand (2001), *The Problems of Philosophy*, Oxford: Oxford University Press.

Ryan, Scott (2003), "A Randian Roundup: A Review of the Objectivist Literature", *Transactions of the Charles S. Peirce Society*, 39 (3): 469-489.

San Diego State University, College of Arts and Sciences (2020), "What is Rhetoric?", rhetoric.sdsu.edu/resources/what_is_rhetoric.htm (accessed October 6, 2020).

Savage, C. Wade (1967), "The Paradox of the Stone", *The Philosophical Review*, 76 (1): 74-79.

Scheffler, Israel (1965), *Conditions of knowledge: An introduction to epistemology and education*, Glenview, IL: Scott, Foresman.

Scalia, Antonin (1989), "Essay: Assorted Canards of Contemporary Legal Analysis," *Case Western Law Review*, (40) 3: 581-597, available online: scholarlycommons.law.case.edu/cgi/viewcontent.cgi?article=1853&context=caselrev (accessed October 2, 2020).

Sciabarra, Chris Matthew (1999a), "Investigative Report: In Search of the Rand Transcript", www.nyu.edu/projects/sciabarra/essays/randt1.htm (accessed September 18, 2020).

Sciabarra, Chris Matthew (1999b), "The Rand Transcript", *The Journal of Ayn Rand Studies*, 1 (1): 1-26.

Sciabarra, Chris Matthew (2013), *Ayn Rand: The Russian Radical*, 2nd ed., University Park: Penn State University Press.

Sellars, Wilfrid (1991), *Science, Perception and Reality*, Atascadero, CA: Ridgeview Publishing.

Shaver, Robert (2019), "Egoism", *The Stanford Encyclopedia of Philosophy* (Spring 2019 Edition), Edward N. Zalta (ed.), plato.stanford.edu/archives/spr2019/entries/egoism/ (accessed September 17, 2020).

Silva, Mary C. (1977), "Philosophy, Science, Theory: Interrelationships and Implications for Nursing Research", *Journal of Nursing Scholarship*, 9 (3): 51-69, available online: doi.org/10.1111/j.1547-5069.1977.tb01604.x (accessed September 14, 2020).

Silva, Mary C. and Daniel Rothbart (1984), "An analysis of changing trends in philosophies of science on nursing theory development and testing", *Advances in Nursing Theory*, 6 (2): 1-13.

Sinnott-Armstrong, Walter (2019), "Consequentialism", *The Stanford Encyclopedia of Philosophy* (Summer 2019 Edition), Edward N. Zalta (ed.), plato.stanford.edu/archives/sum2019/entries/consequentialism/ (accessed September 14, 2020).

Smith, Barry, *et al.* (1992), Letter to *The Times* (London), May 9, 1992: letters page.

Sokal, Alan (2008), *Beyond the Hoax: Science, Philosophy and Culture*, Oxford: Oxford University Press.

Sokal, Alan, and Jean Bricmont (1998), *Fashionable Nonsense: Postmodern Intellectuals' Abuse of Science*, New York: Picador.

Stalker, Douglas and Clark Glymour (1989), *Examining Holistic Medicine*, Buffalo: Prometheus Books.

Strimbu, Kyle, and Jorge A. Tavel (2010), "What are biomarkers?", *Current Opinion in HIV and AIDS*, 5 (6): 463-466, available online: dx.doi.org/10.1097%2FCOH.0b013e32833ed177 and (author manuscript) www.ncbi.nlm.nih.gov/pmc/articles/PMC3078627/.

Taylor, Richard (1992), *Metaphysics*, Englewood Cliffs: Prentice Hall.

Tuckness, Alex (2016), "Locke's Political Philosophy",*The Stanford Encyclopedia of Philosophy (Summer 2019 Edition)*, Edward N. Zalta (ed.), plato.stanford.edu/archives/sum2019/entries/locke-political/ (accessed September 14, 2020).

U.S. Department of Justice (2019), "Jury Finds Nxivm Leader Keith Raniere Guilty of All Counts", www.justice.gov/usao-edny/pr/jury-finds-nxivm-leader-keith-raniere-guilty-all-counts (accessed September 17, 2020).

U.S. District Court (2009), "Videotaped Deposition of: Keith A. Raniere (Volume I)", transcript, March 11, 2009, No. 2:06-ev-01051, District of New Jersey, culteducation.com/pdf/nxivm/FILED%202009-03-11_K.%20Raniere%20Deposition%20Transcript%20(Confidential).pdf (accessed September 17, 2020).

References

U.S. District Court (2016), "NXIVM CORPORATION, f/k/a/ EXECUTIVE SUCCESS PROGRAMS, INC., and FIRST PRINCIPLES, INC., Plaintiffs v. Estate of Morris Sutton, *et al.*, Civil Action No. 2:06-cv-1051-KSH-CLW", United States District Court, Newark, NJ, www.govinfo.gov/content/pkg/USCOURTS-njd-2_06-cv-01051/pdf/USCOURTS-njd-2_06-cv-01051-5.pdf" (accessed September 17, 2020).

University of Western Australia (2015a), "Fraud & Corruption – Appendix A – Definition of Misconduct", available online: www.hr.uwa.edu.au/__data/assets/pdf_file/0018/2802420/Fraud-and-Corruption-Appendix-A-Definition-of-Misconduct-Approved-05-10-2015.pdf (accessed September 14, 2020).

University of Western Australia (2015b), "Fraud & Corruption – Appendix D – Possible Indicators", available online: www.hr.uwa.edu.au/__data/assets/pdf_file/0010/2802457/Fraud-and-Corruption-Appendix-D-Possible-Indicators-Approved-05-10-2015.pdf (accessed September 14, 2020).

University of Western Australia (2015c), "University Policy on: Fraud and Corruption", available online: www.hr.uwa.edu.au/policies/policies/conduct/fraud-policy (accessed September 14, 2020).

Van Laer, P. Henry (1963), Philosophy of Science: An introduction to some general aspects of science, 2nd ed., Pittsburgh: Duquesne University Press.

Waldor, Cathy L. (2017), "Re: NXIVM Corporation, *et al* v. Sutton, *et al.*, Civil Action No. 2:06-cv-1051-KSH-CLW", United States District Court, Newark, NJ, www.govinfo.gov/content/pkg/USCOURTS-njd-2_06-cv-01051/pdf/USCOURTS-njd-2_06-cv-01051-8.pdf (accessed September 17, 2020).

Wikipedia contributors (2020a), "Aristotle's theory of universals", *Wikipedia, The Free Encyclopedia,* en.wikipedia.org/w/index.php?title=Aristotle%27s_theory_of_universals&oldid=945694873 (accessed September 14, 2020).

Wikipedia contributors (2020b), "David Malet Armstrong", *Wikipedia, The Free Encyclopedia,* en.wikipedia.org/w/index.php?title=David_Malet_Armstrong&oldid=968877309 (accessed September 14, 2020).

Wikipedia contributors (2020c), "Deepak Chopra", *Wikipedia, The Free Encyclopedia,* en.wikipedia.org/w/index.php?title=Deepak_Chopra&oldid=977649586 (accessed September 14, 2020).

Wikipedia contributors (2020d), "Epistemology", *Wikipedia, The Free Encyclopedia,* en.wikipedia.org/wiki/Epistemology (accessed September 14, 2020).

Wikipedia contributors (2020e), "Fallacy of the undistributed middle", *Wikipedia, The Free Encyclopedia,* en.wikipedia.org/wiki/Fallacy_of_the_undistributed_middle (accessed September 18, 2020).

Wikipedia contributors (2020f), "Jacques Derrida", *Wikipedia, The Free Encyclopedia,* en.wikipedia.org/w/index.php?title=Jacques_Derrida&oldid=977246254 (accessed September 14, 2020).

Wikipedia contributors (2020g), "List of paradoxes", *Wikipedia, The Free Encyclopedia,* en.wikipedia.org/w/index.php?title=List_of_paradoxes&oldid=978079422 (accessed September 16, 2020).

Wikipedia contributors (2020h), "Perpetual Motion", *Wikipedia, The Free Encyclopedia,* en.wikipedia.org/w/index.php?title=Perpetual_motion&oldid=977994132 (accessed September 14, 2020).

Wikipedia contributors (2020i), "Problem of evil", *Wikipedia, The Free Encyclopedia,* en.wikipedia.org/w/index.php?title=Problem_of_evil&oldid=978894559 (accessed September 18, 2020).

Wikipedia contributors (2020j) "Pseudohistory", *Wikipedia, The Free Encyclopedia*, en.wikipedia.org/w/index.php?title=Pseudohistory&oldid=977464342 (accessed September 14, 2020)

Wikipedia contributors (2020k)"Pseudomathematics", *Wikipedia, The Free Encyclopedia,* en.wikipedia.org/wiki/Pseudomathematics (accessed September 14, 2020)

Wikipedia contributors (2020l)"Pseudophilosophy", *Wikipedia, The Free Encyclopedia,* en.wikipedia.org/wiki/Pseudophilosophy (accessed October 15, 2020)

Wikipedia contributors (2020m), "Pseudorealism", *Wikipedia, The Free Encyclopedia,* en.wikipedia.org/w/index.php?title=Pseudorealism&oldid=936980373 (accessed September 14, 2020).

Wikipedia contributors (2020n), "Pseudoscience", *Wikipedia, The Free Encyclopedia,* en.wikipedia.org/w/index.php?title=Pseudoscience&oldid=976911114 (accessed September 14, 2020).

Wikipedia contributors (2020o), "Teleological argument", *Wikipedia, The Free Encyclopedia,* en.wikipedia.org/w/index.php?title=Teleological_argument&oldid=973035638 (accessed September 17, 2020).

Wikipedia contributors (2020p), "Theory of forms", *Wikipedia, The Free Encyclopedia,* en.wikipedia.org/w/index.php?title=Theory_of_forms&oldid=978225459 (accessed September 14, 2020).

Wikipedia contributors (2020q), "A Theory of Justice", *Wikipedia, The Free Encyclopedia,* en.wikipedia.org/w/index.php?title=A_Theory_of_Justice&oldid=974937988 (accessed September 14, 2020).

References

Wikiquote contributors (2020), "Star Trek II: The Wrath of Khan", *Wikiquote,* en.wikiquote.org/wiki/Star_Trek_II:_The_Wrath_of_Khan (accessed September 14, 2020).

Wiley, Keith (2020), "Voyages of The Ship of Theseus", www.youtube.com/watch?v=t_935gCpPVw (accessed December 15, 2020).

Williams, Susan M. (1989), "Holistic Nursing", in Stalker, Douglas and Clark Glymour (eds), 1989, *Examining Holistic Medicine*, 49-63, Buffalo: Prometheus Books.

Xenophon (2013), *The Sportsman: On Hunting, A Sportsman's Manual, Commonly Called Cynegeticus*, trans. H. G. Dakyns, Project Gutenberg, www.gutenberg.org /files/1180/1180-h/1180-h.htm (accessed September 18, 2020).

Zalta, Edward N. (2019), "Gottlob Frege", *The Stanford Encyclopedia of Philosophy* (Fall 2020 Edition), Edward N. Zalta (ed.), plato.stanford.edu/archives/fall2020/entries/frege/ (accessed September 14, 2020).

Zalta, Edward N. (2020), ed., *Stanford Encyclopedia of Philosophy,* plato.stanford.edu/.

Index

abduction, 87, 155
   and aggregation of markers, 85
   enhanced constraints, 157
   inference to the best explanation, 164
ambiguity, 68, *See* equivocation
   weaponization of, 133, *See* rhetoric
anti-sophistical stance, 150, 160, 173, 182, 192, 218, 258, 267, 314, 323
Aristotle
   and dialectic, 70
   and formal logic, 29
   features of his logic, 65
   his use of *qua*, 330
   limitations of his logic, 65
   Rand's attitude towards, 255, 258, 277, 297, 308
   The Knife Of, 222
   the nature of wisdom and philosophy, 19
bad faith, 126
borrowing
   and misappropriation, 140
   of philosophy for other purposes, 108, 191, 217, 328
bullshit and pseudo-philosophy, 194, 332, 333
Carnap, Rudolf, 56, 273, 274, 275, 330, 336
Chambers, Whitaker, 267, 278
Collingwood, R. G., 3, 108, 110, 111, 112, 142, 320, 332, 336
consistency, 110, 216
   a marker of genuine philosophy, 90
   and counterexamples, 74
   and harm, 64
   and Pseudo, 120
   and small minds, 59

   and truth, 58
   as a norm, 307
   as a value for Philo, 79
   assumed by philosophers, 37
   Emerson's view, 59
   foolish, 59, 326
   in philosophy vs. rhetoric, 97
   Scalia's view, 61
counterexamples, 73, 74, *See also* Raniere, Keith, *See also* Silva, Mary Cipriano
   Eric Mack on Ayn Rand, 299
   in Rand's Shuffle, 302
   Rand's response to, 286, 289
criteria of adequacy, 4, 11, 81, 82, 89, 91, 102, 105, 153, 154, 161, 210, 318, 321, 324, 332, 333
   as a measure of success, 82, 89
criticism
   and discouraging inquiry, 127
   and the Pseudo persona, 118, 119
   and theories, 72
   as a reaction to pseudo-philosophy, 149
   avoiding, 128, 129, 130
   of self and others, 37, 79, 89, 90
   Pseudo's response to, 125
definitions, 69
dialectic, 70
Elliot, Marc, 225, 227, 232, 233, 237, *See* Raniere, Keith
epistemology, 28
   and abduction, 87, 155
   Introduction to Objectivist Epistemology, 250
equivocation, 133
ethics, 26
   in Rand's Shuffle, 295
   Rand's principles of, 281

Raniere's odd view of, 222
gobbletygook, 214, 215, 219, 220, 233
Hume, David, 21, 102, 212, 264, 265, 268, 269, 270, 277, 327
irrationalism, 264, 285
    and Philo, 79
    and pseudo-philosophy, 111
    and rhetoric, 99
Isocrates, 6, 14, 111, 142, 319
Kant, 98
    and Ayn Rand, 248, 271
logic, 29, 65
    Aristotelian. *See* Aristotle
    informal, 66
    Rand's ignorance of, 277
Mack, Allison, 225, 227, 228, *See* Raniere, Keith
Mack, Eric, 280, 281, 288, 291, 295, 299, 302, 303, 304, 307, 322, 323, 324, 330, 331, 332, 334
markers, 83
    constituitive of pseudo-philosophy, 83
    effect of aggregation, 84, 85
    fallibility of, 84
    in biomedicine, 83
    in business and finance, 84
    in philosophy, 85
    objectivity of, 83, 86
    of genuine philosophy, 88
        competence, 90
        integrity, 89
        the pursuit of wisdom, 88
    of pseudo-philosophy, 120
        incompetence, 134
        language abuse, 131
        manipulation, 126
        standards, 135
        trickery, 122
    their roles, 86
    use of, 121, 162
masquerade
    and mimicry, 115, 118
    by Ayn Rand, 280
    by Keith Raniere, 195, 196, 218, 235, 239
    by pseudo-philosophers, 110, 111
    by pseudo-scientists, 108
    obscured by inspiration, 322
metaphilosophy, 30
metaphysics, 24
models, 71
    and abduction, 157
    application of, 147, 157, 159, 164, 319
    dimensions of the pseudo, 112
    in mimicry, 115
    personas as, 78
    used in guiding scrutiny, 151
Nevares, Ivy, 200, 203, 205, 208, *See* Raniere, Keith
    exaggerated claims, 204
    misrepresentation, 207
Nozick, Robert, 322, 323, 324, 334
Nursing Theory. *See* Silva, Mary Cipriano
ontology, 55, 101, 325
    meaning of, 325
paradox, 48, 73, 94
    and intuition, 184
    approaches to solving, 51, 53
    lessons of, 56
    Omnipotence Paradox, 66
    Paradox of the Stone, 66
    Ship of Theseus, 49, 132
persona, 77
    a literary persona, 103
    a poet persona, 105
    a psychologist persona, 102
    a scientist persona, 100
    as a representation, 78
    as part of the genuine philosopher and pseudo-philosopher models, 147
    building a *subject* persona, 151
    matching a work or writer to, 159, 162, 164
        Rand, 279, 304
        Raniere, 237, 276

Silva, 192
of the genuine philosopher, 77
Rand, 263, 279, 304, 306, 322
Raniere, 207, 224, 237
Silva, 175, 179, 188, 192
the Philo (genuine philosopher) persona, 79
the Pseudo (pseudo-philosopher) persona, 118
not the anti-Philo, 119
use in abduction, 159
philosopher
as a tradesman or artisan, 40
being one, 41, 45
philosophy
as a discipline, 19
as a matrix, 94
as a skilled trade, 41
as an intellectual conscience, 142
markers of. *See* markers of genuine philosophy
the *anything goes* view, 36
vs. not philosophy, 13, 105, 269, 317
what it does, 45
what it is, 17
Plato, 14, 20, 111, 131, 142, 149, 248, 255, 259, 261, 262, 263, 264, 319, 325, 330
a slave, a prisoner, a professional wrestler, 21
against poetry, 104
against rhetoric, 97
and definitions, 69
and dialectic, 70
his rough career path, 21
Principle of Charity, 80, 89, 134, 180, 219, 258
pseudo, the, 3
dimensions of, 112
mimicry and masquerade, 114
perspectives on, 107
pseudo-philosopher
as a predator, 116
goals and motivation, 114, 148

goals and motivations, 111
what he offers, 110
pseudo-philosophy. *See also* mimicry
accusation as a warning, 5, 7, 247, 314
and dishonesty, 141
and incompetence, 110, 111, 112, 134
and personal gain, 7, 97, 98, 195, 239, 313
consequences of, 7, 148, 170, 186, 192, 239, 282, 327
its accusation as a warning, 321
its ascription as a moral judgment, 321
not merely incompetence, 142, 188
of Keith Raniere, 239
on a sliding scale, 85
Rand, Ayn
consequences of her pseudo-philosophy, 282
criticism of, 245
deceit, 313
incompetence, 312, 313
incompetence and exploitation, 278
pseudo-philosophy, 300
Raniere, Keith. *See* Nevares, Ivy, *See* Mack, Allison, *See* Elliot, Marc
consequences of his pseudo-philosophy, 239
failure to deal with counterexamples, 216
undermining science and knowledge, 213, 214, 216, 217, 327
Rescher, Nicholas, 110, 111, 112, 114, 142, 313, 320, 332
rhetoric, 97
about thought control, 97
deceitful, 98
independent of truth and wisdom, 97
Schopenhauer, Arthur, 6, 14, 142
Silva, Mary Cipriano

argument for the fallibility of science, 183
consequences of her pseudo-philosophy, 192
failure to deal with counterexamples, 185
failure to pursue, 190
ignorance and exploitation, 178
intuition as knowledge, 180, 181
motives, 189
Nursing Theory, 165
   controversy, 167
perspectives on philosophy, 179
philosophical support for pseudo-science, 192
problems with intuition, 185, 186
pseudo-philosophical blurring of boundaries, 194
   undermining science and knowledge, 188
Sophists, 6, 7, 14, 97, 142, 199, 313
   and rhetoric, 6
the pseudo. *See* pseudo, the
theories, 71
wisdom, 5, 6, 19, 37, 38, 47, *See* Aristotle
   and definitions, 69
   and goofy arguments, 48
   and historians, 92
   and inconsistency, 63, 64
   and pseudo-philosophy, 7
   and the Sophists, 6
   not yielded by rhetoric, 99
Xenophon, 20, 97, 98, 111, 142

About the Author

I grew up in Oneonta – a small city on the Susquehanna river in the foothills of the Catskill mountains in New York State. My BS in philosophy, with a concentration in mathematical logic, is from Rensselaer Polytechnic Institute (RPI), and my Master's and PhD degrees (with concentrations in logic, philosophy of language, and philosophy of science) are from the University of Rochester. I spent a decade at Loyola University of Chicago, teaching undergraduate and graduate courses and performing the standard professorial tasks associated with research and publication. Although a tenured associate professor of philosophy, I found myself drawn to the rapidly advancing fields of computer science and information technology. There, I saw interesting real-world problems whose understanding and solutions could be approached with the skills and knowledge my background in philosophy provided.

I decided to leave academia and moved into the world of business and industry. Over a period of about 15 years I designed and developed a range of applications including commercial compilers, software development tools, and formal languages; and I managed software development teams and departments. From tech companies such as Bell Laboratories and SAS Institute, I moved on to the pharmaceutical industry – Glaxo Wellcome, then later Novartis and GlaxoSmithKline – to focus on AI and knowledge engineering systems for drug development and drug safety. This work culminated in the SafetyWorks project at GSK which resulted in the development of innovative methods employed to discover adverse drug reactions by analyzing very large health system, insurance, government, and prescription data bases.

In 2004 I also began a fruitful and enjoyable collaboration with the North Carolina State University Department of Philosophy to create their Logic and Cognitive Science Initiative in conjunction with my GSK Undergraduate Internship in Knowledge Exploration. Over the next five years, my interns and I published a number of papers in refereed journals, books, and national and international conferences in the areas of drug development, drug safety, artificial intelligence, data and text mining, knowledge representation, and the use of semantic methods and formal ontologies in the empirical sciences.

I retired from GSK in 2009 to focus on other interests. My list of publications on topics in philosophy, logic, computer science, cognitive science, computational linguistics, artificial intelligence, methodology, drug discovery, and drug safety can be found at PhilPapers (philpapers.org), ResearchGate (researchgate.net), and Google Scholar (scholar.google.com).

www.ingramcontent.com/pod-product-compliance
Lightning Source LLC
Chambersburg PA
CBHW071236160426
43196CB00009B/1078